ACCOUNTING PRINCIPLES
WORKBOOK

JAMES S. REECE, D.B.A., C.M.A.

Professor
Graduate School of Business Administration
The University of Michigan
and

ROBERT N. ANTHONY, D.B.A.

Professor Emeritus
Graduate School of Business Administration
Harvard University

SIXTH EDITION

 1983

**RICHARD D. IRWIN, INC.
HOMEWOOD, ILLINOIS**

ISBN 0-256-02786-2

Printed in the United States of America

1 2 3 4 5 6 7 8 9 0 ML 0 9 8 7 6 5 4 3

Contents

Sources of Cases

The 67 cases published in this workbook are listed below in alphabetical order, together with their authors' names. Cases with no author's name shown were written by, or under the supervision of, James S. Reece or Robert N. Anthony. Unless otherwise indicated, the copyright on all cases is held by Osceola Institute. No case herein may be reproduced in any form or by any means without the permission of the copyright holder.

Permission to reproduce Osceola Institute cases should be sought through Professor Reece at the Graduate School of Business Administration, The University of Michigan, Ann Arbor, MI 48109. Comments on the text, cases, or teacher's guide, or new ideas for teaching the cases, would be welcomed and should be sent to Professor Reece.

ABC Company--Prof. Harvey Yu, c Business Week,

Banning, Julie,
Bartlett, John, (A)--Profs. R. G. Walker and J. S. Reece, c Harvard University,
Bartlett, John, (B)-- c Harvard University,
Bates Boat Yard--Prof. C. B. Nickerson, c Harvard University,
Bedford Manufacturing Company (A)--Prof. R. G. Walker, c Harvard University,
Bedford Manufacturing Company (B)-- c Harvard University,
Bedford Manufacturing Company (C)-- c Harvard University,
Bennett Body Company--Profs. C. A. Bliss and R. N. Anthony,
     c Harvard University,
Bernhart Dress Shop-- c Harvard University,
Black Meter Company--Profs. J. Dearden and R. N. Anthony, c Harvard University,
Braydon Corporation (A)--Profs. T. F. Bradshaw and J. S. Reece,
     c Harvard University,
Braydon Corporation (B)-- c Harvard University,

Cascade Cafe (A),
Cascade Cafe (B),
Coburg, Baron--Prof. W. T. Andrews, Guilford College, c The Accounting Review,
Coffin, Jean--Profs. C. B. Nickerson and R. N. Anthony, c Harvard University,
Collin, Chris,
Conan Company--Profs. J. W. Horowitz and D. H. Davenport, c Harvard University,
Conrad Taxi,
Cotter Company--Prof. R. F. Vancil, c Harvard University,
Crompton Limited--Prof. G. Shillinglaw, c IMEDE,

Early Years Day Care Center,

Freeson's Gift Gallery,

Gallup Company,
Glencoe Hospital-- c Institute of Management Accounting,
Government Contracts,

Hardin Tool Company,
Hill Associates, Inc.--Prof. C. J. Christenson, c Harvard University,
Horton Press,

Import Distributors, Inc.,
Imports Boutique,

Johnson Company-- c Harvard University,

Lake Erie Table Company--Prof. T. E. Lynch,
Lewis Landscaping Servide--C. T. Sharpless and Prof. M. E. Barrett,
     c M. E. Barrett,
Liberty Electronics,
Liquid Chemical Company--Prof. D. Solomons, c University of Bristol
     (Great Britain),

MacDonald's Farm--J. Brown and Prof. J. K. Shank, c Harvard University,
Mammoth Manufacturing--Prof. J. Dearden, c Harvard University,
Marion Music Company--Prof. V. Boyd, c Northwestern University,
Mason Automotive Company,
Mavioli, Charles--Profs. R. G. Walker and C. A. Bliss, c Harvard University,
Michigan Avenue Furriers--D. S. Howard and Prof. C. M. Williams,
     c Harvard University,
Mogielnicki, Bob--Prof. C. J. Christenson, c Harvard University,
Monroe Stamping Corporation--Profs. J. Dearden and J. S. Reece,
     c Harvard University,

Peale, Ruby--J. A. Doehrman and Prof. M. E. Barrett, c M. E. Barrett,
Penn Electronics--Prof. J. Dearden, c Harvard University,
Pilbeam Company,
Pinkham Motel,
Piqua Products--Prof. J. K. Shank, c Harvard University,

Radcliffe Company,

Salem Funiture Company-- c Institute of Management Accounting,
Sheridan Carpet Company,
Shuman Automobiles, Inc.--A. M. McCosh, Profs. D. F. Hawkins, J. R. Yeager,
     J. S. Reece, c Harvard University,
South American Coffee Company--Prof. R. H. Hassler, c Harvard University,
Sullivan, F. J. Insurance Agency--Prof. J. Dearden, c Harvard University,
SunAir Boat Builders--W. Earner, Profs. M. E. Barrett and J. S. Reece,
     c Harvard University,
Sylvan Pools, Inc.--J. Mudge and Prof. R. A. Howell, c Harvard University,

Thurber Company--Prof. S. I. Buchin, c Harvard University,
Tru-Fit Parts, Inc.,

Upstate Fuel Oil-- c Neil C. Churchill,

Vandiver Equipment Sales-- c Harvard University,

Wheat Company-- c Institute of Management Accounting,
Whiz Calculator Company-- c Harvard University,
Wilkinson & Gould--Prof. D. Smith, c The University of Western Ontario,
Woodside Products, Inc.,

Zephyr Research Company,

Chapter 1

The Nature and Purpose of Accounting

Key Terms

Operating information
Management accounting information
Financial accounting information
Control
Planning
Budgeting
Generally accepted accounting principles

FASB
Relevance
Objectivity
Feasibility
Status reports
Flow reports

Discussion Questions

1. As a child you may have set up a sidewalk lemonade stand on a hot summer day. What information would be needed to assess the economic success of such a lemonade stand?

2. Does a coach "control" his or her team in the sense that this word is used in the text?

3. What quantitative information is available for appraisal of, say, a basketball player? In what way is this information like accounting data for a business?

4. Distinguish between the nature of financial accounting statements and management accounting statements.

5. What is the relative importance of (a) accuracy and (b) timeliness in the preparation of financial accounting statements? Of management accounting statements?

6. Distinguish between the rules of financial accounting and those of management accounting.

7. In reading a company's financial statements, what must the reader know about these statements in order to draw meaningful conclusions from them?

8. Must every company prepare statements in accordance with generally accepted accounting principles? Explain.

9. Classify each of the following as either a "flow" figure or a "status" figure:

    a. The attendance of last year's Army-Navy football game.
    b. The number of cars using the San Francisco Bay Bridge yesterday.
    c. The balance in your checking account.
    d. Your weight.
    e. The amount of hot water you used when you last took a shower.
    f. A baseball scoreboard in the top of the ninth inning.
    g. Last Tuesday's revenues at the campus bookstore.
    h. The number of people on your school's faculty as of registration day.

10. Listed below are certain data about companies. For each item, rank its rele-

vance (to an investor), its objectivity, _and_ its measurement feasibility as being either relatively high or low.

    a. The value of the Coca-Cola trademark.
    b. The number of spark plugs on hand at a certain Ford Motor engine assembly plant.
    c. Next year's earnings per share of Allied Chemical.
    d. The backlog of orders for model 747 aircraft at Boeing.
    e. The number of employees at Western Electric's Hawthorne, Illinois plant.
    f. The value of the patents on the Polaroid SX-70 camera.
    g. The number of barrels of crude oil and cubic feet of natural gas under land for which Texaco owns the oil and gas rights.
    h. The amount of long-term debt owed by American Telephone and Telegraph.

11. What information should the financial statements provide to the user?

12. Why does the income statement's amount of pretax profit or loss often differ from the amount of profit or loss shown on the taxpayer's income tax return?

13. Why is it often useful to express accounting numbers as ratios or percentages?

CASES

Case 1-14: Charles Mavioli

    In the fall of 1982, Charles Mavioli, a general carpenter living in one of the suburbs, decided to invest a part of his savings in woodworking machinery and in a building which had formerly been used as a small garage. His plan for some time had been to prepare himself for contracting work of a modest sort, including small-home construction. He had always wanted to build low-priced dwellings "all on his own." Such an activity would be limited, he knew, by his ability to carry his share of the total investment load necessary for such an undertaking. So far in his career, Mavioli had been extraordinarily successful as a general carpenter, working at a wide variety of jobs. At times he had been hired as "boss carpenter" on large and important constructions. For this kind of work he had received a very good salary, a large part of which he and his wife had been able to save against the time when he could have a business of his own.

    By October 1982, Mavioli had his shop completely fitted and had hired two mill hands and a shop mechanic to help him in his new undertaking. As a "fill-in" between big jobs, it was his expectation to be able to provide fairly uniform employment for these people through making window and door frames, kitchen cabinets, and similar construction parts both for stock and on order.

    In that same month, in connection with a substantial order for cabinets requiring six to eight weeks of shop activity, Mavioli talked with the credit officer of his bank about his need for some temporary financial assistance in the purchase of necessary materials and supplies. This assistance the bank was glad to extend to him. In granting the loan, however, the credit officer suggested that Mavioli would now need to spend more time and money on financial and operating records than had been necessary when his work was almost entirely a matter of personal services. "More paper work will be a painful necessity from now on," he said, "not only to make it easier for you to do a good job in managing your new business, but also in making your tax returns and in later dealings with this or other banks." The banker suggested that Mavioli talk with some qualified person about this problem. Mavioli said that he had a friend who was controller of a manufacturing business, and that he was sure this friend would give him some practical suggestions.

    A week or so after the conference at the bank, Mavioli had a long and satisfactory talk with his friend about his need for additional records. At the outset he emphasized that up to this point he had gotten along pretty well with the stubs of his checkbook, plus some odds and ends of memoranda which he and his wife had been careful to keep for reference purposes. The controller agreed that it is easy to overdo "this business of keeping records," and said that in his opinion it would be best for them to make a small start and feel their way along for a few months before attempting anything that would call for much work.

He suggested that, as a starter, Mavioli and his wife might well spend an evening drawing up a list of the properties used in operating their shop and contracting business, and a corresponding list of the debts which had grown out of this business, together with the amounts of money that Mavioli had invested in it. The controller explained that the list of "properties used" should be confined to things having a money value in this particular business. "With these two lists," he said, "we can draw up a beginning financial statement of your assets and liabilities, which should be helpful in talking over your need for figures." To this he added: "Generally speaking, the problem of useful and understandable accounting information is built around this statement, and the job is to keep such a statement (or its supporting records) more or less continuously adjusted to what takes place in the affairs of the business it represents, with enough supplementary facts about resulting changes to help the owner to be a better manager than would be possible without such tools to help him."

The controller assured Mavioli that he did not believe the cost of keeping the necessary records would be a very important consideration. He pointed out that he knew of experts in accounting procedures who specialized in making periodic visits to small concerns such as Mavioli's for the very purpose of relieving their clients of much of the clerical burden of keeping

operating records. But he said it would nevertheless be necessary for Mavioli or his wife to keep a memorandum record or daybook of transactions practically as they occurred. The controller suggested that as time went on Mavioli might want to give some attention to the accepted ways of keeping accounting records; but, he said, there was no need for Mavioli to be apprehensive about the cost of supplying his simple requirements.

Questions

1. Why did Mavioli need any records? What did he need?

2. See what you can do to draw up a list of Mavioli's assets and liabilities, as the controller suggested, making any assumptions you consider useful. How should Mavioli go about putting a value on his assets?

3. Among the changes in the assets, liabilities, and proprietary claims of a business which the controller spoke of as the subject matter of accounting is an important variety growing out of "profit and loss" or "trading" operations. What would be the general construction of a profit and loss analysis for Mavioli's new business? How frequently would he wish to provide himself with such an analysis?

4. What other kinds of changes in assets, liabilities, and proprietary claims will need careful recording and reporting if Mavioli is to keep in control of his job as manager?

* * * * *

Case 1-15: Baron Coburg

Once upon a time many, many years ago, there lived a feudal landlord in a small province of Western Europe. The landlord, Baron Coburg, lived in a castle high on a hill. He was responsible for the well-being of many peasants who occupied the lands surrounding his castle. Each spring, as the snow began to melt and thoughts of other, less influential men turned to matters other than business, the Baron would decide how to provide for all his peasants during the coming year.

One spring, the Baron was thinking about the wheat crop of the coming growing season. "I believe that 30 acres of my land, being worth five bushels of wheat per acre, will produce

enough wheat for next winter," he mused, "but who should do the farming? I believe I'll give Ivan and Frederick the responsibility of growing the wheat." Whereupon Ivan and Frederick were summoned for an audience with Baron Coburg.

"Ivan, you will farm on the 20-acre plot of ground and Frederick will farm the 10-acre plot," the Baron began beg. "I will give Ivan 20 bushels of wheat for seed and 20 pounds of fertilizer. (Twenty pounds of fertilizer are worth two bushels of wheat.) Frederick will get 10 bushels of wheat for seed and 10 pounds of fertilizer. I will give each of you an ox to pull a plow but you will have to make arrangements with Feyador, the Plowmaker, for a plow. The oxen, incidentally, are only three years old and have never been used for farming, so they should have a good ten years of farming ahead of them. Take good care of them, because an ox is worth 40 bushels of wheat. Come back next fall and return the oxen and the plows along with your harvest.

Ivan and Frederick genuflected and withdrew from the Great Hall, taking with them the things provided by the Baron.

The summer came and went, and after the harvest Ivan and Frederick returned to the Great Hall to account to their master for the things given them in the spring. Ivan said, "My Lord, I present you with a slightly used ox, a plow, broken beyond repair, and 223 bushels of wheat. I, unfortunately, owe Feyador, the Plowmaker, three bushels of wheat for the plow I got from him last spring. And, as you might expect, I used all the fertilizer and seed you gave me last spring. You will also remember, my Lord, that you took 20 bushels of my harvest for your own personal use."

Frederick spoke next. "Here, my Lord, is a partially used-up ox, the plow for which I gave Feyador, the Plowmaker, three bushels of wheat from my harvest, and 105 bushels of wheat. I, too, used all my seed and fertilizer last spring. Also, my Lord, you took 30 bushels of wheat several days ago for your own table. I believe the plow is good for two more seasons."

"You did well," said the Baron. Blessed with this benediction the two peasants departed.

After they had taken their leave, the Baron began to contemplate what had happened. "Yes," he thought, "they did well, but I wonder which one did better?"

Questions

1. For each farm, prepare blance sheets as of the beginning and end of the growing season, and an income statement for the season. (Do not be concerned that you do not have much understanding of what a balance sheet and income statement are; just use your intuition as best you can.)

2. Which peasant was the better farmer?

Chapter 2

Basic Accounting Concepts:
The Balance Sheet

Key Terms

Money measurement concept
Entity concept
Going-concern concept
Cost concept
Dual-aspect concept
Balance sheet
Assets
Current assets
Monetary assets

Property, plant and equipment
Equities
Liabilities
Current liabilities
Owners' equity
Contributed capital
Retained earnings
Transaction

Discussion Questions

1. What advantage is there in expressing accounting facts only in monetary terms?

2. Why does financial accounting not give a complete accounting of all happenings in an organization?

3. Give some examples of important facts about a company that do not appear in its accounting records.

4. If land purchased for $30,000 in 1978 now has a market value of $70,000, at what amount will it be recorded in the financial records of the business?

5. What difficulty sometimes arises in the application of the entity concept?

6. Under what circumstances are a company's assets reported at their liquidation value?

7. At what value are resources that have been acquired, but not yet used, shown on the accounting records?

8. Which assets <u>are</u> recorded at their "actual" value in the accounting records?

9. When does an account called "goodwill" appear on a balance sheet?

10. Why is it that accounting records and reports do not attempt to report market values on a continuing basis?

11. Why is the accounting system you are studying known as a "double-entry" system?

12. Distinguish between the two ways of interpreting the two sides of the balance sheet.

13. Kramer Co. paid $2,400 for a three-month lease on a new truck. Does the truck constitute an asset? Explain.

14. Distinguish between marketable securities and the noncurrent asset, "Investments."

15. Comment on the statement, "The company's cash dividends should be immediately increased, because its retained earnings are at the highest level in history!

Problems

2-1. As of December 31, Henry Company had $10,000 in cash, held $80,000 of inventory, and owned other items which originally cost $15,000. Henry Company had also borrowed $35,000 from First City Bank. Prepare a balance sheet for Henry Company as of December 31. Be sure to label each item and each column with appropriate terms.

2-2. The Excelsior Company has $80,000 in cash, $272,000 in accounts receivable, and $976,000 in fixed assets. Its equities consist of $160,000 due a bank, $800,000 in capital stock, and $320,000 in retained earnings. Accumulated depreciation is $368,000. Assuming that these figures measure everything the company owes or owns besides inventory, find the value of the inventory.

2-3. Prepare a balance sheet as of June 30, for the R.D. Morison Company, using the following data:

Accounts payable	$ 260,000	Cash	$ 84,000
Accounts receivable	500,000	Equipment (at cost)	741,000
Accrued expenses	115,000	Estimated tax liability	130,000
Accumulated depreciation on buildings	546,000	Inventories	546,000
Accumulated depreciation on equipment	390,000	Investment in the Peerless Company	325,000
Bonds payable	650,000	Land (at cost)	227,000
Buildings (at cost)	1,040,000	Marketable securities	366,000
Capital stock	975,000	Notes payable	195,000
		Retained earnings	?

2-4. The January 1 balance sheet of the Weldon Company, an unincorporated business, is as follows:

WELDON COMPANY
Balance Sheet as of January 1

Assets		Equities	
Cash	$30,000	Notes payable	$15,000
Inventory	40,000	Capital	55,000
Total	$70,000	Total	$70,000

The following transactions took place in January:

Jan. 4: Merchandise was sold for $10,000 cash that had cost $6,000.
Jan. 6: To increase inventory, Weldon placed an order with Star Company for merchandise that would cost $2,000.
Jan. 8: Weldon received merchandise ordered from Star, and agreed to pay the $2,000 in 30 days.
Jan. 11: Merchandise costing $1,000 was sold for $1,600 in cash.
Jan. 16: Merchandise costing $1,500 was sold for $2,400 on 30-day open account.
Jan. 26: Weldon paid employees for the month $3,000 in cash.
Jan. 29: Purchased land for $17,500 in cash.
Jan. 30: Weldon purchased a two-year insurance policy for $2,000 in cash.

Required: Describe the impact of each transaction on the balance sheet, and prepare a new balance sheet as of January 31.

2-5. On a sheet of paper, set up in pencil the balance sheet of Music Mart as it appears after the last transaction described in the text, leaving considerable space between each item. Record the effect, if any, of the following events on the balance sheet. The basic equation, Assets = Equities, must be preserved at all times. Errors will be minimized if you make a separate list of the balance sheet items affected by each transactions and the amount (+ or -) by which each is to be changed.

After you have finished recording these events, prepare a balance sheet in proper form. Assume that all these transactions occurred in January and that there were no other transactions in January.

(1) The store purchased and received merchandise for $5,000, agreeing to pay within 30 days.
(2) Merchandise costing $1,250 was sold for $2,000, which was received in cash.
(3) Merchandise costing $1,500 was sold for $2,250, the customer agreeing to pay $2,250 within 30 days.
(4) The store purchased a three-year fire insurance policy for $500, paying cash.
(5) The store purchased two lots of land of equal size for a total of $25,000. It paid $5,000 in cash and gave a 10-year mortgage for $20,000.
(6) The store sold one of the two lots of land for $12,500. It received $2,500 cash and, in addition, the buyer assumed $10,000 of the mortgage; that is, Music Mart became no longer responsible for this half.
(7) Smith received a bona fide offer of $37,500 for the business, and although his equity was then only $26,750, he rejected the offer. It was evident that the store had already acquired goodwill of $10,750.
(8) Smith withdrew $1,250 cash from the store's bank account for his personal use.
(9) Smith took merchandise costing $1,000 from the store's inventory for his personal use.
(10) Smith learned that the person who purchased the land (No. 6 above) subsequently sold it for $20,000. The lot still owned by Music Mart was identical in value with this other plot.
(11) The store paid off $5,000 of its note payable (disregard interest).
(12) Music Mart was changed to a corporation, Music Mart, Inc. Smith received common stock with a par value of $24,500 in exchange for his equity in the store. (Disregard costs of organizing the corporation. Note that this event creates a new business entity.)
(13) Smith sold one fourth of the stock he owned in Music Mart, Inc., for $7,500 cash.
(14) Merchandise costing $750 was sold for $1,125, which was received in cash.

2-6. The January 1 balance sheet of the Matten Company was as follows:

Balance Sheet as of January 1

Assets		Equities	
Cash	$12,000	Notes payable	$ 6,000
Inventory	9,000	Common stock	7,000
		Retained earnings	8,000
Total	$21,000	Total	$21,000

After a month of operations, Matten Company had the following balance sheet:

Balance Sheet as of January 31

Assets		Equities	
Cash	$14,000	Common stock	$ 7,000
Inventory	9,000	Retained earnings	16,000
Total	$23,000	Total	$23,000

Required: Explain what occurred during January.

2-7. D. Swanson and F. Bergsma formed a partnership on June 1 to operate a shoe store. Swanson contributed $40,000 cash and Bergsma contributed $40,000 worth of shoe inventory. During the month of June the following transactions took place:

(1) Additional shoe inventory was purchased at a cost of $20,000.
(2) Total cash sales for the month were $25,000. The inventory which was sold had a cost of $12,500.
(3) Swanson withdrew $5,000 of cash drawings. Bergsma withdrew only $3,000 of cash drawings.
(4) The partnership borrowed $40,000 from Third National Bank.

(5) Land and a building were purchased at a cost of $20,000 and $40,000, respectively.

Required:

    a. Prepare a balance sheet as of June 1.
    b. Prepare a reconciliation of the beginning and ending balances for each owner's capital account.
    c. Prepare a balance sheet as of June 30.

2-8. Assume that Swanson and Bergsma in Problem 2-7 had chosen to incorporate their business rather than operate as a partnership. Prepare a balance sheet as of June 30. Describe the similarities and differences between the balance sheets prepared in 2-7c and in this problem.

2-9. As of December 31, Quayle Company had the following account balances:

Accounts payable................	$4,000	Long-term investments.........	$1,500
Accounts receivable............	5,000	Marketable securities.........	4,000
Bonds Payable..................	2,000	Plant and equipment...........	7,500
Cash...........................	3,000	Wages payable..................	1,000
Current portion of bonds payable......................	1,000		

Required:

    a. What was the current ratio?
    b. Explain what the current ratio measures.

2-10. Prepare a balance sheet in proper format from the following list of December 31 account balances for Norman Company:

Accounts payable..............	$25,000	Goodwill....................	$ 10,000
Accounts receivable...........	40,000	Income tax payable..........	1,500
Accrued interest payable......	500	Inventory...................	?
Accumulated depreciation......	?	Land........................	30,000
Building......................	60,000	Notes payable...............	25,000
Cash..........................	20,000	Retained earnings...........	?
Common stock.................	43,000	Total assets................	155,000
Current assets...............	75,000		

2-11. a. If assets equal $75,000 and liabilities equal $30,000, then owners' equity equals _____.

    b. If assets equal $45,000 and owners' equity equals $30,000, then liabilities equal _____.

    c. If current assets equal $20,000, liabilities equal $30,000, and owners' equity equals $35,000, the noncurrent assets equal _____.

    d. If the current ratio is 2:1, current assets are $30,000 and noncurrent assets equal $50,000, then owners' equity is _____. (Assume that all liabilities are current.)

    e. What is the current ratio if noncurrent assets equal $50,000, total assets equal $90,000, and owners' equity equals $70,000? (Assume that all liabilities are current.)

2-12. Indicate the net effect on assets, liabilities and owners' equity resulting from each of the following transactions:

(1) Stock was issued for $85,000 cash.
(2) Bonds payable of $17,000 were refunded with stock.
(3) Depreciation on plant and equipment equaled $5,950 for the year.
(4) Inventory was purchased for $13,600 cash.
(5) $8,500 worth of inventory was purchased on credit.
(6) Inventory costing $3,400 was sold for $6,800 on credit.
(7) $2,550 in cash was received for merchandise sold on credit.
(8) Dividends of $3,400 were declared.

(9) The declared dividends of $3,400 were paid.
(10) The company declared a stock split, and replaced each outstanding share with two new shares.

2-13. At the beginning of July the accounts of PC Corporation showed the following balances:

Cash.........................$7,000   Accounts payable..............$6,000
Accounts receivable.......... 3,000   Notes payable................. 1,500
Inventory.................... 3,000   Common stock.................. 8,000
Supplies..................... 500   Retained earnings............. 7,500
Equipment.................... 9,500

During July the following transactions occurred:

(1) Inventory was purchased for $5,000 on credit.
(2) Supplies were purchased for $300 with cash.
(3) Cash sales were $14,000.
(4) A new machine was purchased with common stock valued at $12,000
(5) Trade vendors were paid $9,000.
(6) Cost of goods sold was $6,000.
(7) Notes payable of $1,000 were paid.
(8) Equipment depreciation of $600 was recorded.

Required: Prepare a balance sheet as of the end of July.

2-14. Prepare a balance sheet for Belsky Corporation as of the end of May, its first month of operations. The following transactions took place during May:

(1) Stock was issued for $104,000 cash.
(2) Stock was issued for land valued at $39,000.
(3) Stock was issued for $45,500 worth of plant and equipment.
(4) Inventory was purchased for $58,500.
(5) All inventory was sold to customers during the year for $91,000 cash.
(6) Management decided to invest all but $2,000 of available cash in marketable securities.
(7) Depreciation of $650 was recorded for the plant and equipment.

2-15. Using the January 1 and January 31 balance sheets of Gosman Cmpany explain what occurred during the month of January. Assume the only item of expense was cost of goods sold.

	January 1	January 31
Cash..................................	$10,800	$10,530
Accounts receivable..................	0	2,700
Inventory............................	2,700	9,450
Plant and equipment (net)............	13,500	13,500
Total Assets	$27,000	$36,180
Accounts payable.....................	$ 5,400	$13,500
Notes payable........................	5,400	5,130
Common stock.........................	16,200	16,200
Retained earnings....................	0	1,350
Total Liabilities and Owners' Equity....................	$27,000	$36,180

Note: There is a 100% markup on inventory; i.e., the selling price of an item is two times its cost.

CASES

Case 2-16: Cascade Cafe (A)*

On March 31, 1983, the partnership that had been organized to operate the Cascade Cafe was dissolved under unusual circumstances, and in connection with its dissolution, preparation of a balance sheet became necessary.

The partnership was formed by Mr. and Mrs. Frank Rayburn and Mrs. Grace Harris, who had become acquainted while working in a Portland, Oregon, restaurant. On November 1, 1982, each of the three partners contributed $9,000 cash to the partnership. The Rayburns' contribution represented practically all of their savings. Mrs. Harris' payment was the proceeds of her late husband's insurance policy.

On that day also the partnership signed a one-year lease to the Cascade Cafe, located in a nearby recreational area. The monthly rent on the cafe was $1,100. They were attracted to this facility in part because there were living accommodations on the floor above the restaurant. One room was occupied by the Rayburns and another by Mrs. Harris.

They borrowed $11,000 from a local bank, and used this plus $21,400 of partnership funds to buy out the previous operator of the cafe. Of this amount, $30,600 was for equipment, and $1,800 was for the food and beverages then on hand. The partnership paid $430 for local operating licenses, good for one year beginning November 1, and paid $900 for a new cash register. The remainder of the $38,000 was deposited in a checking account.

The partners opened the restaurant shortly after November 1. Mr. Rayburn was the cook and Mrs. Rayburn and Mrs. Harris waited on customers. Mrs. Rayburn also ordered the food, beverages, and supplies, operated the cash register, and was responsible for the checking account.

The restaurant operated throughout the winter season of 1982–83. It was not very successful. On the morning of March 31, 1983, Mrs. Rayburn discovered that Mr. Rayburn and Mrs. Harris had disappeared. Mrs. Harris had taken all her possessions, but Mr. Rayburn had

left behind most of his clothing, presumably because he could not remove it without warning Mrs. Rayburn. The new cash register and its contents were also missing. Mrs. Rayburn concluded that the partnership was dissolved. (The court subsequently affirmed that the partnership was dissolved as of March 30.)

Mrs. Rayburn decided to continue operating the Cascade Cafe. She realized that an accounting would have to be made as of March 30, and called in Frank Whittaker, an acquaintance who was knowledgeable about accounting.

In response to Mr. Whittaker's questions, Mrs. Rayburn said that the cash register had contained $198, and that the checking account balance was $662. Ski instructors who were permitted to charge their meals had run up accounts totaling $517. (These accounts subsequently were paid in full.) Cascade Cafe owed suppliers amounts totaling $943. Mr. Whittaker estimated that depreciation on the assets amounted to $1,440.

Food and beverages on hand were estimated to be worth $1,450. During the period of its operation, the partners drew salaries at agreed-upon amounts and these payments were up to date. The clothing that Mr. Rayburn left behind was estimated to be worth $540. The partnership had also repaid $900 of the bank loan.

Mr. Whittaker explained that in order to account for the partners' equity, he would prepare a balance sheet. He would list the items that the partnership owned as of March 30, subtract the amounts that it owed to outside parties, and the balance would be the equity of the three partners. Each partner would be entitled to one third of this amount.

Questions

1. Prepare a balance sheet for the Cascade Cafe as of November 2, 1982.

2. Prepare a balance sheet as of March 30, 1983.

3. Disregarding the marital complications, do you suppose that the partners received the equity determined in Question 2? Why?

---

*Based on a case decided by the Supreme Court of the State of Oregon (216 P2d 1005).

Case 2-17: Early Years Day Care Center

After six months of operations, Mrs. Frances Nissen wanted to analyze the performance of Early Years Day Care Center. She wanted to know where the company stood as of December 31, 1982, and what its future prospects were.

Early Years Day Care Center was a company organized by Mrs. Nissen early in 1982 to provide supervised care, preschool education, a snack, and a noonday meal, primarily for children of working mothers. For its initial capital, Mrs. Nissen took out a $24,000 mortgage on her own house. She invested $21,000 of this in common stock of the center. Friends of hers invested $11,000 in cash, receiving stock in return. A government agency made a one-year loan of $6,500 to the center.

With these funds, the center purchased property for $40,000 of which $8,000 was for land and $32,000 was for a building on the land. The purchase was financed in part with a $27,000 mortgage, the remainder being paid in cash. Interest on the mortgage was to be paid quarterly, but no principal repayment was required until the company had become established. The center also purchased $13,200 of furniture and equipment for cash.

During the first six months of operations, which ended December 31, 1982, the center paid out the following additional amounts in cash:

Salary* to Mrs. Nissen........	$ 8,000
Salaries* of part time employees....................	5,120
Insurance and taxes...........	1,340
Utilities....................	1,019
Food and supplies............	4,370
Interest and miscellaneous....	3,642
Total paid out..........	$23,491

*Includes payroll taxes.

The center received $16,880 of fees in cash. In addition, the center was owed $600 of fees from parents. As of December 31, 1982, Mrs. Nissen estimated that $320 of supplies were still on hand. The center owed food suppliers $520.

In thinking about the future, Mrs. Nissen estimated that for the next six months, ending June 30, student fees received (in addition to the $600 of fees that applied to the first six months) would be $25,600. This was higher than the amount for the first six months because enrollments were higher.

She estimated that the center would pay $13,120 for salaries; $1,280 cash for utilities (which was higher than the first six months because of expected colder weather); $5,600 for additional food and supplies (higher because of the higher enrollment); and $2,720 for interest and miscellaneous (lower than the first six months because certain start-up costs were paid for during the first six months). She also expected to pay back the government loan.

She estimated that food and supplies on hand as of June 30 would be $320, and that nothing would be owed suppliers. She did not include any additional amounts for insurance or taxes because the amounts paid in the first six months covered these costs for the whole year.

She knew that many companies recorded depreciation on buildings, furniture, and equipment; however, she had a firm offer of $56,000 cash for these assets from someone who wanted to buy the center, so she thought that under these circumstances depreciation was inappropriate.

Questions

1. Prepare a balance sheet for Early Years Day Care Center as of December 31. (In order to minimize errors, it is suggested that you treat each event separately; show the items that are affected and the amount of increase or decrease in each item. For events that affect shareholders' equity, other than the initial investment, increase or decrease the item "Retained Earnings." This item will have a minus amount, which should be indicated by enclosing it in parentheses. Show noncurrent assets at their original cost.)

2. Prepare another balance sheet as of the following June 30.

3. Should the noncurrent assets be reported on the December 31 balance sheet at their cost, at $56,000, or at some other amount (the amount need not be calculated)? If at some amount other than cost, how would the balance sheet prepared in Question 1 be changed?

4. Does it appear likely that Early Years Day Care Center will become a viable company; that is, is it likely to be profitable if Mrs. Nissen's estimates are correct?

Chapter 3

Basic Accounting Concepts:
The Income Statement

Key Terms

Income statement
Revenues
Expenses
Net income
Time period concept
Conservatism concept
Realization concept
Matching concept
Consistency concept

Materiality concept
Expenditure
Gains and losses
Cost of goods sold
Gross margin
Cash-basis accounting
Economic income
Gross margin percentage
Profit margin

Discussion Questions

1. How does the time period concept aid management and other interested parties in making business decisions?

2. J. Winters & Company was aware of the business conditions described below as of December 31. Using the conservatism concept, determine when the revenues or expenses should be recognized and describe how each condition should be recorded on the balance sheet.

   a. Currently the selling price of certain goods in inventory is lower than the acquisition cost of these goods. The total difference between the selling price and the cost is $2,000, but it is highly probable that the selling price will exceed the cost by June of next year.

   b. Rent on a warehouse in the amount of $500 has been collected in advance for January of next year.

   c. $3,000 of repair service was supplied to a new customer, but no payment has been received.

   d. A loan was granted to a major customer on November 1 of the current year. The loan will yield $2,400 of interest revenue every six months beginning next May.

3. Indicate how each of the following affects owner's equity. Then show the overall effect of the transactions on owner's equity:

   a. Owner invested an additional $1,000 in the business.
   b. Owner borrowed $1,000 from the First National Bank.
   c. Owner made a sale of $1,000 for cash.
   d. The cost of goods sold in transaction (c) was $700.
   e. Owner paid rent bill of $200.
   f. Owner paid back the bank loan of $1,000 [transaction (b) -- ignore interest].
   g. Owner took $500 from the business for personal use.

4. Distinguish between "revenues" and "receipts."

5. Distinguish between "costs" and "expenses."

6. Norris Stores had sales in May totaling $50,000. Of these, $40,000 were credit sales. Norris' belief is that 5 percent of the credit sales will not be collectible. What should Norris show as its May revenues?

7. Describe how the realization concept is used to determine the total revenue recognized within a given time period.

8. How does the matching concept impact the amount of expense recognized during an accounting period?

9. Four types of transactions need to be considered in distinguishing between amounts that are properly considered as expenses of a given accounting period and the expenditures or cash payments made in connection with these items. These are:

   a. Expenditures that are also expenses.
   b. Assets that become expenses.

   c. Expenditures that are not yet expenses.
   d. Expenses not yet paid.

   Give a clear example of each of these types of transactions.

10. J. Weiss & Company had the following transactions in June. Using the matching concept, decide which of these transactions represented expenses for June.

    a. Received orders for goods with prices totaling $22,000; goods to be delivered in July.
    b. Paid office staff $9,750 for work performed in June.
    c. Products in inventory costing $1,725 were found to be obsolete.
    d. Sold goods with a cost of $25,000 in June.
    e. Paid $750 for radio advertising in June.
    f. Purchased additional inventory for $695.

11. It is customary to set up a liability for "expenses not yet paid." It has been said that "the incurrence of these expenses reduces owners' equity; the subsequent payment of the obligation does not affect owners' equity." Explain what this remark means.

12. Discuss the rationale behind the consistency concept.

13. Electra Company purchases a number of magazines and technical journals for its library. In doing so, Electra usually takes advantage of the lower per-year cost afforded by multiyear subscriptions. Despite the fact that typically Electra buys multiyear subscriptions, it does not show these as a prepaid expense on its balance sheet. Is this improper accounting?

14. Describe the differences between accrual accounting and cash-basis accounting. What distinguishes cash-basis accounting from modified cash-basis accounting?

15. Why are financial accounting income and taxable income typically different?

16. Why do economists deduct an additional equity interest expense from a business entity's income?

Problems

3-1. The E. Stahbenfeldt Company had July sales of $190,000. The cost of goods sold was $114,000 and other cash expenses were:

Rent.................$ 2,280		Taxes.................$ 950
Salaries............. 19,000		Other................. 34,770

Required: What were the company's (1) revenues, (2) expenses, and (3) net income in July?

3-2. The Clerbrook Corporation expended $182,000 for supplies during 1982. On December 1, it ordered $122,500 worth of supplies to be received on January 3, 1983. On December 31, 1982, the amount of supplies inventory on hand was $61,250.

Required:

    a. What was the supplies expense for 1982?
    b. What is the amount of supplies cost in 1982 that will become an expense in 1983?

3-3. The R. N. Johanson Computer Company purchased a two-year fire insurance policy, paying the $18,000 premium in October 1982. The policy was dated October 1, 1982 and expired on September 30, 1984. With respect to this policy, what were the expenses applicable to 1982, 1983, and 1984, and what was the asset value (prepaid insurance) as of December 31, 1982, 1983, and 1984?

3-4. Lowland Rental Company requires the first year and a half of rent for a five-year lease on its townhouse apartments to be paid in advance. On November 1, 1983 Lowland collected $45,000 of advance rental payments, but also incurred the following costs in cleaning and renovating the newly-leased apartments:

Paint....................$2,000
Fixtures................. 1,500
Carpeting................ 4,250
Labor.................... 1,250
Total..............$9,000

With respect to 1983 and 1984, what are the revenues and expenses for the new rentals from November 1, 1983?

3-5. On October 1, 1982 the Weafer Company borrowed $68,000 on a five-month, 14% note; the note and related interest will fall due on March 31, 1983. Determine:

    a. The amount of cash received by the company on October 31, 1982.
    b. The amount of interest expense applicable to 1982.
    c. The amount of interest accrual as of December 31, 1982.
    d. The amount of interest expense applicable to 1983.
    e. The amount of cash to be paid on March 31, 1983.
    f. The effect on owners' equity of each of the above and the overall effect.

3-6. The Dandes Company borrowed $45,000 on a four-month note discounted at a rate of 12% on November 30, 1982.

    a. What was the amount of the liability, Notes Payable, as of November 30, 1982? (Assume no other notes were outstanding.)
    b. What was the amount of cash Dandes received on November 30, 1982?
    c. Determine the interest expense applicable to 1982.
    d. What is the amount of prepaid interest expense as of December 31, 1982?
    e. Determine the interest expense applicable to 1983.
    f. What is the amount of cash to be paid on March 31, 1983?
    g. What is the effect of each of (a)-(f) above on owners' equity, and the overall effect?
    h. Suppose that instead of the note described, Dandes' note was for three months, discounted at 10%, and Dandes received $75,000 in cash. Determine the face value (principal) of this note.

3-7. Schiffli Company's July balance sheet was as follows:

Assets		Equities	
Cash.......................$ 5,750		Notes payable............$11,500	
Accounts receivable....... 5,750		Capital, J. Schiffli..... 23,000	
Inventories............... 23,000			
Total..............$34,500		Total..............$34,500	

During July, the following transactions occurred:

(1) Acquired $23,000 additional inventory on trade credit; payment due August 10.
(2) Sold goods carried in inventory at $4,600 for $11,500 cash.
(3) Paid rent for July 1 to September 30 at $1,150 per month.

(4) Sold on credit goods carried in inventory at $9,200 for $23,000; payments due August 15.
(5) Collected all of the July 1 balance in accounts receivable.
(6) Repaid $6,900 of the note payable (ignore interest).
(7) Collected $4,600 of the receivables due on August 15.
(8) Ms. Schiffli, the owner, withdrew $2,300 for her personal use.
(9) Other expenses in July totaled $13,800, all paid in cash.

Required: Prepare a July income statement, including a reconciliation of Schiffli's capital, and a balance sheet as of July 31.

3-8. Tower Grove Bank had the following transactions in December. How much revenue does each represent to Tower Grove Bank in December? Explain.

(1) A customer repaid his $6,000 auto loan.
(2) Interest of $675,000 on outstanding loans for the month of December was received.
(3) N. K. Inc. paid $12,000 interest on its outstanding loan from Tower Grove. Of this amount, $9,375 was interest applicable to future months.
(4) On January 2, Tower Grove Bank was to receive $1,200,000 in interest from government securities held during December.
(5) On December 31, the bank made a $225,000 loan to the J. W. Company.
(6) On December 31, $60,000 in service charges on checking accounts for the month of December were billed.

3-9. What is cost of goods sold for the period, given the following information?

```
Purchases for the period............$65,000
Beginning inventory................. 25,000
Ending inventory.................... 35,000
```

3-10. KSR Electronics Company had the following transactions during August while conducting its television and stereo repair business.

(1) A new repair truck was purchased for $14,000.
(2) Parts with a cost of $1,200 were received and used during August.
(3) Service revenue for the month was $26,750, but only $17,250 was cash sales. Typically, only 95% of sales on account are realized.
(4) Interest expense on loans outstanding was $650.
(5) Wage costs for the month totaled $7,350; however, $1,050 of this had not yet been paid to the employees.
(6) Parts inventory from the beginning of the month was depleted by $1,500.
(7) Utility bills totaling $900 were paid. $500 of this amount was associated with July's operations.
(8) Depreciation expense was $2,000; however, income tax regulations require a deduction of $3,000 for computing taxable income.
(9) Selling expenses were $1,400.
(10) A provision for income taxes was established at $2,700, while payments to the Federal government totaled at $2,500.
(11) Administrative and miscellaneous expenses were recorded at $3,000.

Required: Prepare a detailed August income statement.

3-11. What expense items are associated with the following transactions? When and how is the income statement affected by each one?

(1) Purchased equipment for $20,000 that has a useful life of 4 years.
(2) Purchased land for $125,000.
(3) Purchased $6,000 worth of inventory on December 21. On December 29 sold one half of the inventory for $8,000. On January 4, sold the remainder for $7,500. The company uses the calendar year for its fiscal year.
(4) On January 1, subscribed to a magazine for two years. The cost was $64.

3-12. Sandy Corporation has the following income statement for the year:

Income Statement
for the year ended December 31

```
Sales revenues................................$60,000
Expenses:
    Cost of goods sold........................ 35,000
    Selling and administrative expenses...... 15,000
    Income taxes..............................  1,000
Total expenses................................ 51,000
Net income....................................$ 9,000
```

Required:

a. Calculate:
    (1) Gross margin (in dollars)
    (2) Gross margin percentage
    (3) Profit margin percentage
b. Interpret the results of the above calculations.

3-13. Determine the amount of total assets at the end of the period from the following data:

Sales.....................$120,000

Expenses other than cost
    of goods sold........... 70,000

Total liabilities,
    ending balance......... 80,000

Retained earnings,
    beginning balance.........$55,000
Common stock, ending
    balance.................. 40,000
Gross margin percentage.....   50%

3-14. Determine the amount of total assets, current assets, and noncurrent assets at the end of the period, given the following data:

Current liabilities,
    ending balance..........$ 40,000
Current ratio, ending.....   1.5:1
Owners' equity, beginning
    balance................$100,000
Inventory, beginning
    balance................$ 25,000

Purchases during the
    period....................$30,000
Inventory, ending balance...$20,000
Gross margin percentage.....   40%
Profit margin...............   10%
Long-term debt, ending
    balance...................$30,000

3-15. During September, Newan, Inc., a retail store, had the following transactions. Prepare an income statement for the month of September (ignore taxes).

(1) Sales were $30,000. The gross margin percentage was 40%.
(2) Purchased a 12-month fire insurance policy for $1,200 on September 1.
(3) Purchased a 12%, $10,000 bond for investment purposes on September 1. Interest will be paid on January 1 and July 1.
(4) Paid August payroll. In August, 1,000 hours were worked at an average salary of $9 per hour.
(5) During September, 800 hours were worked at an average salary of $9 per hour. This will not be paid until October 2.
(6) General and administrative expenses totaled $2,000.
(7) Depreciation charges were $500.

3-16. Prepare an income statement on the cash basis using the transactions from Problem 3-15. Assume all sales are for cash, and all expenses are paid immediately. Would this statement be of use to management? Compare and contrast the uses of income statements prepared on the cash basis with those prepared on the accrual basis.

3-17. PKO Corporation's January 1 balance sheet was as follows:

Assets		Equities	
Cash.....................$ 8,100		Accounts payable............$ 9,450	
Accounts receivable....... 2,700		Notes payable (9%, inter-	
Inventory................. 18,900		est payable on 12/31).......5,600	
Prepaid insurance......... 1,296		Common stock................ 5,200	
Supplies.................. 54		Retained earnings........... 10,800	
$31,050		$31,050	

During January, the following transactions occurred.:

(1) Collected $2,430 of accounts receivable. The remainder of the January 1 receivables balance was written off as bad debts.
(2) Purchased $135 worth of supplies
(3) Purchased $8,100 worth of inventory.
(4) Sales totaled $16,200.
(5) A physical inventory on January 31 disclosed a balance in inventory of $15,660 and supplies of $27.
(6) Prepaid insurance as of January 1 was a policy that would be in force for six more months.
(7) Declared a $2,000 dividend on January 20, payable to shareholders of record on February 15.
(8) Issued 200 shares of common stock for $10 per share.

Required: Prepare an income statement for January that includes a disclosure of the effect on retained earnings. Ignore taxes.

CASES

Case 3-18: Cascade Cafe (B)

In addition to preparing the balance sheet described in Cascade Cafe (A), Mr. Whittaker, the accountant, agreed to prepare an income statement. He said that such a financial statement would show Mrs. Rayburn how profitable operations had been, and thus help her to judge whether it was worthwhile to continue operating the restaurant.

In addition to the information given in the (A) case, Mr. Whittaker learned that cash received from customers through March 30 amounted to $23,651 and that cash payments were as follows:

Monthly payments to partners....$11,300
Wages to part-time employees..... 2,490
Interest...................... 270
Food and beverage suppliers...... 4,707
Telephone and electricity........ 1,617
Miscellaneous.................... 556
Rent payments................... 5,400

Questions

1. Prepare an income statement.

2. What does this income statement tell Mrs. Rayburn?

* * * * *

Case 3-19: John Bartlett (A)

John Bartlett was the inventor of a switching device that enabled a videogame or home computer to be connected to the antenna terminals of an ordinary television set. The switch would soon be given a patent, whose legal life was 17 years. Having confidence in the switch's commercial value, but possessing no excess funds of his own, he sought among his friends and acquaintances for the necessary capital to put the switch on the market. The proposition which he placed before possible associates was that a corporation, Bartlett Manufacturing Company, should be formed with capital stock of $50,000 par value.

The project looked attractive to a number of the individuals to whom the investor presented it, but the most promising among them -- a retired manufacturer -- said he would be un-

willing to invest his capital without knowing what uses were intended for the cash to be received from the proposed sale of stock. He suggested that the inventor determine the probable costs of experimentation and of special machinery, and prepare for him a statement of the estimated assets and liabilities of the proposed company when ready to begin actual operation. He also asked for a statement of the estimated transactions for the first year of operations, to be based on studies the inventor had made of probable markets and costs of labor and materials. This information Mr. Bartlett consented to supply to the best of his ability.

After consulting the engineer who had aided him in constructing his patent models, Mr. Bartlett drew up the following list of data relating to the transactions of the proposed corporation during its period of organization and development.

1. The retired manufacturer would pay the corporation $20,000 cash for which he would receive stock with a par value of $20,000. The remaining stock (par value, $30,000) would be given to Mr. Bartlett in exchange for the patent on the switch.
2. Probable cost of incorporation and organization, including estimated officers' salaries during developmental period, $3,300.
3. Probable cost of developing special machinery, $10,000. This sum includes the cost of expert services, materials, rent of a small shop, and the cost of power, light, and miscellaneous expenditures.
4. Probable cost of raw materials, $1,000, of which $600 is to be used in experimental production.

On the basis of the above information, Mr. Bartlett prepared the estimated balance sheet shown in Exhibit 1.

EXHIBIT 1

BARTLETT MANUFACTURING COMPANY
Estimated Balance Sheet
As of Date Company Begins Operations

Assets

```
Cash.........................$ 5,700
Inventory....................    400
Machinery................... 10,000
Organizational costs........  3,300
Experimental costs..........    600
Patent......................  30,000
        Total Assets.........$50,000
```

Equities

```
Shareholders' equity........$50,000
        Total Assets......... $50,000
```

Mr. Bartlett then set down the following estimates as a beginning step in furnishing the rest of the information desired:

1. Expected sales, all to be received in cash by the end of the first year of operations, $168,000.
2. Expected additional purchases of raw materials and supplies during the course of operating year, all paid for in cash by the end of the year, $54,000.
3. Expected borrowing from the bank during the year but loans to be repaid before the close of the year, $4,000. Interest on these loans, $300.

4. Expected payroll and other cash expenses and manufacturing costs for the operating year: $66,000 of manufacturing costs (excluding raw materials and supplies) plus $12,000 for selling and administrative expenses, a total of $78,000.
5. New equipment to be purchased for cash, $2,000.
6. Expected inventory of raw materials and supplies at close of the period, at cost, $10,000.
7. No inventory of unsold switches expected as of the end of the period. All products to be manufactured on the basis of firm orders received; none to be produced for inventory.
8. All experimental and organization costs, previously capitalized, to be charged against income of the operating year.
9. Estimated depreciation of machinery, $1,200.
10. Dividends paid in cash, $6,000.
11. Estimated tax expense for the year, $8,450. Ten percent of this amount would not be due until early in the following year.

It should be noted that the transactions summarized above would not necessarily take place in the sequence indicated. In practice, a considerable number of separate events, or transactions would occur throughout the year, and many of them were dependent on one another. For example, operations were begun with an initial cash balance and inventory of raw materials, products were manufactured, and sales of these products provided funds for financing subsequent operations. Then, in turn, sales of the product subsequently manufactured yielded more funds.

Questions

1. Trace the effect on the balance sheet of each of the projected events appearing in Mr. Bartlett's list. Thus, Item 1, taken alone, would mean that cash would be increased by $168,000 and that (subject to reductions for various costs covered in later items) shareholders' equity would be increased by $168,000. Notice that in this question you are asked to consider all items in terms of their effect on the balance sheet.

2. Prepare an income statement covering the first year of planned operations and a balance sheet as of the end of that year.

3. Assume that the retired manufacturer received capital stock with a par value of $16,000 for the $20,000

cash he paid to the corporation, John Bartlett still receiving stock with a par value of $30,000 in exchange for his patent. Under these circumstances, how would the balance sheet in Exhibit 1 appear?

4. Assume that the management is interested in what the results would be if no products were sold during the first year, even though production continued at the level indicated in the original plans. The following changes would be made in the 11 items listed above: Items 1, 6, 7, 10, and 11 are to be disregarded. Instead of Item 3, assume that a loan of $156,000 is obtained, that the loan is not repaid, but that interest thereon of $18,700 is paid during the year. Prepare an income statement for the year and a balance sheet as of the end of the year. Contrast these financial statements with those prepared in Question 2.

* * * * *

Case 3-20: Ruby Peale

Ruby Peale retired in early 1981. Her last few years at work had been frustrating ones, and it had seemed to her that retirement could not come soon enough. Since after her husband's death in 1977, Mrs. Peale had considered moving to a warmer climate after she retired. After settling on a course of action, she withdrew $60,000 of her savings in order to purchase a modest three-bedroom house in a fast growing Sunbelt city. The house was located on a main thoroughfare on the north side of town, and there were a number of businesses, primarily restaurants, located on the same street. Shopping was convenient and the level of public transportation was the best in the city.

Ruby's early experience with retirement turned out to be a mixed blessing. While she enjoyed the moderate weather of her newly-found city, the suddenly increased amount of leisure time left her ill at ease and often downright uncomfortable. Late in 1981 Mrs. Peale began to explore the possibility of pursuing a childhood dream -- owning and operating her own business.

New Times--Salads 'N' Yogurt. Mrs. Peale soon decided that opening a fast foods shop that featured health foods would be an appropriate course of action. She came to this conclusion after a quick survey of the local business scene, during which she had paid particularly close attention to the apparent trends in the food and restaurant business.

Upon being asked, a local realtor suggested that it would cost around $750 a month to rent a nearby location suitable for use as a small restaurant. This seemed high to Ruby, as she viewed rent as being "lost money." When a friend suggested that she consider using her own home for the site of the proposed restaurant, Ruby decided to look in depth at this idea.

After further research, she discovered that the city would allow her to operate a small restaurant in her house. They would, however, require that she make some minor structural modifications to the building. They also said that she would need to provide a paved parking area capable of holding ten automobiles. The required renovations and additions, costing some $18,000, were completed in late December. Upon installation of some $9,000 worth of furniture and fixtures, Salads 'N' Yogurt was formally inaugurated in mid-January 1982.

Minnie Gibson, an old friend of Ruby's agreed to work for her in a combined waitress and cashier role. While business was slow at first, she and Ruby watched with great pride as the sales volume grew steadily throughout the first half of the year. In late summer, they placed advertisements with coupons in the neighborhood press and in the campus newspaper of a nearby university. In the early autumn, Ruby hired her nephew and niece, both students at the local university, in order to enable her to extend the restaurant's business hours into Friday and Saturday evenings. Both of the above actions were followd by noticeable increases in the total volume of business.

Measuring Performance--Mixed Views. By the end of 1982, the cumulative sales of Salads N' Yogurt had reached a level of nearly $180,000. Ruby was clearly delighted with the progress of her business. She noted that her personal withdrawals from the business of $18,000 were only $4,500 less than a friend of hers had been paid for managing a small chain restaurant down the street. This, she thought, indicated the great progress that had been made during the firm's first year of operations.

Early in January 1983, Ruby decided that she would put together a profit and loss statement covering her firm's first year of operations. Her efforts, and some advice from Minnie, resulted in the statement shown as Exhibit 1. Somewhat uncertain of her accounting ability but proud of her achievements, Ruby went over the financial summary with her nephew.

The nephew, sensing an opportunity to demonstrate his own accounting skills, asked if he could review the firm's records and prepare his own version of the profit and loss statement. Ruby, appreciative of her nephew's interest in the business, consented to the request.

The nephew soon derived an alternative income statement which he left with Ruby one day on his way to class (see Exhibit 2). Shortly after reading this statement, Ruby stormed out of her office to find Minnie. "Look what my nephew has done!", she said. "He's charged my firm with a rent figure that we didn't pay. He's treated my withdrawals from the business as salary. And, he couldn't even get that right! He's boosted them from $18,000 to $22,500. Finally, he's removed the depreciation figure that I had on there for the renovations and parking and for half of the building and my estimated personal income tax. What are they teaching him at that university? Creative accounting?"

With that tirade, Ruby sat down to reflect upon the numbers contained in the two financial statements.

Questions:

1. How much profit did Salads 'N' Yogurt earn in 1982?

2. How do you explain the difference between the amount shown for net

EXHIBIT 1

SALADS 'N' YOGURT
1982 Income Statement
(as prepared by Ruby Peale)

Gross sales	$117,623
Less: Sales discounts	5,835
Net sales	171,788
Cost of sales	73,203
Gross margin	98,585
Operating Expenses:	
Advertising	9,300
Depreciation (building)*	1,200
Depreciation (renovations and parking)	1,800
Depreciation (furniture and fixtures)	1,500
Insurance**	1,572
Janitorial services	4,500
Miscellaneous	4,074
Payroll	25,185
Payroll taxes	2,798
Personal income taxes (estimated)	3,000
Property taxes**	1,479
Service contracts (on appliances)	1,539
Supplies	6,270
Utilities	9,300
Total operating expenses	73,517
Net Income	$25,068

---

*This represents depreciation of half of the house over 20 years. The building is presumed to constitute 80% of the purchase price of the land and building.

**This represents fifty percent of actual amount spent, as the restaurant occupies about half of the building.

EXHIBIT 2

SALADS 'N' YOGURT
1982 Income Statement
(as prepared by the Nephew)

Gross sales	$177,623
Less: Sales discounts	5,835
Net sales	171,788
Cost of sales	73,203
Gross margin	98,585
Operating expenses:	
Advertising	9,300
Depreciation (furniture and fixtures)	1,500
Janitorial services	4,500
Miscellaneous	4,074
Payroll	25,185
Payroll taxes	2,798
Rent of Premises	9,000
Salary, Ruby Peale*	22,500
Service contracts (on appliances)	1,539
Supplies	6,270
Utilities	9,300
Total operating expenses	95,966
Net Income	$ 2,619

---

*This represents the approximate market value of services performed.

profit in the two exhibits? What accounting principles are at issue in the dispute?

3. Should Ruby continue to operate her own business? Has she been successful?

Chapter 4

Accounting Records and Systems

Key Terms

Account
Debit and credit
Ledger
Chart of accounts
Journal
Posting

Trial balance
Adjusting entries
Contra account
Temporary accounts
Closing entries

Discussion Questions

1. Why is the "T account" a useful device in recording transactions?

2. What would it mean if, in the trial balance, the sum of the debit balances did not equal the sum of the credit balances?

3. Can each of the following characteristics exist in a given transaction? For any "yes" answers, give an example.

   a. Decrease in owners' equity and decrease in an asset.
   b. Increase in revenue and decrease in a liability.
   c. Decrease in a liability and increase in an asset.
   d. Decrease in an asset and decrease in an expense.
   e. Increase in owners' equity and decrease in a liability.

4. How is it that a debit entry can increase an asset, which is a "good" thing, and also increase an expense, which is a "bad" thing?

5. How many accounts should a company maintain?

6. Distinguish among "original" entries, "adjusting" entries, and "closing" entries.

7. For the transactions which follow, indicate whether each is an original, adjusting, or closing entry.

a.	dr.		Bad Debts......................................	100	
		cr.	Allowance for Doubtful Accounts............		100
b.	dr.		Accounts Receivable...........................1,000		
		cr.	Sales......................................		1,000
c.	dr.		Purchases.....................................2,000		
		cr.	Accounts Payable...........................		2,000
d.	dr.		Depreciation Expense..........................	150	
		cr.	Accumulated Depreciation...................		150
e.	dr.		Income Summary...............................5,000		
		cr.	Retained Earnings..........................		5,000

- 23 -

```
f.   dr.         Interest Expense.............................   50
          cr.        Accrued Interest.............................        50

g.   dr.         Insurance Expense............................  100
          cr.        Prepaid Insurance............................       100

h.   dr.         Cash.........................................  980
                 Sales Discounts..............................   20
          cr.        Accounts Receivable..........................     1,000

i.   dr.         Accounts Payable.............................2,000
          cr.        Purchase Discounts...........................        20
                     Cash.........................................     1,980

j.   dr.         Income Summary...............................9,000
          cr.        Cost of Goods Sold...........................     9,000

k.   dr.         Income Tax Expense...........................  750
          cr.        Income Taxes Payable.........................       750

l.   dr..        Sales Discounts..............................   50
          cr.        Allowance for Sales Discounts...............        50
```

8. Prepare adjusting entries to record the following:

   a. Depreciation expense for the period is $1,000.
   b. The estimated amount of uncollectible accounts receivable is $300.
   c. One year's coverage on a four-year insurance policy has been received; the policy was paid in full for $400 cash on its effective date.
   d. Employees have earned $2,000 since their last payday.
   e. Six months have passed since the company borrowed $10,000. The $10,000 plus interest at 8 percent will be due in six more months.
   f. A customer has placed a $50 deposit on goods that are being specially ordered for her.

9. Record the following transactions, related to (b), (d), (e), and (f) in Question 8:

   b. Management decides to write off a customer's account receivable of $75 as uncollectible.
   d. On their next payday, employees are paid $5,000.
   e. The $10,000 loan and a year's interest at 8 percent are paid.
   f. The customer's goods, with a retail price of $200, are delivered to the customer. Her $50 deposit is applied against the purchase price, and she pays cash for the balance.

10. The text describes the closing process, whereby revenue and expense accounts are closed to Income Summary and then Income Summary is closed to Retained Earnings. Suppose that _instead_ of this process, the debits and credits in the expense and revenue accounts were summarized on a piece of scrap paper, and the net amount was entered into Retained Earnings. If a balance sheet were then prepared, would it balance? If so, why bother with a more formal closing process?

11. What is the primary purpose of a work sheet?

12. Fill in the blank space for each item. Your answer will be either _debit_ or _credit_.

   a. A _____ will increase an owners' equity account.

   b. A _____ will decrease a liability account.

   c. A _____ will increase an asset account.

   d. A _____ will decrease an expense account.

   e. A _____ will decrease an owners' equity account.

   f. A _____ will decrease an asset account.

g. A _____ will increase a revenue account.

h. A _____ will increase a liability account.

i. The normal balance of a liability account is _____.

j. The normal balance of an expense account is _____.

k. The normal balance of an asset account is _____.

l. The normal balance of an owners' equity account is _____.

13. What are the four objectives that the "best" accounting system for a company would fulfill?

14. Describe the purpose and operation of an imprest fund.

15. What impact has the Foreign Corrupt Practices Act of 1977 had upon financial accounting?

16. Why is the matrix concept practical only when employed within a computerized accounting system?

17. Briefly describe the advantages and disadvantages of a computer-based accounting system vis-a-vis a manual system.

Problems

4-1. Set up the following in T-account form and determine the ending balances insofar as these accounts are concerned. (Not all balance sheet accounts are shown.)

	Beginning balances	
Account	Dr.	Cr.
Cash...	$ 750	
Accounts Receivable...............................	3,000	
Inventory...	6,000	
Accounts Payable..................................		$3,750
Notes Payable.....................................		750

Transactions:

(1) Purchased inventory on account.............$2,250
(2) Sold goods on account: sale price......... 6,000
    Cost of goods sold........................ 3,750
(3) Paid creditors............................ 3,000
(4) Collected from customers.................. 5,250
(5) Paid off note payable..................... 750

4-2. Set up the following columns on a piece of paper:

Transaction	Assets	=	Liabilities	+	Owners' Equity
a	-1,150		-1,150		
b					
c					
Etc.					

For each of the following transactions, indicate the effect on the balance-sheet equation by inserting the amount in the appropriate column, and by indicating whether the effect is + or -. (For example, a check for $1,150 paid to a trade creditor would be shown as indicated above under transaction a.)

a. Paid trade creditor $1,150.
b. Paid rent, $690.
c. Purchased $4,600 merchandise on account.

d. Sold merchandise on account $3,450, cost $2,300.
e. Purchased $230 ofice supplies for cash. All office supplies were

used during the period.
f. Proprietor withdrew $460 for personal use.
g. Received a check for $3,450 from customer in payment of his account. No discount involved.
h. Paid trade creditor $4,600 less 2 percent prompt-payment discount.

4-3. Ajax Company had a four-month, 12 percent note receivable of $15,000 dated October 1, 1983, due February 1, 1984. Ajax's fiscal year ends December 31.

Required: What entries related to this note should be made on Ajax's books on December 31, 1983 and February 1, 1984?

4-4. Compute the net income or loss for the year, given the following information:

Assets:
Beginning of year.................................$190,000
End of year....................................... 235,000
Liabilities:
Beginning of year................................ 109,000
End of year....................................... 112,000
Dividends paid during the year................... 12,000
Issuance of additional capital stock.............. 30,000

4-5. From the following data, compute the amount of Cash:

Total current liabilities...........................$ 30,000
Owners' equity at end of year....................... 94,000
Total fixed assets.................................. 125,000
Goodwill.. 5,000
Long-term debt...................................... 55,000
Total current assets, exclusive of cash............. 41,000

4-6. Ryan Corporation's accounts had the following beginning balances:

Account	Dr.	Cr.
Accounts Payable...............................		$2,130
Accounts Receivable............................	$1,500	
Accumulated Depreciation.......................		2,000
Allowance for Doubtful Accounts................		50
Cash...	1,000	
Fixed Assets (at cost).........................	4,300	
Inventories....................................	1,200	
Note Payable (current).........................		400
Owners' Equity.................................		3,420
	$8,000	$8,000

During the period, the following transactions occurred:

(1) Purchased inventory on account, $900.
(2) Paid employees, $510.
(3) Sold goods for cash, $1,350.
(4) Sold goods on credit, $1,260.
(5) Overhead and other expenses paid in cash, $630.
(6) Collection of accounts receivable, $1,050.
(7) Paid certain accounts payable, $1,200.
(8) Received cash for revenue applicable to the next period, $450.
(9) Increased the current note payable by $150.
(10) Physical inventory showed ending balance of $1,200.
(11) Depreciation expense, $300.

Required:

a. Journalize the transactions.
b. Set up T-accounts and post beginning balances and transactions.
c. Determine the cost of goods sold.
d. Prepare an ending balance sheet.
e. Prepare an income statement for the period (ignore taxes).

4-7. The account balances in the ledger of the Chapman Company on February 28 (the end of its fiscal year), before adjustments, were as follows:

Debit balances		Credit balances	
Cash........................	$ 38,300	Accumulated depreciation	
Accounts receivable.........	52,250	on store equipment........	$ 12,000
Merchandise inventory.......	225,300	Notes payable...............	46,000
Store equipment.............	69,000	Accounts payable............	38,000
Supplies inventory..........	4,975	Common stock................	100,000
Prepaid insurance...........	12,300	Retained earnings...........	35,000
Selling expense.............	8,000	Sales.......................	230,525
Sales salaries..............	34,000		
Miscellaneous general			
expense...................	10,000		
Sales discounts.............	2,000		
Interest expense............	3,000		
Social Security tax expense.	2,400		
Total.................	$461,525	Total.................	$461,525

The data for the adjustments are:

(1) Cost of merchandise sold, $97,425.
(2) Depreciation on store equipment, $4,100.
(3) Supplies inventory, February 28, $1,675. (Purchases of supplies during the year were debited to the Supplies Inventory account.)
(4) Expired insurance, $1,500.
(5) Interest accrued on notes payable, $1,200.
(6) Sales salaries earned but not paid to employees, $1,150.
(7) Interest earned on savings account, but not recorded, $125.

Required:

a. Set up T-accounts with the balances given above.
b. Journalize and post adjusting entries, adding other T-accounts as necessary.
c. Journalize and post closing entries.
d. Prepare an income statement and balance sheet.

4-8. Prepare a May income statement for Alessi Corporation from the following May data. Indicate any adjusting or closing entries. (Ignore taxes.)

Sales revenues..............	$100,000	Cost of goods sold..........	$132,000
Accounts receivable, gross,		Purchased six-month insur-	
May 31 balance (2% esti-		ancy policy on May 1......	3,960
mated to be uncollect-		Wages payable, May 1	
ible; no allowance for		balance...................	6,600
bad debts as of May 1)....	66,000	Wages paid during May.......	75,900
Plant and equipment (10-		Wages payable, May 31	
year life, straight-		balance...................	3,300
line depreciation).......	49,500	Dividends declared..........	49,500

4-9. Kruse Company had the following transactions in November:

(1) Allowance for Bad Debts, November 1 balance, $125.
(2) Accounts Receivable, November 1 balance, $3,000.
(3) Sold goods for $1,000 on credit to R. Company.
(4) Sold goods on credit to other customers for $1,400.
(5) Collections of receivables, $2,100.
(6) Estimated that $100 worth of receivables booked in November will not be collected.
(7) R. Company paid its receivable promptly, and was thereby able to take a 2% discount.

Required: Prepare journal entries for the above. Determine the ending balance of Accounts Receivable, net of bad debt allowance.

4-10. Write journal entries for the following transactions that occurred at Lakeview Company during March, and explain how each would be disclosed in Lakeview's financial statements.

(1) The company prepaid $5,670 rent for the period March 1 - August 31.
(2) Sales discounts and allowances were $13,500.
(3) A loan for $1,400 at 12% interest continued to be owed to the company by one of its employees, who made no payments related to this loan during March.
(4) Depreciation expense was $5,400.
(5) Customers paid $1,080 for services they will not receive until sometime in April.
(6) Purchased $68 worth of stamps, and used $40 worth of them.
(7) The allowance for doubtful accounts was increased by $540, reflecting a new estimate of uncollectible accounts.

4-11. Show how the following account balances are closed to the owner's equity accounts.

	Dr.	Cr.
Sales...		$24,700
Interest Revenue..............................		650
Cost of Goods Sold............................	$12,350	
Wages...	1,950	
Supplies Expense..............................	325	
General and Administrative....................	195	
Depreciation Expense..........................	130	

4-12. At the beginning of June, the accounts of Beta Company had the following balances:

	Dr.	Cr.
Cash..	$ 8,000	
Accounts Receivable...........................	2,000	
Allowance for Bad Debts.......................		$ 20
Inventory.....................................	9,000	
Building (at cost)............................	60,000	
Accumulated Depreciation......................		9,000
Accounts Payable..............................		10,000
Notes Payable.................................		12,000
Common Stock..................................		20,000
Retained Earnings.............................		27,980

During June the following occurred:

(1) Sales were $82,000. All sales were on credit.
(2) Purchased $35,000 worth of merchandise on credit.
(3) Paid $38,000 worth of accounts payable.
(4) Collected $78,000 worth of accounts receivable.
(5) Paid $20,000 to employees for their services.
(6) Specific accounts receivable of $20 were determined to be uncollectible. The remaining accounts were all deemed to be collectible.
(7) A physical inventory determined that the ending balance of inventory was $7,000.
(8) Estimated life of the building is 20 years, with zero residual value at the end of 20 years. Straight-line depreciation is used.
(9) Interest on the notes payable is at 13% per annum. No interest was paid during June.
(10) General and administrative expenses totaled $4,000, paid in cash.

Required: Write journal entries for June's transactions. Then prepare financial statements as of the end of June. (Ignore taxes.)

4-13. MKO Corporation has the following year-end (December 31) balances before adjusting and closing entries:

	Dr.	Cr.
Cash...............................$	4,300	
Accounts Receivable (gross)........	17,200	
Inventories........................	21,500	
Equipment (net)....................	193,500	
Building (net).....................	43,000	
Accounts Payable...................		$ 21,500
Notes Payable (12%)................		43,000
Common Stock.......................		86,000
Retained Earnings, beginning.......		64,500
Sales..............................		344,000
Cost of Goods Sold.................	215,000	
Other Expenses.....................	64,500	

Further transactions and information are as follows:

(1) During the year, $2,500 for supplies purchases was debited to Other Expenses. At year end, $200 of these supplies remain unused. There were no supplies on hand at the beginning of the year.

(2) Estimated uncollectibles equal 3% of the ending gross balance of accounts receivable. (The balance in Allowance for Bad Debts at the beginning of the year was zero.)

(3) Depreciation charges are $20,000 for equipment and $3,000 for the building.

(4) Interest on notes payable is paid annually on June 30.

(5) Dividends of $10,000 were declared on December 31 and are payable on January 15.

(6) MKO estimates that of the year-end accounts receivable, $344 will not be received in cash because some customers will take advantage of a discount to which they are entitled if they pay within 10 days.

Required:

    a. Prepare the necessary adjusting entries.
    b. Prepare financial statements.

4-14. Perry Franklin, though not well-versed in accounting, attempted keeping the books for his new business, Franklin's TV Service. The trial balance he prepared for March does not balance, and he has asked you to correct it. In examining Franklin's records, you have discovered the following:

(1) The first two digits of FICA Taxes Payable as shown in the trial balance had been transposed when copied from the ledger.

(2) A $250 check given as payment to a vendor had not been posted to the Accounts Payable account.

(3) The March 1 balance in Parts Inventory was $15,400; during March purchases of parts totaled $62,750. The month-end physical inventory appeared to have been counted and costed correctly.

(4) Although Franklin did not usually offer credit to his customers, one of them, a close friend, owed $125 for a repair job for which the revenue and related costs had been recorded in the accounts.

Franklin's incorrect trial balance is shown below.

FRANKLIN'S TV SERVICE   Trial Balance
March 31

	Dr.	Cr.
Cash..$	10,175	
Parts inventory............................	17,500	
Prepaid insurance..........................	600	
Accounts payable...........................		$ 5,800
FICA taxes payable.........................		258
Notes payable..............................		2,000
Capital....................................		10,650
Sales revenues.............................		87,000
Cost of parts used in repair jobs........	60,560	
Administrative expenses..................	4,363	

	Dr.	Cr.
Salaries and wages........................	$ 10,000	
FICA tax expense..........................	450	
Advertising expense.......................	1,050	
Miscellaneous expenses....................	950	
Nonoperating revenue......................	235	
Interest expense..........................		100
Totals...............................	$106,338	$105,808

4-15. The following are the business transactions of Joan Forner for the month of March:

March 1 Ms. Forner invested $14,000 in cash and $12,000 in store equipment in order to start her own business (credit Joan Forner, Equity).
 4 Paid $900 rent for the month of March.
 6 Purchased $16,000 worth of merchandise from the Acme Company on account.
 8 Sold merchandise to Black Company on account; sales price, $14,000.
 12 Purchased office equipment for $5,000 from Thurston Company on account.
 15 Issued check for payment due the Acme Company.
 18 Received check from Black Company in settlement of bill.
 20 Paid $375 for advertising placed in the Newtowne Chronicle on March 10.
 25 Ms. Forner withdrew $550 for her personal use.*
 26 Paid salaries and wages of $4,800 for March (ignore all taxes and deductions).
 27 Sold merchandise to White Company on account, $9,000.
 28 Paid to Protector Insurance Company $420 for a one-year fire insurance policy that was effective as of March 1.
 31 Cost of goods sold to:
 Black Company...............$7,200
 White Company.............. 6,000

---

*The account "Joan Forner, Drawings" is a temporary account used to record Forner's withdrawals during the month. At the end of the month it is closed into her capital account.

Adjustments necessary as of March 31:

(1) Estimated life of store equipment is five years, and of office equipment, ten years. Straight-line depreciation is used.
(2) Insurance partially expired. Compute amounts.
(3) Assume combined state and federal income tax liability to be $450.

Required:

a. Prepare current journal entries for March on the journal pages provided.
b. Post current entries to the ledger; rule off Cash and Accounts Receivable accounts for practice.
c. Take off a trial balance on the work sheet provided.
d. Prepare and post adjusting entries to the work sheet.
e. Extend the work sheet to financial statement sections.
f. Prepare an income statement for March.
g. Prepare a balance sheet as of March 31.

CASES

Case 4-16: Freeson's Gift Gallery

In January, Carla Freeson opened a gift store. The following transactions and transaction summaries constituted her operations for the first year of

JOAN FORNER
JOURNAL

DATE	ACCOUNT TITLES AND EXPLANATION	FO-LIO	DEBIT	CREDIT

DATE	ACCOUNT TITLES AND EXPLANATION	FO-LIO	DEBIT	CREDIT

GENERAL LEDGER

CASH

Date	Explanation	R	Amount	Date	Explanation	R	Amount

ACCOUNTS RECEIVABLE

Date	Explanation	R	Amount	Date	Explanation	R	Amount

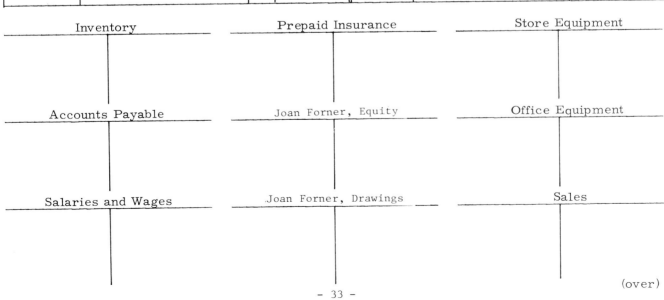

Inventory   Prepaid Insurance   Store Equipment

Accounts Payable   Joan Forner, Equity   Office Equipment

Salaries and Wages   Joan Forner, Drawings   Sales

(over)

Rent Expense		Advertising Expense

JOAN FORNER
WORK SHEET FOR MARCH

	Trial Balance		Adjustments		Income Statement		Balance Sheet	
	Dr.	Cr.	Dr.	Cr.	Dr.	Cr.	Dr.	Cr.
Cash								
Accounts receivable								
Inventory								
Prepaid insurance								
Store equipment								
Office equipment								
Accounts payable								
Joan Forner, Equity								
Joan Forner, Drawings								
Sales								
Salaries and Wages								
Rent expense								
Advertising expense								

business.

1. Ms. Freeson invested $90,000 in cash.
2. She paid $60,000 cash for a store building, including fixtures, and gave a mortgage note of $54,000 on the building. (No mortgage payments were due during the year.)
3. She bought merchandise of $372,750 on account.
4. For every sale a slip was made out showing both the selling price and, in code, the cost of the article sold. Thus, at the close of each day Ms. Freeson could, if she so wished, take totals of these figures and calculate her gross margin for the day. The summary of these figures for the year showed:

       Sales for cash...........$192,900
       Sales on credit.......... 189,450
             Total Sales......... 382,350
       Cost of goods sold....... 287,010

5. She paid $38,550 for wages. (Ignore social security and withholding taxes.)
6. She paid $21,450 for other expenses.
7. She received $2,700 net for rent of storage space in her store loft.
8. She paid $235,500 of her accounts payable, $208,500 with cash and the remainder with notes payable.
9. Her customers paid her $130,500 on the amounts owed her.
10. During the year Ms. Freeson withdrew for her own use $72,000 in cash.*

_____

*The account "Carla Freeson, Drawings" is a temporary account used to record Ms. Freeson's withdrawals during the year. At the end of the year, it is closed into her capital account.

On December 31, Ms. Freeson scrutinized her accounts carefully to see whether they fully reflected the business situation, and discovered the following items requiring entries:

11. She estimated that her buildings and fixtures had depreciated $3,900.
12. At the end of the year she owed her employees $600 for wages.
13. She found that miscellaneous supplies were still on hand and unused to the amount of $2,502. These supplies had been charged (debited) to the Other Expense account when they were purchased.
14. A physical inventory of merchandise on hand was taken on December 31, and was determined to be $85,230. The discrepancy between this figure and the balance shown by the inventory account was assumed to be caused by (a) errors in recording cost prices on sales tickets, (b) breakage, and (c) shoplifting. The amount was not considered unreasonable for a year's operation. Debit "Other Expense" for the difference.

Required:

a. Journalize the fourteen transactions; then post them in the T-accounts provided.
b. Prepare an income statement for the year and a year-end balance sheet.

* * * * *

Case 4-17: Pinkham Motel

Mr. and Mrs. George Treml had purchased the Pinkham Motel in 1973 with their life savings, supplemented by a loan from a close personal friend. The motel consisted of 15 units (i.e., rentable rooms), and was located near a vacation area which was popular during both the summer and winter seasons. The Tremls had entered the motel business because Mrs. Treml had long wanted to run a business of her own.

Both Mr. and Mrs. Treml felt that they had been successful. Each year

saw a growth in revenues from room rentals. Furthermore, their bank balance had increased. They noted that many of their customers returned year after year. This was attributed to their location and their efforts to provide consistently clean rooms and up-to-date furnishings. Fortunately, no significant competition had arisen along the route on which the Pinkham Motel was situated.

The Tremls had no formal business training, but felt their experience

FREESON'S GIFT GALLERY
Ledger

Cash

Accumulated Depreciation

Accounts Receivable

Accounts Payable

Merchandise Inventory

Cost of Goods Sold

Buildings & Fixtures

Wages Expense

Supplies Inventory

Notes Payable	Carla Freeson, Drawings

Depreciation Expense	Income Summary

Other Expense	Mortgage Payable

Accrued Wages	Rent Revenue

Carla Freeson, Capital	Sales

since acquiring the motel had alerted them to the management problems involved. Both Mr. and Mrs. Treml devoted full time to operating the motel. In addition, they hired part-time help for cleaning and chambermaid work. They had no dining facilities, but had installed coffee, cigarette, and candy vending machines to supplement room rentals. The vending machines posed no inventory or maintenance problem as the vending machine company provided servicing and maintenance.

A frequent guest at Pinkham Motel was Mr. Fernando Garcia, controller of a large company. Mr. Garcia visited a company branch plant near the motel several times a year. As he stayed at the motel during these trips, he became acquainted with the Tremls.

In August 1978, Mr. Treml showed Mr. Garcia the July issue of the Motel/ Motor Inn Journal, a trade journal which contained operating percentages of motels for the calendar year 1977. Data were given for motels with 40 or fewer units. Mr. Treml commented: These figures show a profit of 21 percent. Our profit last year was $32,106 on sales of $58,329 or 55 percent. We think 1977 was our best year to date, but we can't make our figures jibe with those in the magazine, and we wonder if we really are 34 percent ahead of the industry average. Can you help us?"

Mr. Garcia was interested and willing to help. He told Mr. Treml to get the available figures for 1977 so that he could look them over that evening. The principal records the Tremls kept to reflect the motel's financial transactions were a record of receipts, taken from the cash register, and a checkbook describing cash paid out. In addition, certain rough notations of other expenses incurred were available.

That evening Mr. Treml showed Mr. Garcia the cash summary for the year 1977, as given in Exhibit 1. Mr. Garcia immediately noted that the difference between receipts and expenditures was $11,371, and asked Mr. Treml to explain why he had stated the profit was $32,106. Mr. Treml replied, "Oh, that's easy. Our drawings aren't expenses; after all, we are the owners. My wife and I have consistently taken only about $20,000 a year out because we want the rest of the profits to accumulate in the business. As I said, our bank balance has steadily risen. Furthermore, I have a local accountant make out the annual income tax statements so I don't have to worry about

EXHIBIT 1

Cash Register and Checkbook Summary During 1977

Receipts

From rooms.........................	$56,371
From vending machines.............	1,958
Total.........................	$58,329

Checks Drawn

Owners' drawings..................	$20,735
Salaries and wages...............	6,263
Paid to laundry..................	2,095
Replacement of glasses, bed linens and towels.............	395
Advertising......................	556
Payroll taxes and insurance.....	694
Fuel for heating.................	2,906
Repairs and maintenance.........	2,138
Cleaning and other supplies.....	1,624
Telephone and telegraph.........	664
Electricity......................	1,336
Real estate and property taxes..	2,269
Insurance.......................	2,758
Interest........................	2,525
Total.........................	$46,958

EXHIBIT 2

1977 Operating Data for Motels with 40 or Fewer Units*
(expressed as percentage of total revenues)

Revenues:	
Room rentals....................	98.7
Other revenue	1.3
Total revenues.................	100.0
Operating expenses:	
Payroll costs...................	22.5
Administrative and general......	4.2
Direct operating expenses.......	5.9
Fees and commissions............	3.3
Advertising and promotion.......	1.2
Repairs and maintenance.........	4.8
Utilities.......................	7.5
Total..........................	49.4
Fixed expenses:	
Property taxes, fees............	4.4
Insurance.......................	2.5
Depreciation....................	12.5
Interest........................	7.7
Rent............................	2.8
Total..........................	29.9
Profit (pre-tax).................	20.7

*Copyright July 1978 issue of Motel/ Motor Inn Journal, Temple, Texas. Further reproduction in part or in whole prohibited unless written permission obtained from the copyright owner.

them. That income tax business is so complicated that I avoid it."

Mr. Garcia worked with the Motel/ Motor Inn Journal figures (Exhibit 2) and the cash summary (Exhibit 1) that evening and quickly found he needed more information. He told Mr. Treml that he was returning to the home office the next morning but would be back in two weeks for another visit to the branch plant. Meanwhile, he wanted Mr. Treml to get together some additional information. Mr. Garcia suggested to Mr. Treml that an important noncash expense was depreciation. Mr. Garcia also wanted to know about expenses that had been incurred in 1976 but not paid until 1977. He told Mr. Treml to check up on wages and salaries, insurance, advertising, taxes, utilities, and any other items paid in 1977 but applicable to 1976.

In addition, Mr. Garcia instructed Mr. Treml to try to find items of expense properly chargeable to 1977 but not paid by December 31, 1977. Mr. Treml told Mr. Garcia the same types of expenses were involved, that is, wages and salaries, insurance, advertising, taxes, and so forth. Also Mr. Garcia inquired about income from room rentals. He asked if any of the cash receipts during 1977 related to rentals during 1976 and if there were any rentals during 1977 that had not been collected.

During the two weeks Mr. Garcia was back at the home office, Mr. Treml checked the records and compiled the additional information requested by Mr. Garcia. The evening Mr. Garcia returned to the Pinkham Motel, Mr. Treml gave him a summary of the information he had gathered (Exhibit 3). With all the additional information, Mr. Garcia constructed an operating statement that matched in form the one appearing in the Motel/Motor Inn Journal. He calculated both the dollar amounts and percentage composition of each expense for more useful comparison with the Journal figures.

Questions

1. Prepare an operating statement such as Mr. Garcia prepared.

2. As Mr. Garcia, what comments would you make to the Tremls regarding their progress to date?

EXHIBIT 3

Additional Information About the Business

Chargeable in 1976, but paid in January, 1977:

Wages and salaries................$240
Advertising....................... 200
Fuel for heating................. 303
Telephone and telegraph.......... 33
Electricity...................... 120
Real estate and property taxes... 335
Insurance........................ 689
Interest......................... 229
Payroll taxes and insurance...... 26

Chargeable in 1977, but not paid by December 31, 1977:

Wages and salaries................$360
Advertising...................... 332
Fuel for heating................. 280
Cleaning and other supplies...... 26
Telephone and telegraph.......... 46
Electricity...................... 164
Real estate and property taxes... 373
Interest......................... 193
Payroll taxes and insurance 40

Also, 1977 depreciation charges of $7,365. Also, 1977 cash receipts included a $395 payment from a company which had rented several units during December 1976 for a convention in the nearby city. There were no such uncollected rentals as of December 31, 1977.

Chapter 5

Revenue and Monetary Assets

Key Terms

Delivery method
Percentage-of-completion method
Completed-contract method
Installment method
Bad debt expense
Aging schedule
Warranty costs
Unexpired cost

Realizable value
Certificate of deposit
Marketable securities
Investments
Current ratio
Acid-test ratio
Days' cash
Days' receivables

Discussion Questions

1. Describe how Illustration 5-1 should be modified so as to apply to a retail department store.

2. Why is revenue, and hence gross margin, for products recognized at a specific time, rather than recognized in "pieces" throughout the production-sales process?

3. Given your answer to Question 2, how can the practice of recognizing revenues on precious metals and agricultural commodities before their sale be defended?

4. Try to think of an instance where an argument can be made for not recognizing revenue until some point well after the time of the sale.

5. Describe how the delivery method affects the recognition of revenue in the following situations:

   a. Goods are shipped by a manufacturer to a wholesaler, but are not received until one week later.

   b. A consignor delivers 20 color television sets to an authorized dealer.

   c. Membership in a tennis club is granted upon receipt of a $700 yearly membership fee.

   d. A franchisor requires a payment of $10,000 upon the signing of the franchise contract for training and professional advice which will be provided at a later date.

6. The text states that many companies use the installment method for tax purposes. Why is this so? Can you imagine a set of circumstances under which a retailer would pay more taxes under the installment method than if it were recognizing revenues at the time goods were sold?

7. Baker Company sold goods to Aldrich Company and received a $10,000, one-year, 8 percent note from Aldrich as "payment." How much revenue should Baker record on this sale?

8. Dunster Company sold goods to Elliot Company, receiving a $10,000, one-year, non-interest-bearing note as "payment." How much revenue should Dunster recognize on this sale?

9. Why would a company go through the extra bookkeeping work of recognizing long-term contract revenue on the percentage-of-completion method rather than using the simpler completed-contract method? Under what conditions would it not make much difference in reported results which of these two methods a company used?

10. What is the basic purpose of providing an estimated Bad Debt Expense account?

11. Why is the Allowance for Doubtful Accounts set up as a contra account, rather than a direct reduction in Accounts Receivable?

12. Two methods used for the bad debts adjustment are the "direct write-off" method and the "doubtful accounts" method. When is each used? Give a journal entry to illustrate each method.

13. Sadler Stores' June 1 balance sheet shows Accounts Receivable (gross) of $49,500 and Allowance for Doubtful Accounts of $1,600. On June 2, Sadler is informed that a customer has filed for bankruptcy, and hence his $400 account with Sadler will not be paid. Prepare a journal entry to record this transaction. How would the accounts receivable information appear if Sadler prepared a June 2 balance sheet?

14. What difference does it make whether a company regards sales discounts, returns, and bad debts as expenses rather than as revenue adjustments?

15. Marketable equity securities are classified as either current or noncurrent. How does this classification affect the income statement and the amounts reported on the balance sheet?

16. Ballarin Company owns stock in two companies. Ballarin intends to sell these stocks when it needs the cash. The original cost of each and market values as of two dates are as follows:

Stock	Original Cost	Market Value July 1	October 1
Dahlia Co.	$10,000	$ 9,000	$ 8,000
Elm Corp.	15,000	17,000	16,000

How much should Ballarin show for marketable securities on its July 1 balance sheet? On its October 1 balance sheet?

17. What does it mean for a company to have an "adequate" current ratio, and why is an adequate current ratio important?

Problems

5-1. Below is a schedule of monthly credit sales and collections for Marcotte Company. Assuming Marcotte's cost of goods sold is always 60 percent of sales, calculate how much gross margin Marcotte will report each month (a) if revenues are recognized when the sale is made, and (b) if the installment method is used.

	Jan.	Feb.	Mar.	Apr.	May	June
Sales.........$ 8,000		$12,000	$13,000	$11,000	$ 9,000	$13,500
Collections.... 10,000		11,000	11,500	10,500	10,500	9,500

5-2. The Kuhn Construction Company primarily builds houses, and only rarely is a house only partially completed as of December 31. However, this year Kuhn is also building a motel, which it started in March and expects to complete next April. The motel contract calls for a fee of $1 million. Expected total costs are $700,000 and $400,000 of these had been incurred as of December 31.

Required: Assume that, excluding the motel project, Kuhn's income before taxes will be $250,000 both this year and next. What will each year's income before taxes be, including the motel project, (a) if Kuhn uses the completed-contract method, and (b) if they use the percentaye-of-completion method?   (Assume actual motel costs in fact turn out to be $700,000.) Which method should Kuhn use?

5-3.   Woburn Company decided to write off the $2,000 Morkel Corporation receivable as uncollectible.   Subsequently, Morkel makes a $750 payment on the account. Prepare journal entries for these two transactions.

5-4.   (C.M.A. adapted.)   Erie Corporation operates in an industry which has a high rate of bad debts. On December 31, before any year-end adjustments, the balance in Erie's accounts receivable account was $500,000 and the allowance for doubtful accounts had a balance of $25,000. The year-end balance reported in the statement of financial position for the allowance for doubtful accounts will be based on the aging schedule shown below.

Days Account Outstanding	Amount	Probability of Collection
Less than 15 days	$300,000	.99
Between 16 and 30 days	100,000	.94
Between 31 and 45 days	50,000	.80
Between 46 and 60 days	30,000	.65
Between 61 and 75 days	10,000	.50
Over 75 days	10,000	.00

Required:

    a. What is the appropriate balance for the allowance for doubtful accounts on December 31?
    b. Show how accounts receivable would be presented on the balance sheet prepared on December 31.
    c. What is the dollar effect of the year-end bad debt adjustment on the before-tax income for the year?

5-5.   Green Lawn Chemical Company sells lawn and garden chemicals through several hundred garden supply stores and department store garden shops. It was Green Lawn's policy to ship goods to these retailers in late winter on a consignment basis. Periodically a Green Lawn field representative would count the Green Lawn products on hand at a retailer; based on this count, the previous count, and intervening shipments, it was determined how many items the retailer had sold since the previous count, and the retailer was billed for these goods by Green Lawn.

Required:

    a. Assume Green Lawn shipped goods costing Green Lawn $3,400 and with a wholesale price (i.e., price to the retailer, not the end user) of $5,100, to Abbott's Garden Shop. Prepare journal entries to record this entry (1) on Green Lawn's books and (2) on Abbott's books.
    b. Later, the field representative's count indicated that Abbott's had sold some of these goods, totaling $2,720 at retail, $2,040 at wholesale, and $1,360 at Green Lawn's cost. Prepare journal entries to reflect these sales (1) on Green Lawn's books and (2) on Abbott's books.

5-6.   SCB Corporation has the following balance sheet:

Assets

Current Assets:
Cash.................$	5,000	
Marketable securities..	10,000	
Accounts receivable.....	20,000	
Inventories...........	13,000	
Prepaid expenses.......	2,000	
Total Current Assets.	50,000	
Noncurrent assets........	75,000	
Total Assets.......$125,000		

Equities

Current liabilities...........$	35,000
Common stock..................	40,000
Retained earnings............	50,000
	$125,000

Required.

     a. Calculate the current ratio and the quick ratio.
     b. Interpret the above ratios, both in general and in the context of SCB Corporation.

5-7. MLB Company has the following account balances at the end of the year, before adjusting and closing entries. (All numbers are thousands of dollars.)

	Dr.	Cr.
Accounts receivable (gross; terms, net 30 days)	$ 14,850	
Accounts payable		$ 16,500
Allowance for doubtful accounts		1,650
Accumulated depreciation		26,400
Bonds payable (being refunded at $1,000 per year)		82,500
Cash	9,900	
Common stock		99,000
Cost of goods sold	69,300	
Depreciation expense	6,600	
Goodwill	16,500	
Interest payable		9,900
Inventory, beginning	19,800	
Other expenses	29,700	
Plant and equipment	148,500	
Purchases of inventory	79,200	
Retained earnings, beginning		19,800
Sales (23% were for cash)		138,600

Required: Calculate and interpret the current and quick ratios for the year.

5-8. Use the data from Problem 5-7 to calculate the number of days' cash on hand, and interpret the results.

5-9. Use the data from Problem 5-7 to calculate the number of days' worth of sales represented in accounts receivable.

5-10. Karwin Company's marketable securities portfolio is given below.

	Original Cost	Market Value as of Dec. 31
Bar Company 14% bonds	$ 54,000	$ 52,500
Maybar Company common stock	30,000	31,000
*Lowride, Inc. preferred stock	12,000	13,000
U.S. Treasury bills, 90-day	90,000	89,000
Stembrite Company common stock	70,000	64,000
G.R. Calvin 12% bonds	25,000	24,500
Cuestar Company common stock	55,000	53,000
ETA, Inc. 90-day commercial paper	42,000	43,000
	$378,000	$370,000

*These securities, in management's opinion, will be sold within one month. The remaining securities will be held indefinitely or until maturity.

Required:

     a. Record the necessary adjusting entries related to the marketable securities portfolio for December 31.
     b. On January 15 of the next year, the Cuestar Company common stock was sold by Karwin for $59,000. What is the journal entry for this transaction?

5-11. Quick-Fab Construction Company entered into a long-term construction contract at a fixed contract price of $3,500,000 on September 1, 1980. Work has proceeded since that time with the following results:

	1980	1981	1982
Costs incurred (this year)...........$	515,000	$ 850,000	$1,225,000
Cost of work yet to be completed (at year-end).......................	2,450,000	1,600,000	375,000
Cash collections (this year).........	400,000	800,000	1,100,000
Year-end percent complete...........	20%	50%	95%

Required: Determine the amount of revenues, expenses, and income for 1980. 1981, and 1982 by using the percentage-of-completion method.

5-12. The detail for the receivables of Alpha Company is as follows:

	Amount	
	Dr.	Cr.
A Company............... $	4,000	
B Company...............		$2,000
H. Hall.................	750	
S. Levine..............	1,500	
ISB Company...........	2,500	
	$ 8,750	$2,000

Additional information:

(1) The balance in Allowance for Doubtful Accounts is $60. Management believes that 2% of the current accounts receivable outstanding will be uncollectible.
(2) H. Hall is president of the Alpha Company. The $750 balance is a 90-day loan.
(3) B Company expects to have its credit balance remitted in cash within the next 30 days.

Required:

a. Record the necessary adjusting entries related to receivables.
b. Indicate how receivables and related accounts would be disclosed in the financial statements.

5-13. Hi-Tech, Inc. manufactures sophisticated metal processing equipment, and provides maintenance service on a contract basis if desired. Hi-Tech's bookkeeper, who graduated with a philosophy major from a local college, has been unable to record the transactions listed below. You are requested to record, as necessary, the initial transactions and respective adjusting entries as of December 31, 1983.

(1) Delivered high-speech polishers on December 31, 1983, which cost $25,000 and currently have a market value of $50,000. The terms of the contract call for payment of $35,000 by January 25 and final payment of $10,000 by February 15. However, the payments are subject to a 2.5% discount if they are paid 20 days before the due date. Hi-Tech consistently records sales revenue at the net amount.

(2) On November 15, 1983, Hi-Tech agreed to provide $45,000 of maintenance service for six months starting December 1, 1982 for a major customer. $15,000 was paid in advance and a trade account was created for the balance.

(3) Repair work at a customer's plant with a cost (to the customer) of $20,000 was completed on December 31, 1983, except for a few necessary tests of the repaired equipment. The tests will be completed on January 2, 1984.

(4) On October 1, 1983, parts inventory was shipped on consignment to authorized trade representatives. The cost of the parts totaled $385,000. By December 31, 1983, $250,000 of these parts had been sold at a retail price of $645,000. Hi-Tech normally required a 30% profit margin above cost.

(5) Received orders for $125,000 of automated lathes from a reliable customer on November 20, 1983. A $40,000 profit is anticipated on this order and

delivery is to be completed on January 5, 1984.

(6) Sold, on account, $200,000 of metal-pressing equipment to a steel-processing company on September 15, 1983. However, due to depressed economic conditions in the steel industry, the total amount to be received is uncertain. Hi-Tech chooses to account for this sale on the pure installment method. Payment of $40,000 was received on December 15, 1983.

5-14. Record the following transactions:

(1) It is estimated that warranty costs of 1.5% of sales will be incurred. The warranty period on goods sold is one year. Sales this year were $950,000.
(2) During the following year, $7,600 worth of warranty work was performed. This amount was comprised of $2,850 labor costs, $4,370 parts inventory, and $380 cash refunds.
(3) The following year, sales totaled $1,045,000. Estimated warranty costs were again 1.5% of sales, and the warranty period was still one year.

5-15. Record the following transactions:

(1) A furniture store sold a couch on credit for $990, payable in 90 days. The couch would have sold for $960 if the customer had paid cash.
(2) On January 1, the Bank of Otterville loaned $1,200 to a customer at 14% simple interest. The interest and $1,200 principal are due on December 31 of that year. What are the entries on the bank's books for the life of the note?
(3) Reperform part 2, assuming that the customer owes $1,200 as of December 31, but received only $1,053 cash when the loan was taken out the preceding January 1.

5-16. Klein Suppliers had the following transactions during February and early March:

(1) Sales for the month, all on credit, were $65,000. Cost of goods sold was $39,000. Klein's credit policy also allowed for the following:

   a. Sales charged on bank credit cards were $32,000. The bank's credit fee to retailers was 3.5% of gross sales on credit cards.
   b. $20,000 of the credit sales not on bank cards were entitled to a 3% discount if paid within 7 days of the sale. $5,000 of such sales did not receive the discount due to late payment. Sales revenues are recorded net of the cash discount allowances.

(2) Sales returns are normally 1% of recorded sales revenues. The balance in the Provision for Returns and Allowances account was $250 as of February 1.

(3) Warranty costs are estimated to be 2% of recorded sales revenues. The Allowance for Warranties account had a $400 balance as of February 1.

(4) Sales returns of nonresalable goods during the month of February were $700.

(5) Merchandise was replaced under warranty at a cost of $1,400.

(6) Bad debt expense is estimated to be 2.5% of recorded credit sales except for sales charged on bank cards. The February 1 balance in Allowance for Doubtful Accounts was $200 in excess of 2.5% of the February 1 balance of non-bank-card Accounts Receivable.

(7) On March 3, a customer who owed the company $400 left town and left no forwarding address.

(8) On March 5, the company received from a bankruptcy trustee a check for $75 related to an account for $150 that the company had previously written off.

Required:

    a. Prepare journal entries for all of the above transactions.
    b. Prepare two income statements for February, one using the revenue adjustment approach and the other using the expense approach. Assume that general expenses are $6,490 and that income taxes equal $5,398.
    c. As a user of financial statements, which of the two income statements you prepared would you find more useful? Explain.

5-17. Cobo Company has the following balance sheet as of January 1:

Assets

Current Assets:		
Cash	$16,750	
Accounts receivable	30,500	
Provision for sales returns	(3,000)	
Allowance for doubtful accounts	(1,250)	
Marketable securities	87,500	
Inventory	25,000	
Prepaid insurance	2,000	
Total Current Assets		$157,500
Noncurrent Assets (net)		205,000
Total Assets		$362,500

Equities

Liabilities:		
Current	$ 75,000	
Bonds (20 year, 10%)	100,000	
Total Liabilities		$175,000
Owners' Equity:		
Common stock	125,000	
Retained earnings	62,500	
Total Owners' Equity		187,500
Total Equities		$362,500

During the year the following occurred:

(1) Total sales were $250,000, of which $150,000 were credit sales.
(2) Specific credit accounts totaling $5,000 were written off during the year.
(3) Of the above, $1,250 were subsequently collected.
(4) Collections on receivables equaled $162,500 during the year.
(5) A specific receivable equaling $1,875 has a credit balance.
(6) It is estimated that 2.5% of the ending receivables balance will not be collected.
(7) The portfolio of marketable securities at the beginning of the year was sold for $95,000. The portfolio at the end of the year was purchased for $75,000 and has a value of $87,500 at December 31.
(8) Merchandise purchases during the year, paid in cash, equaled $112,500. The ending balance of inventory is $17,500.
(9) The current insurance policies expired on April 30. They were renewed for one year. The cost was $2,700.
(10) Depreciation charges during the year totaled $12,500.
(11) During the year, sales returns were $12,500, all involving cash refunds. $2,000 of these returns were associated with prior year sales.
(12) Sales returns for next year are estimated to be $2,500.
(13) Dividends of $75,000 were declared and paid on December 30.
(14) All other expenses were paid for with cash and totaled $25,000.

Required:

    a. Journalize the above.
    b. Prepare financial statements. Disregard income taxes.

5-18. Haessler Home Builders was a small construction company formed on March 1 by Jeff Haessler, who had recently resigned his position as general foreman for another construction company in order to start his own business. Currently he was building six houses on a six-acre wooded parcel he had purchased; each home was to be built on a one-acre site. On July 1, before extending him further construction loans, Haessler's banker asked for an income statement of operations to date. Haessler's data showed the following through June 30:

```
Land cost.................................................$126,000
Site improvement costs to date..............................  63,280
Home construction costs to date............................. 423,935
Interest on construction loans to date......................  12,500
Estimated costs to complete site improvements...............  34,320
Estimated costs to complete home construction............... 340,255
Estimated future interest costs.............................   8,985
```

House	Selling Price	Status
1	$165,000	Unsold; construction net yet started
2	203,850	Sold; construction 75% complete
3	172,000	Unsold; construction 60% complete
4	159,000	Unsold; construction complete
5	211,850	Sold; house complete
6	180,000	Unsold; construction net yet started
	$1,091,700	

Unfortunately, Haessler had not kept track of costs on a house-by-house basis. He does not anticipate discounting (or raising) any of the selling prices listed above.

Required: Prepare an income statement that you feel fairly reflects Haessler's operations from March 1 through June 30.

CASES

Case 5-19: Marion Music Company

Marion Music Company, a retail music store, was organized in 1968 by Thomas and Emily Marion. The business operated as a sole proprietorship until 1972 when it was incorporated, with Mr. and Mrs. Marion as stockholders. Gross sales (sales before returns) had risen from $40,000 in 1969 to $600,000 in 1980. Sales of instruments accounted for about $400,000 of this total. In 1980 the company had 15 full-time employees and 14 part-time teachers.

The Purchase Plan. Since competition in the music business was keen, the Marions were constantly alert for any promotional device that would aid in the sale of instruments. In 1980 a special type of purchase agreement was adopted to overcome some of the resistance of parents to acquiring band instruments for their children. The plan permitted the customer to rent a new or used instrument at a low cost for a three-month period prior to the actual purchase. At the end of the three-month period, the customer had three options:

1. To return the instrument without further obligation.
2. To pay for the instrument in full with an allowance given for the amount already paid as rent for the three months; and
3. To pay for the instrument on an installment basis over the next ten months. If this plan was elected, the customer paid a carrying charge.

Exhibit 1 is part of a typical contract signed for each such agreement.

During 1980 gross placements (before returns) on this plan were approximately $300,000. The average sales price of the instruments sold was $259. The typical markup on selling price was 50 percent. Almost all of the instruments were placed during October since most of the instruments were to be used by children entering band and orchestra programs in various grammar schools. From December, 1980 to February, 1981 about 40 percent of these instruments were returned.

Considerable planning and expense were involved in the placing of the instruments. During the spring and summer months the company sent salespersons to all grammar schools within a radius of 100 miles of the store. Inquiries were made about the band programs at these schools, and the cooper-

EXHIBIT 1

This certifies that I have rented from Marion Music Company for a period of <u>three</u> months the above described instrument for a total rental fee of..............$38.68, payable upon the signing of this agreement.

In the event that the instrument is not returned by me by the end of the rental period, it is agreed that I have purchased it and I promise to pay Marion Music Company, or its assigns, the purchase price of the instrument as follows, WITH FULL ALLOWANCE FOR THE RENTAL ALREADY PAID:

Full Payment by End of of Rental Period	First Payment Due at End of Rental Period
Price of instrument.......$259.00 State tax..................$ 7.77 Total...............$266.77	Cash price (after rental allowance)........ $227.91 Carrying charge.............$ 22.79 Total..................$250.70 Payable in ten monthly payments of..............$ 25.07

ation of band teachers and school officials was solicited. If such cooperation was obtained, a date in October was set for a display. When children returned to school in the fall, those interested in music were asked by the school officials to notify their parents of the display date. The display was held in the evening at the school with the school officials describing the school program and the company salespersons exhibiting the various instruments. No sales were made at the display; instead appointments were made to see the parents at the school at a later date. All instruments placed were delivered to the school within one week.

Accounting for the Plan. In the case of the sale of instruments on the special-purchase plan, the initial payment was credited to Rental Revenues. Instruments were not recorded as sales or accounts receivable until the return privileges had expired and the sales price or the first installment had been received. At the time the first installment was received a receivable was set up for the amount still owed. The payments that had previously been received as rent were transferred from the Rental Revenues account to the Instrument Sales account. Thus, the total original selling price was recognized as a sale at the time that the customer gave evidence of his or her decision to purchase by paying the first installment. Subsequent collections were credited to Accounts Receivable. On the other hand, if the customer elected to return the instrument, the initial payment remained in the Rental Revenues account, which was closed to Profit and Loss at the end of the accounting per-

iod. Cost of goods sold was determined by physical inventories at the close of each accounting period. Instruments that were in customers' possession but which had not yet been purchased were included in inventory at original cost. When an instrument was returned, its cost valuation was reduced by $10.00 and its selling price by $20.00. Salespersons' commissions were not recognized in the books until the return privilege expired.

Problems. The Marions were convinced that this plan was essential to the continued growth of the firm, but they realized that the plan introduced many problems. Some of these problems were apparent from financial statements that were prepared at the end of 1980; see Exhibits 2, 3, and 4.

In spite of the Marions' efforts, the inventory had continued to increase in size. About 50 percent of the increase in inventory during 1980 was attributed to an increase in returned instruments. The other 50 percent increase was a result of an error in estimating the number of particular kinds of instruments that were needed to meet the fall demand.

The rate of return on instruments placed on the plan had varied slightly from year to year; from the last five years returns had been 35 percent to 40 percent of the instruments placed. As sales increased, the dollar amount of the returns increased each year. The Marions were not sure whether this indicated that some immediate action should be taken.

The Marions were also concerned with the adequacy of their financial statements. They felt the statements were deficient because (1) the placements and returns of purchase-plan instruments were not shown; (2) net income did not reflect the sales activity during the period; (3) the income statement failed to show the real expense activity of the business in the sense that the salespersons' commissions, 7 percent of selling price, were not shown until the third month had expired on the purchase-plan instruments; and (4) the inventory shown on the statements was not the amount on hand.

Questions

1. What is your opinion of the financial statements? Are they useful in solving the problems that confronted the Marions? Could the statements be made more useful? How?

2. In what way would you modify the accounting for sales on this special-purchase plan?

3. Do you agree with the method of valuing returned instruments?

4. Outline briefly how you would control inventory.

EXHIBIT 2

MARION MUSIC COMPANY
Comparative Statements of Financial Condition at December 31

ASSETS

	1979		1980	
Current Assets:				
Cash.............................		$ 37,880		$ 36,620
Accounts receivable:				
Purchase plan....................	$ 88,740		$100,980	
Other............................	74,960		87,140	
	163,700		188,120	
Less: Allowance for				
doubtful accounts.........	8,460	155,240	7,400	180,720
Inventory........................		183,080		236,080
Prepaid expenses.................		5,660		2,320
Total Current Assets........		381,860		455,740
Fixed Assets:				
Truck............................	15,700		15,700	
Less: Depreciation.............	5,260	10,440	10,460	5,240
Furniture and fixtures...........	36,900		36,900	
Less: Depreciation.............	8,640	28,260	12,330	24,570
Total Assets		$420,560		$485,550

LIABILITIES AND CAPITAL

	1979	1980
Current Liabilities:		
Accounts payable..................	$226,640	$250,640
Accrued sales and employee taxes..	16,840	16,240
Income taxes payable.............	25,060	27,100
Total Current Liabilities...	268,540	293,980
Loan from Thomas Marion..........	30,000	30,000
Capital stock....................	110,000	110,000
Retained earnings................	12,020	51,570
Total Liabilities and		
and Capital...............	$420,560	$485,550

EXHIBIT 3

MARION MUSIC COMPANY
Income Statement, 1980

```
Sales of merchandise:
  Instruments--purchase plan.................$184,000
               --other........................ 118,200
  Music and accessories........................ 65,800
            Total...................................        $368,000
Cost of merchandise sold:
  Inventory, January 1...................... 183,080
  Purchases................................. 263,000
                                             446,080
  Inventory, December 31.................... 236,080
            Total...................................         210,000
Gross margin on merchandise sold.............               158,000
Sales of services:
  Repairs....................................                72,600
  Rental income..............................                17,400
  Lessons....................................                39,400
  Other......................................                 4,000
Total gross margin...........................               291,400
Operating expenses:
  Salaries................................... 132,800
  Commissions................................  18,200
  Employee taxes.............................   3,780
  Delivery expense...........................   7,880
  Advertising and promotion..................  10,520
  Postage and office supplies................   7,620
  Rent and utilities.........................  19,080
  Insurance..................................   3,340
  Depreciation...............................   8,890
  Bad debt expense...........................   4,760
  Miscellaneous..............................   7,880
            Total...................................         224,750
Income before income taxes...................                66,650
Income taxes.................................                27,100
Net Income...................................              $ 39,550
```

EXHIBIT 4

MARION MUSIC COMPANY
Placements on Purchase Plan

	Total	Received as Rent		Received on Account		
		1979	1980	1979	1980	1981
1979 Placements:						
Conversions:						
In year of placement	$140,000	$21,000		$30,260	$ 88,740	
In year following placement	22,000	3,300			18,700	
Returns:						
In year of placement	76,000	11,400				
In year following placements	32,000	4,800		30,260	107,440	
1980 Placements:						
Conversions:						
In year of placement	162,000		$24,300		36,720	$100,980
In year following placement	16,000		2,400			13,600
Returns:						
In year of placement	96,000		14,400			
In year following placement	26,000		3,900			
Total 1980 Placements	350,000		45,000		36,720	114,580
Totals	$570,000	$40,500	$45,000	$30,260	$144,160	$114,580

Case 5-20: MacDonald's Farm

Early in 1983, Denise Grey was notified by a lawyer that her recently deceased uncle had willed her the ownership of a 2,000-acre wheat farm in Iowa. The lawyer requested information as to whether Grey wanted to keep the farm or sell it.

Grey was an assistant vice president in the consumer credit department of a large New York bank. Despite the distance between New York and Iowa, Grey was interested in retaining ownership of the farm if she could determine its profitability. During the last ten years of his life, Jeremiah MacDonald had hired professional managers to run his farm while he remained in semiretirement in Florida.

Keeping the farm as an investment was particularly interesting to Grey for the following reasons:

1. Recent grain deals with Communist countries had increased present farm commodity prices substantially; many experts believed these prices would remain high for the next several years.
2. While the number of small farms had decreased markedly in the last 20 years, large farms such as MacDonald's using mechanization and new hybrid seed varieties could be extremely profitable.
3. The value of good farm land in Iowa was appreciating at about 10 percent a year.

Included in the lawyer's letter were data on revenues and expenses for 1982 and certain information on balance sheet items, which are summarized below:

Inventory:

```
Beginning inventory.....   0 bushels
1982 wheat
   production........210,000 bushels
Sold to grain
   elevator..........180,000 bushels
Ending inventory.....  30,000 bushels
```

Prices:

The average price per bushel for wheat sold to the grain elevator operator in 1982 was $3.30. The price per bushel at the time of the wheat harvest was $3.15. The closing price per bushel at December 31, 1982 was $3.42.

Accounts Receivable:

At year end, the proceeds from 20,000 bushels had not yet been received from the elevator operator. The average sales price of this wheat had been $3.33 per bushel. There were no uncollected proceeds at December 31, 1981.

Cash:

The farm has a checking account balance of $8,700 and a savings account balance of $22,500

Land:

The original cost of the land was $375,000. It was appraised for estate tax purposes at $1,050 per acre.

Buildings and Machinery:

Buildings and machinery with an original cost of $412,500 and accumulated depreciation of $300,000 are employed on the farm. The equipment was appraised at net book value.

Current Liabilities:

The farm has notes payable and accounts payable totaling $33,000.

Owner's Equity:

Common stock has a par value of $7,500 plus additional paid-in capital of $450,000. There was no record of retained earnings although it was known that Jeremiah MacDonald withdrew most of the earnings in the last few years in order to continue the life style to which he had become accustomed in Florida.

1982 Expenses for the MacDonald Farm

A. Variable costs per bushel:
```
Seed........................ $0.053
Fertilizer and chemicals...... 0.315
Machinery costs, fuel
   and repairs.............. 0.097
Part-time labor and
   other costs................ 0.038
      Variable cost per
      bushel..................$0.503
```

B. Annual costs not related to the volume of production:
```
Salaries and wages..........$ 67,500
Insurance....................   6,000
Taxes*.......................  22,500
Depreciation.................  28,500
Other expenses...............  45,000
                             $169,500
```

*This figure excludes income taxes since the corporation was taxed as a sole proprietorship.

Looking over the data on revenues and expenses Grey discovered that there were no monetary numbers for 1982's total revenues or for the ending inventory. The lawyer's letter explained that there was some doubt in his mind about when revenue for the farm should be recognized and about the appropriate way to value the grain inventory. There are at least three alternative states in the wheat growing cycle at which revenue could be counted.

First, the production method could be used. Since wheat has a daily valuation on the Chicago Commodity Exchange, any unsold inventory as of December 31 could be valued at market price very objectively. In this way, revenue can be counted for all wheat produced in a given year, regardless of whether it is sold or not. A decision not to sell this wheat before December 31 is based on speculation about future wheat price increases.

Second, the sales method could be used. This would recognize revenue when the grain is purchased from the farm by the grain elevator operator in the neighboring town. In this instance, the owner of the grain elevator had just sold control to a Kansas City company with no previous experience in running such a facility. The manager of the MacDonald Farm had expressed some concern about selling to an operator.

Third, the collection method could

be used. Under this approach revenue is counted when the cash is actually received by the farm from the grain elevator operator. Full collection often took several months because a grain elevator operator might keep wheat for a considerable time in the hope that prices would rise so he could sell at a greater profit.

Questions

1. repare the 1982 income statement and related ending balance sheet for the MacDonald Farm recognizing revenue by the:

   a. Production method
   b. Sales method
   c. Collection method

   Which method would you recommend?

2. Assume that the MacDonald Farm had received a firm offer of $225,000 for 100 acres of the farm which would be used as the site of a new housing development. This development would have no effect on the use of the remaining acreage as a farm, and Ms. Grey planned to accept it. How would you account in the 1982 financial statements for the economic gain represented by this appreciation in land values?

3. Should Grey retain ownership of the farm?

* * * * *

Case 5-21: F.J. Sullivan Insurance Agency

Frederick J. Sullivan operated an insurance agency in Monson, a town of about 5,000 inhabitants. Mr. Sullivan, an independent agent representing several fire and casualty companies, sold principally fire and automotive insurance to businesses and residents of Monson and surrounding towns. The

agency was a small one, employing, in addition to Mr. Sullivan, only a part-time secretary.

The business had grown steadily since its founding in 1958 and so had outstanding accounts receivable. Exhibit 1 indicates gross premiums and

EXHIBIT 1

Gross Premiums and Accounts Receivable

	Gross Premiums	Accounts Receivable as of 12/32
1978	$103,792	$17,300
1979	121,048	16,176
1980	153,424	34,452
1981	162,532	39,142
1982	181,724	43,888
1983	201,300	49,856

EXHIBIT 2

Accounts Receivable

	December 31	
	1982	1983
1 month	$ 8,600	$13,640
2 to 3 months	19,888	23,928
3 to 6 months	6,560	3,360
6 months to 1 year	4,140	5,848
1 to 2 years	3,572	2,520
Over 2 years	1,118	560
Total	$43,888	$49,856

- 53 -

accounts receivable for past 5 years. Exhibit 2 shows the accounts receivable as of December 31, 1982 and 1983 broken down by the age of the account. The balance in the Allowance for Doubtful Accounts on December 31, 1982 was $480.

Questions

1. Make the appropriate adjusting entry to the Allowance for Doubtful Accounts for December 31, 1982. (Mr. Sullivan uses the following rates to calculate his Allowance for Doubtful Accounts: 1 month or less, 1%; 2 to 6 months, 10%; 6 months to a year, 25%; over 1 year, 50%.)

2. On February 15, 1983, Mr. Sullivan discovered that one of his customers had left town without leaving a forwarding address. This customer owed $1,300. What entry, if any, would you make?

3. In March of 1983, Mr. Sullivan turned over $9,720 in delinquent accounts to his lawyer for collection. By April, the lawyer had collected $6,300. The remainder, the lawyer believed, could not be collected.

What entries would you make to reflect these transactions?

4. In July, a customer owing $1,000 was adjudged a bankrupt. It was expected that she would pay her creditors $.10 on the dollar. Make any required entry.

5. In September, the customer who had left town in February returned. He had no money, however, and made no indication that he would pay. What entry should be made?

6. In October, a customer owing $600 which had been written off as a bad debt in April, paid $200 on his account. He promised to pay the remaining amount within the next few months. What entry should be made?

7. No other entries to the Allowance for Doubtful Accounts were made during the remainder of the year. Exhibit 2 shows the balance of the accounts receivable, by age group, as of December 31, 1983. Make the appropriate adjusting entry to the Allowance for Doubtful Accounts for December 31, 1983.

*   *   *   *   *

Case 5-22: Lewis Landscaping Service

Lewis Landscaping Service was a small company that specialized in residential landscaping, lawn care, and pest control. Mr. Lewis, seduced by the comfortable life of retirement, decided that it was time to train a family member to run the business. He chose his nephew, Jack, and decided that the wisest thing would be to create a partnership until Jack got a firm grip on running the business. The firm's operating headquarters were at the Lewis home. The two partners' wives shared the responsibilities for general office duties, advertising, and recordkeeping. These records consisted basically of payments received from contract and noncontract customers, and cash payments made to suppliers and subcontractors.

The company's reputation was excellent. In order to stay abreast of the continuing demand, Lewis had hired an additional full-time employee and several part-time employees. These employees served as a crew for a new truck that had been purchased in January, 1983. The addition of several staff members and a new truck allowed Lewis to provide improved service.

Neighborhood children were often employed to clean the tools and mowers and to wash the pick-up trucks.

As long as the firm showed a profit, Mr. Lewis had demonstrated little desire to maintain complex financial records. He had always relied on his neighbor, Mr. Ludlum, to figure out his annual income and his tax liability. In 1981, Jack was initiated as a partner. As time passed, he began to press his uncle to keep more accurate financial records. The expansion of the firm, along with the creation of the partnership, had brought to light certain facts. The firm's need for financial data was no longer limited to billing and taxes; it was necessary to measure each partner's share of the profits annually. The firm was also legally responsible for reporting payroll and tax information to state and local authorities.

Having studied accounting and finance at a prominent university, Jack knew the value of accurate financial data. Due to his educational background, Mr. Lewis had begun to allow him to perform the duties of chief financial officer for the small firm. His duties consisted of: a review of monthly financial transactions; posting these transactions to accounts in the general ledger; producing quarterly and annual income statements; and, keeping definitive tax and payroll records.

EXHIBIT 1

LEWIS LANDSCAPING SERVICE
Balance Sheet
as of December 31, 1982

ASSETS

Current Assets:
Cash..................		$14,660
Accounts receivable..		13,784
Inventory:		
Plants, trees, and shrubs............$11,200		
Fertilizer and insecticide........ 2,330		13,530
Total Current Assets..........		41,974

Fixed Assets:
Furniture and fixtures.......... 2,400		
Less: Accumulated depreciation. 720		1,680
Trucks and lawn equipment 40,300		
Less: Accumulated depreciation. 17,360		22,940
Buildings............ 13,400		
Less: Accumulated depreciation. 5,360		8,040
Land.................		14,000
Total Fixed Assets..........		46,660

Total Assets.......... $88,634

EQUITIES

Current Liabilities:
Accounts payable.....	$14,340
Other liabilities....	680
Total Current Liabilities......	15,020

Partners' Capital:
Robert Lewis,
Capital, 1/1/82....$34,570
Less: 1982 Drawings. 12,360
Subtotal 22,210
Plus: 1982 Profit
share......... 15,152   37,362
Jack Lewis,
Capital, 1/1/82.... 33,460
Less: 1982 Drawings. 12,360
Subtotal 21,100
Plus: 1982 Profit
share......... 15,152   36,252

Total Equities........ $88,634

Jack reviewed copies of the 1982 financial statements -- Exhibits 1 and 2. He observed the methods by which Lewis had transacted business and what recordkeeping methods were employed. He became satisfied that the records were consistent and fair. Jack formulated some general observations and developed the following ground rules:

1. Customers were billed monthly for services provided, but the service was not reflected in any other manner unless cash payment was received. Sales were always recorded when payments were received.

2. These cash receipts were recorded under the name of the client at the time of collection.

3. Cash disbursements were recorded by Mrs. Lewis as she issued the check.

4. The two journals, receipts and disbursements, were totaled and balanced monthly.

EXHIBIT 2

LEWIS LANDSCAPING COMPANY
Income Statement
Year Ended December 31, 1982

Revenue from Services:
Noncontract clients.........$105,680	
Contract customers.......... 97,960	
Spraying and pest control.... 25,750	
Total Revenues........... 229,380	

Cost of Services:
Plants, trees, and shrubs.... 120,630	
Fertilizer and insecticide... 25,655	
Subcontractor charges........ 5,540	
Total Cost of Services.... 151,825	
Gross Margin................. 77,555	

Operating Expenses:
Depreciation.................	6,780
Equipment repairs............	1,820
Wages and salaries...........	26,355
Office, printing, and advertising.................	4,484
Utilities and telephone......	876
Property taxes...............	898
Payroll taxes................	1,306
Uniforms and supplies........	691
Professional fees............	2,500
Miscellaneous expenses.......	1,541
Total Operating Expenses..	47,251

Income (before tax)*.........$ 30,304

*As this was a partnership, no figure is shown for income taxes. All such taxes would be paid individually by the two partners.

5. The payroll was prepared each month from a record of the number of hours an employee had worked.

6. A list of accounts receivable was prepared at the end of each operating year in order to adjust sales by that portion of revenue that remained uncollected.

A large part of yearly revenue was provided by customers taking part in the firm's contract plan. Each customer participating in the plan contracted to make equal monthly payments for nine months during the year (March through November). Participants in this plan had all their lawn needs taken of on a year-round basis. The services included were mowing, edging, minor landscaping, and Fall clean-up, and the time period covered was March 1 to February 28.

Contract plan customers also were obligated to purchase an annual spraying service contract for a fee of $30. This amount became the initial entry against their account. The contract covered fertilization, shrub and tree spraying, and pest control performed once a year.

The remaining customers of the firm were billed for only those services actually performed. Cash receipts from these customers were divided into normal revenue -- which represented such things as mowing, edging, and landscaping -- and spraying and insect control. The latter business was believed to be very profitable as the total cost of the fertilizer and insecticides was covered by revenue from noncontract clients, even though nearly fifty percent of the work was done for contract customers.

The 1983 Financial Statements

During the early part of January, 1984, Jack Lewis had begun to construct financial statements for 1983. These statements were based on the 1982 year ending statements and the 1983 operating data (Exhibit 3). On Sunday evening, about the middle of the month, the following conversation occurred at a Lewis family dinner:

Mr. Lewis: Jack, this is no reflection on your work, but, quite frankly, I'm worried about those preliminary financial reports you showed me. Our revenues are up about 20 percent, but these reports have us making about 30 per-

cent more profit than last year. That seems strange, given our new truck and the break-in period for our new people.

Jack: Well, I'm not quite sure what to say. I'm certain that the entries that I've made to produce the trial balance are correct.

EXHIBIT 3

LEWIS LANDSCAPING COMPANY
Operating Data, 1983

Cash Receipts Journal:
Noncontract customers........$133,200
Contract customers...........117,800
Spraying and insect control.. 22,400
Total.................... 273,400

Cash Disbursements Journal:
1982 accounts payable........ 14,340
Other 1982 liabilities....... 680
Withdrawn by Robert Lewis.... 14,600
Withdrawn by Jack Lewis...... 18,000
Paid for new truck........... 11,500
Wages and salaries........... 35,277
Office, printing, and
advertising............... 3,966
Miscellaneous expenses....... 1,685
Property taxes............... 1,370
Uniforms and supplies........ 794
Equipment repairs............ 1,483
Payroll taxes............... 1,315
Professional fees........... 1,787
Utilities and telephone...... 923
Plants, trees, and shrubs.... 136,500
Fertilizer and insecticide... 17,300
Paid out to subcontractors... 1,100
Total.................... 262,620

Accounts Payable, as of 12/31/82
Plants, trees, and shrubs.... 13,700
Fertilizer and insecticide... 800
Utilities.................... 100
Advertising.................. 300

Other Liabilties, as of 12/31/83
Payroll taxes............... 900

Accounts Receivable, as of
12/31/83
Noncontract customers........ 11,600

Ending Inventory, as of 12/31/83
Plants, trees and shrubs..... 9,890
Fertilizers and insecticide.. 1,810

Depreciation Formulas
Furniture and fixtures: Straight-
line at 12-1/2% (8 yrs.)
Trucks and lawn equipment: Straight-
line at 20% (5 yrs.)
Buildings: Straight-line at 4% (25
yrs.)

Mr. Lewis: I noticed, for example, that the depreciation expense was up over last year by nearly two-thirds. That alone should have had some negative impact.

Jack: Yeh, I'd have to agree with you. Let me review the data and see what explanations I can come up with.

Questions:

1. Prepare an income statement and balance sheet for 1983 using Lewis' operating data.

2. What explanation(s) can you offer for the seemingly disproportionate rise in pretax income?

Chapter 6

Cost of Goods Sold and Inventories

Key Terms

Gross margin
Periodic inventory method
Perpetual inventory method
Retail method
Inventory shrinkage
Cost accounting system
Product costs
Period costs
Production overhead

Full cost of a product
Specific identification method
Average cost method
First-in, first-out (FIFO)
Last-in, first-out (LIFO)
Net realizable value
Inventory turnover
Days' inventory

Discussion Questions

1. Distinguish among service, merchandising, and manufacturing firms. How do these differences affect the meaning of gross margin as reported by each type of company?

2. During a one-month accounting period, a clothing store's records showed: purchases, $45,000; cost of sales, $40,000; freight-in, $2,500; cost of pressing and marking goods before putting them on display, $1,000; supplies purchased, $500; sales returns at cost, $850; salespersons' salaries, $7,000. What is the total amount of the debits which reflect the month's additions of goods to inventory?

3. Kort's Shoe Palace consistently orders shoes on credit terms of 2/10, n/30 from several manufacturers and records purchases at the net amount. Shipping charges are 5 percent of the manufacturer's price. A $28,00 shipment of shoes was recently received with an invoice marked "f.o.b. destination." How much will Kort's Shoe Palace record as Purchases for this shipment?

4. Briefly distinguish between the perpetual and periodic inventory methods, considering how each measures the inventory asset amount and the amount for cost of goods sold. Why must a physical inventory be taken if a periodic inventory system is used?

5. Describe the three advantages the perpetual inventory method has over the periodic method.

6. Winsom Department Stores estimates monthly income statements by using the retail method. Purchases for July totaled $12,500 at cost and $210,000 at retail. Beginning inventory had a value of $30,000 for cost and $45,000 at retail. What is the cost of goods sold for the month of July if sales for the month are $190,000?

7. What are the three inventory accounts used by a manufacturing firm? In what ways do they differ? Why is it said that costs "flow" through these accounts?

8. Distinguish between "cost of goods manufactured" and "cost of goods sold."

9. What are the product costing differences between professional service firms and building trade firms?

10. What difference does it make whether an item of manufacturing cost is treated as a product cost or a period cost?

11. Distinguish between product costs and period costs for each of the three types of service organizations.

12. Suppose that two manufacturing companies in the same industry have finished goods inventories which are identical in physical substance; that is, the type of items and number of each item are the same for both companies. Explain concisely, but thoroughly, why these two companies' balance sheets might show quite different dollar amounts for finished goods inventory.

13. For what items in a jewelry store would the store be likely to use the specific identification method rather than one of the other three inventory measurement methods?

14. During the highly inflationary years of 1975 to 1981, many U.S. companies changed from the FIFO method to the LIFO method. (This change, if made, must be made both for financial accounting and tax-reporting purposes.) Why would there have been such an unusually high number of companies making this switch during these years?

15. What are the risks to a company of changing from FIFO to LIFO during an inflationary period?

16. Why does the use of LIFO result in a gross margin which closely approximates the "true" margin when compared to the FIFO method of inventory accounting?

17. It has been said that the choice between using FIFO and LIFO "depends on whether you want a misleading balance sheet or a misleading income statement." Explain.

18. An item of inventory originally cost $42 to make, but currently can be replaced at a cost of $29. The selling price of this item is estimated to be $45, but $6 of cost will be incurred to complete the sale. If a 20 percent profit margin is normally earned on a sale of such inventory, what is the amount at which this item will be reported on the balance sheet?

19. What is the rationale for using cost of goods sold rather than sales revenues in computing days' inventory?

20. How do days' inventory and inventory turnover differ, and how are they related?

Problems

6-1. In the table below there appear income statements for four hypothetical companies. Each income statement is missing three numbers; you are to determine these missing numbers. (Assume taxes are part of "period expenses.")

	Co. A	Co. B	Co. C	Co. D
Sales	$1,500	$1,200	$900	$1,400
Cost of goods sold:				
Beginning inventory	200	150	?	200
Plus: Purchases	650	?	550	800
Less: Ending inventory	150	200	225	?
Cost of goods sold	?	600	?	?
Gross margin	?	?	?	500
Period expenses	200	275	100	?
Net Income (Loss)	$?	$?	$150	$ (100)

6-2. The Parkwood Pharmacy uses the periodic inventory method. In its most recent fiscal year, Parkwood had: beginning inventory of $70,000; gross purchases of $140,000; freight-in of $3,000; purchases returned to suppliers totaling $5,000; and ending inventory of $80,000. MMake the year-end adjusting and closing entries to reflect the above information in the inventory, cost of goods sold, and income summary accounts. Then, assuming sales of $250,000, other expenses (excluding taxes) of $80,000, and a tax rate of 30 percent, prepare an income statement for the year, including the derivation of the cost of goods sold amount.

6-3. Dudas Company makes a single product, and uses the perpetual inventory method. At the end of each accounting period, a physical inventory is taken to verify the perpetual inventory records. For its most recent accounting period, Dudas' records showed: beginning inventory of 400 units; goods added to finished goods inventory during the period, 2,700 units; and sales during the period of 2,400 units. Finally, during the period 50 units in resalable condition were returned by Dudas' customers. The unit cost was $12 throughout the period.

Required:

   a. Assuming Dudas sells this item for $17 per unit, prepare summary journal entries for the period's purchases, sales, and sales returns.
   b. Prepare an income statement down to the gross margin line.
   c. Assume that after the entries in part (a) were made, a physical count revealed that ending inventory was actually 670 units. What additional entry is required? How does this affect your income statement?

6-4. You are given the following inventory-related figures for the Loumus Company:

```
Materials inventory:
   Beginning balance..................................$126,500
   Purchases.......................................... 315,100
   Ending balance..................................... 140,300
Work in process:
   Beginning balance..................................  55,660
   Labor and overhead charged to work in process....... 363,400
   Ending balance.....................................  87,860
Finished goods:
   Beginning balance..................................  32,890
   Ending balance.....................................  37,490
```

From this information, prepare a detailed cost of goods sold schedule like the one which appears on the income statement in Illustration 6-5 of the text (Hint: you will find it easier to prepare this schedule if you first refer to Illustrations 6-3 and 6-4.)

6-5. Karlin Retailers maintains a perpetual inventory system. As of December 31, Merchandise Inventory had a balance of $257,000. During the month of January, the following transactions occurred.

   (1) Purchased $1,100,000 of merchandise on account, terms 2/15, n/30. Purchases are recorded at the net amount.
   (2) Shipping charges of $38,950 for merchandise sold during the month were paid.
   (3) Returned $34,000 of merchandise (at manufacturer's prices) due to defective packaging.
   (4) Sales revenue totaled $2,300,000. Of these sales, $1,855,000 were cash sales.
   (5) Recorded $132,000 of depreciation expense on the retail outlets.
   (6) On January 31, $8,725 of bad debts were written off. The allowance for doubtful accounts had a $10,345 credit balance as of December 31. Normally, 2.5 percent of credit sales are uncollectible.
   (7) Sales returns of $28,000 (at retail prices) were refunded with cash. Karlin Retailers does not use the allowance method for returns. The returned goods were placed back in inventory.
   (8) Wages paid to sales clerks totaled $197,000.
   (9) General and administrative expenses totaled $345,000.

   Required: Assuming a 40 percent income tax rate and a 100 percent mark-up over cost (i.e., 50 percent gross margin) on merchandise sold, prepare:

a. journal entries for the above transactions.
b. T-accounts for any of the items affecting inventory or income statement accounts.
c. closing entries for the month of January.
d. an income statement for the month of January.

6-6. The balances of the inventory accounts of the Blanchard Bindery as of June 30 were:

Materials inventory..............$ 4,000
Work in process................... 9,000
Finished goods................... 11,000

The following transactions apply to the month of July:

(1) Purchased materials, $21,000, on account.
(2) Incurred $40,000 direct labor costs, not yet paid.
(3) Spent a total of $53,000 for manufacturing overhead items (for example, rent, heat, light, repairs, indirect labor).
(4) Factory equipment depreciation expense for the month, $6,000.
(5) Issued $23,000 of materials for processing.
(6) Transferred goods with a cost of $120,000 from work in process to finished goods.
(7) Sold goods on account: sales value, $183,000; cost, $112,000.
(8) Incurred selling and administrative expenses, $65,000.

Required:

a. Prepare journal entries.
b. Post to T-accounts any of the items affecting the inventories or income statement accounts.
c. Prepare closing entries.
d. Prepare an income statement for the month of July, ignoring income taxes.

6-7. Electron-Wizard Company retails electronic merchandise, including a personal computer which retails for $775. Due to a holiday special in late December, the personal computer was completely sold out by December 31. Sales of personal computers for the next six-month period (ending June 30) totaled $46,500. Purchase records indicate the following on the amounts purchased and prices paid by Electron-Wizard:

Purchase date	Units	Cost
January 15	10	$450
February 20	8	445
March 23	14	452
April 15	20	448
May 31	17	435

Required: Prepare a statement of gross margin for the six-month period ending June 30 using the FIFO, average cost, and LIFO inventory methods.

6-8. On January 1, the Oakley Store had no hair dryers on hand. During the next six months, it first purchased 40 dryers for $11 each, and then 60 more for $12 each. During the six months, 90 dryers were sold.

Required: What will the June 30 hair dryer inventory amount and the six months' cost of goods be if the Oakley Store uses the periodic inventory method and: (a) average cost; (b) FIFO; (c) LIFO?

6-9. Whiting's Store has just completed taking a physical inventory. Most of the items, whose aggregate cost was $50,000, raised no inventory valuation problem. However, there are several items shown below, for which inventory valuation is not straightforward.

Item A: there are 5 units on hand, with an original cost of $15 each. Because of a style change, this item is felt to be unsalable, and has no scrap value.

Item B: there are 20 units on hand for which a cost of $7 each has been paid. The supplier of this item has just dropped the wholesale cost to $6 per unit, which is lower than Whiting's net realizable value, but higher than net realizable value less the normal profit margin.

Item C: there is one unit on hand, which originally cost $80 and which has been used as a "floor sample." It is estimated that this unit can be sold for $60; whichever salesperson sells it will receive a 5 percent commission.

Item D: there are 10 units on hand, with an original unit cost of $21. Because of general economic conditions, the supplier has raised the wholesale price to $23 and the suggested retail price from $29 to $32.

Item E: there are three units on hand with an original cost of $29 each. This item has been discontinued by the manufacturer; accordingly, Whiting expects to be able to sell the three on hand for cost, $29 each. The salespersons will receive their usual 5 percent commission on this item.

Item F: there are four units on hand, originally costing $25 each. These units can now be replaced for $24 each. This item is expected to be sold at retail by Whiting for $40 each. For each unit sold, Whiting will earn a gross margin (before selling commissions) of 30 percent ($12) and will pay a 5 percent sales commission.

Required:

    a. Determine the <u>unit</u> cost at which each of the above items should be valued for inventory valuation purposes.

    b. What will be the <u>total</u> valuation of Whiting's inventory?

6-10. You are given the following data for Alfred Company:

        Inventory, beginning balance...............$ 33,000
        Inventory, ending balance.................. 16,500
        Purchases during the period............... 132,000

Required:

    a. Calculate inventory turnover (based on average inventory) and days' inventory (based on ending inventory).

    b. What do the above ratios measure?

    c. How could they be utilized in managerial planning and control?

6-11. You are given the following unit cost data for Sound-Power Company:

Item:	A	B	C	D
Historical cost...................................	$100	$122	$89	$75
Current replacement cost.........................	97	118	84	77
Net realizable value.............................	100	115	89	85
Net realizable value less profit margin.........	95	110	87	81
Number of units on hand.........................	20	35	15	43

Required: Determine the carrying cost of each item, and record the adjusting entry to the inventory account.

6-12. Higgins Manufacturing Company has the following beginning balances:

        Materials inventory.......................$ 75,000
        Work in process........................... 265,000
        Finished goods............................ 45,000

During the period the following occurred:

(1) Purchased for cash $654,000 worth of raw materials. Delivery charges on these materials equaled $16,500.

(2) Used $423,500 worth of direct labor in the production process.

(3) Used $675,000 worth of materials in the production process.

(4) The following costs were incurred:
    Indirect labor..........$20,000   Factory utilities........$110,000

Factory supplies used...$35,000   Depreciation--non-
Property taxes and   manufacturing..........$ 35,000
   insurance............. 10,000   Selling and administrative 50,000
Depreciation--factory... 40,000

(5) Transferred $1,525,000 worth of work in process inventory to finished goods inventory.
(6) Sales were $1,950,000.
(7) The ending balance in Finished Goods Inventory was $70,000.

Required:

    a. Journalize the above transactions.
    b. Prepare an income statement in the format of Exhibit 6-5. (Disregard income taxes.)

6-13. Record the following transactions using (a) the net method and (b) the gross method.

   June   1: Purchased $3,000 worth of goods on credit from Vendor A, terms 2/10, n/30.
   June   3: Purchased $4,000 worth of goods on credit from Vendor B, terms 0.5/15, n/30.
   June   4: Purchased $3,500 worth of goods on credit from Vendor C, terms 3/10, n/45.
   June 10: Paid Vendor A for the June 1 purchase.
   June 11: Returned one third of the merchandise purchased on June 4 from Vendor C for credit.
   June 13: Paid Vendor C for the other two thirds of the June 4 purchase.
   July   2: Paid Vendor B for the June 3 purchase.

What considerations should be made when deciding whether to take advantage of the available discounts?

6-14. You are given the following data for Boyle's Sporting Goods store:

        Sales........................ 900 units @ $90
        January 1 inventory........... 200 units @ 60
        Purchases:
           January 12................. 250 units @ 58
           March 18.................. 100 units @ 60
           September 18.............. 250 units @ 62
           October 15................ 150 units @ 65
           December 27............... 100 units @ 70

   Required: Prepare comparative gross margin statements and gross margin percentages under the assumptions of (a) FIFO, (b) weighted-average cost, and (c) LIFO as the basis for inventory valuation.

6-15. (C.M.A. adapted.) The management of Gemini Products Company has asked its accounting department to describe the effect upon the company's financial position and its financial statements of accounting for inventories on the LIFO rather than FIFO basis during 1981 and 1982. The accounting department is to assume that the change to LIFO would have been effective on January 1, 1981, and that the initial LIFO base would have been the inventory value on December 31, 1980. Presented below are the company's financial statements and other data for the years 1981 and 1982 when the FIFO method was in fact employed.

Balance Sheet as of December 31

Assets

	1980	1981	1982
Cash..........................	$203,100	$ 363,900	$ 528,150
Accounts receivable..........	120,000	162,000	185,250
Inventory....................	207,000	225,000	252,000
Other assets.................	342,000	342,000	342,000
Total assets..............	$872,100	$1,092,900	$1,307,400

Equities

	1980	1981	1982
Accounts payable	$ 69,000	$ 90,000	$ 109,200
Other liabilities	120,000	120,000	120,000
Common stock	420,000	420,000	420,000
Retained earnings	263,100	462,900	658,200
Total Equities	$872,100	$1,092,900	$1,307,400

Income Statements

	1981	1982
Sales	$1,620,000	$1,852,500
Less:		
Cost of goods sold	882,000	1,065,000
Other expenses	405,000	462,000
	1,287,000	1,527,000
Income before taxes	333,000	325,500
Income taxes (40%)	133,200	130,200
Net Income	$ 199,800	$ 195,300

Other Data

1. Inventory on hand at 12/31/80 consisted of 30,000 units valued at $6.90 each.
2. Sales (all units sold at the same price in a given year):
   1981 -- 120,000 units @ $13.50 each
   1982 -- 130,000 units @ $14.25 each.
3. Purchases (all units purchased at the same price in a given year):
   1981 -- 120,000 units @ $7.50 each
   1982 -- 130,000 units @ $8.40 each.
4. Income taxes at the effective rate of 40 percent are paid on December 31 each year.

Required: Name the account(s) presented in the financial statements which will have different amounts for 1982 if LIFO rather than FIFO had been used and state the new amount for each account that is named.

6-16. You are given the following data for Tartars Inc.:

	At Cost	At Retail
Sales	--	$66,000
Beginning inventory	$19,800	26,400
Purchases	33,000	49,500

Required: Using the retail method, determine the:

a. Gross margin percentage
b. Cost of goods sold
c. Ending inventory

CASES

Case 6-17: Bedford Manufacturing Company (A)

The management of Bedford Manufacturing Company prepared annually a budget of expected financial operations for the ensuing calendar year. The completed budget provided information on all aspects of the coming year's operations It included a projected balance sheet as of the year and a projected income statement.

The final preparation of statements was accomplished only after careful integration of detailed computations submitted by each department. This was done to insure that the operations of all departments were in balance with one another. For example, the finance department needed to base its schedules of loan operations and of collections and disbursements on figures that were dependent upon manufacturing, purchasing, and selling expectations. The level of production would be geared to the forecasts of the sales department, and purchasing would be geared to the proposed manufacturing schedule. In short, it was necessary to integrate the estimates of each department and to revise them in terms of the overall effect on operations to arrive at a well-formulated and profitable plan of operations for the coming year. The budget statements ultimately derived from the adjusted transactions would then serve the company as a reliable guide and measure of the coming year's operations.

At the time the 1983 budget was being prepared, in November of 1982, projected 1982 financial statements were compiled for use as a comparison with the budgeted figures. These 1982 statements were based on nine months' actual and three months' projected transactions. They appear as Exhibits 1, 2, and 3.

Below is the summary of expected operations for the budget year 1983 as finally accepted:

1. Sales: All on credit, $2,445,000; sales returns and allowances, $21,000; sales discounts taken by customers, $45,000. (The sales figure is net of expected bad debts.)

2. Purchases of goods and services:
   a. New assets:
      Purchased for cash: manufacturing plant and equipment, $99,000; prepaid manufacturing taxes and insurance, $36,000.
      Purchased on accounts payable: raw materials, $681,000; supplies, $75,000.
   b. Services used to convert raw materials into goods in process,* all purchased for cash: direct manufacturing labor, $456,000; indirect manufacturing labor, $168,000; social security taxes

---

*In a manufacturing company, inventory is assumed to increase in value by the amounts spent to convert raw material into salable products. These amounts include the items listed in 2(b) plus the items listed in 3.

EXHIBIT 1

Projected Balance Sheet
December 31, 1982

Assets

Current Assets:
Cash and securities...		$ 196,600
Accounts receivable (net of allowance for doubtful accounts)...		369,000
Inventories:		
Materials...$ 177,000		
Work in process................................... 141,000		
Finished goods.................................... 46,500		
Supplies.. 27,000		463,500
Prepaid taxes and insurance...............................		27,000
Total Current Assets.................................		1,056,100
Other Assets:		
Manufacturing plant at cost........................... 1,860,000		
Less: Accumulated depreciation................... 630,000		1,230,000
Total Assets...................................		2,286,100

Liabilities and Shareholders' Equity

Current Liabilities:
Notes payable..$ 192,000		
Accounts payable.. 81,000		
Income taxes payable...................................... 15,000		
Total Current Liabilities...........................		$ 288,000
Shareholders' Equity:		
Contributed capital................................... 1,530,000		
Retained earnings.................................... 468,100		1,998,100
Total Liabilities and Shareholders' Equity...........		$2,286,100

EXHIBIT 2

Projected 1982 Statement of Cost of Goods Sold

Finished goods inventory, 1/1/82...............		$ 501,000
Goods in process inventory, 1/1/82.............	$ 156,000	
Materials used.................................	543,000	
Plus: Factory expenses:		
Direct manufacturing labor...................	291,000	
Factory overhead:		
Indirect manufacturing labor...............$118,500		
Power, heat, and light..................... 81,000		
Depreciation of plant...................... 87,000		
Social security taxes...................... 16,500		
Taxes and insurance, factory.............. 15,000		
Supplies................................... 47,400	365,400	
	1,355,400	
Less: Goods in process inventory, 12/31/82...	141,000	
Cost of goods manufactured (i.e., completed)...		1,214,400
		1,715,400
Less: Finished goods inventory, 12/31/82....		46,500
Cost of Goods Sold.............................		$1,668,900

EXHIBIT 3

Projected 1982 Income Statement

Sales..		$2,190,000
Less: Sales returns and allowances.........................$16,800		
Sales discounts allowed............................ 42,000		58,800
Net sales..		2,131,200
Less: Cost of goods sold (per schedule)..................		1,668,900
Gross margin..		462,300
Less: Selling and administrative expense..................		360,600
Operating income..		101,700
Less: Interest expense......................................		18,000
Income before federal income tax............................		83,700
Less: Estimated income tax expense........................		25,100
Net Income..		$ 58,600

---

on labor, $28,200; power, heat, and light, $124,800. (Accrued payroll was ignored in these estimates.)

c. Sales and administrative services, purchased for cash: $702,000.

3. Conversion of assets into work in process: This appears as an increase in the "value" of work in process and a decrease in the appropriate asset accounts. Depreciation of building and equipment, $78,000; expiration of prepaid taxes and insurance, $24,000; supplies used in manufacturing, $87,000; raw materials put into process, $777,000.

4. Transfer of work in process into finished work: This appears as an increase in finished goods and a decrease in work in process. Total cost accumulated on goods that have been completed and transferred to finished goods inventory, $1,647,000.

5. Cost of finished goods sold to customers: $1,497,000.

6. Financial transactions:
   a. $180,000, borrowed on notes payable to bank.
   b. Bank loans paid off (i.e., retired), $210,000.
   c. Cash payment to bank of $20,000 for interest on loans.

7. Cash receipts from customers on accounts receivable: $2,431,500.

8. Cash payments of liabilities:
   a. Payment of accounts payable, $747,000.
   b. Payment of 1982 income tax, $15,000.

9. Estimated federal income tax on 1983 income: $53,350, of which $5,335 is estimated to be unpaid as of December 31, 1983.
10. Dividends declared for year and paid in cash: $33,000.

This summary presents the complete cycle of the Bedford Manufacturing Company's budgeted yearly operations from the purchase of goods and services through their various stages of conversion to completion of the finished product to the sale of this product. All costs and cash receipts and disbursements involved in this cycle are presented, including the provision for federal income tax and the payment of dividends.

Questions

1. Journalize each of the projected transactions. Set up T-accounts with balances as shown on the balance sheet for December 31, 1982, and post the journal entries to these accounts.

2. Prepare a projected statement of cost of goods sold for 1983, a projected income statement for 1983, and a projected balance sheet as of December 31, 1983.

3. Describe the principal differences between the 1983 estimates and the 1982 figures as shown in Exhibits 1, 2, and 3. In what respects is 1983 performance expected to be better than 1982 performance, and in what respects is it expected to be poorer?

* * * * *

Case 6-18: Upstate Fuel Oil

"My accountant, Sharon Palmer, said I should go on FIFO this year," said Dave Williams, "in order to save tax money. As I understand it, I could save even more if I filled my tanks this month [May], even though I have one million gallons in storage and only estimate sales of 200,000 for the rest of this fiscal year -- June and July, 1980. The profit and loss figures Sharon has prepared have convinced me that LIFO is the way to go [see Exhibit 1]. But with interest at 20 percent, I don't know whether it is wise to buy one million gallons this month to 'top off my tanks.' What do you think?"

EXHIBIT 1

UPSTATE FUEL OIL

Projected Profit and Loss Statement
For the Fiscal Year Ended July 31, 1980

	FIFO		LIFO	
Sales......................		$8,492,900		$8,492,900
Cost of Sales:				
Beginning inventory......$ 934,200			$ 934,200	
Purchases................ 6,856,200			6,856,200	
	7,790,400		7,790,400	
Less: Ending inventory.... 1,398,900*	6,391,500		934,200**	6,856,200
Gross margin...............	2,101,400			1,636,700
Operating expenses........	1,000,000			1,000,000
Profit before taxes........	1,101,400			636,700
Federal income taxes (46%).	506,640			292,880
Net Income................	$ 594,760			$ 343,820

```
*    500,000 @ 73.7¢ = $  368,500
     300,000 @ 76.8¢ =    230,400
   1,000,000 @ 80.0¢ =    800,000
                      $1,398,900
```

**1,800,000 @ 51.9¢ = $934,200 (beginning inventory)

- 68 -

EXHIBIT 2

UPSTATE FUEL OIL

Purchases and Sales of Fuel Oil
For the Fiscal Year Ended July 31, 1980

| Month | PURCHASES | | | SALES | | | ENDING INVENTORY |
	Price Per Gal.	Gal. in 000's	Total Purchases	Price Per Gal.	Gal. in 000's	Total Purchases	Gal. in 000's
July 1979	53.0¢						1,800
August	55.2¢	--		69.0¢	100	$ 69,000	1,700
September	57.6¢	--		71.9¢	200	143,800	1,500
October	60.0¢	700	$ 420,000	75.0¢	700	525,000	1,500
November	62.5¢	1,500	937,500	78.1¢	1,000	781,000	2,000
December	65.1¢	1,700	1,106,700	81.4¢	1,700	1,383,800	2,000
Jan. 1980	67.9¢	2,000	1,358,000	84.8¢	2,500	2,120,000	1,500
February	70.7¢	2,000	1,414,000	88.4¢	2,100	1,856,400	1,400
March	73.7¢	800	589,600	92.1¢	1,100	1,013,100	1,100
April	76.8¢	300	230,400	96.0¢	300	288,000	1,100
May	80.0¢	1,000	800,000	100.0¢	100	100,000	1,000
June	83.4¢*	--	--	104.2¢*	100*	104,200	1,900*
July	86.9¢*	--	--	108.6¢*	100*	108,600	1,800*
		10,000	$6,856,200		10,000	$8,492,900	

*Estimates

Upstate Fuel Oil distributed heating oil in upper New York state. The company had a two-million-gallon storage capacity which it filled each year prior to the closing of the Hudson River to barge traffic in order to keep down its transportation costs. It also tried to fill its customers' fuel oil tanks in October and November, both to save transportation costs and to spread delivery schedules. Exhibit 2 shows sales and purchases in gallons for fiscal 1980.

In the winter of 1979-80, fuel prices rose steadily from 51¢ a gallon in the summer of 1979 to 80¢ a gallon in May, 1980. Upstate Fuel Oil establishes its retail prices as 125 percent of the wholesale price in the month delivered.

"You know," Dave Williams continued, "I am negotiating the purchase of Centre Fuel Oil in the next county. It has three million gallons of fuel oil in its tanks right now. If buying one million gallons of fuel oil is good, maybe buying Centre's oil before my year end would be even better."

Questions:

1. What would the fiscal 1980 profit and loss statement of Upstate Fuel Oil look like if Dave Williams purchased the 1,000,000 gallons of fuel oil in August 1980 instead of in May 1980 (LIFO basis)? What are the tax savings? Should he make the May purchase?

2. If Dave Williams acquires the three million gallons of Centre's fuel oil at 80¢ a gallon prior to the end of this fiscal year, what will be the tax savings (over and above any produced by the one million gallon May purchase)? What percent is this of the purchase price of the oil? Why does this happen?

* * * * *

Case 6-19: Bernhart Dress Shop

For over 20 years, Murray Bernhart had owned and operated a women's specialty shop in a suburban town. Early in 1983, Marion Wilson, a representative of Stylway Stores Inc., discussed with Bernhart the possibility of selling his business to Stylway Stores, which owned 16 specialty shops in the same metropolitan area. Over the past several years, several other chains had approached Bernhart with similar propositions, but the Stylway proposal was the first one that he seriously considered.

After a series of conversations, Bernhart told Wilson that he would consider selling his business provided they could agree on a fair price and provided Stylway would agree to employ him as store manager. Wilson assured him Stylway would certainly be happy to have Bernhart continue as manager of the store and the discussion then turned to the problem of deciding the selling price. Wilson asked what financial information was available, and Bernhart replied:

The only formal statements I have are balance sheets and my income tax returns, which I have a tax expert prepare for me. I expect him to work up the returns for 1982 within the next month. I know what is going on in the business well enough so that I don't need other statements. Of course, I have a checkbook, a file of charge slips showing what customers owe me, and a file of unpaid invoices from suppliers. On New Year's day, or the preceding afternoon, I take a physical inventory and determine the purchase cost of goods on hand.

I have two salespersons helping me, but I am at the store most of the time, and I try to keep a close tab on everything that takes place. There are two cash registers which everyone uses regardless of the kind of merchandise sold. None of us specializes in the sale of any particular kind of goods.

Wilson replied that the lack of financial statements for 1982 probably would not prove to be any great obstacle to the conclusion of negotiations. All that was necessary was permission from Bernhart to examine whatever records were available, from which it was highly probable that Stylway could ascertain all the operating facts about the business that were needed. Bernhart agreed with this arrangement.

Wilson was able to gather the data presented in Exhibits 1 and 2. In going over this information with Bernhart, Wilson commented: "If Stylway takes over this store, even if you stay on as manager, we will need more figures than you have been gathering for yourself."

EXHIBIT 1

BERNHART DRESS SHOP
Balance Sheet
As of December 31, 1973

Assets

Current Assets:
Cash... $ 38,757
Notes receivable.. 6,000
Accounts receivable... 25,686
Merchandise inventory... 67,803
    Total Current Assets.. 138,246

Other Assets:
Furniture and fixtures.....................................$20,610
    Less: Accumulated depreciation.........................11,739
Office equipment.. 5,760
    Less: Accumulated depreciation.......................... 5,760
    Total Assets.. 0
                                               $147,117

Equities

Current Liabilities:
Salaries payable.. $ 2,460
Notes payable... 22,800
Accounts payable.. 12,564
    Total Current Liabilities....................................... 37,824

Owner's Equity:
M. W. Bernhart, prop.. 49,500
Retained earnings... 59,793
    Total Equities... $147,117

EXHIBIT 2

Cash Record for 1982

Receipts:
Cash sales.....................$209,286
Collection of accounts
    receivable............... 117,354
  Total receipts.............$326,640
Plus cash balance,
    December 31, 1981........ 38,757
  Total......................$365,397

Expenditures:
Payroll.......................$ 79,467
Rent.......................... 12,900
Advertising...................   7,296
Taxes.........................   5,223
Supplies...................... 11,670
Travel........................   2,430
Telephone.....................   2,736
Repairs to building...........   2,150
Insurance.....................   1,350
Miscellaneous expenses........   2,934
Paid on accounts payable
    for merchandise.......... 222,873
  Total expenditures.........$351,009
Plus cash balance,
    December 31, 1982........ 14,388
  Total......................$365,397

Other Information

The expenditure for payroll includes Bernhart's salary of $48,000. Social security and withholding taxes may be disregarded since the expense portion was included in the payroll figure and amounts due to the government were immediately deposited in a separate bank account that does not appear on the financial statements.

Wages payable (including taxes
  thereon) as of
  December 31, 1982.............$ 4,344
Accounts payable represented
  only invoices for merchandise
  purchased on credit. As of
  December 31, 1981, these
  unpaid invoices amounted to... 29,688
Amounts due from customers on
  December 31, 1982 totaled..... 51,930
Merchandise inventory,
  December 31, 1982............113,808

The note receivable carried a 9 percent rate of interest. The note payable carried an 8 percent rate of interest. The note receivable was not collected in 1982, nor was the note payable paid in 1982.

Miscellaneous expenses included $1,800 paid to Ajax Truck Rental for a three-month lease on a delivery truck. The lease began on December 1, 1982.

Depreciation on furniture and fixtures was computed at 10 percent of cost.

Questions

1. From the information given in Exhibits 1 and 2, determine (a) sales, (b) the cost of merchandise sold, and (c) the expenses for the year.

2. Prepare an income statement for 1982 and a balance sheet as of December 31, 1982.

3. Why should more figures apparently be justifiable under chain responsibility than when the store was owned by Mr. Bernhart?

4. How should the parties proceed to decide on a fair selling price for the business?

Chapter 7

Long-Lived Assets and Their Amortization

Key Terms

Long-lived tangible asset
Capitalized expenditure
Amortization
Intangible asset
Depreciation
Depletion
Betterment
Capital lease
Service life

Residual value
Straight-line method
Declining-balance method
Sum-of-years'-digits method
Units-of-production method
Net book value
ACRS
Deferral and flow-through methods

Discussion Questions

1. Distinguish between asset maintenance and asset betterments.

2. Distinguish between an operating lease and a capital lease.

3. Why is interest capitalized when a company constructs a building or item of equipment for its own use? How much interest is normally capitalized on self-constructed assets?

4. Explain why depreciation expense is an estimate rather than an amount which can be determined with precision.

5. Under what circumstances is an asset's service life shorter than its physical life?

6. Many people unfamiliar with accounting think that depreciation represents the "wearing out" of a long-lived tangible asset. Others think depreciation reflects the decrease in the asset's market value. Discuss these two viewpoints.

7. Explain the conceptual differences between determining depreciation expense for financial reporting and determining cost recovery allowances for income tax purposes.

8. Distinguish between the effects on net income of the deferral method and the flow-through method of accounting for the investment tax credit.

9. On January 1, 1977, Mathews Company bought for $100,000 an asset which at the time was expected to have a service life of ten years and no residual value. On January 1, 1983, the company decided that this asset would provide benefits to the company for another eight years, that is, four years longer than originally anticipated. Assuming Mathews uses straight-line depreciation, what were the annual depreciation charges from 1977 to 1982? What should the annual depreciation charge be from 1983 to 1986? Beyond 1986?

10. PDB Company purchased an asset with a ten-year estimated service life and no expected residual value, for $10,000 on October 1. The following adjusting entry was made in PDB's books at the close of its fiscal year on December 31:

```
Depreciation Expense........................ 500
     Accumulated Depreciation.............        500
     ($10,000/10 years x 1/2 year = $500)
```

Since the asset was used only three months during this fiscal year, shouldn't the above entry have been for $250?

11. Wilbur Company depreciates its equipment assets on an individual basis (i.e., not group depreciation) using the straight-line method. On December 31, it disposed of an asset it had acquired five years previously. The original cost of this asset was $50,000, and at the time of acquisition it was estimated that the asset would have a service life of ten years and residual value of $5,000. Disposal proceeds were $10,300. Prepare a journal entry which reflects the disposal transaction.

12. Explain what you think the account "Gain (or Loss) on Sale of Fixed Assets" means.

13. Why are annual depreciation charges based on an asset's original cost minus residual value, if any, rather than just on its original cost?

14. Why is there no recognition of gain or loss when an old asset is traded in for a new similar asset?

15. What is meant by "group" depreciation? How does it differ from "item" depreciation? If a company using the straight-line depreciation method disposed of a machine halfway through its estimated service life, where the machine had original cost of $20,000 and disposal proceeds were $12,000, what would be the accounting entry to reflect the disposal transaction under group depreciation?

16. The following quotation appeared in Business Week: "...In terms of economic reality, depreciation should not be considered as part of cash flow which can be used to pay dividends; rather, it should be considered as a source of funds to replace plant." Comment on this statement.

17. In their accounting usage, why aren't the terms "depreciation" and "appreciation" opposites?

18. Explain how the FASB's required accounting for research and development costs illustrates a conflict among accounting principles.

Problems

7-1. On January 1, a company spent $22,000 for preventive maintenance on Machine A and $46,000 on Machine B. It was estimated that the $46,000 expenditure would extend the life of Machine B for five years. Both machines had a ten-year estimated life when purchased for $200,000 each six years previously.

Required: Prepare entries for the January 1 maintenance expenditures and for the year's depreciation (straight-line basis.)

7-2. Diesel-Power Motor Company agreed to provide a new truck to Speed-Rite Trucking Company under a five-year lease. The lease requires five annual payments (beginning upon receipt of the truck) of $35,000. The market value of the truck is $125,000. The present value of the stream of minimum lease payments is $120,000.

Required:

a. Explain why this lease is a capital lease.
b. Assume that the first annual payment consists of $18,000 of interest expense and $17,000 to reduce the obligation, and that the second annual payment consists of $15,450 of interest expense and $19,550 to reduce the obligation. Prepare the lessee's journal entries for the first two years of the lease.

7-3. Bradley Corporation purchased a machine costing $210,000 which had an estimated useful life of six years and residual value of $18,000. The machine is expected to produce 3.2 million units during its useful life, as follows:

Year	Units
1	830,000
2	715,000
3	535,000
4	465,000
5	385,000
6	270,000
	3,200,000

Required:

a. What will be each year's depreciation charge if Bradley uses the units-of-production method?
b. Will this give significantly different depreciation charges in each year than the sum-of-the-years' digits method?

7-4. During 1983, Swenk Company purchased the following assets:

Asset	Value
Light-duty delivery truck................$ 9,000	
Grinding machine........................ 28,000	
Conveyor-belt system.................... 125,000	
Fork-lift............................... 5,500	

Required:

a. Compute the amount of the investment tax credit allowable under the 1981 Tax Act.
b. Prepare the 1983 journal entries relating to the investment tax credit under both the deferral method and the flow-through method.

7-5. Arlington Corporation owned two branch sales offices of which it wanted to dispose. Office A, which had a net book value of $65,000 and an appraised value of $117,000, was transferred to Fairfax Company along with $39,000 cash in exchange for a larger Fairfax Company sales office, Office C, in a different city. This Fairfax office had a net book value of $97,500 on Fairfax's balance sheet, and was appraised at $162,500. Arlington's Office B, which had a net book value of $169,000 and appraised value of $195,000, was transferred to McLean Company. In exchange, McLean gave Arlington three trucks, with an aggregate market value of $46,800 and carried at $39,000 (net) on McLean's balance sheet, plus a promissory note for $149,500.

Required: Prepare journal entries which will record these transactions on the books of each of the three companies.

7-6. Williams Company owns the following noncurrent assets:

Asset	Original Cost	Residual Value	Useful Life
Machinery......	$ 65,000	$1,000	8 years
Goodwill.......	100,000	0	25 years
Patent.........	34,000	0	17 years

Required:

a. Prepare depreciation and amortization schedules for the first four years, using (1) straight-line depreciation and (2) 150% declining-balance depreciation and (3) sum-of-the-years' digits depreciation for the tangible assets. Assume all assets were purchased as of January 1.
b. Assume that after four years of operating the machinery, Williams Company decides that the machinery will last only two more years, at which time its residual value will be zero. Prepare the journal entries for year five by using the straight-line method.

7-7. On June 1, Claremont Corporation purchased land and a vacant factory building thereon from the Newport Company for $600,000. The appraised value of this property was $800,000, of which $600,000 was attributed to the land. Claremont had been able to acquire the property at less than the appraised value because the surrounding community wanted to encourage new economic development, and accordingly had "subsidized" the sale by paying Newport Company the $200,000 difference between the appraised value and purchase price paid by Claremont.

It had been clear all along that the vacant factory building was not suitable for Claremont's purposes, so Claremont paid $25,000 on June 30 to have it torn down so that a new building could be constructed. In July, when "core samples" were taken prior to siting of the new building, a valuable mineral deposit was discovered. Although Claremont decided not to mine this deposit, two independent appraisers determined that the deposit increased the value of the land to $3,000,000.

Required: Show the carrying cost of the land on Claremont's balance sheet as of:

a. June 1, the purchase date;
b. June 30, when the building was torn down; and
c. July, when the mineral deposit was discovered.

7-8. Trebco Company had the following transactions for the month of April:

(1) Paid $1,100,000 for land and a building. Recent appraisals have estimated the fair market value of the purchase at $1,200,000, with $540,000 of value attributed to the building.

(2) Ordered and received machinery with a total purchase price of $120,000, subject to terms of 1/15, n/60. Trebco records purchases at the net amount.

(3) Repaired the drainage system for the parking lot at a cost of $3,500, which was paid in cash.

(4) An insurance premium of $1,500 was paid in cash. The insurance policy had provided protection against possible damage to the new machinery described in (2) above while in-transit.

(5) Taxes were assessed in the amount of $2,500 for repair work on the county road which provides access to the property.

(6) Remodeled the office at a cost of $45,000, which included a $200 charge for a building permit and $2,200 in architect's fees. All costs will be paid next month.

(7) Installed $15,000 of protective air-filtering devices due to the fine dust created by the new machinery when operating. These costs were paid in cash.

Required: Prepare journal entries for the above transactions.

7-9. On January 1, 1982, the Mann Corporation purchased all of the assets of the Ash Company for $2,816,500 cash, and the Ash Company was disbanded. At the time of this purchase, Ash's assets were valued by an independent appraiser. These values and the Ash balance sheet book values are shown below:

THE ASH COMPANY
Assets as of January 1, 1982

	Book Value	Appraised Value
Cash	$344,000	$344,000
Accounts receivable (net)	508,500	508,500
Inventories	399,900	484,000
Fixed assets (net)	638,000	880,000
Other tangible assets	111,800	140,000

Required:

    a. Give the journal entry for Mann's books to record Mann's purchase of the assets of Ash.

    b. Assuming the acquired fixed assets have a remaining useful life of eleven years, and that both companies use straight-line depreciation, how much larger will Mann's 1982 depreciation expense for the acquired fixed assets be than Ash's 1982 depreciation would have been?

    c. Assuming Mann uses the maximum allowable amortization period, how large will the 1982 goodwill write-off be?

    d. Assuming a 40 percent tax rate for both companies, and assuming that Ash's assets would have generated the same income in 1982 under either set of owners, how much less will Ash's net income be with Ash owned by Mann than it would have been had Ash retained its previous ownership?

7-10. During the month of July, Quickworth Company constructed an addition to its office with its own employees. The following information about the construction costs is available:

(1) Purchased $65,000 of building materials, subject to terms of 2/15, n/30. Company policy requires all purchases to be recorded at the net amount. Purchases are always paid for within the discount period.

(2) Labor expense for the addition totaled $45,000.

(3) Office lights were purchased at a cost of $4,000. A private contractor installed the fixtures for a fee of $1,200.

(4) On July 15, carpeting was purchased and installed for a total cost of $35,000. A three month, 12 percent promissory note was issued to satisfy payment requirements. Interest of $1,700 on a $127,500 bank loan was the only other amount of interest expense for the month of July. The loan is typical in respect to interest rates charged to Quickworth.

(5) Miscellaneous expenses totaled $30,925.

(6) The addition was complete as of July 31.

Required: Determine the amount that Quickworth Company should capitalize for the new addition to its office. Show supporting computations.

7-11. Alvin Company had the following transactions during the year:

(1) Land was purchased for $50,000 cash. This land was to be used for a new office building. It was agreed that Alvin Company would pay for the razing of a building currently on the land; this would cost $3,500, to be paid in cash.

(2) Alvin Company contracted with Wallis Construction to build the new office building. It was agreed that Alvin would pay Wallis with 2,000 shares of Alvin common stock, a $10,000 note, and $20,000 in cash. Alvin's common stock was currently selling for $30 a share.

(3) Alvin purchased some office equipment from Central Office Equipment for $6,000 cash. Mr. Alvin was a close personal friend of the owner of Central Office Equipment, and accordingly was sold this equipment at a price lower than normally would be charged. The prices charged to "normal" customers were as follows:

    Desks and chairs................$5,600
    Bookcases....................... 1,600
    Filing cabinets.................   800
                           $8,000

Required: Prepare journal entries for the above transactions.

7-12. Slowburn Coal Company purchased coal-leasing land which contains 500,000 tons of coal for $14,000,000. Soil tests by geologists cost $23,000 for the purchased land, but tests at other sites which yielded negative results cost $75,000. Slowburn uses the full cost method for exploration costs. Test permits were issued by the federal government at a cost of $27,000 to Slowburn. The estimated salvage value of the purchased land will be $1,500,000 once the coal is removed. The coal is expected to be mined within 10 years.

Before mining could begin, the company had to remove trees and undergrowth at a cost of $250,000. In addition, storage facilities and a field office were constructed at a total cost of $175,000. These facilities will last an estimated 25 years, but will serve no purpose once the coal is removed; hence, they have no residual value. Machinery which cost $750,000 was installed, but its service life is limited to the time required to remove the coal. The buildings will be depreciated on a straight-line basis, while the machinery will be depreciated by using the sum-of-the-years' digits method.

In the first year of operation, Slowburn mined 20,000 tons of coal; in the second year, 45,000 tons; and in the third year, 60,000 tons.

Required: Prepare a schedule showing (1) unit and total depletion and (2) depreciation for the first three years of operation. Assume that the purchase occurred on January 1 and that Slowburn uses a calendar fiscal year.

7-13. Kensington Company has been evaluating the usefulness of several of its major assets. During the year, Kensington carried out the following decisions to improve its operating efficiency:

(1) A computer, which had been purchased for $375,000, was traded in for a new computer on December 31. The old computer had a book value of $125,000. Kensington paid $300,000 to the manufacturer in addition to the trade-in.
(2) The service life on the $2,950,000 bottling machine was decreased by two years. At the end of the current year, the bottling machine will have: accumulated depreciation of $1,450,000; estimated residual value of $450,000; and a remaining practical life of 15 years. When originally purchased six years ago, the estimated service life was 10 years and the estimated residual value was $600,000. Depreciation is calculated on a straight-line basis.
(3) A new roof was put on the south wing of the plant, which will add 10 years to the physical life of this portion of the building. Kensington's accounting records show that this wing was built 15 years ago for a cost of $12,635,000. At that time, the estimated service life of the plant was 35 years. As of this year, Kensington decided to use the building for only 16 more years due to an anticipated property tax increse. The roof was replaced at a cost of $1,895,000. Straight-line depreciation is used for all buildings.

Required: Prepare any journal entries as of December 31 which are required for the decisions listed above. Also, assume that December 31 is the end of Kensington's fiscal year.

7-14. Unger Company had the following disposals of production equipment during 1982:

Equipment ID Number	Purchase Date	Original Cost	Date of Disposal	Disposal Proceeds	Useful Life	Depreciation Method
103	3/11/74	$40,500	8/5/82	$ 8,100	10	straight line
213	9/18/81	81,000	10/1/82	54,000	5	double declining balance
318	4/ 8/80	67,000	3/3/82	27,000	8	sum of the years' digits

Unger's policy is to charge a full year's depreciation in the year of purchase if an asset is purchased before July 1. For assets purchased after July 1, only one-half year's depreciation is charged. During the year of disposal, one-half year's depreciation is charged if the asset is sold after June 30. No depreciation is charged during the year of disposal if the asset is sold before July 1. In all three cases above, estimated residual value at the time of acquisition was zero.

Required: Write journal entries to record the above disposals.

7-15. During the year, Aisen Company traded an automobile plus $5,000 in cash to Haron Company for another automobile. The car Aisen used as a trade-in originally had cost $6,000, of which $4,500 had been depreciated.

Aisen also purchased new office furniture during the year. The list price of the furniture was $6,800. Aisen paid $2,550 cash plus gave the furniture company a used truck. This truck had a net book value of $4,250; it had originally cost $9,860, and had recently been appraised at $3,910.

Required: Record the above transactions on Aisen Company's books.

CASES

Case 7-16: Jean Coffin

"Your course unfortunately doesn't give me the answer to a great many real-life problems," said Jean Coffin to an accounting professor. "I've read the text and listened to you attentively, but every once in a while I run across something that doesn't seem to fit the rules."

"Not all of life's complications can be covered in a first course," the professor replied. "As is the case with law, medicine, or indeed any of the professions, many matters are dealt with in advanced courses, and others are not settled in any classroom. Nevertheless, some problems that are not specifically discussed can be solved satisfactorily by relating them to principles that you already have learned. Let's take fixed asset capitalization as a case in point. If you will write down some of the matters about which you are now uncomfortable, I'd be glad to discuss them with you; that is, after you have given some thought as to the most reasonable solution."

A week later, Coffin returned and said to the accounting instructor, "The general principle for arriving at the amount of a fixed asset that is to be capitalized is reasonably clear, but there certainly are a great many problems in applying this principle to specific situations. Following are some situations I've made up."

1. Suppose that the Bruce Manufacturing Company used its own maintenance crew to build an additional wing on its existing factory building. What would be the proper accounting treatment of the following items:

a. Architects' fees.
b. The cost of snow removal during construction.
c. Cash discounts earned for prompt payment on materials purchased for construction.
d. The cost of building a combined construction office and tool shed which would be torn down once the factory wing had been completed.
e. Interest on money borrowed to finance construction.
f. Local real estate taxes for the period of construction on the portion of land to be occupied by the new wing.
g. The cost of mistakes made during construction.
h. The overhead costs of the maintenance department which include: supervision; depreciation on buildings and equipment of maintenance department shops; heat, light, and power for these shops; and allocations of cost for such items as the cafeteria, medical office, and personnel department.
i. The cost of insurance during construction, and the cost of damages or losses on any injuries or losses not covered by insurance.

2. Assume that the Archer Company bought a large piece of land, including the buildings thereon, with the intent of razing the buildings and constructing a combined hotel and office building in their place. The existing buildings consisted of a theater and several stores and small apartment buildings, all in active use at the time of the purchase.

a. What accounting treatment should be accorded that portion of the purchase price considered to be the amount paid for the buildings which were subsequently razed?
b. How should the costs of demolishing the old buildings be treated?
c. Suppose that a single company had owned this large piece of land, including the buildings thereon, and instead of selling to the Archer Company had decided to have the buildings razed and to have a combined hotel and office building constructed on the site for its own benefit. In what respects, if any, should the accounting treatment of the old buildings and the cost of demolishing them differ from your recommendations with respect to (a) and (b) above?

3. Midland Manufacturing Company

purchased a new machine. It is clear that the invoice price of the new machine should be capitalized and it also seems reasonable to capitalize the transportation cost to bring the machine to the Midland plant. I'm not so clear, however, on the following items:

a. The new machine is heavier than the old machine it replaced; consequently the foundation under the machine has had to be strengthened by the installation of additional steel beams. Should this cost be charged to the building, added to the cost of the machine, or be expensed?

b. The installation of the machine took longer and was more costly than anticipated. In addition to time spent by the regular maintenance crew on installation, it became necessary to hire an outside engineer to assist in the installation and in "working out the bugs" to get the machine running properly. His costs included not only his fee but also his transportation, hotel expense, and meals. Moreover, the foreman of the department and the plant superintendent both spent a considerable amount of time assisting in the installation work. Before the new machine was working properly a large amount of material had been spoiled during trial runs.

c. In addition to the invoice price and transportation, it was necessary to pay a sales tax on purchasing the machine.

d. In connection with payment for the new machine the machine manufacturer was willing to accept the Midland Company's old machine as partial payment. The amount allowed as a trade-in was larger than the depreciated value at which the old machine was being carried in the books of the Midland Company. Should the difference have been treated as a reduction in the cost of the new machine or a gain on disposal of the old one?

4. A computer manufacturing company sold outright about 25 percent of its products (in terms of dollar volume) and leased 75 percent. On average, a given computer was leased for four years. The cost of leased computers was initially recorded as an asset and was depreciated over four years. The company assisted new customers in installing the computer and in designing the related systems. The "applications engineering" services were furnished without charge, and the company's cost was reported as part of its marketing expense. Applications engineering costs averaged about 5 percent of the sales value of a computer, but about 20 percent of the first-year rental revenue of a leased computer. Recently, the company's installation of computers grew rapidly. Because the applications engineering cost was such a high percentage of lease revenue, reported income did not increase at all. Research and development costs must be expensed as incurred. Does the same principle apply to applications engineering costs, or could these costs be added to the asset value of leased computers and amortized over the lease period? If so, could other marketing costs related to leased computers be treated in the same way?

5. Using the deferral method of accounting for the investment tax credit in effect reduces the capitalized cost of the asset that gave rise to the credit, whereas the flow-through method reduces reported income tax expense for the period in which the asset was acquired. While I can understand permitting accounting alternatives such as FIFO vs. LIFO, and straight-line vs. accelerated depreciation, I cannot understand the rationale for permitting two different treatments for the investment tax credit. What _is_ the latter rationale?

* * * * *

Case 7-17: Horton Press

Horton Press was founded in 1972 as a one-man job printing firm in a small southwestern town. Shortly after its founding, the owner decided to concentrate on one specialty line of printing. Because of a high degree of technical proficiency, the company experienced a rapid growth.

However, the company suffered from a competitive disadvantage in that the major market for its specialized output was in a metropolitan area over 300 miles away from the company's plant. For this reason, the owner, in 1982, decided to move nearer his primary market. He also decided to expand and modernize his facilities at the time of the move. After some investigation, an attractive site was found in a suburb of his primary market, and the move was made.

A balance sheet prepared prior to the move is shown in Exhibit 1. The transactions that arose from this move are described in the following paragraphs:

1. The land at the old site together with the building thereon was sold for $104,800.

2. Certain equipment was sold for $19,600 cash. This equipment appeared on the books at a cost of $51,500 less accumulated depreciation of $28,600.

3. A new printing press was purchased. The invoice cost of this equipment was $78,400. A 2 percent cash discount was taken by Horton Press, so that only $76,832 was actually paid to the seller. Horton Press also paid $314 to a trucker to have this equipment delivered. Installation of this equipment was made by Horton Press employees who worked a total of 60 hours. These workers received $10.00 per hour in wages, but their time was ordinarily charged to printing jobs at $20.00 per hour, the difference representing an allowance for overhead ($7.80) and profit ($2.20).

EXHIBIT 1

HORTON PRESS
Condensed Balance Sheet
As of December 31, 1982

Assets

Current Assets:

Cash.................		$ 87,320
Certificates of deposit........		200,000
Other current assets.............		176,076
Total Current Assets...		463,396
Property and Equipment:		
Land.................		23,800
Buildings...........$244,800		
Less: Accumulated depreciation....	139,200	105,600
Equipment...........	185,380	
Less: Accumulated depreciation....	125,120	60,260
Total Assets......		$653,056

Equities

Current liabilities...	$112,044
Common stock.........	308,000
Retained earnings.....	233,012
Total Equities...	$653,056

4. The city to which the company moved furnished the land on which the new plant was built as a gift. The land had an appraised value of $98,000. The appraisal had been made recently by a qualified appraiser. The company would pay property taxes on its assessed value, which was $62,700.

5. Horton Press paid $14,850 to have an old building on the gift plot of land torn down. (The value of this building was not included in the appraised or assessed values named above.) In addition, the company paid $9,500 to have permanent drainage facilities installed on the new land.

6. A new composing machine with an invoice cost of $19,600 was purchased. The company paid $14,600 cash and received a trade-in allowance of $5,000 on a used piece of composing equipment. The used equipment could have been sold for not more than $8,400. It had cost new, and accumulated depreciation on it was $3,600.

7. The company erected a building at the new site for $392,000. Of this amount, $294,000 was borrowed on a mortgage.

8. After the equipment had been moved to the plant, but before operations began there, extensive repairs and replacements of parts were made on a large paper cutter. The cost of this work was $3,900. Prior to this time, no more than $280 had been spent in any one year on the maintenance of this paper cutter.

9. Trucking and other costs associated with moving equipment to the new location and installing it were $5,900. In addition, Horton Press employees worked an estimated 125 hours on that part of the move that related to equipment.

10. During the moving operation, a piece of equipment costing $7,000 was dropped and damaged; $1,900 was spent to repair it. The management believed, however, that the salvage value of this equipment had been reduced to $980. Up until that time, the equipment was being depreciated at $560 per year, representing a 10 percent rate after deduction of estimated salvage of $1,400. Accumulated depreciation was $2,240.

11. The $200,000 certificates of deposit matured and were cashed.

Questions

1. Analyze the effect of each of these transactions on the items in the balance sheet and income statement. For transactions that affect owners' equity, distinguish between those that affect the net income of the current year and those that do not. In most cases, the results of your analysis can be set forth most clearly in the form of journal entries.

2. Prepare a balance sheet showing the effect of these transactions. (Assume a date as of December 31, 1982, and ignore any usual closing entries.)

* * * * *

Case 7-18: Imports Boutique

On September 1, Jan Turcotte started a new retail business specializing in imported merchandise. The store was called Imports Boutique. During September, the following transactions took place:

1. Turcotte invested $100,000 cash in the new business.

2. Store fixtures were purchased for $53,500; $5,350 was paid in cash and the remainder left on account.

3. Inventory purchases for the month totaled $93,500; $14,000 worth of this inventory was paid for in cash; the remainder was on account.

4. Store supplies of $2,000 and office supplies of $175 were purchased on account.

5. Sales for the month consisted of $15,000 in cash sales and $47,500 charge (i.e., credit) sales.

6. Accounts receivable collected in the first month amounted to $10,500 plus others mentioned below).

7. Turcotte took out a two-year fire and theft insurance policy costing $1,800, paid for in cash.

8. Customers returned $700 worth of merchandise for which they received full credit. Of this, $450 worth was returned by charge account customers; the rest was returned for a cash credit. (The merchandise was not resalable.)

9. Turcotte withdrew $2,000 for personal use.

10. In order to receive discounts for prompt payment, Turcotte paid suppliers for inventory purchased earlier in the month. This inventory had a gross cost of $37,500;

the total discounts amounted to $750.

11. The store paid $8,025 cash on account with the store fixtures dealer.

12. Freight paid to the Ace Freight Company for transporting goods to the store amounted to $240.

13. Salespersons' salaries paid in cash were $3,225.

14. A used delivery truck worth $14,400 new and having a book value of $9,600, according to the seller's accounting records, was purchased by Turcotte for $9,000. Of this, $6,000 was paid for in cash, and Turcotte gave a 90-day, 12 percent note for the remaining $3,000.

15. A factory overhauled engine was purchased and installed in the truck at a cost of $1,500, plus the trade-in of the old truck engine. Turcotte paid cash.

16. Rent of $1,650 for the store building was paid in cash at the end of the month.

17. During the month, Turcotte decided to set up an allowance for doubtful accounts of $900.

18. The utilities for the month, amounting to $625, were paid in cash.

19. A check for $100 was received from a customer for payment of 50 percent of his account. The balance was considered as uncollectible because a court had declared the customer to be bankrupt.

20. A customer who was unable to meet her bills sent in a 120-day non-interest-bearing note for the full amount of her account, which was $275.

21. Miscellaneous general expenses paid in cash amounted to $375.

22. Salespersons' salaries accrued, but not yet paid, at the end of the month amounted to $160.

23. On Saturdays, Turcotte hired an extra employee for the day, who was paid $128 cash during September. (This was not included in item 13 above.)

24. Miscellaneous selling expenses of $240 were incurred. These were paid in cash.

25. Depreciation on the fixtures (item 2 above) was estimated to be 1 percent per month.

26. Depreciation on the used truck (items 14 and 15 above) was estimated to be 2 percent per month. (Assume the truck and its replacement engine have been in use for half a month.)

27. At the end of the month interest had accrued for 15 days on the $3,000 note Turcotte gave to the previous owner of the truck (item 14 above). The interest was not to be paid until the note was due.

28. Turcotte wanted to adjust the allowance for doubtful accounts to 3 percent of monthly credit sales. The balance in the allowance at the end of the month was $800.

29. Jan Turcotte made the usual monthly $575 payment to the bank for the mortgage on the Turcotte family's house.

30. Store supplies used during the month totaled $725.

31. Office supplies used totaled $70.

32. Gas and oil for the delivery truck amounted to $112. This was paid in cash.

33. The two-year insurance policy (item 7 above) had been in effect for one month.

34. Turcotte sold the wooden crates in which the store fixtures were packed to a junk dealer for $20.

35. At the end of the month a $50 check was received as payment on an account which Turcotte had written off as a bad debt.

36. Cash of $130 was paid to a printer for handbills.

37. Repairs costing $230 cash were made on the rented building. Turcotte did not expect to be able to persuade the landlord to reimburse these repair costs.

38. During the month Turcotte returned to importers $425 worth of merchandise purchases for which full credit was given by the importers.

39. Turcotte took $15 worth of trinkets out of inventory and distributed them free to the children of customers in order to build up customer goodwill.

40. At the end of the month Turcotte purchased a small computer on account for $650.

Required: Write journal entries for the above transactions. Ignore social security, withholding, and income taxes.

Chapter 8

Liabilities and Interest Expense

Key Terms

Contingency
Term loan
Bond
Mortgage bond
Debenture
Sinking fund bond
Callable bond
Convertible bond
Bond par value
Coupon rate

Bond discount and premium
Refund a bond issue
Debt/equity and debt/capitalization ratios
Times interest earned
Compound interest
Discounting
Present value
Debt amortization
Current yield
Yield to maturity

Discussion Questions

1. A store that leases its building from year to year does not show the obligation to make future rent payments as a liability. Why not?

2. Why is the bad debt allowance for accounts receivable shown on the balance sheet as a contra-asset, whereas an allowance for future warranty costs is shown as a liability?

3. If you purchase a multiyear magazine subscription, the publisher will record part of your payment as a liability called "unearned subscriptions revenue." Why is this a liability? Why does a three-year subscription generally cost less than three times the cost of a one-year subscription?

4. When is a contingency recorded as a liability?

5. As a test of your understanding of liability and equity terminology, explain what a "callable sinking fund debenture" is.

6. Viking Corporation issued some bonds with a face value of $1,000 each and a coupon rate of 8 percent. At the time, the prevailing rate of interest for bonds of similar risk was 10 percent. Were the bonds issued at a discount or a premium?

7. Randlett Corporation has outstanding some 8 percent debentures (face value $1,000 each) and some 8 percent convertible debentures (also $1,000 face value each). Both of these securities are traded on a major stock exchange. Which would you expect to have the higher price? Explain.

8. Comment on this statement: "Interest expense on outstanding liabilities should always be computed by using the stated rate of interest."

9. Why are different amortization methods used for the asset and the liability amounts in a capital lease?

10. Contrast a sales-type lease with a direct financing lease.

11. Defining "debt" to be only long-term debt, why do the debt/equity and debt/capitalization ratios for a given company convey exactly the same information? If you knew a company's debt/equity ratio was 50%, what would its debt/capitalization ratio be?

12. Why is a dollar received today more valuable than a dollar received tomorrow?

13. Describe why interest compounding can be thought of as the "reverse" of discounting.

14. Balance sheet liabilities often can be properly interpreted as a present value amount, as well as the dollar amount of the principal obligation. Why is this so?

15. What is achieved by using the compound interest method of debt amortization?

16. How does the current yield on a bond differ from the yield to maturity?

Problems

8-1. How would the following be disclosed on R&S Company's financial statements? The balance sheet was dated December 31, 1982 and the financial statements were issued February 9, 1983.

(1) The Internal Revenue Service has claimed that R&S Company owes $275,000 of additional taxes for the first quarter of 1982; the claim was made in a suit filed on January 25, 1983. R&S Company's tax advisor estimates that the actual amount that will be paid is between $165,000 and $195,000.

(2) On January 19, 1983, a fire destroyed one of R&S Company's warehouses. The warehouse had a net book value of $2,225,000 on the year-end balance sheet.

(3) During 1982, a lawsuit was filed against R&S Company that claimed $800,000 in punitive damages and $350,000 for personal injury, which the plaintiff alleges occurred when using one of R&S Company's products. The suit was not settled as of December 31, 1982, but the company's attorney is convinced that the court will award approximately the requested amounts.

(4) Several dissident shareholders had informed the company that they intended to sue the R&S board of directors for $4,500,000 because the board had rejected a merger offer proposed by a major supplier. The company has indemnified the directors; thus, any judgment against the directors would be paid by the company. R&S Company's attorney felt any such suit would be without merit.

8-2. On March 1, 1983, the Sixdor Company issued bonds with a face value of $200,000 for $210,000 cash. These bonds paid an annual interest of 14 percent. The interest was paid semiannually on March 1 and September 1. The bonds were to be repaid on March 1, 1993. Record the entries that should be made on the following dates: March 1, 1983; September 1, 1983; December 31, 1983; and March 1, 1984. (Assume for simplicity that the bond premium is to be amortized on a straight-line basis.)

8-3. During the year, Lang Company issued several series of bonds. For each bond, record the journal entry that must be made upon the issuance date. (Round to the nearest dollar.)

(1) On January 25, a 15-year, $10,000 par value bond series with annual interest of 15 percent was issued. Two thousand of these bonds were issued at a price of 97. Interest is paid semiannually.

(2) On April 10, a series of 20-year, $1,000 par value bonds with annual interest of 14 percent was issued at a price giving a current yield of 12.5 percent. Issuance costs for the 5,000 bonds issued were $100,000. Interest is paid annually.

(3) On November 15, a 5-year, $1,000 par value bond with annual interest of 11

percent was issued at a price to give a current yield of 12.5 percent. Interest on the 3,000 bonds issued is paid semiannually.

8-4. On January 1, 1978, the Sevdor Company issued callable bonds with a face value of $1,000,000 for $950,000 cash. These bonds paid an annual interest of 12 percent semiannually on January 1 and July 1. The bonds were to be repaid on January 1, 1988. On January 1, 1983, the bonds were called and redeemed for $1,050,000. Make the journal entries for January 1, 1978, and January 1, 1983. (Assume that the bond discount was being written off on a straight-line basis. Ignore bond issuance and reacquisition costs.)

8-5. On January 1, 1962, Wheeler Corporation issued 2,000 bonds with face value of $1,000 each and a coupon rate of 5 percent. The bonds were purchased by investors at a price of $1,020. Wheeler incurred costs of $60,000 in issuing the bonds. On January 1, 1982, which was five years prior to the bond's maturity date, Wheeler redeemed the bonds at a call price of $1,100. Wheeler also spent $45,000 in calling the bonds. What accounting entries should Wheeler make to reflect this early redemption?

8-6. Wright Corporation leased equipment requiring annual payments of $6,000 for 6 years. The lease met the criteria for a capital lease. The present value of the stream of minimum lease payments was $22,110. Wright Corporation uses the straight-line depreciation method.

Required: Prepare journal entries to record the lease obligation and the first year's depreciation expense (assume a 6-year useful life).

8-7. Marlu Company leased office furniture requiring annual payments for $8,000 for five years. The lease met the criteria for a capital lease. The present value of the lease payments was $26,816. The capital lease obligation reduction for each of the five years is:

Year	Amount
1	$3,977.60
2	4,574.24
3	5,260.38
4	6,049.43
5	6,954.35

Marlu depreciates such assets on a straight-line basis over five years. Assume all lease payments are made at the end of the year.

Required: Prepare the necessary journal entries for the inception and duration of this capital lease.

8-8. On January 1, Winters Company agreed to lease a new car from Lease-All Corporation for two years. The lease requires two payments of $1,475. At the end of the lease, the car will be returned to Lease-All. The present value of the stream of minimum lease payments is $2,398.35. New cars of this type have an average useful life of 5 years and a market value of approximately $7,500. Lease-All never includes bargain price options in their leases.

Required:

   a. Determine the proper classification for this lease.
   b. Prepare any necessary journal entries for the first year of the lease. Winters always depreciates on a straight-line basis.

8-9. The following information was taken from the balance sheet of Palder Company (amounts are thousands of dollars):

Current Liabilities*...................	$ 13,600
Long-Term Debt........................	40,800
Common Stock, par value...............	34,000
Paid-In Capital.......................	8,500
Retained Earnings.....................	39,100
	$136,000

*Includes $3,400 current portion of long-term debt.

Required:

    a. Calculate the debt/equity and debt/capitalization ratios.
    b. What do these ratios measure?

8-10. James Company's income statement disclosed the following:

    Lease Payments (Long-term lease).........$ 27,600
    Interest Expense......................... 41,400
    Federal Income Taxes..................... 73,600
    Net Income............................... 165,600

Required:

    a. Calculate times interest earned and times fixed charges earned.
    b. What do the above ratios measure?

NOTE: The remaining problems may require the use of the present value tables found in the textbook appendix. Hand-held calculators may yield slightly different results due to the rounding of factors used in the tables.

8-11. As a manager in charge of information processing for a fast-growing company, you realize that your current computer will only serve your needs for the next seven years. At that time, you will replace it with a more efficient model which at that time will cost an estimated $500,000. If the anticipated rate of interest is 14 percent for the next seven years, how much money should you place in a special investment fund today so that you will have a balance of $500,000 seven years from now? (Assume annual compounding.)

8-12. In 1983, a record album costs $7. If the price of record albums continues to increase at an annual compound rate of 10 percent, how much will an album cost in 10 years? 25 years? 50 years?

8-13. For each of the following situations, the present value concept should be applied:

    (1) Your wealthy aunt has established a trust fund for you that will accumulate to a total of $35,000 in ten years. Interest on the trust fund is compounded annually at a 12 percent interest rate. How much is in your trust fund today?

    (2) On January 1, you will purchase a new car. The automobile dealer will allow you to make increasing annual December 31 payments over the following four years. The amounts of these payments are: $2,000; $2,250; $3,000; $3,500. On this same January 1, your father will lend you just enough money to enable you to meet these payments. Interest rates are expected to be 15 percent for the next five years. Assuming that you can earn annual compounding of interest by depositing the loan from your father in a bank, what is the minimum amount your father must loan you to enable you to meet the car payments?

    (3) In settlement of a claim for your recently wrecked car, your insurance company will pay you either a lump sum today or three annual payments of $1,700 starting one year from now. Interest rates are expected to be 14 percent for the next five years. What is the least amount of money that you should be willing to accept today?

    (4) What is the present value of $3,000 a year to be received in Years 4 through 9, assuming a 15 percent discount rate?

8-14. Chemrite Company borrowed $120,155 with interest at 14 percent to be repaid in equal annual amounts at the end of each of the next five years. Prepare a loan amortization schedule for the repayment of this obligation. Round to the nearest whole dollar.

8-15. Goldmar Company issued a 5-year, 14-percent bond with a face value of $1,000. Interest is paid annually at end of each year. However, upon issuance, other bonds of similar risk were earning a 15 percent rate of return. What is the expected price of Goldmar's bond at the date of issuance?

8-16. Wington Company's 10-percent bond is currently selling for $895.50. The 20-year bond was issued with a face value of $1,000 and interest is paid semian-nually. Your broker has told you that the bond has 10 years until maturity and that the present value of the bond redemption proceeds is $322. What is the bond's yield to maturity?

CASES

Case 8-17: Piqua Products

On December 31, 1973, Piqua Products issued 10-year bonds having a maturity value of $5,000,000. The bonds carried an 8 percent coupon, and the proceeds (ignoring issuance costs) were $4,444,444.

The Piqua bonds required semiannual interest payments and they were redeemable between June 30, 1979 and June 30, 1982 at 104; thereafter until maturity they were redeemable at 102. They were also convertible into Piqua's $10 par value common stock according to the following schedule:

Before June 30, 1979: 50 shares of common per $1,000 face value of bonds.
July 1, 1979 to June 30, 1982: 40 shares of common per $1,000 face value of bonds.
After June 30, 1982: 30 shares of common per $1,000 face value of bonds.
The following transactions occurred in connection with the bonds:

December 31, 1978:
Bonds having a face value of $1,000,000 were converted into common stock.

December 31, 1979:
Bonds having a face value of $1,000,000 were reacquired by Piqua on the open market at a price of 90. The reacquired bonds were canceled immediately.

Questions

1. Show how the proceeds from the bond issue would be carried on the balance sheet as of December 31, 1973.

2. Determine the amount of interest expense to be deducted in arriving at net income for the year ended December 31, 1974. (Assume straight-line amortization of discount.)

3. Show the entries to record the conversion of the bonds in 1978.

4. Show the entries to record the retirement of the bonds in 1979.

* * * * *

Case 8-18: Julie Banning

Julie Banning was graduating from business school in the spring of 1982. She had accepted a fine job offer, and planning for her future was much on her mind. She had recently noticed several bank and savings and loan association advertisements for Individual Retirement Accounts (IRAs). The ads stressed the extremely large values regular deposits in an IRA would amount to at retirement. An often-heard promise was that IRA accounts would grow to over $1 million at retirement. Ms. Banning wondered if this promise was really true. She began to gather more information on IRAs.

She found that as of January 1, 1982, every income earner became eligible to start an IRA. Annual deposits were tax deductible from current income up to certain limits. These limits were $2,000 a year for individuals, $2,250 a year for couples with one working spouse, and $4,000 a year for two-income couples. Earnings from IRA accounts were not taxable until withdrawals began after age 59 1/2. At this point, upon retirement, it was expected the wage earner(s) would be in a lower tax bracket. Early withdrawals were taxable and also subject to a 10 percent penalty.

In the first quarter of 1982, banks were offering fixed 2 1/2-year rates of approximately 14 percent and 18-month rates of approximately 15 percent on IRAs.

Questions

1. Assuming current rates (14 percent and 15 percent) continue, deposits

are made once a year at the beginning of the year for the maximum $2,000 tax-deductible amount, and interest is compounded annually, should Ms. Banning open her IRA at age 30 in order to be a millionnaire at age 60 when she retires? What happens to this goal if she waits until she is 35? Or 40?

2. Under the same assumptions as Question 1, if Ms. Banning marries, at what age must she and her husband, both working, open their IRA account to assure themselves joint membership in this "Millionnaire's Club"? At age 30, 35, or 40? When should the account be opened if Ms. Banning's family is a one-income family and the maximum deposit becomes $2,250?

3. One bank's advertisement based its calculations on a continuing 12 percent interest rate. What requirements does this change put on the number of years of deposits and family circumstances required to achieve $1 million in an IRA at a retirement age of 60?

4. What would be the lowest interest rate that would fulfill the banks' "millionnaire" promise, assuming age 20 is the youngest one would be to start an IRA? For how long would the saver(s) have to maintain his or her (their) IRA deposits?

5. In early 1982, inflation was approximately 10 percent and a loaf of bread cost $0.65. If this inflationary trend continues, how much will a loaf of bread cost by the year 2002? 2012? 2022?

Chapter 9

Other Expenses, Net Income, and Owners' Equity

Key Terms

Personnel costs
Normal costs
Past service cost
Unfunded cost
Permanent tax difference
Timing tax difference
Deferred income taxes
Extraordinary item
Discontinued operations
Prior period adjustment
Single proprietorship

Partnership
Corporation
Stock certificate
Preferred stock
Book value of common stock
Contributed capital
Paid-in capital
Treasury stock
Reserve
Stock options and warrants
Earnings per share

Discussion Questions

1. Why is only a portion of the social security taxes remitted by an employer to the government considered to be a personnel cost?

2. During June, Lynn Winkler worked on the final assembly line at Hi-Tec Electronics Company. Winkler's spouse, Chris, worked in the company's executive offices. In which month will each of the following costs appear on Hi-Tec's monthly income statement?

   a. Lynn's and Chris' June salaries.
   b. Hi-Tec's share of Lynn's and Chris' June social security taxes.
   c. Hi-Tec's cost of the employee medical insurance plan for which both Lynn and Chris are eligible.
   d. Lynn's and Chris' June withheld income taxes.

3. Distinguish among these three pension-related costs: normal cost, past service costs, and unfunded cost. Which of these costs involves an accounting entry on the employee's books?

4. Why are unused compensated absences accrued as a liability at the end of the year?

5. Explain the difference between a permanent tax difference and a timing tax difference.

6. Comment on this statement and question: "Using different depreciation methods for financial accounting and tax accounting requires additional recordkeeping, and results in a confusing balance sheet item called deferred taxes. Why don't corporations simply use the same method for both purposes?"

7. Some people argue that "deferred taxes" are not really a liability, whereas "taxes payable" are. Defend or refute this argument.

8. Under what circumstances might a company pay <u>more</u> taxes for the year than it

shows as the provision for income taxes on its income statement? Under these same circumstances, would the company's year-end balance in its deferred tax account necessarily be a debit balance? Explain.

9. Using the definition of an "extraordinary item" that is cited in the text, which of the following do you think would constitute extraordinary items for a multibranch retail store?

a. Write-off of inventory of an ususual style of women's skirts that did not sell at all well.
b. Proceeds from a life insurance policy on a key officer who died.
c. Fire loss not covered by insurance.
d. Collection of a large receivable which had previously been written off.
e. Write-off of inventory of children's pajamas which did not meet the standards of a newly enacted safety law, and thus must be destroyed.
f. Foreign currency loss associated with purchases of shoes from Italy.
g. Loss on closing of a branch store.
h. Capital gain on branch store taken by eminent domain in order that a new highway could be built.
i. Refund of customer deposits on certain television sets because of a prolonged strike at the television manufacturer's plants.
j. Damage caused by roof collapse at Orlando, Florida branch after a six-inch snowstorm.

10. In November 1982, International Electric Corporation decided, effective March 1, 1983, to discontinue its business segment that made automobile highway radar detectors. In December 1982, the company also decided to sell one of several plants, all of which made microwave ovens. The plant sale was consummated on December 28, 1982. What is the correct accounting treatment of these two events in International Electric's 1982 financial statements?

11. Which of the following may be treated as prior period adjustments? Explain your rationale for each response, and assume each item is material.

a. The estimated useful life of a building has been extended from 30 years to 40 years.
b. The company has changed its depreciation method from double declining balance to straight line.
c. A mathematical mistake was made when the previous year's ending balance in Retained Earnings was calculated.
d. The previous year's allowance for uncollectible accounts has proven to be too small.
e. Last year the company used LIFO on its federal income tax return and FIFO in its published financial statements.
f. The company has changed from capitalizing research and development costs to expensing them as incurred.
g. In preparing the previous year's financial statements, the company did not show the effect of discontinuing a business segment that was disposed of this year, but the disposal decision for which was made the previous year.
h. Inventory written down last year because it was believed to be obsolete, was sold this year at a price well in excess of the written-down amount.

12. What are the relative advantages of unincorporated and incorporated business entities?

13. What is the difference between cumultive and noncumulative preferred stock?

14. Under what circumstances does the par value of (a) bonds, (b) preferred stock, and (c) common stock have meaning to the holders of these securities?

15. It has been said that a company's acquiring treasury stock represents an alternative to the company's paying a dividend. Explain.

16. If stock split-ups and stock dividends do not change each shareholder's fraction of owners' equity in a business, why would a firm ever split its stock or issue a stock dividend?

17. Under what circumstances would a corporation report primary earnings per share that were significantly higher than its fully diluted earnings per share?

Problems

9-1. Sal Amato received a paycheck from her employer in the amount of $605.50. The paycheck stub indicated that in calculating her $605.50 net pay, $112.10 had been withheld for federal income tax, $28.80 for state income tax, and $53.60 for FICA. Assuming that Sal's employer had to match her share of FICA tax, and in addition had to pay unemployment insurance tax of $31.40, prepare journal entries which would record these transactions in Sal's employer's accounts.

9-2. Larry's Snack Shacks, Inc. began a pension plan for certain of its employees, effective January 1, 1983. The actuarially determined amount to fund future pension benefits earned by employees in 1983 was $26,700. In addition, the plan was made retroactive to January 1, 1978, for all present employees who had worked full time for the company during those five years. Had the pension plan actually been started on January 1, 1978, these retroactive benefits would have required $73,800 to fund them as of January 1, 1983. The company intends to fund these retroactive benefits uniformly over the next 20 years.

Required:

   a. Write a journal entry for the company's 1983 pension cost.
   b. What was the 1983 normal cost?
   c. What is the amount of the unfunded cost as of January 1, 1984?

9-3. Newton Design Group is an incorporated architectural firm that reports to its shareholders on the accrual basis, but to the Internal Revenue Service on the cash basis. Below is a schedule of its 1979-1982 revenues, expenses, receipts, and disbursements. For each year shown, calculate the company's income tax payment, income tax expense (provision for income taxes), and year-end balance in its deferred tax account. Assume the 1978 deferred tax balance was zero, and that in all four years the effective tax rate was 40 percent.

	1979	1980	1981	1982
Revenues....................	$380,000	$580,000	$700,000	$650,000
Expenses....................	225,000	560,000	665,000	515,000
Receipts....................	280,000	530,000	745,000	575,000
Disbursements..............	240,000	440,000	625,000	505,000

Based on your calculations, do you feel the company was wise in using the cash basis for its tax returns? Explain.

9-4. (C.M.A. adapted.) Gordon Inc., which started operations in 1982, reported income before federal income taxes of $435,000 on its income statement and taxable income of $375,000 on its federal income tax return for fiscal year 1982. The difference in income figures was solely due to the use of the installment sales method for tax purposes, which differed from the recognition "at time of sales" method used in the financial statements. For 1983, the company reported income before federal income taxes of $815,000 on its income statement and $650,000 of taxable income on its federal income tax return. Again, the use of the installment sales method for income tax purposes accounted for all of the difference. Gordon Inc. has an effective income tax rate of 40 percent.

Required:

   a. What amounts would be shown for income tax expense on the income statements of Gordon Inc. for 1982 and 1983?
   b. The management of Gordon Inc. wants to know if a deferred income tax account is necessary. If it is necessary, indicate the amount and classification of the deferred income tax account that would be shown on the balance sheets of Gordon Inc. as of December 31, 1982 and 1983, and justify your classification of the account. If a deferred tax account is not necessary, explain why one is not required.

9-5. During 1982, Bellaire company had pretax income of $19 million from its continuing operations. From the operations of a division that was sold during the year, Bellaire had a pretax loss of $3.5 million, but realized a pretax gain of $2.2 million on the disposal of the division. In addition, before income tax effects, Bellaire had an extraordinary loss of $1.5 million because a hurricane destroyed an uninsured building the company owned. Assuming that the gain or disposal of the division and the hurricane loss would have a 30 percent tax rate applied, and that the other items were subject to a 46 percent tax rate, prepare in proper format an income statement starting with the line, "Income from continuing operations before income taxes."

9-6. Lenox Ski Manufacturing had the following transactions during the year:

(1) Sales were $1,200,000.
(2) A physical inventory disclosed that $7,000 worth of inventory and supplies had been stolen.
(3) Operating expenses, including cost of goods sold, totaled $850,000.
(4) The company's patent on a special bonding process was successfully challenged in court. It was valued on the balance sheet at $15,000, and had to be written off.
(5) A small factory in Maine was closed. It had a net book value of $52,000. There were no proceeds from the closing.
(6) A new product safety law affecting ski bindings was enacted by the government. This resulted in a pretax write-off of $24,000 worth of inventory.
(7) A pretax gain of $12,000 was realized when a bond issue was refunded.
(8) The company reclassified certain period costs as inventoriable product costs. The cumulative effect of this change in accounting principle was to increase net income by $35,000.

Required: Prepare an income statement for the year. Use a 40 percent income tax rate.

9-7. The Thredor Corporation was organized on January 1 with authorized capital stock of 100,000 no-par value shares. The stock had a stated value, however, of $10 a share. On February 1, 25,000 shares were issued for $300,000. An additional 1,000 shares were issued on February 1 to the founder, M. A. Thredor, for his efforts in organizing the corporation. On February 20, 10,000 shares were issued for $130,000 and 5,000 shares were issued to E. Z. Getaway in payment of a building taken over by the new corporation.

Required: Analyze the above transactions and prepare journal entries to record them.

9-8. During its fiscal year, Furey corporation had outstanding 500,000 shares of $4.50 preferred stock and 1,000,000 shares of common stock. Furey's net income for the year was $9,700,000. What were Furey's earnings per share?

9-9. Murphy Company had 145,000 shares of common stock outstanding throughout the year. The company had no other outstanding equity securities. Net income for the year was $725,000 before extraordinary items, and $797,500 including extraordinary items. Calculate Murphy's earnings per share.

9-10. Record the following personnel cost transactions for Freed Company:

a. During March, 400 hours were worked at an average wage rate of $9.50 an hour.
b. On April 2, the employees were paid their March earnings.
c. On April 12, the employment taxes related to March earnings were remitted to the government.

Additional information: (1) The FICA rate was 6.70 percent; (2) unemployment taxes were 2 percent of gross wages; and (3) federal withholding taxes were $825.

9-11. During 1983, Kirkpatrick Corporation purchased a new electric generator for $1,750,000. The generator is expected to have a five-year useful life and will be disposed of in 1988 without any anticipated residual value. The company uses straight-line depreciation on its income statement, but only takes half a year's depreciation in the year of acquisition and year of disposal. For tax purposes, the generator falls into an ACRS five-year cost recovery class. The ACRS cost recovery percentage rates as applicable to the generator are as follows:

Year	ACRS Rate
1983	15%
1984	22%
1985	21%
1986	21%
1987	21%

Kirkpatrick expects its income before depreciation and income taxes to be $1,500,000 for years 1983 through 1988. The combined federal and state income tax rate is 60 percent. (Ignore the investment tax credit, for simplicity.)

Required: Prepare a schedule showing:

    a. Each of the six years' income tax payments, starting in 1983.
    b. Each year's provision for income taxes; and
    c. The balance in the deferred tax account at the end of each year. (Assume a zero beginning balance.)

As you develop your schedule, for each year make a posting to the following T-accounts: Cash (for payments), Income Tax Expense, and Deferred Taxes. In what year does the timing difference reverse?

9-12. During the period 1978-1982, Seybold Stores, Inc., a department store chain, reported to the Internal Revenue Service on the same basis as it reported income to its shareholders. In 1983, Seybold's new accounting firm suggested that Seybold file its tax return using the "installment method." With this method, the amount of gross margin on Seybold's tax return would be based on the company's cash collections during the year, rather than on its accrual revenues and cost of goods sold. For example, if in 1983, Seybold were to have revenues of $80 million, a gross margin percentage of 40 percent, and cash collections of $70 million, then the gross margin for tax purposes would be $28 million ($70 million x 40 percent) rather than the $32 million ($80 million x 40 percent) reflected on the income statement. Except for gross margin, other income statement items would be the same under either method.

In considering the accountant's suggestion, Seybold's controller collected the following information for 1978-1982 (dollar figures are millions):

	1978	1979	1980	1981	1982
Revenues..................................	$176	$190	$195	$200	$215
Gross margin percentage*.................	30%	32%	30%	31%	34%
Expenses other than cost of goods sold...	$42.9	$37.7	$45.5	$48.3	$55.6
Increase in accounts receivable**........	$ 4.0	$ 6.0	$ 3.6	$ 4.5	$ 9.8

---

*Gross margin (revenues minus cost of goods sold) expressed as a percentage of revenues.

**For example, between January 1, 1978 and December 31, 1978, accounts receivable went up by $4.0 million.

Required:

    a. Assuming a 50 percent tax rate, how much could Seybold Stores have saved in income taxes between 1978 and 1982 if they had used the installment method for tax reporting rather than reporting the same income before taxes to both the IRS and to shareholders?
    b. Can you imagine a set of conditions that would make it advisable for Seybold not to change to the installment method for tax purposes starting in 1983?

9-13. Stern Company had the following transactions during the year (all dollar amounts are thousands):

(1) Sales were $90,000
(2) Cost of goods sold was $35,000.
(3) Other operating expenses were $17,000.

(4) The company changed depreciation methods. Both the old and new methods are generally accepted accounting principles (GAAP). The effect is to increase prior years' depreciation charges $6,000 after taxes.

(5 The company's new CPA firm informed Stern that an accounting policy used for the first time in the preceding year was not in accordance with GAAP. The effect of changing to an acceptable method was to increase last year's net income by $3,000.

(6) A plant valued at $20,000 was completely destroyed by fire after the balance sheet date. Proceeds from the insurance company were $14,000.

(7) An arithmetic error resulted in a cumulative overstatement of retained earnings by $1,500.

(8) The income tax rate for this year is 40 percent.

(9) The preceding year's ending retained earnings balance was $140,000.

(10) Dividends of $5,000 were declared.

Required: Prepare an income statement that incorporates a statement of changes in retained earnings.

9-14. Two recent business school graduates, Jan Johnson and Lou Swartz, started a shop called Imports Unlimited on January 1. Their partnership agreement stipulated that each would receive 12 percent on capital contributed and that they would share equally any net income in excess of this 12 percent payment. Jan had contributed $25,000 and Lou, $40,000. They also agreed that Jan, who could devote only part time to the venture, would receive a salary of $8,000, while Lou would receive $23,000. Net income for the first year (after deducting both partners' salaries) was $56,000. What was each partner's total income (including salaries) from the business?

9-15. The Owners' Equity section of the balance sheet of Nodor Corporation on December 31, 1982, was as follows:

$6.00 preferred stock (20,000 shares, par value $100)......$ 2,000,000
Common stock (no par value, 1,000,000 shares issued
   and outstanding)... 6,000,000
Retained earnings.. 7,000,000
    Total Owners' Equity...................................$15,000,000

The Board of Directors took the following actions:

December 31, 1982:
(a) A 2-for-1 stock split of common stock was declared.
(b) 4,000 shares of its outstanding preferred stock were purchased by Nodor at $115 per share.

January 1, 1983:
(a) The preferred dividend of $6.00 was declared.
(b) A cash dividend of $.25 a share on common stock outstanding on January 1 was declared.
(c) A stock dividend of 1/10 of a share was declared on common stock, effective February 1.

February 1, 1983: The dividends declared in January were paid.

Required: Prepare journal entries to record the transactions.

9-16. As of January 1, Pierpont Corporation had outstanding 200,000 shares of $8.00 preferred stock and 2,000,000 shares of common stock. The preferred stock dividend was payable January 1, April 1, July 1, and October 1. On June 30, Pierpont purchased and retired 60,000 shares of its preferred stock, thus avoiding payment of the July 1 dividend on these 60,000 shares. On September 1, Pierpont issued an additional 600,000 shares of common stock. Reported net income for the year was $11,150,000. What were Pierpont's earnings per share?

9-17. The owners' equity section of Wilson Company's balance sheet was as follows at the beginning of the year (i.e., as of January 1):

```
Preferred stock:  $12 cumulative; $100 par............$  250,000
Common stock:  $1 par value..........................   700,000
Common stock:  excess paid in over par value......... 1,300,000
Retained earnings....................................   885,000
      Total Owners' Equity...........................$3,135,000
```

During the year the following occurred:

(1) Net income before preferred stock dividends was $400,000.
(2) The company did not pay its second and third quarter preferred stock dividends, which normally would have been paid a few days after the end of the respective quarters. This was the first year Wilson had ever missed a quarterly preferred stock dividend payment.
(3) Late in December, common stock dividends of $75,000 were declared, payable early next year to holders of record as of December 31.
(4) On April 1, 10,000 shares of common stock were issued for $18 a share.
(5) On October 1, Wilson purchased 3,000 shares of its own stock for $14 a share.
(6) On November 1, 2,000 of the shares acquired on October 1 were resold for $17 a share.
(7) On December 31, another 150 shares of treasury stock were sold for $13 a share.
(8) On January 3 of the next year, shareholder dividends were paid.

Required:

a. Journalize the above transactions.
b. Show the owners' equity section at the end of the year.
c. Calculate the year's earnings per share.

CASES

Case 9-18: Braydon Corporation (A)

The accounts of the Braydon Corporation contained the following balances at the beginning of the year:

Accounts with Debit Balances

```
Cash...............................................$  16,625
Accounts receivable................................   34,700
Raw materials and supplies inventory...............   25,000
Goods in process inventory.........................   15,250
Finished goods inventory...........................   17,250
Land and buildings (at cost).......................   50,000
Machinery and equipment (at cost)..................   60,000
                                                     $218,825
```

Accounts with Credit Balances

```
Accounts payable...................................$  13,765
Notes payable......................................    5,000
Accrued wages......................................    1,465
FICA taxes payable.................................    1,771
Withholding taxes payable..........................    3,040
Accumulated depreciation...........................   12,900
Capital stock......................................  150,000
Retained earnings..................................   30,884
                                                     $218,825
```

During the first half of the year, the operations of the corporation consisted of the transactions indicated below:

```
1. Credit sales......................................... $183,602
2. Discounts given on sales............................     2,400
```

```
 3. Executive salaries paid*.............................................  24,996
 4. Factory wages paid**..............................................  39,400
 5. FICA tax (employer's share) expense was accrued...................   4,315
 6. Materials and supplies purchased on account (net)................  97,500
 7. Light and power on account.......................................   7,536
 8. Interest on notes payable paid...................................     300
 9. Donated to charity..............................................   1,200
10. Sales force commissions paid....................................   4,380
11. Selling expenses incurred on account...........................   1,375
12. Insurance premium paid by cash.................................     900
13. Machinery repairs paid by cash................................   1,950
14. FICA and withholding taxes paid in cash........................  16,990
15. Sales returns***...............................................   2,100
16. General administrative expense ($750 on account)...............   3,280
17. Collections from customers..................................... 196,800
18. Payments made to open account creditors........................  98,000
19. Factory wages accrued but not paid.............................   2,950
20. Depreciation on plant and equipment (charged to manufacturing)....   2,500
21. Estimated loss from bad debts..................................     730
22. Additional capital stock issued for cash.......................  20,000
```

     *FICA taxes of $1,675 and withholding taxes of $3,498 were withheld from this total.
     **FICA taxes of $2,640 and withholding taxes of $3,035 were withheld from this total.
     ***Goods returned were scrapped, as they were not suitable for resale.

    The transactions represented by the above summaries were journalized with the following debits and credits:

```
                                                          Debit      Credit

 1. Accounts Receivable..................................183,602
      Sales Revenues.....................................              183,602

 2. Cash Discount on Sales...............................  2,400
      Accounts Receivable...............................                2,400

 3. Executive Salaries................................... 24,996
      Cash.................................................             19,823
      FICA Taxes Payable..................................              1,675
      Withholding Taxes Payable...........................              3,498

 4. Factory Wages........................................ 37,935
    Accrued Wages.......................................... 1,465
      Cash.................................................             33,725
      Accrued FICA Taxes..................................              2,640
      Accrued Withholding Taxes...........................              3,035

 5. FICA Tax Expense--Wages..............................  2,640
    FICA Tax Expense--Salaries............................  1,675
      FICA Taxes Payable..................................               4,315

 6. Materials and Supplies Purchases..................... 97,500
      Accounts Payable....................................              97,500

 7. Light and Power Expense..............................  7,536
      Accounts Payable....................................               7,536

 8. Interest Expense.....................................    300
      Cash................................................                300

 9. Donations............................................  1,200
      Cash................................................                1,200

10. Sales Force Commissions..............................  4,380
      Cash................................................                4,380
```

	Debit	Credit
11. Selling Expense..	1,375	
Accounts Payable...		1,375
12. Insurance Expense..	900	
Cash..		900
13. Machinery Repairs..	1,950	
Cash..		1,950
14. FICA Taxes Payable...	9,330	
Withholding Taxes Payable.......................................	7,660	
Cash..		16,990
15. Sale Returns...	2,100	
Accounts Receivable...		2,100
16. General Administrative Expense.......................................	3,280	
Cash..		2,530
Accounts Payable..		750
17. Cash..196,800		196,800
Accounts Receivable...		
18. Accounts Payable...	98,000	
Cash..		98,000
19. Factory Wages..	2,950	
Accrued Wages...		2,950
20. Depreciation Expense (Manufacturing).................................	2,500	
Accumulated Depreciation..		2,500
21. Bad Debt Expense...	730	
Allowance for Doubtful Accounts.................................		730
22. Cash...	20,000	
Capital Stock...		20,000

Questions

1. Fill in the blank spaces opposite journal entries 23 through 30 (below), posting to the T-accounts as your work progresses.

2. Prepare a balance sheet as of June 30, and an income statement for the six months ending June 30. Your income statement (or a schedule thereto) should show how you determined the amount for cost of goods sold.

The following entries were made to close the books at the end of the six months' period:

	Debit	Credit
23. Cost of Goods Sold.. _____		_____
Raw Material and Supplies Inventory...............		_____
Goods in Process Inventory........................		_____
Finished Goods Inventory..........................		_____
To close inventories on hand January 1 into Cost of Goods Sold.		
24. Raw materials and Supplies Inventory...................	21,000	
Goods in Process Inventory............................	17,505	
Finished Goods Inventory..............................	20,811	
Cost of Goods Sold................................		59,316
To record inventories as of June 30.		

25. Cost of Goods Sold...................................._____

        Materials and Supplies Purchases...................   _____
To close Materials and Supplies Purchases into Cost of
Goods Sold.

26. Cost of Goods Sold...................................._____

        Factory Wages......................................   _____

        Light and Power....................................   _____

        Insurance Expense..................................   _____

        Machinery Repairs Expense..........................   _____

        Depreciation Expense (Manufacturing)...............   _____

        FICA Taxes--Factory Wages..........................   _____
To close the manufacturing expense accounts into Cost of
Goods Sold.

27. Expense and Revenue Summary.........................._____

        Cost of Goods Sold.................................   _____
To close Cost of Goods Sold into Expense and Revenue
Summary.

28. Sales.._____

        Cash Discounts on Sales............................   _____

        Sales Returns......................................   _____

        Expense and Revenue Summary........................   _____
To close Sales, Cash Discounts on Sales, and Sales
Returns into Expense and Revenue Summary.

29. Expense and Revenue Summary.........................._____

        Sales Force Commissions............................   _____

        Selling Expenses...................................   _____

        Executive Salaries.................................   _____

        FICA Taxes--Executive Salaries.....................   _____

        General Administrative Expense......................   _____

        Bad Debt Expense...................................   _____

        Interest Expense...................................   _____

        Donations..   _____
To close the operating expense accounts into Expense and
Revenue Summary.

30. Retained Earnings...................................._____

        Expense and Revenue Summary........................   _____
To close Expense and Revenue Summary into Retained
Earnings.

Cash

*	16,625	19,823	(3)
(17)	196,800	33,725	(4)
(22)	20,000	300	(8)
		1,200	(9)
		4,380	(10)
		900	(12)
		1,950	(13)
		16,990	(14)
		2,530	(16)
		98,000	(18)

Accounts Receivable

*	34,700	2,400	(2)
(1)	183,602	2,100	(15)
		196,800	(17)

Allowance for Doubtful Accounts

	730	(21)

Land and Buildings

*	50,000

Machinery and Equipment

*	60,000

Accumulated Depreciation

	12,900	*
	2,500	(20)

Accounts Payable

(18)	98,000	13,765	*
		97,500	(6)
		7,536	(7)
		1,375	(11)
		750	(16)

Machinery Repairs Expense

(13)	1,950

Depreciation Expense--Manufacturing

(20)	2,500

Raw Material and Supplies Inventory

*	25,000

Goods in Process Inventory

*	15,250

Finished Goods Inventory

*	17,250

Materials and Supplies Purchases

(6)	97,500

Notes Payable

	5,000

Bad Debt Expense

(21)	730

Interest Expense

(8)	300

Executive Salaries

(3)	24,996

Donations

(9)	1,200

General Administrative Expense

(16)	3,280

Sales Force Commissions

(10)	4,380

Selling Expenses

(11)	1,375

FICA Taxes Payable

(14)	9,330	1,771	*
		1,675	(3)
		2,640	(4)
		4,315	(5)

Factory Wages

(4)	37,935
(19)	2,950

Light and Power

(7)	7,536

Insurance Expense

(12)	900

*Balance on January 1.

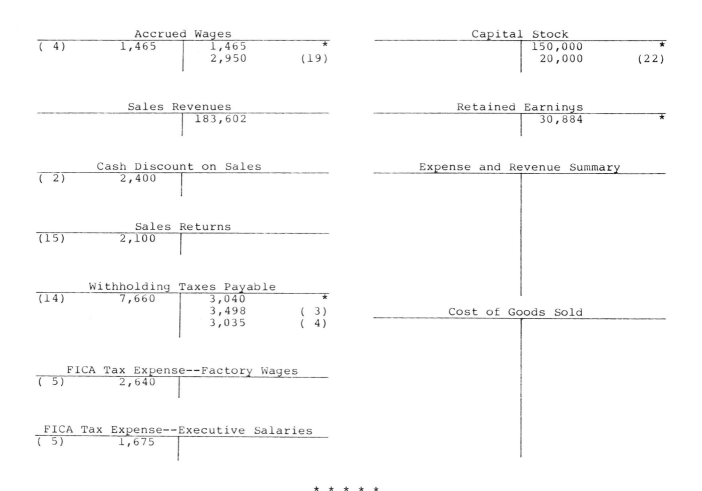

```
          Accrued Wages                                    Capital Stock
( 4)    1,465  |  1,465        *                          |  150,000        *
               |  2,950      (19)                          |   20,000      (22)


          Sales Revenues                                   Retained Earnings
               |  183,602                                  |   30,884        *


       Cash Discount on Sales                       Expense and Revenue Summary
( 2)    2,400  |


          Sales Returns
(15)    2,100  |


      Withholding Taxes Payable                         Cost of Goods Sold
(14)    7,660  |  3,040        *
               |  3,498      ( 3)
               |  3,035      ( 4)


   FICA Tax Expense--Factory Wages
( 5)    2,640  |


  FICA Tax Expense--Executive Salaries
( 5)    1,675  |
```

* * * * *

Case 9-19: Monroe Stamping Corporation

In 1975, Regi Bennett resigned as plant superintendent for a large automobile company, and formed Monroe Stamping Company to produce metal-stamping parts in a small plant on the outskirts of Detroit. The new business was financed as follows: Regi Bennett contributed $50,000; Joseph McDonald, Regi's brother-in-law, contributed $100,000; and Janet McDonald, Regi's mother-in-law, allowed them to use, rent free, a building that she owned.

Regi Bennett and Joseph McDonald were to be equal partners; that is, each was to receive one half of the profits. Regi was to work full time for the partnership. Joseph was to work little or no time on partnership business. With the money that the partners had put up and with funds borrowed from the bank, Regi purchased equipment, had it installed in the mother-in-law's building, hired workers, obtained several contracts, and started to produce metal stampings.

The partnership prospered and the partners "plowed back" much of the profits into the business. By 1983, they decided that it was time to incorporate. Accordingly, they hired an attorney and made plans to organize the Monroe Stamping Corporation as of January 1, 1983. Exhibit 1 is the partnership's balance sheet as of December 31, 1982, prior to the adjustments described below.

The Monroe Stamping Corporation was to be incorporated with an authorized capital of 500,000 shares at $2.50 per share par value. The new corporation was to take over the assets and liabilities of the partnership. Stock was to be issued to the partners, at par value, based on their share of the book value in the partnership. Before transferring the assets to the new corporation, it was decided to adjust the values to realistic market values. Accordingly, the following adjustments were made to the partnership assets:

1. An allowance for bad debts of $6,250 was established.
2. Obsolete inventory worth $23,400 was written off.
3. The net book value of the machinery and equipment was increased by $73,500 by debiting the accumulated depreciation account.

EXHIBIT 1

THE BENNETT-McDONALD PARTNERSHIP
Balance Sheet as of December 31, 1982

Assets

Cash...............	$ 71,710
Accounts receivable.......	54,650
Inventory.........	142,410
Machinery and equipment........$878,405	
Accumulated depreciation.. 402,095	
Net machinery and equipment.......	476,310
Total Assets.	$745,080

Equities

Accounts payable...	$ 48,480
Note payable.......	100,000
Bennett, capital...	357,150
McDonald, capital..	239,450
Total Equities....	$745,080

Janet McDonald agreed to accept $97,500 worth of stock for the land and building that the partnership had been using.

The note payable was held by the Johnson Corporation, a customer of the partnership. Win Johnson, president of the Johnson Corporation, agreed to accept $50,000 worth of stock at par in partial payment of the note.

Chris Moore, a local businessperson, offered to pay $32,500 for 10,000 shares of stock. The offer was accepted and Moore purchased the stock.

Organizational expenses amounted to $2,490; this was treated as an asset.

Questions

1. Make the necessary journal entries to close the partnership books. (Assume all transactions took place on December 31, 1982.)

2. Make the necessary entries to open the books of the new corporation. (Assume all transactions took place on January 1, 1983.)

3. Prepare a balance sheet for the Monroe Stamping Corporation after the above entries have been made.

4. Prepare a schedule showing the shares held by each stockholder.

Chapter 10

Funds Flow Statements

Key Terms

Statement of changes in financial
  position
Funds flow statement
Sources of funds
Use of funds
Funds generated by operations
Net current monetary assets
Working capital

Permanent capital
Receipts and disbursements
Cash flow statement
Working capital flow statement
All financial resources principle
Depreciation
Cash flow earnings

Discussion Questions

1. Compare funds flow statements with the balance sheets and income statements studied in previous chapters.

2. What are the arguments favoring net current monetary assets as the definition of funds?

3. What is the rationale for using working capital (rather than cash) as "funds" in a statement of changes in financial position?

4. Explain the differences between a statement of receipts and disbursements, and a cash flow statement. Why is the latter more informative?

5. Does an increase in accounts receivable represent a decrease or an increase in cash generated by sales? Why?

6. How should a change in inventory level be accounted for in a cash flow statement?

7. What effect does a change in accounts payable have on the computation of cash disbursed for expenses?

8. What is the concept of "all financial resources" and what value does it have in preparing a statement of changes in financial position?

9. Why is depreciation expense added back to net income in determining the amount of funds generated by operations in a funds flow statement?

10. What effect will changing from a straight-line depreciation to ACRS allowances on its tax return have on an entity's total sources of funds?

11. Each year, the Retained Earnings account increases by the amount of the year's net income less any dividends declared to owners. This change in Retained Earnings is often referred to as "the portion of profits plowed back into the business." Explain why the annual change in Retained Earnings actually <u>understates</u> the amount of funds "plowed back into the business."

12. Following along the lines of the preceding question, one might hear a manager

say, "This increase in assets was financed out of Retained Earnings." What is a more accurate way of expressing what this manager means?

13. When is it appropriate to use a projected cash flow statement as opposed to a projected working capital flow statement?

14. Below is a list of accounting events. (The events are unrelated to one another.) For each one, answer the following questions:

   a. Does the transaction involve a flow of cash?
   b. Does the transaction involve a flow of working capital?
   c. How will the transaction be reflected in a cash flow statement?
   d. How will the transaction be reflected in a working capital flow statement?

(1) An account receivable is collected.
(2) Goods for inventory are purchased on account.
(3) Shares of common stock are issued.
(4) Employees are paid on June 2 for working the last two week in May.
(5) A new plant is acquired by issuing shares of common stock to the former owners.
(6) The year's depreciation on fixed assets is recorded.
(7) A vehicle with several years' useful life is purchased on 90-day credit.
(8) Goodwill is amortized.
(9) A 30-day note payable is repaid.
(10) Goods are sold on 30-day credit.
(11) A convertible bond is convert- into common stock.

(12) The final annual installment on a five-year term loan will be due one year from today.
(13) A machine is bought by making a cash down payment and giving a three-year mortgage.
(14) Raw materials are issued from the stockroom to the factory floor.
(15) The final annual installment on a five-year term loan is paid.
(16) An interest payment due January 15, 1984 is accrued at the end of the fiscal year, December 31, 1983.
(17) A cash dividend on a marketable security is received.
(18) Company X owns 40 percent of Company Y's common stock; Company X "spins off" this investment by distributing its shares of Y to X's stockholders as a dividend.

Problems

10-1. The B & U Company shows the following account amounts:

	1982	1981
Sales	$6,245,000	$5,955,000
Accounts receivable, 12/31	365,000	315,000

Required: Determine how much cash was generated from sales during 1982.

10-2. Toys for Tots, a children's clothing store, had the following cash receipts and disbursements for its first year of operations:

Receipts	
Cash sales	$103,000
Loan proceeds	15,000
Total receipts	118,000

Disbursements:	
Merchandise purchases	56,000
Wages	21,000
Rent and lease payments	14,500
Other operating outlays	5,200
Loan payment	7,500
Total disbursements	104,200
Increase in Cash Balance	$ 13,800

The store has no accounts receivable (it accepts only cash or bank cards for payment). At year end, an employee had earned $200 which she had not yet been paid by the store. Also, at year end, the store had not paid its most recent utilities bills, which totaled $150.

Required: Prepare a cash flow statement for the year.

10-3. Harlow's Tax Service had the following operating expenses in its income statement for its most recent fiscal year ended December 31:

Depreciation expense............................$ 4,000
Supplies..   850
Utilities.......................................   3,000
Interest expense................................   700
Salaries.. 225,000
Rent expense.................................... 12,000
Auto expense....................................   4,000
Miscellaneous...................................   375
    Total...................................... $249,925

Supplies are expensed when purchased. No inventory accounts are maintained. Interest expense arises from a $5,000, five-year note due in three years; interest is 14 percent per year, payable in two installments on January 1 and July 1. An analysis of accounts payable shows the following:

	December 31 This Year	December 31 Last Year
Utilities payable..........	$ 220	$ 200
Interest payable...........	350	350
Salaries payable...........	3,000	2,500
Rent payable..............	--	500
Auto expense payable.......	150	300

Supplies are always purchased for cash. Miscellaneous expenses are paid from petty cash.

Required: Determine how much cash was used for operating expenses in the current year.

10-4. Jan Pruitt owns a small trucking operation. The bookkeeper presented Pruitt with the following income statements and balance sheets for 1981 and 1982:

Income Statements		1982		1981
Revenues...................		$87,000		$83,000
Operating expenses:				
Depreciation..............	$12,000		$12,000	
Fuel.....................	35,000		21,000	
Drivers' salaries.........	20,000		16,000	
Tax and licenses..........	10,000		8,000	
Repairs..................	14,000		9,000	
Miscellaneous.............	1,000	92,000	500	66,500
Income (Loss)..............		$(5,000)		$16,500

Balance Sheets	12/31/82	12/31/81
Cash......................	$ 10,000	$ 2,000
Accounts receivable.........	4,000	12,000
Net fixed assets...........	90,000	102,000
Total Assets.............	$104,000	$116,000
Accounts payable...........	$ 14,000	$ 10,000
Accrued salaries...........	4,000	2,500
Other accruals.............	1,500	500
Long-term debt.............	45,500	59,000
Pruitt, capital...........	39,000	44,000
Total Liabilities and Capital...............	$104,000	$116,000

Pruitt does not understand how the company can be $8,000 ahead of last year in terms of cash on hand and yet show a $5,000 loss for the year.

Required: Prepare a cash flow statement to use in explaining this to Jan Pruitt.

10-5. The owner of a small business has asked you to prepare a statement that will show him where his firm's cash came from and how it was used this year. He gives you the following information based on the Cash account in his general ledger:

Balance at beginning of year......................		$ 2,300
Collections of accounts receivable.............		23,000
Interest on savings account....................		230
Sale of old machine............................		2,070
Cash sales.....................................		18,400
Total.......................................		46,000
Payment on vendor accounts.....................$11,500		
Cash purchase of supplies......................	230	
Cash purchase of inventory.....................	11,500	
Down payment on new truck......................	2,300	
Rent payments..................................	5,750	
Utilities......................................	1,380	
Interest payments..............................	690	
Other miscellaneous expenses...................	1,150	
Payment on debt................................	2,300	
Part-time help.................................	4,600	41,400
Balance at end of Year.........................		$ 4,600

In addition, the following information is available from company records:

(1) Sales were $40,940 for the year.
(2) The accounts receivable balance decreased by $460.
(3) Operating expenses totaled $36,110 (including cost of sales, supplies, rent, utilities, interest payments, part-time help, $1,150 depreciation, and other miscellaneous expenses).
(4) Accounts payable decreased by a net of $1,840 during the year.
(5) The inventory balance remained constant throughout the year.

Required: Prepare a cash flow statement for the year.

10-6. You have been given the balance sheet of Flow Co. shown below. You have determined that net income for the year ended December 31, 1982, was $85,000. During 1982, cash dividends of $30,000 were paid. The depreciation expense for the year was $175,000. Flow Co. borrowed $500,000 on September 1, 1982, repayable in full on September 1, 1983. The company also purchased a new plant for $900,000 with $600,000 cash plus 10,000 shares of Flow's stock.

Required: Prepare a working capital flow statement for the year ended December 31, 1982.

FLOW COMPANY
Balance Sheets (Condensed)
As of December 31, 1982 and 1981
(thousands of dollars)

	1982	1981
Current assets...........................$ 775		$ 600
Net fixed assets......................... 1,725		1,000
Total Assets.........................$2,500		$1,600
Current liabilities.....................$ 445		$ 400
Long-term liabilities................... 1,000		500
Common stock and paid-in capital....... 600		300
Retained earnings...................... 455		400
Total Liabilities and		
Owners' Equity....................$2,500		$1,600

10.7. The Amwatt Company balance sheet as of January 1 is as follows (000 omitted):

Assets

Current Assets:
Cash.......................$ 2,500
Marketable securities.....   150
Accounts receivable....... 4,350
Inventories............... 11,795
Prepaid expenses..........   105
  Total Current Assets.... 18,900

Fixed Assets:
Property, plant, and
  equipment............... 25,000
Less: accumulated
  depreciation........(12,500)
  Net fixed Assets........ 12,500

Other Assets:
Goodwill..................   150
Patent....................   450
  Total Other Assets......   600
   Total Assets.........$32,000

Equities

Current Liabilities:
Accounts payable..........$ 6,000
Estimated tax liability... 1,450
Accrued expense payable...   585
Deferred income...........   175
  Total Current
   Liabilities........... 8,210

Other Liabilities:
Mortgage bonds payable.... 3,790
Stockholders' Equity:
Common stock.............. 12,000
Retained earnings......... 8,000
  Total Stockholders'
   Equity.............. 23,790
   Total Equities........$32,000

Required:

a. Compute working capital as of January 1.
b. Explain what effect the following transactions would have on working capital and how they would be shown in a working capital flow statement.

  (1) A $2,000,000 piece of equipment is purchased with the proceeds of a new 12-month note.
  (2) The mortgage bonds are retired with $790,000 cash and the proceeds of an issue of 150,000 shares of common stock.
  (3) $2 million of inventory is purchased on account.
  (4) A dividend of $0.25 per share is declared on the 750,000 outstanding shares.
  (5) A piece of machinery is sold for $1,500,000 cash. When originally purchased, it cost Amwatt $4,000,000, and currently has $2,500,000 of accumulated depreciation.

10-8. Joan Hadley, president of Hadley Inc., was concerned about her company's liquidity. She contemplated that the firm would continue to grow, and she wanted to know if the firm had enough liquid assets to meet the financial needs associated with such growth. Ms. Hadley knows the company has been profitable, but is not sure that profitability alone insures liquidity. In addition to having the balance sheets for 1982 and 1983 (below), you note that the following took place during 1983:

  (1) A new wing was added to the plant during the year at a cost of $67,800. This addition was funded by issuance of 2,000 shares of common stock with net proceeds of $15 per share, a six-month $15,000 note, and the remainder in cash.
  (2) A new machine was purchased for $45,000 cash plus trade-in of a similar old machine which had an original cost of $30,000 and $15,000 accumulated depreciation.
  (3) Total depreciation expense for the year was $24,000.
  (4) Net income was $67,500.
  (5) A $0.75 per share dividend was declared and paid during 1983. There were 50,000 outstanding shares at the time.

Required: Prepare a working capital flow statement for Hadley, Inc. for the year ended December 31, 1983. Assuming this year is typical, what, if any, liquidity problems would you foresee for Hadley?

HADLEY, INC.
Balance Sheets as of December 31

	1983	1982
Assets		
Cash..	$ 36,600	$ 30,300
Accounts receivable (net)................................	225,900	76,500
Inventory...	297,000	360,000
Total Current Assets....................................	559,500	651,300
Land..	60,000	60,000
Buildings..	284,100	216,200
Equipment...	168,000	138,000
Accumulated depreciation................................	(93,000)	(84,000)
Net Fixed Assets...	419,100	330,300
Total Assets..	$978,600	$981,600

Liabilities and Owners' Equity		
Accounts payable...	$ 29,100	$ 92,100
Accrued expenses..	78,000	76,500
Note payable...	15,000	--
Current portion of long-term debt.......................	16,500	16,500
Total Current Liabilities...............................	138,600	185,100
Long-term debt...	180,000	196,500
Common stock ($1 par).....................................	150,000	144,000
Additional paid-in capital................................	60,000	36,000
Retained earnings...	450,000	420,000
Total Owners' Equity.....................................	660,000	600,000
Total Liabilities and Owners' Equity...............	$978,600	$981,600

10-9. Rule Corporation incurred the following transactions during its fiscal year, ended December 31:

(1) Dividends of $75,000 were declared; however, only $25,000 was paid to the shareholders as of Decmeber 31.
(2) A long-term loan of $325,000 was arranged during September, to be repaid in 5 years.
(3) Eight new trucks were added to the company's fleet for a cash purchase price of $585,000.
(4) 12,000 shares of common stock were issued with net proceeds of $480,000.
(5) Interest payments for the year totaled $125,000.
(6) Funds generated from operations (before interest and taxes) were $368,000.
(7) Income taxes paid for the year totaled $69,000.
(8) A 10-year bond issue was retired for a total payment of $275,000.

Required: Prepare a working capital flow statement similar to the format as found in Illustration 10-13. What does this format reveal about Rule Corporation's financing activities?

10-10. Prepare a working capital flow statement for 1983 for MIS Company, given the following information:

	December 31	
Assets	1983	1982
Cash..	$ 12,500	$ 12,500
Marketable securities......................................	15,000	7,500
Accounts receivable..	42,500	30,000
Property, plant, and equipment at cost.................	100,000	100,000
Less: Accumulated depreciation..........................	(40,000)	(50,000)
Total Assets..	$125,000	$100,000

	1983	1982

Equities

Accounts payable.......................................$ 20,000		$ 25,000
Long-term liabilities................................. 30,000		25,000
Capital stock... 25,000		12,500
Retained earnings..................................... 50,000		37,500
Total Equities...................................$125,000		$100,000

Additional information for 1983:

(1) Net income...$16,500
(2) Gain on sale of marketable securities................................. 1,250
(3) Gain on sale of plant sold for $13,750 cash........................ 1,250
(4) Depreciation expense.. 2,500
(5) Dividends... 3,750
(6) Equipment costing $25,000 was purchased, and financed as follows: Capital stock, $12,500; long-term notes payable, $5,000; and Cash, $7,500.

10-11. Prepare a 1982 funds flow statement for JMK Company, given the following data:

	December 31	
Assets	1982	1981
Cash...$ 45,500		$ 29,900
Accounts receivable.................................. 60,450		48,100
Inventory.. 58,500		52,000
Plant and equipment at cost.......................... 156,000		130,000
Less: Accumulated depreciation....................... (85,800)		(78,000)
Goodwill... 5,850		6,500
Total Assets....................................$240,500		$188,500

Equities

Accounts payable.....................................$ 71,500		$ 65,000
Long-term liabilities................................ 52,000		45,500
Capital stock.. 52,000		32,500
Retained earnings.................................... 65,000		45,500
Total Equities...................................$240,500		$188,500

Additional information for 1982:

(1) Net income...............$26,000
(2) Dividends................ 6,500
(3) There was a 2 for 1 stock split during the year.
(4) $19,500 worth of long-term debt was refunded with common stock.
(5) A long-term debt issue of $26,000 was used to purchase new equipment.

10-12. Prepare a balance sheet as of December 31, 1981, for Van Wick Company, given the following:

Balance Sheet as of December 31, 1982

Assets		Equities	
Cash.....................$ 6,900		Accounts payable...........$ 32,200	
Accounts receivable....... 18,400		Long-term liabilities...... 46,000	
Inventory................. 23,000		Capital stock............. 69,000	
Land..................... 11,500		Retained earnings.......... 27,600	
Plant and equipment (net). 115,000		Total Equities..........$174,800	
Total Assets...........$174,800			

Income Statement for 1982

```
Sales revenues...........$276,000
Operating expenses.......(241,500)
Operating income.........  34,500
Gain on sale of land......   6,900
Loss on sale of equipment. (16,100)
    Net Income...........$ 25,300
```

Additional information:

(1) Cash and accounts receivable each increased four-fold (i.e., by 300 percent) between December 31, 1981 and December 31, 1982.
(2) Accounts payable increased by 40 percent during the same period.

Working Capital Flow Statement
for 1982

Sources:

```
    Operations................$ 46,000
    Sale of land..............  23,000
    Additional long-term debt.  34,500
    Issuance of capital stock.  23,000
    Sale of equipment.........  126,500
        Total sources.........$253,000
```

Uses:

```
    Purchase of equipment.....  230,000

Increase in Working Capital.$ 23,000
```

10-13. Alcott Paint Supplies, Inc. has developed the following financial statements for 1982:

ALCOTT PAINT SUPPLIES, INC.
Balance Sheets as of December 31

Assets	1982	1981
Cash..$	20,000	$ 60,000
Marketable securities (at cost).............	240,000	100,000
Accounts receivable.........................	225,000	115,000
Inventory...................................	410,000	400,000
Buildings...................................	550,000	500,000
Accumulated depreciation....................	(150,000)	(250,000)
Total Assets...............................$1,295,000		$925,000

Equities		
Accounts payable.............................$	250,000	$150,000
Long-term debt..............................	400,000	350,000
Capital stock...............................	150,000	100,000
Retained earnings...........................	495,000	325,000
Total Equities...........................$1,295,000		$925,000

Income Statement for 1982

```
Sales revenues....................................................$1,400,000
Gain on sale of marketable securities.....................  10,000
Gain on sale of building..................................  10,000
Expenses..................................................(1,250,000)
    Net Income............................................$  170,000
```

Additional information for 1982:

(1) All sales were on account. The company expects to collect all of its receivables, and therefore does not maintain an allowance for doubtful accounts.
(2) Marketable securities costing $100,000 were sold for cash.
(3) The company uses the LIFO inventory valuation method.
(4) The original cost of the building that was sold was $250,000. It was sold for $135,000 cash. No 1982 depreciation expense was charged on this building prior to its sale.
(5) All operating costs are initially credited to Accounts Payable.
(6) Capital stock was issued for $50,000 cash.
(7) A $50,000 ten-year note was issued for cash.

Required: Prepare a 1982 cash flow statement.

10-14. Use the information given in problem 10-13 to prepare a 1982 working capital flow statement.

10-15. Prepare a 1982 SCFP with "net current monetary assets" as the definition of funds, using the information given in problem 10-13. Net current monetary assets = Cash + Marketable Securities + Accounts Receivable - Accounts Payable. What advantage, if any, does this funds flow concept have over the more common working capital definition of funds?

CASES

Case 10-16: ABC Company*

Bill Jones of the ABC Company started the year in fine shape. His company made widgets -- just what the customer wanted. He made them for $0.75 each, sold them for $1. He kept an inventory equal to shipments of the past 30 days, paid his bills promptly, and billed his customers 30-days net. The sales manager predicted a steady increase of 500 widgets each month. It looked like his lucky year, and it began this way:

Jan. 1: Cash, $875; receivables, $1,000; inventory, $750.

January

In January, he sold 1,000 widgets; shipped them at a cost of $750; collected his receivables -- winding up with a tidy $250 profit and books like this:

Feb. 1: Cash, $1,125; receivables, $1,000; inventory, $750.

February

This month's sales jumped, as predicted, to 1,500. With a corresponding step-up in production to maintain his 30-day inventory, he made 2,000 units at a cost of $1,500. All receivables from January sales were collected. Profit so far, $625. Now his books looked like this:

---

*Adapted from an article in Business Week.

Mar. 1: Cash, $625; receivables, $1,500; inventory, $1,125.

March

March sales were even better: 2,000 units. Collections: on time. Production, to adhere to his inventory policy: 2,500 units. Operating results for the month, $500 profit. Profit to date: $1,125. His books:

Apr. 1: Cash, $250; receivables, $2,000; inventory, $1,500.

April

In April, sales jumped another 500 units to 2,500, and Jones patted his sales manager on the back. His customers were paying right on time. Production was pushed to 3,000 units, and the month's business netted him $625 for a profit to date of $1,750. He took off for Florida before he saw the accountant's report. Suddenly he got a phone call from his treasurer: "Come home! We need money!" His books had caught up with him.

May 1: Cash, $000; receivables, $2,500; inventory, $8,75.

Questions:

1. Why did the ABC Company need money?

2. Assume that business keeps growing at 500 widgets per month. How much cash will the company need, month by month, through December?

* * * * *

Case 10-17: John Bartlett (B)

Referring to Case 3-19, John Bartlett (A), prepare the following for the accounting period beginning when Bart- lett first began to organize his firm (the $20,000 investment by the retired manufacturer) and ending with the last event (#11) of the case:

a. A statement of cash receipts and cash expenditures.
b. A cash flow statement.
c. A working capital flow statement.

Compare and contrast (a) with (b) and (b) with (c). Which of the three would you find most useful as a shareholder? As a bank being asked by Bartlett for a 90-day loan? As a manager of Bartlett Manufacturing?

* * * * *

Case 10-18: Bedford Manufacturing Company (B)

Refer to the situation in Bedford Manufacturing Company (A) (Case 6-17).

Prepare a cash flow statement and a working capital flow statement.

* * * * *

Case 10-19: Braydon Corporation (B)

Refer to the situation described in Braydon Corporation (A) (Case 8-16). Prepare the following for the six months ending June 30:

a. A statement of cash receipts and disbursements.
b. A cash flow statement.
c. A working capital flow statement.

* * * * *

Case 10-20: Salem Furniture Company*

Salem Furniture Company was an established firm specializing in the manufacture of wood furniture. The company was well known nationally for its high-quality furnishings.

The company's accounting department was in the process of preparing the financial statements for the fiscal year just completed on December 31, 1982. The comparative statements of income and financial position for 1981 and 1982 appear below.

The state of the furniture industry was influenced greatly by the economy and the number of housing starts. Consequently, the industry as a whole had been suffering the past few years.

Salem Furniture Company was able to show a modest increase in sales over 1981 levels. The company's management expected that its operations in 1983 would be similar to those in 1982. Even if the economy and housing starts should improve during 1983, Salem would not benefit from the recovery until 1984.

Salem's manufacturing process was labor intensive. The present labor contract had an additional 18 months to run before it expired. The cost of

---

*Adapted from a C.M.A. examination.

Income Statement
For the Years Ended
December 31, 1981 and 1982
(000 omitted)

	1981	1982
Revenues:		
Sales (net)............	$5,850	$6,320
Interest and dividends	20	8
Total revenues........	5,870	6,328
Costs and expenses:		
Cost of goods sold....	4,330	4,740
Selling expenses......	610	620
Administrative		
expenses............	510	515
Interest expense......	90	83
Loss on sale of		
investments.........	--	10
Total costs and		
expenses............	5,540	5,968
Net Income............	$ 330	$ 360

lumber, especially high-quality hardwoods, had risen in recent years, but company officials expected that these costs would stabilize at their present levels.

The following additional data regarding Salem's operations had been assembled by the accounting department:

1. The allowance for uncollectible

Statement of Financial Position
December 31, 1981 and 1982
(000 omitted)

	1981	1982
Assets		
Cash...................$	220	$ 46
Marketable securities	80	40
Accounts receivable (net)...	960	1,152
Inventories..........	1,580	1,802
Current assets..	2,840	3,040
Investments.........	320	135
Property, plant and equipment (net)....	1,320	1,370
Total assets........$	4,480	$4,545
Liabilities and Stockholders' Equity		
Short-term notes payable......$	350	$ 430
Accounts payable.....	450	450
Cash dividends payable...........	--	30
Accrued and other liabilities........	120	130
Current portion of long-term debt.....	200	200
Current liabilities...	1,120	1,240
Serial bonds payable.	1,000	800
Convertible bonds payable...........	150	95
Total liabilities...	2,270	2,135
Common stock, $4 par.	1,120	1,164
Paid-in capital......	280	291
Retained earnings....	810	1,020
	2,210	2,475
Less treasury stock..	--	(65)
Total stockholders' equity........	2,210	2,410
Total liabilities and stockholders' holders' equity....$	4,480	$4,545

accounts had a balance of $50,000 on December 31, 1981, and a balance of $63,000 on December 31, 1982. A total of $52,000 in accounts receivable was written off as uncollectible during 1982. Provisions for uncollectible accounts amounting to $60,000 in 1981 and $65,000 in 1982 were included in the selling expenses.

2. The company liquidated some of its investments during 1982 in order to raise cash. Marketable securities were sold at their recorded cost of $40,000. In addition, Salem sold its interest in Nova Products Co., a promising new company in contemporary furniture and related accessories, for $175,000. Management regretted this action, but this was the only long-term investment which could be sold easily and quickly.

3. Equipment costing $215,000 was purchased during 1982 as part of management's project to improve the manufacturing facilities and to replace obsolete equipment. This upgrading of the manufacturing facilities which was started in 1981, was expected to be completed next year when a similar amount would be expended on equipment. Used equipment was sold at its book value of $25,000. Annual depreciation on plant and equipment included in the operating expenses amounted to $130,000 and $140,000 for 1981 and 1982 respectively.

4. At the end of the current year holders of Salem's short-term notes agreed to extend the maturities through 1983. The serial were being retired on schedule at the rate of $200,000 per year. A total of 55 convertible bonds were exchanged for common stock during 1982.

5. The company purchased $65,000 of its own common stock; the cost method was used to record this purchase of treasury stock.

6. Salem declared cash dividends of $150,000 during 1982; a total of $120,000 was paid during 1982.

7. A large operating loss was incurred by the Salem Furniture Co. in 1979. As a result of this loss, the company has not had to pay any federal or state income taxes on its earnings for the past three years (1980-1982).

Questions

1. Using the data provided, prepare a funds flow statement for the year ended December 1982.

2. Using the statement prepared in Question 1 and the data provided in the case, identify and briefly discuss the significant funds movements that should be of concern to the management of Salem Furniture Co.

Chapter 11

Acquisitions and Consolidated Statements

Key Terms

Cost method
Equity method
Parent and subsidiary
Horizontal combination
Vertical combination
Conglomerate combination

Pooling of interests
Purchase accounting
Goodwill
Consolidated financial statements
Minority interest

Discussion Questions

1. What are the two basic methods of accounting for unconsolidated subsidiaries and how do they differ?

2. Distinguish among horizontal, vertical, and conglomerate business combinations.

3. What are the two methods of accounting for business combinations, and when is it appropriate to use each?

4. How does "goodwill" arise and how must it be accounted for?

5. What is "negative goodwill"?

6. What basic differences arise in a consolidated balance sheet prepared using the purchase versus the pooling-of-interests method?

7. Prior to the issuance of APB Opinion No. 16, a business combination effected by an exchange of stock generally could be accounted for on either the purchase or the pooling-of-interests basis, at the discretion of the acquiring company's management. In most of these instances, the pooling treatment was chosen. Explain why this was the case.

8. What is the criterion for consolidating the statements of a parent company and its subsidiaries?

9. What is the concept underlying the adjustments made when consolidating two firms' financial statements; i.e., why aren't the statements simply added together?

10. What effect does the payment of dividends by the subsidiary to the parent have on the consolidated entity? What adjustment, if any, need be made?

11. The equity method is sometimes said to be, in effect, a "one-line consolidation." Explain.

12. Beta Company is a wholly owned subsidiary of Alpha Company. Alpha's published financial statements consolidate Beta. During the year, Beta sold to Alpha goods for $100,000; these goods had cost Beta $80,000 to produce. During this same year, Alpha sold only half of these goods to its customers, earning reve-

nues on these sales of $65,000. How much gross margin has the consolidated entity made on these transactions? How dos this differ from the sum of the two firms' gross margins if they were separate accounting entities? Prepare journal entries to reflect the adjustments that would have to be made on Alpha's consolidation balance sheet work sheet.

13. Why isn't book value used as the valuation amount in all acquisitions?

Problems

11-1. On January 1, Company P purchased 30 percent of the voting stock of Company S for $800,000 cash. Company P exercises significant influence over Company S. During the year, Company S had net income of $150,000 and declared and paid dividends of $50,000. What accounting method should Company P use to record this investment? Why? Show how Company P would account for this investment on January 1, and for the subsequent income and dividends of Company S, using journal entries. Show the explanations of the journal entries and your calculations. How would the investment apppear on Company P's books as of December 31?

11-2. During its fiscal year Company P purchased 20,000 shares of voting stock of Company S for $400,000. Company S has 125,000 shares of voting stock outstanding. Company S had a profit of $62,500 for the current year. Both companies have the same fiscal year. Company S paid dividends of $0.25 per share during the year. What accounting method should be used by Company P to account for this investment and why? Show the journal entries with explanations to record the original investment and make any adjustments necessary for Company S's profits and dividends.

11-3. ABC Company had the following transactions related to XYZ Company over a two-year period:

Year 1

(1) On January 1, ABC purchased 40% ownership of XYZ Company for $800,000 cash.
(2) XYZ Company had net income of $80,000 for the year.
(3) At year end, XYZ Company paid its shareholders dividends of $40,000.

Year 2

(1) ABC Company purchased on January 1 an additional 5% of XYZ Company's stock for $100,000 cash.
(2) XYZ Company declared a 10% stock dividend.
(3) XYZ Company had net income of $90,000 for the year.
(4) At year end, XYZ Company paid its shareholders dividends of $70,000.

Required: Prepare the journal entries for ABC Company's books for the above transactions.

11-4. Conglomerate Co. acquired for cash all of the outstanding stock of Smallfry Co. on December 31 for $725,000. The balance sheets of the two companies just prior to the acquisition were as follows:

	Conglomerate	Smallfry
Current assets	$ 1,645,000	$115,000
Net fixed assets	27,345,000	448,000
Other assets	12,010,000	112,000
Total Assets	$41,000,000	$675,000
Current liabilities	$ 3,000,000	$ 35,000
Long-term debt	12,985,000	125,000
Common stock	20,000,000	385,000
Paid-in capital	4,515,000	100,000
Retained earnings	500,000	30,000
Total Equities	$41,000,000	$675,000

An independent appraiser valued the assets of Smallfry Co. as follows:

Market Value

```
Current assets.......................  $125,000
Net fixed assets.....................   463,000
Other assets.........................   112,000
```

Required: Prepare a consolidated balance sheet as of the acquisition date. Assume that no intercompany transactions have occurred in the past and that Conglomerate will assume Smallfry's liabilities.

11-5. Chemblast Company is a wholly owned subsidiary of Fallout, Inc. Each company maintains its own financial statements, but consolidated statements are prepared at the end of each fiscal year. At the end of the present fiscal year, the following items will affect the consolidated statements:

(1) During the year, Chemblast sold chemicals to Fallout at a total price of $465,000; Chemblast's cost of these chemicals was $337,000. Fallout has sold all of these goods to outside customers.
(2) Fallout owes Chemblast $58,000 of accounts payable.
(3) Chemblast is indebted to Fallout on a long-term loan for $352,000. Fallout realized $48,000 of interest revenue from this long-term loan during the year.
(4) As of the beginning of the year, Chemblast was carried at an equity amount of $2.5 million on Fallout's balance sheet.

Required: Prepare the elimination entries (in journal entry form) that would be needed in preparing consolidated statements.

11-6. The X Company and the Y Company decided to merge their companies. The merger was completed by exchange of all of Y Company's stock for X Company stock on a one-for-one basis, and qualified for pooling-of-interests treatment. The balance sheets for the two companies just prior to the merger are shown below. Included in these balance sheets were two intercompany financial transactions:

(1) X Company had $5,000 accounts receivable owed by Y Company.
(2) $50,000 of Y Company's long-term debt was owed to X Company. X Company included this receivable in its Other Assets account.

Required: Prepare the consolidated balance sheet as of the date of the merger, showing the appropriate intercompany eliminations.

	X Company	Y Company
Current assets...............................	$ 200,000	$ 90,000
Net fixed assets.............................	1,700,000	300,000
Other assets.................................	100,000	10,000
Total Assets.............................	$2,000,000	$400,000
Current liabilities..........................	$ 100,000	$ 30,000
Long-term debt...............................	800,000	180,000
Capital stock................................	700,000	150,000
Retained earnings............................	400,000	40,000
Total Liabilities and Owners' Equity.....	$2,000,000	$400,000

11-7. (C.M.A. adapted.) After much analysis, Company A is considering the acquisition of Company B. Two alternative methods of acquisition are available to Company A. It can either buy all of Company B's stock on the market for a cash outlay of $425,000, or Company A can exchange authorized but unissued shares with a value of $425,000 (currently selling for $50 per share) for all of the outstanding shares of Company B. In either case, Company A will assume Company B's liabilities, and Company B will be preserved as a wholly owned subsidiary. The following data were collected immediately before the acquisition:

	Company A		Company B	
	Book Value	Market Value	Book Value	Market Value
Current Assets	$ 500,000	$ 635,000	$150,000	$175,000
Fixed Assets	700,000	840,000	250,000	325,000
Totals	$1,200,000	$1,475,000	$400,000	$500,000
Current Liabilities	$ 250,000		75,000	
Long-term Liabilities	175,000		50,000	
Capital Stock, $20 par	400,000		--	
Capital Stock, $10 par	--		170,000	
Additional Paid-in Capital	125,000		60,000	
Retained Earnings	250,000		45,000	
Totals	$1,200,000		$400,000	

Required:

    a. Present the balance sheet that would result immediately after the acquisition assuming a stock exchange is consummated and "pooling" accounting is to be followed. Use only the facts given and assume no others.

    b. Present the balance sheet that would result immediately after the acquisition is consummated assuming that the Company B stock is purchased for cash rather than exchanged. Assume that of the $425,000 purchase price, Company A took out a term loan for $350,000 of the total, and used $75,000 cash on hand for the remainder.

11-8. Mammoth Co. acquired for cash all the outstanding stock of Petite Co. on December 31 for $315,000. An independent appraiser valued the fixed assets of Petite Co. at $1,500,000 as of December 31. All other assets and liabilities on the Petite Co. balance sheet were valued at fair market value. The balance sheets of the two companies just prior to the acquisition were as follows (000s omitted):

	Mammoth Co.	Petite Co.
Current assets....................................	$ 750	$ 75
Net fixed assets.................................	6,675	1,425
Other assets......................................	75	--
Total Assets...............................	$7,500	$1,500
Current liabilities..............................	$ 375	$ 225
Long-term debt...................................	2,250	1,050
Common stock and paid-in capital................	3,000	450
Retained earnings................................	1,875	(225)
Total Liabilities and Owners' Equity.......	$7,500	$1,500

Required:

    a. What business combination accounting method should be used? Why?

    b. Prepare a consolidated balance sheet as of the acquisition date. Assume that although Mammoth and Petite are in the same industry, no intercompany transactions have transpired in the past.

11-9. Corporation P is about to acquire Corporation Q. At the moment, the companies' balance sheets are as follows (thousands of dollars):

	Corporation P	Corporation Q
Assets:		
Cash..................................	$ 48,000	$ 27,000
Accounts receivable..................	54,000	30,000
Inventories..........................	195,000	132,000
Fixed assets (net)...................	270,000	156,000
	$567,000	$345,000

	Corporation P	Corporation Q
Liabilities and Owners' Equity:		
Accounts payable...................	$ 81,000	$ 39,000
Other current liabilities..........	33,000	12,000
Long-term debt.....................	--	60,000
Common stock*......................	75,000	60,000
Retained earnings..................	378,000	174,000
	$567,000	$345,000
*Shares outstanding................	3,000,000	1,500,000

Corporation P is considering two methods of making the acquisition:

Method 1: Issue 1,500,000 new shares of P common stock in exchange for all of Q's common stock. P's accountant says this method will qualify for treatment as a pooling of interests.

Method 2: Purchase Q's net assets, paying Q's owners $30 million cash and issuing them $300 million worth of debentures. It is believed this method would require purchase accounting.

During the negotiations between the two companies, the following information has been presented:

(1) Q's fixed assets have been appraised at $186 million.
(2) Q's estimated pretax income for the coming year, assuming it were not to be combined with Corporation P, is $60 million.
(3) P's estimated pretax income for the coming year, assuming no acquisition of Q, is $105 million.
(4) Both corporations have a combined state and federal income tax rate of 60 percent.
(5) P plans to depreciate Q's fixed assets over ten years on a straight-line basis.
(6) Under Method 2, goodwill (if any) would be amortized over 20 years.
(7) At present, there are no intercompany transactions, nor are any planned for at least a year after combining.

Required:

a. Prepare a consolidated balance sheet as of immediately after P and Q combined under each of the proposed acquisition methods.
b. Compare the consolidated net income and earnings per share that would result from each of the two methods. For Method 2, ignore interest expense on the newly issued debentures.

11-10. The Able Company is considering acquiring the Baker Company. In exchange for Baker's 60,000 shares of stock, Able will distribute to Baker's shareholders 150,000 shares of Able common stock. This stock is authorized but not issued. In recent talks with Able's investment banker about a possible new public offering of 150,000 shares, the investment banker had expressed a willingness to offer the shares to the public at $8 per share.

Below are Able's and Baker's balance sheets, projected to the proposed acquisition date. Also shown are pro forma income statements for the two firms for a one-year period following the proposed acquisition date; these reflect the best estimates of results of operations if the two firms were not to merge, but were to continue to operate as separate companies. There are no intercompany receivables or payables, and no intercompany sales or other transactions contemplated if the business combination is not consummated.

An appraiser has been retained by the two firms and has appraised Baker's net assets (assets less liabilities) at $900,000. The difference between this amount and Baker's book value is wholly attributable to the appraiser's valuation of Baker's fixed assets. Able's certified public accountant has not yet determined whether the combination would qualify for pooling-of-interests treatment under APB-16.

Condensed Balance Sheet
as of the Proposed Acquisition Date
(thousands of dollars)

	Able	Baker
Assets:		
Current assets..................	$ 600	$ 375
Fixed assets (net)..............	900	450
Total Assets.................	$1,500	$ 825
Equities:		
Current liabilities.............	$ 375	$ 150
Long-term debt..................	150	15
Common stock ($1 par)...........	150	60
Paid-in surplus.................	450	150
Retained earnings...............	375	450
Total Equities...............	$1,500	$ 825

Condensed Income Statements
for the First Year after Combination
(thousands of dollars)

Sales..............................	$3,000	$2,250
Expenses...........................	2,400	1,800
Income.............................	600	450
Income tax expense.................	240	180
Net Income......................	$ 360	$ 270

Required:

    a. Prepare consolidated balance sheets as of the proposed acquisition date, assuming accounting treatment of the combination: (1) on a pooling-of-interests basis; and (2) on a purchase basis.

    b. Assuming that in its first year of operations a combined Able-Baker company would achieve the same results of operations as the sum of the two firms' independent operations, what would be Able-Baker's net income that year on a pooling basis? What would net income be on a purchase basis, assuming a goodwill amortization period of 40 years and average fixed asset life of 19 years? (Use a 40 percent tax rate and straight-line depreication.)

    c. As Able's president, what would you hope the accountant will conclude regarding accounting treatment of the combination? Why?

11-11. Talbot Company is a wholly owned subsidiary of Bryant Company. Each company maintains its own financial statements, but consolidated statements are prepared at the end of each fiscal year. At the end of the present fiscal year, the following items will affect the consolidated statements:

    (1) As of the beginning of the fiscal year, Talbot was carried on Bryant's balance sheet at an equity of $890,000.

    (2) Talbot owes Bryant $125,000 on a long-term loan.

    (3) Bryant has recognized $15,000 interest revenue for the year on the above loan, and Talbot has recorded $15,000 interest expense; but none of this interest was remitted to Bryant in cash during the year.

    (4) Bryant has a $32,000 account payable owed to Talbot.

    (5) During the year, Talbot sold certain goods to Bryant at a total price of $220,000; Talbot's cost of these goods was $160,000. Bryant sold all of these goods to outside customers for $300,000.

    (6) In addition to the goods described in (5), Talbot sold goods costing $12,000 to Bryant for $18,000. None of these goods had been sold by Bryant as of year end.

Required: Prepare the elimination adjustments in journal entry form which would be needed in preparing consolidated statements.

11-12. On January 1, 1983, the Berk Company paid $789,000 in cash for a 60 percent ownership interest in the Dexter Company. As of December 31, 1982, Dexter's balance sheet showed the following owners' equity account balances:

```
Common stock at par.....................$  180,000
Paid-in surplus.........................   300,000
Retained earnings.......................   660,000
    Total Owners' Equity...............$1,140,000
```

Required:

a. Prepare a journal entry to record Berk's investment in Dexter on Berk's unconsolidated balance sheet as of January 1, 1983.

b. If Berk were to prepare a January 1, 1983 balance sheet consolidating the Dexter Company, what would be the amount shown as goodwill? (Assume Dexter's net assets had a fair market value of $1,140,000 on December 31, 1982.)

c. What is the amount of the minority interest in Dexter as of January 1, 1983?

d. What will be the amount of this minority interest on December 31, 1983 if Dexter has 1983 net income of $225,000 and pays no dividends?

e. What would be the amount of the minority interest in question (d) if Dexter's $225,000 net income included $30,000 in intercompany profit which will be eliminated in preparing Berk's consolidated statements?

11-13. Parent Company purchased 70% ownership in Sub Company on January 1, at which time Sub's balance sheet showed $450,000 common stock (par plus paid-in capital) and $950,000 retained earnings. During the year, Sub's net income was $250,000, of which $25,000 was earnings on sales to Parent Company.

Required: Calculate the year-end minority interest for Sub Company.

CASES

Case 11-14: Penn Electronics Company

The Penn Electronics Company produced various electronic units for both the United States government and for private industrial enterprises. The company had two fully owned subsidiaries:

1. The Resistor Corporation made tubes, resistors, and related parts and sold them to the parent company. This company was organized in 1976 with an authorized capital of 1,000 shares of no-par-value common stock. The entire amount of this stock was purchased by the parent company for $1,000,000.

2. The Penn Sales Company sold all the commercial production of the parent company. This company was also organized in 1976 with an authorized capital of 1,000 shares of no-par-value stock. The entire amount of this stock was purchased by the parent company for $2,000,000.

Exhibits 1 through 6 give the 1982 balance sheets and income statements for the three companies.

EXHIBIT 1

PENN ELECTRONICS COMPANY
Nonconsolidated Balance Sheet
as of December 31, 1982
(Thousands of dollars)

Assets

```
Cash..............................$10,000
Receivables*......................  5,000
Inventories**..................... 10,000
Loan to Resistor Corporation....    500
Fixed assets (net of
   depreciation)................. 40,000
Investment in Resistor
   Corporation...................  1,000
Investment in Penn Sales
   Company.......................  2,000
    Total Assets.................$68,500
```

_____

*Includes $500,000 from Penn Sales Company.

**Includes $1,000,000 purchased from the Resistor Corporation; cost to the Resistor Corporation ws $750,000.

EXHIBIT 1 (concluded)

Equities

Accounts payable and
  accruals***.....................$ 7,000
Bonds payable.................... 10,000
Capital stock................... 40,000
Retained earnings............... 11,500
    Total Equities..............$68,500

***Includes $400,000 owed to the
   Resistor Corporation.

EXHIBIT 2

PENN ELECTRONICS COMPANY
Nonconsolidated Statement of Income
For Year Ended December 31, 1982
(Thousands of dollars)

Sales
   To U.S. government.............$40,000
   To Penn Sales Company......... 30,000
     Total..................... 70,000
   Operating costs............... 60,000
   Operating profit.............. 10,000
   Management fee*................   1,000
     Total..................... 11,000
   Less: Interest on bonds.......   600
   Net Income....................$10,400

---

*$500,000 from the Resistor Corp. and
 $500,000 from the Penn Sales Co.

EXHIBIT 3

RESISTOR CORPORATION
Balance Sheet as of December 31, 1982
(Thousands of dollars)

Assets

Cash.............................$ 100
Accounts receivable*.............   400
Inventories......................   400
Fixed assets (net of
  depreciation)..................   1,500
Bonds of Penn Electronics
  Company........................   100
    Total Assets................$2,500

Equities

Accounts payable and accruals....$ 200
Loan from Penn Electronics
  Company........................   500
Capital stock....................   1,000
Retained earnings................   800
    Total Equities..............$2,500

---

*Due from the Penn Electronics Company

EXHIBIT 4

RESISTOR CORPORATION
Statement of Income
For Year Ending December 31, 1982
(Thousands of dollars)

Sales to Penn Electronics
  Company........................$3,000
Operating costs................... 2,000
  Operating profit............... 1,000
Less: Management fee..............   500
  Net profit.....................   500
Plus: Interest on bonds...........   6
Net Income........................$ 506

EXHIBIT 5

PENN SALES COMPANY
Balance Sheet as of December 31, 1982
(Thousands of dollars)

Assets

Cash.............................$ 500
Receivables......................   1,500
Inventories*.....................   1,500
Fixed assets (net of
  depreciation)..................   5,050
    Total Assets................$8,550

Equities

Accounts payable**...............$ 500
Accruals.........................   150
Capital stock....................   2,000
Retained earnings................   5,900
    Total Equities..............$8,550

---

*Includes $100,000 purchased from the
Penn Electronics Company; the cost to
Penn Electronics was $80,000. The
$80,000 included $10,000 worth of
items purchased from the Resistor
Corporation; the cost to the Resistor
corporation ws $7,000.

**Due to Penn Electronics Company.

EXHIBIT 6

PENN SALES COMPANY
Statement of Income
For Year Ending December 31, 1982
(Thousands of dollars)

Sales............................$40,000
Operating costs................... 36,000
Operating profits................   4,000
Less: Management fee.............   500
Net Income.......................$ 3,500

Questions

Prepare a consolidated balance sheet for Penn Electronics Company as of December 31, 1982 and a consolidated 1982 income statement. (Disregard income taxes.)

* * * * *

Case 11-15: Hardin Tool Company

The management of Pratt Engineering Company had agreed in principle to a proposal from Hardin Tool Company to acquire all its stock in exchange for Hardin securities. The two managements were in general agreement that Hardin would issue 100,000 shares of its authorized but unissued stock in exchange for the 40,000 shares of Pratt common stock. Hardin's investment banking firm had given an opinion that a new public offering of 100,000 shares of Hardin common stock could be made successfully at $8 per share.

Depending on how the details of the acquisition were structured, it could be accounted for either as a purchase or as a pooling of interests.

Condensed balance sheets for the two companies, projected to the date of the proposed acquisition, and condensed income statements estimated for the separate organizations are given in Exhibit 1. The income statements reflect the best estimate of results of operations if the two firms were not to merge but were to continue to operate as separate companies. There were no intercompany receivables or payables, and no intercompany sales or other transactions were contemplated.

An appraiser had been retained by the two firms and had appraised Pratt's net asets (assets less liabilities) at $600,000. The difference between this amount and Pratt's book value was wholly attributable to the appraiser's valuation of Pratt's plant and equipment.

Although an exchange of common stock was the most frequently talked about way of consummating the merger, one Pratt shareholder inquired about the possibility of a package consisting of 50,000 shares of Hardin common stock, and $400,000 of either cumulative preferred stock with a 10 percent dividend or debentures with a 10 percent interest rate. Under either of these possibilities, the transaction would be accounted for as a purchase.

Questions

1. Prepare consolidated balance sheets

EXHIBIT 1

Condensed Balance Sheets
As of the Proposed Acquisition Date
(thousands of dollars)

	Hardin	Pratt
Assets		
Current assets..........	$ 432	$ 246
Plant and equipment.....	690	312
Total Assets.........	$1,122	$ 558
Equities		
Current liabilities.....	$ 263	$ 107
Long-term debt..........	195	10
Common stock ($1 par)...	100	40
Other contributed capital..............	218	94
Retained earnings.......	346	307
Total Equities.......	$1,122	$ 558

Condensed Income Statements
For the First Year after Combination
(thousands of dollars)

	Hardin	Pratt
Sales....................	$2,100	$1,500
Expenses.................	1,620	1,120
Income..................	480	380
Income tax expense......	240	190
Net income..............	$ 240	$ 190

as of the proposed acquisition date, assuming the exchange of 100,000 shares of Hardin common stock (a) on a pooling of interests bsis and (b) on a purchase basis.

2. Assuming that in its first year of operations the combined company would achieve the same results of operations as the sum of the two firms' independent operations, what would be the combined company's net income and earnings per share on a pooling basis? On a purchase basis? (Assume a goodwill amortization period of 40 years, an average plant and equipment life of 10 years, straight-line depreciation, and an income tax rate of 50 percent.)

3. As an advisor to Hardin, would you recommend that the transaction be consummated on a purchase basis or on a pooling basis?

4. What would be the combined net income and earnings per share under (a) the preferred stock package and (b) the debenture package? Is one of these proposals preferable to the all common stock proposal?

Chapter 12

Accounting and Changing Prices

Key Terms

Purchasing power
Consumer Price Index
GNP Deflator
Specific prices
Constant dollar accounting
Holding gain or loss

Current cost accounting
Replacement cost
Inflation-adjusted current cost
Transaction gain or loss
Translation gain or loss

Discussion Questions

1. Why is it difficult to make asset value comparisons within the standards of conventional accounting?

2. Describe the advantages for each of the two approaches that measure price changes.

3. Describe the difference between financial statements based on a "units of money" basis versus financial statements on a "units of general purchasing power" basis.

4. When, if ever, are monetary items restated in terms of units of general purchasing power?

5. What items on a constant dollar income statement are not restated in terms of the current year's average purchasing power? Why?

6. In 19x1, Fendal Company had sales revenues of $460,000. As of December 31 19x1, the CPI was 235, while the 19x1 average CPI was 230. Express Fendal's 19x1 revenues in terms of 19x2 purchasing power if the 19x2 average CPI is 242. Justify your choice of the CPI values you used in arriving at your answer.

7. Why would an investor be interested in knowing the amount of a holding gain or loss for a given company?

8. What three approaches may be used in estimating the current cost for a used asset?

9. At what amount should property, plant, and equipment be reported on the balance sheet within the context of current cost accounting?

10. What is the primary obstacle in making current cost calculations?

11. What are the two factors that cause a change in the price of some specific item?

12. Why do foreign currency transaction gains or losses occur? How are these gains or losses reported on the financial statements?

13. When translating a foreign entity's financial statements, what items are not reported at the year-end exchange rate?

14. How are translation gains or losses reported?

Problems

12-1. Kencher Company had the following historical cost balance sheet as of December 31, 1981:

KENCHER COMPANY
Balance Sheet as of December 31, 1981

Assets		Equities	
Cash	$ 18,500	Accounts payable	$ 31,800
Accounts receivable	49,000	Notes payable	284,000
Inventory	123,700	Common stock	240,000
Fixed assets (net)	461,300	Retained earnings	96,700
Total	$652,500	Total	$652,500

The following additional information is available:

(1) The average CPI for 1981 was 272.3.
(2) The ending inventory balance consists of goods acquired in November, 1981, when the CPI was 279.9. All other nonmonetary items were acquired in 1977 when the CPI was 181.5.
(3) The CPI as of December 31, 1981 was 281.5.

Required: Prepare a 1981 constant dollar balance sheet for Kencher Company using units of average 1981 purchasing power. Round to the nearest dollar.

12-2. Robjan Company had the following historical cost income statement for 1981:

ROBJAN COMPANY
Income Statement
For the year ended December 31, 1981

Sales (net)	$567,500
Cost of sales	228,250
Gross margin	339,250
Expenses:	
Administration	41,000
Depreciation	53,200
Supplies	8,750
Utilities	6,300
Income before income taxes	230,000
Income taxes	92,000
Net Income	$138,000

The following additional information is available:

(1) Depreciation expense was related to equipment purchased in 1971 when the CPI was 121.
(2) All of Robjan's sales were made from inventory. The beginning-of-the-year inventory was $43,000, while the year-end inventory balance was $50,000.
(3) Purchases made during the year amounted to $267,000 (assume an even flow).
(4) Items remain in inventory (on the average) for 2 months.
(5)

Date	CPI
Year-average, 1980	247.0
October 31, 1980	253.9
Year-average, 1981	272.3
October 31, 1981	279.9
December 31, 1981	281.5

Required: Prepare a 1981 constant dollar income statement for Robjan Company in units of average 1981 purchasing power.

12-3. Forner Company was concerned about its eroding purchasing power due to inflation. As a result of this concern, Forner asked you to prepare comparative
1979 and 1980 balance sheets restated on an average 1980 purchasing power
basis. Also, prepare a schedule showing the 1980 holding gain or loss. The
following information is available:

FORNER COMPANY
Balance Sheet as of December 31, 1979 and 1980

Assets

	1980	1979
Cash	$ 13,800	$ 10,700
Receivables	31,400	22,300
Inventory	148,000	59,000
Building	680,000	680,000
Accumulated depreciation, building	(272,000)	(204,000)
Goodwill	26,800	32,600
Total Assets	$628,000	$600,600

Liabilities and Owners' Equity

	1980	1979
Accounts payable	$ 58,000	$ 45,300
Income taxes payable	37,000	42,700
Long-term debt	225,000	225,000
Common stock	250,000	250,000
Retained earnings	58,000	37,600
Total Equities	$628,000	$600,600

Additional information:

(1) The building and goodwill were acquired in December 1976, when the CPI
    was 174.3.
(2) Inventory was acquired in December of each year.
(3)

Date	CPI
Year-average, 1979	217.7
December, 1979	229.9
Year-average, 1980	247.0
December, 1980	258.4

(4) Round to the nearest dollar.

12-4. Harpo Company had the following income statements for its last two years of
operations:

	Year 2	Year 1
Sales	$258,000	$247,000
Cost of sales	85,000	79,000
Gross margin	173,000	168,000
Selling and administrative expenses:		
Salaries	28,000	25,000
Depreciation	45,000	45,000
Income	$100,000	$ 98,000

Harpo Company has provided you with the following information:

(1) Harpo always sells its entire inventory by the end of each year; hence,
    there are no beginning or ending inventory balances.
(2) The only fixed asset is the building from which Harpo's operations are
    conducted. This building was purchased on January 1, Year 1.
(3)

Date	Index
January 1, Year 1	175
Year-average, Year 1	182
December 31, Year 1	187
Year-average, Year 2	196
December 31, Year 2	210

- 129 -

Required: Prepare comparative Year 1 and Year 2 constant dollar income statements using the Year 2 average purchasing power as the basis. Round to the nearest dollar and ignore taxes. Compare these statements with the historical cost ones above.

12-5. PLC Company maintains a perpetual inventory record system on a FIFO basis for its inventory of integrated microprocessors. The following information was gathered from a year's records on this inventory:

	Qty.	Unit Cost
Beginning inventory................... 300		$715
Purchases and sales:		
January -- Purchase................ 400		720
February -- Sale.................... 400		
March -- Purchase.................. 100		722
June -- Purchase................... 50		730
July -- Sale....................... 425		
October -- Purchase................ 550		725
December -- Sale................... 500		

The following schedule shows the year's monthly levels of general purchasing power based upon a standard index:

Month	Index	Month	Index
January	187.0	July	192.9
February	188.5	August	193.4
March	190.0	September	194.0
April	190.7	October	194.6
May	191.0	November	195.0
June	192.3	December	195.8

Required: Prepare a cost of sales schedule using both an historical cost and a December constant dollar basis. Assume that the beginning inventory was acquired when the index was 185.0.

12-6. Chambers Company desires to prepare its balance sheet on a current cost basis. However, management is not certain about how to properly value the ending inventory and the various fixed assets. You have been asked to help determine the proper current costs for these items. The following information is available for your evaluation:

(1)

Asset	Historical Cost
Accounts receivable (net)...............	$ 43,000
Property...............................	238,000
Inventory..............................	461,500
Goodwill...............................	78,000
Machinery (net)........................	359,000
Buildings (net)........................	987,000

(2) A friend at a bank has told you that if the accounts receivables were sold ("factored") today to a third party for cash, the net proceeds would be approximately $39,000.

(3) Property was recently acquired by Chambers Company adjacent to the original property from which Chambers has conducted business for the last 10 years. While the new property is only half the size of the original property, its service potential is alike in all other respects. Its cost was $138,000. These two pieces of property are the only ones that Chambers owns.

(4) The inventory would cost $485,000 if manufactured today. However, Chambers' quality control department has informed you that one fourth of the inventory is approaching obsolescence and is expected to generate only $95,000 of cash when sold. Chambers Company only manufactures one product.

(5) Chambers' machinery supplier has recently informed the company that it would be willing to sell four used machines to Chambers for $180,000 total. These machines are the same age as the machines that Chambers owns and are in the same condition. Chambers currently owns ten such machines.

(6) A recent appraisal placed the market value of the building at $850,000. The cost to replace the building would be $1,785,000.

(7) Management feels the goodwill is worth at least $150,000 today.

Required: For each asset listed in (1), determine the appropriate current cost.

12-7. (a) Vault Company manufactures only one item, small bank vaults. On January 1 of last year, the current cost of a vault was $42,000; but, by December 31, the current cost had risen to $48,000. At the beginning of last year, the inventory balance showed 6 vaults in stock at a cumulative historical cost of $234,000. During the year, 20 vaults were produced and 23 vaults were sold. What was last year's current cost of sales? What was the amount for inventory on December 31 on a current cost basis?

(b) The tools and equipment that Vault Company uses to manufacture its vaults had a current cost (for all new tools and equipment) of $384,000 as of January 1 of last year. The tools and equipment were acquired over two years ago at a cost of $365,000 and are being depreciated on a straight-line basis over a 5-year life. The current cost for the same tools and equipment as of December 31 was $460,000. What was Vault Company's current cost depreciation expense for last year? What was the net current cost of these tools and equipment as of January 1 and December 31, when these items were respectively one and two years old?

12-8. Alles Company has the following balance sheet and income statement for 1981, prepared on a conventional accounting basis:

ALLES COMPANY
Balance Sheet as of December 31, 1982

Assets		Equities	
Cash......................	$ 493,000	Accounts payable.........	$ 580,000
Accounts receivable.......	479,000	Notes payable............	1,845,000
Marketable securities.....	253,000	Common stock.............	2,000,000
Inventory.................	602,000	Retained earnings........	500,000
Building (net)............	2,610,000		
Property..................	488,000		
Total.................	$4,925,000	Total.................	$4,925,000

Income Statement for 1982

Sales..........................		$3,468,000
Cost of sales.................		1,516,000
Gross margin..............		$1,952,000
Expenses:		
Depreciation...............	$435,000	
Salaries...................	628,000	
Pensions...................	175,000	
Utilities..................	39,000	
Insurance..................	51,000	1,328,000
Income before income taxes....		624,000
Income taxes.................		280,000
Net Income................		$ 344,000

The company's staff has provided the following data:

(1) Cost of sales consisted of the following units of inventory, which were sold evenly throughout the year:

Item	Units Sold	Historical Cost	Current Cost Jan. 1	Current Cost Dec. 31
A	3,400	$190	$190	$195
B	4,200	120	122	128
C	3,660	100	107	115

(2) The ending inventory consisted of 1,600 units of A, 1,300 units of B, and 1,420 units of C. Alles Company intends to sell these units at a 50 percent gross margin.

(3) The building's current replacement cost as of January 1, 1982, was $4,975,000; and as of December 31, 1982, $5,335,000. The building has a 10-year life, with 6 years remaining as of December 31, 1982. It is being depreciated on a straight-line basis.

(4) The fair market value of the property as of December 31, 1982, was $547,000.

Required: Prepare a current cost income statement and determine the amount of current cost net assets for Alles Company as of December 31, 1982.

12-9. For each of the items given below, determine (a) the price change due to inflation, and (b) the "real" price change. The index of general prices was 182 on January 1, 19x3 and 200 on January 1, 19x4. (Round to the nearest cent.)

Item	Price 1/1/x3	Price 1/1/x4
A	$247	$ 282
B	35	29
C	125	135
D	92	125
E	922	1,025

12-10. Lonite Company prepared the following comparative conventional accounting balance sheets for 1980 and 1981:

LONITE COMPANY
Balance Sheet as of December 31

Assets

	1981	1980
Cash	$ 428,000	$ 353,000
Accounts receivable	917,000	579,000
Marketable debt securities	969,000	434,000
Inventory	1,804,500	1,622,800
Property, plant (net)	4,856,250	5,180,000
Equipment (net)	1,408,800	1,643,600
Goodwill	215,450	240,600
Total	$10,599,000	$10,053,000

Liabilities and Owners' Equity

	1981	1980
Accounts payable	$ 314,000	$ 119,000
Taxes payable	158,000	59,000
Mortgage payable	1,200,000	1,250,000
Bonds payable	625,000	625,000
Common stock	3,000,000	3,000,000
Additional paid-in capital	4,000,000	4,000,000
Retained earnings	1,302,000	1,000,000
Total	$10,599,000	$10,053,000

Required: Prepare comparative 1980 and 1981 constant dollar balance sheets using units of 1981 average purchasing power as the basis, and determine the holding gain or loss for 1981, using the following information (round to the nearest dollar):

(a) Inventory turnover is 4 times a year.
(b) Property and plant were acquired for $7,593,750, when the CPI was 175. Depreciation is on a straight-line basis.
(c) Equipment is depreciated on a straight-line basis and was acquired when the CPI was 187 for a price of $2,348,000.
(d) The goodwill was acquired through the purchase of a small supplier's business assets when the CPI was 198.

(e)

Date	CPI	Date	CPI
10/1/79	223.4	Average 1980	247.0
1/1/80	229.9	4/1/81	265.1
4/1/80	239.8	7/1/81	272.6
7/1/80	247.6	10/1/81	278.3
10/1/80	251.7	12/31/81	281.5
12/31/80	258.4	Average 1981	271.3

12-11. Prepare a 1981 current cost balance sheet for Lonite Company using the conventional accounting balance sheets given in Problem 12-10. Ignore any additional information given in 12-10; instead, use the following year-end information:

(a) The plant could be rebuilt on a similar piece of property for a combined plant-and-property total price of $12,450,000. The old plant cost $7,093,750, while the property was purchased for $500,000. As of December 31, 1981, the plant is 40 percent depreciated.
(b) Similar equipment could be purchased from a local rebuilt-equipment dealer for $1,500,000. The used equipment would have the same service potential as Lonite's.
(c) The year-end inventory would cost $2,000,000 to manufacture at current costs.

12-12. In February, 1980, a microprocessor cost $1,500. By February, 1982, the same microprocessor cost only $875. The CPI was 236.4 in February, 1980, and 283.4 as of February, 1982. What was the "real" price change?

12-13. Bograd Company received an invoice from a firm in the Philippines for 10,000 pesos. On the date the invoice was received and journalized, the exchange rate was $0.1440 per peso. Sixty days later, when Bograd paid the invoice in pesos, the rate had dropped to $0.1425.

Required: Write journal entries reflecting the receipt and payment of the invoice.

12-14. Peaches International, a U.S. corporation, purchased a plant in Canada on January 1, 1975, when the Canadian dollar was equivalent to 1.04 U.S. dollars. The cost was 10 million Canadian dollars, and is being depreciated over 20 years using straight-line depreciation. During 1982, Peaches incurred 180,000 Canadian dollars maintenance expense on the Canadian plant. On December 31, 1982, the exchange rate was 0.79 U.S. dollars per Canadian dollar. The average exchange rate during 1982 was 0.81 U.S. dollars per Canadian dollar.

Required: Using the current rate method required by FASB Statement No. 52:

a. Calculate the amount of 1982 Canadian plant maintenance expense for Peaches' income statement.
b. Calculate the 1982 depreciation expense on the Canadian plant for Peaches' income statement.
c. Calculate the amounts for original cost, accumulated depreciation, and net book value of the Canadian plant for Peaches' December 31, 1982 balance sheet.

12-15. Repeat parts a-c of problem 12-14 using the monetary/nonmonetary method that was required by FASB Statement No. 8. Compare your results with those from problem 12-14.

CASE

Case 12-16: Liberty Electronics Company

Liberty Electronics Company produced various types of household electronic equipment, which it sold primarily through two large retail store chains in the United States. On October 1, 1981, Liberty established a wholly owned subsidiary in South Korea, called Liberty-Korea, for the purpose of assembling a small home version of a video arcade game that Liberty had been licensed to produce. The Korean subsidiary sold its output directly to the U.S. retailers that carried the game (as opposed to selling its output to its U.S. parent for re-sale to U.S. retailers).

Exhibit 1 shows the subsidiary's condensed balance sheet as of September 30, 1982 (fiscal year-end), and an income statement for its first year of operations. Liberty's controller, Marion Rosenblum, asked a member of the accounting staff to translate these statements into dollars, following the standards of FASB Statement No. 52. The controller also was interested in how the statements translated in accord with FASB-52 might differ from those prepared using the method formerly required by FASB-8.

The accounting staffperson assembled the following information to assist in preparing the two sets of translated statements:

1. The South Korean unit of currency is the won (abbreviated W). As of October 1, 1981, the exchange rate was one won = $0.00146; as of September 30, 1982, the rate was one won = $0.00130.

2. As of October 1, 1981, Liberty-Korea's assets were W400 million cash and W600 million fixed assets. No additional fixed assets were acquired during the first year of operations. On average, the year-end inventories had been on hand 1 1/2 months; the exchange rate on August 15, 1982 was one won = $0.00132.

3. The capital stock of Liberty-Korea had been issued to Liberty Electronics on October 1, 1981; no additional capital stock transactions had taken place during the fiscal year.

EXHIBIT 1

LIBERTY-KOREA
Balance Sheet
as of September 30, 1982
(millions of won)

Assets

Cash..............................	W 591
Receivables......................	1,182
Inventories......................	552
Fixed assets.....................	575
	W2,900

Liabilities and Owners' Equity

Current liabilities..............	W 624
Capital stock....................	1,000
Retained earnings................	1,276
	W2,900

Income Statement
for the year ended September 30, 1982
(millions of won)

Revenues.........................	W7,990
Cost of sales....................	4,415
Other expenses...................	1,399
Net Income.......................	W1,276

Questions

1. Prepare translated year-end statements for Liberty-Korea using the net investment method, as required by FASB-52.

2. Prepare translated statements using FASB-8's monetary/nonmonetary method. (Note: Under FASB-8, any translation gain or loss was included as an item in the translated income statement. You may treat any such gain or loss as a "plug" figure; i.e., you are not expected to calculate it in detail.)

3. Compare your two sets of translated statements, and comment on any differences between them. If the company were permitted a choice as to which method to use, which method do you think they would prefer?

Chapter 13

Financial Statement Analysis

Key Terms

Return on assets
Return on owners' equity
Return on invested capital
Return on tangible investment
Price/earnings ratio
Profit margin
Investment turnover

Capital intensity
Working capital turnover
Cash conversion cycle
Liquidity
Solvency
Dividend yield
Dividend payout

Discussion Questions

1. What is the overall objective of a business?

2. What is return on assets and when is it appropriate to use it as a measure of return on investment?

3. What is the difference between return on owners' equity and return on invested capital, and when is each a more appropriate measure for evaluation of a business?

4. From a shareholder's point of view, what are the benefits and corresponding risks involved in a company's incurring additional liabilities?

5. What does a rise over time in the price/earnings ratio of a company indicate about how investors judge the company's performance?

6. In calculating return on investment, why is interest expense, net of tax, added back to net income when total assets or invested capital is the measure of investment, but not when shareholders' equity is used as the investment base?

7. How do profit margin and investment turnover interact to affect return on investment?

8. Some people treat net income percentage or return on sales as the single most important measure of overall profitability. Is it valid to measure profitability using this measure alone? Explain.

9. As a review, define and explain the liquidity and solvency ratios that were described in earlier chapters: current ratio, acid-test ratio, debt/equity, debt/capitalization, and times interest earned.

10. Why does equity capital have a higher cost to a company than debt capital?

11. Explain why net income (as calculated according to generally accepted accounting principles) is an amount smaller than profit <u>before</u> capital costs, but larger than profit <u>after</u> capital costs.

12. What would be suggested by a company's capital intensity ratio being lower this year than last?

13. What are some of the basic problems of comparing financial ratios?

14. If financial performance fails to meet the established budgets, does this always indicate poor performance?

15. What is the value of comparing a company's financial performance for the year with its historical performance?

16. Why might an older company's ROI be higher than a newer company's ROI? Is the older company necessarily more profitable?

17. What actions could a company take near year end to improve its ratios? What does this suggest about ratios calculated from annual report financial statements?

18. What is the principal value of ratio analysis? What is the inherent weakness in such an analysis?

Problems

13-1. You are given the following data on two companies, A and B (figures are millions):

	A	B
Sales	$720	$810
Net income	36	81
Investment	120	270

Required:

a. Which company has the higher profit margin?
b. Which company has the higher investment turnover?
c. Based solely on the data given, in which firm would you prefer to invest?

13-2. As the manager of Alpha Division of XYZ Corporation, you are interested in determining the division's return on investment. As division manager you have no control over financing assets, but you control acquisition and disposition of assets. The division controller has given you the following data to aid you in calculating return on investment:

Fiscal year, January 1 to December 31 (000 omitted):

Total assets, January 1	$328,000
Total assets, December 31	425,000
Long-term debt, January 1	25,000
Long-term debt, December 31	44,000
Owners' equity, January 1	193,000
Owners' equity, December 31	225,000
Net income for the year	32,000
Interest expense on long-term debt	4,200
Tax rate = 46%	

Required: What method would be most appropriate for calculating the division's return on investment (ROI)? Why? Using this method, what is ROI for the current year?

13-3. The president of Kearney Company is interested in determining how effective the company's new controller has been in controlling cash on hand. You have the following information available from the fiscal year preceding the new controller's arrival, and the current year:

	Current Year	Preceding Year
Cash on hand	$ 3,131,926	$ 3,621,150
Cash expenses	51,961,505	73,430,900

Required: Does it appear that the new controller has been effective in managing cash?

13-4. The treasurer of Black's Stores, Inc. was interested in what effect, if any, new credit terms have had on collections of customer accounts. The usual 30-day payment period was shortened to 20 days in an attempt to reduce the investment in accounts receivable. The following information for the current year and the preceding year (prior to the payment period change) is available:

	Current Year	Previous Year
Accounts receivable (net of bad debt allowance)..	$ 803,790	$ 692,432
Credit sales......................................	7,334,600	6,480,500

Required: What effect has the new credit policy apparently had?

13-5. Pam Pincker was interested in controlling her company's inventory because she knew that excess inventories were expensive in that they tied up funds. On the other hand, insufficient inventory levels could result in lost sales. Ms. Pincker obtained the following inventory information from her trade association, which reported average figures for companies similar to hers:

> Days' inventory............36 days
> Inventory turnover.........10 times

Ms. Pincker had the following information from last year, which she considered to be a typical year for her company:

> Cost of sales............. $250,000
> Beginning inventory....... 47,300
> Ending inventory.......... 49,900

Required: How does Ms. Pincker's company's inventory compare with other similar companies?

13-6. Boyne Company had net income for the year of $14 million. It had 2 million shares of common stock outstanding, with a year-end market price of $56 a share. Dividends during the year were $2.80 a share.

Required: Calculate the following ratios: (1) price/earnings ratio; (2) dividend yield; and (3) dividend payout.

13-7. Measurement Company had sales revenues for the year of $1,000. Average working capital, property, plant, and equipment, and shareholders' equity were $200, $250, and $800, respectively. (All figures are millions.)

Required: Calculate: (1) working capital turnover, (2) capital intensity, and (3) equity turnover.

13-8. Mercury Company had net income for the year of $850,000 on sales of $8.5 million. Assets at the beginning of the year were $5.44 million, and at the end of the year were $4.76 million.

Required:

a. Calculate the profit margin and the investment turnover.
b. How do these ratios relate to ROI? What do these ratios measure?

In Problems 13-9 through 13-15, use the following comparative financial statements prepared for Sherburne Stores, Inc. (000 omitted):

Balance Sheets as of December 31

	1983	1982
Cash	$ 53,200	$ 47,500
Accounts receivable (net)	260,300	138,700
Inventories	611,800	361,000
Equipment (net)	53,200	57,000
Total Assets	$ 978,500	$ 604,200
Current liabilities	$ 765,700	$ 395,200
Long-term debt	45,600	51,300
Capital stock*	142,500	142,500
Retained earnings**	24,700	15,200
Total Liabilities and Owners' Equity	$ 978,500	$ 604,200

Income Statements for years ending December 31

	1983	1982
Sales	$4,503,000	$3,562,500
Cost of goods sold	4,275,000	3,249,000
Gross margin	228,000	313,500
Operating expenses***	290,000	294,500
Income before taxes	38,000	19,500
Income tax expense	17,100	7,600
Net Income	$ 20,900	$ 11,400

Working Capital Flow Statements for years ending December 31

	1983	1982
Sources		
From operations	$26,600	$15,200
Increase in long-term debt	--	5,700
Total Sources	26,600	20,900
Uses		
Equipment acquisitions	1,900	11,400
Decrease in long-term debt	5,700	--
Dividends	11,400	3,800
Total Uses	19,000	15,200
Increase in Working Capital	$ 7,600	$ 5,700

---

*10 million shares were outstanding during both years. The December 31 market price was $6.65 in 1982 and $19 in 1983.

**During 1983, dividends totaling $11.4 million were declared and paid. In 1982, dividends totaled $3.8 million.

***Includes interest and depreciation expenses as follows (000 omitted):

	1983	1982
Interest expense	$22,800	$11,400
Depreciation	5,700	3,800

13-9. For each item in Sherburne's 1983 financial statements, show the amount of increase (decrease) over 1982 and the percent increase (decrease). (This is one type of "horizontal" analysis.) Round percentages to the nearest whole percent.

13-10. In each year's Sherburne income statement, treat sales as 100 percent and calculate the percentages of the other income statement items. (This is a "vertical" analysis.) Round percentages to the nearest tenth of 1 percent.

13-11. Do a vertical analysis of each year's working capital flow statement, treating total sources as 100 percent. Again, round to the nearest tenth of 1 percent.

13-12. Using Sherburne's statements, calculate the ratios listed in Illustration 13-4 for 1983. For each one, be prepared to give a brief explanation of its meaning. Base your calculations on year-end (not average) balance sheet amounts and year-end stock prices.

13-13. Repeat problem 13-12, calculating the ratios for 1982.

13-14. Using your calculations for 1983 from problem 13-12, prepare a diagram like the one in Illustration 13-2 of the text. Then add the pertinent ratios for 1982 (problem 13-13) to your diagram. Be prepared to use your diagram and other data to explain to Sherburne's top management group why 1983's return on invested capital differed from 1982's.

13-15. Chocley Corporation had the following 1983 income statement and balance sheets for 1982 and 1983:

Income Statement for the Year 1983

Sales(net)..	$1,451,200
Cost of sales..	1,015,800
Gross margin..	435,400
Selling, administrative and general*...............	267,900
Income from operations.............................	167,500
Interest expense**.................................	12,500
Income before taxes................................	155,000
Provision for income taxes.........................	74,600
Net Income...	$ 80,400

---

*Includes $29,200 of depreciation and amortization expense.
**This is $15,300 interest expense, net of $2,800 of interest revenue.

Balance Sheets as of December 31

	1983	1982
Assets		
Cash and short-term investments.....................	$ 53,900	$ 48,900
Accounts receivable.................................	56,200	46,000
Inventories...	151,900	113,700
Other current assets................................	25,000	12,800
Total current assets.............................	287,000	221,400
Property, plant, and equipment at cost..............	598,000	515,000
Less: accumulated depreciation.....................	157,800	135,600
Total fixed assets...............................	440,200	379,400
Goodwill..	53,900	55,200
Investments and other assets........................	25,700	28,500
Total Assets.....................................	$806,800	$684,500
Liabilities and Stockholders' Equity		
Accounts payable....................................	$ 48,100	$ 52,500
Accrued liabilities.................................	67,000	57,500
Current portion of long-term debt...................	2,100	1,600
Total current liabilities........................	117,200	111,600
Long-term debt......................................	158,200	158,800
Deferred income taxes...............................	61,700	52,500
Total liabilities................................	337,100	322,900
Common stock ($1 stated value).....................	15,700	14,200
Additional paid-in capital..........................	54,000	2,300
Retained earnings...................................	400,000	345,100
Total stockholders' equity.......................	469,700	361,600
Total Liabilities and Stockholders' Equity......	$806,800	$684,500

Required:

a. For Chocley Corporation in 1983, calculate the ratios listed in Illustration 13-4, making these changes:

(1) Calculate the returns on <u>tangible</u> assets, invested capital, and equity.
(2) For return on investment and turnover ratios, use the <u>average</u> balance sheet amounts rather than the December 31, 1983 amounts.
(3) The December 31, 1983 market price was $36 per share.

Note: Certain information needed in calculating the ratios, which was given to you in Sherburne Stores, might have to be deduced for Chocley Corporation.

b. Based on your calculations from part (a), what questions concerning Chocley's 1983 financial performance would you want to ask Chocley's management? Speculate as to what the answer to each of your questions might be.

CASES

Case 13-16: Radcliffe Company

Sarah Radcliffe, aged 50, president of Radcliffe Company, was concerned about the business which her father, Gilbert Radcliffe, had started 50 years ago. Now age 72, he was still active in the business, currently being chairman of the board. The company was completely family owned, and the board of directors consisted of Gilbert, Sarah, and Sarah's two brothers who, though equal shareholders with Sarah, were not active in the business. Radcliffe Company had been successful for many years but for the last two years had suffered losses. Sarah Radcliffe was gavely concerned about the decline in profits and believed that something was seriously wrong. Her father, how-

ever, was much more optimistic and felt that 1981 and 1982 were temporary declines in the business and that in 1983 the company would again show substantial profits.

Since the elder Radcliffe had always run the business with a firm hand, he was not particularly amenable to Sarah's suggestion that they engage a financial consultant, nor to her proposal that they hire a professional manager to run the business.

Exhibit 1 shows the company's balance sheets, income statements, and statements of retained earnings for the past five years.

EXHIBIT 1

RADCLIFFE COMPANY
Balance Sheets as of December 31
(000 omitted)

	1978	1979	1980	1981	1982
Assets					
Current Assets:					
Cash	$1,446	$1,520	$1,450	$1,600	$1,400
Marketable securities	1,500	1,685	2,164	1,120	1,057
Accounts receivable	725	820	816	1,170	1,300
Inventories	1,320	1,470	1,700	2,250	2,400
Total Current Assets	4,991	5,495	6,130	6,140	6,157
Fixed Assets	3,120	3,120	3,320	4,050	4,963
Less: Accumulated depreciation	1,677	1,989	2,300	2,700	3,100
Net	1,443	1,131	1,020	1,350	1,863
Total Assets	$6,434	$6,626	$7,150	$7,490	$8,020

	1978	1979	1980	1981	1982
Equities					
Current Liabilities:					
Accounts payable...................$	826	$ 880	$1,060	$1,573	$2,555
Notes payable.......................	400	350	450	500	550
Dividends payable...................	63	56	46	55	50
Accrued taxes.......................	230	196	140	--	--
Accrued expenses....................	145	150	138	148	140
Total Current Liabilities........	1,664	1,632	1,834	2,276	3,295
Long-Term Debt........................	800	800	1,000	1,500	2,000
Shareholders' Equity:					
Capital stock.......................	1,500	1,500	1,500	1,500	1,500
Retained earnings...................	2,470	2,694	2,816	2,214	1,225
Total.............................	3,970	4,194	4,316	3,714	2,725
Total Equities...............$	6,434	$6,626	$7,150	$7,490	$8,020

Income Statements for the years ended December 31
(000 omitted)

	1978	1979	1980	1981	1982
Sales.................................$	7,365	$7,450	$6,800	$6,000	$6,200
Cost of sales.........................	4,345	4,470	4,148	3,884	4,454
Gross margin..........................	3,020	2,980	2,652	2,116	1,746
Operating expenses:					
Selling.............................	1,031	1,118	1,156	1,450	1,200
Administrative......................	884	894	816	1,046	1,230
Total expenses....................	1,915	2,012	1,972	1,396	2,430
Operating income.....................	1,105	968	680	(380)	(684)
Interest expense.....................	60	54	68	122	95
Income before taxes..................	1,045	914	612	(502)	(789)
Income taxes.........................	543	466	306	--	--
Net Income...........................$	502	$ 448	$ 306	$ (502)	$ (789

Statements of Retained Earnings as of December 31
(000 omitted)

	1978	1979	1980	1981	1982
Balance, January 1...................$	2,219	$2,470	$2,694	$2,816	$2,214
Net income...........................	502	448	306	(502)	(789)
Total.............................	2,721	2,918	3,000	2,314	1,425
Dividends............................	251	224	184	100	200
Balance, December 31.................$	2,470	$2,694	$2,816	$2,214	$1,225

Questions

1. Determine the current status of the business using such financial ratios and analysis that you deem appropriate.

2. Does the analysis indicate whether or not the owners should consider hiring an outside professional manager?

3. What are the implications if the company were to hire a professional manager?

* * * * *

Case 13-17: Michigan Avenue Furriers

In early May 1983, Richard Bowers, vice president of a large Chicago bank, was considering opposing points of view on a loan request by Michigan Avenue Furriers expressed by two of his credit department trainees following their independent computation of selected financial data. Bowers had asigned to

William Dickenson, a recent liberal arts college graduate, and to Roberta Woods, an accounting major in college, the task of analyzing the recently received financial statements of Michigan Avenue Furriers (see Exhibits 1 through 3), comparing them with past figures, and recommending what action the bank should take on renewing the company's existing $1 million line of credit. The two trainees had come to the bank direct from college with no practical experience in financial analysis.

Michigan Avenue Furriers was one of Chicago's more exclusive fur salons. The company had been in existence since the early 1920s; the present owner-managers purchased it in 1974. The company's sales and reputation had been established on its line of expensive, custom-styled furs. The company had only one store, located on Michigan Avenue near Chicago's "loop" district, and sold only to the retail trade. The company designed all the furs in its line, but had the garments made by two or three independent contractors. The company also engaged in storage of furs on a contract basis with a local warehouse, but this activity contributed little to earnings and was regarded primarily as a customer service. The business of Michigan Avenue Furriers was highly seasonal with most sales made in late August and early September or during the Christmas buying season. Typically, the company's borrowing obligations reached a peak about the end of October or early November, and were at a minimum in the period between the middle of February and the first of May. It had been the company's policy to be out of debt to the bank, except for the loan secured by life insurance, for at least one month during this latter period. Despite its reputation as one of Chicago's finest furriers, the company had suffered a net loss in three of the past seven years.

The borrowing line for Michigan Avenue Furriers was composed of two parts: the first was a $112,500 loan secured by the cash surrender value of the life insurance held by the company on the lives of its chief executives; the remaining line was secured by all accounts receivable less than one year outstanding up to 95 percent of their book value to a maximum of $900,000. The portion of the credit line secured by life insurance carried an interest rate of 10 percent, the line secured by accounts receivable, 13 percent. The average combined balances of Michigan Avenue Furriers and the company owners' personal accounts with the bank amounted to about $150,000.

Bowers had requested Dickenson and Woods to compute the following figures for Michigan Avenue Furriers: the "quick" assets to current liabilities ratio; working capital; current ratio; and the debt to equity ratio.

Bowers was surprised to find that Dickenson and Woods arrived at quite different figures and conclusions from the same basic information (see Exhibit 4). Dickenson included in current assets all asset items except furniture and fixtures, leasehold improvements, and goodwill. He defended his position stating that these items would be converted into cash in the next year through normal operations of the business, or were redeemable for cash on very short notice. In computing owners' equity, Dickenson added to total capital the reserves for doubtful accounts, depreciation, and amortization of leasehold improvements. He defended the addition of the reserves on the basis that they represented simply a segregation of surplus and were actually part of the shareholders' equity.

Woods, on the other hand, took a narrow viewpoint on the current assets. She included only cash, inventories, and accounts receivable outstanding less than one year. She defended the exclusion of unexpired insurance and other prepaid accounts with the explanation that these items, having to be replaced in the normal course of business, represented a fixed commitment rather than a current one. She stated also that the cash surrender value of life insurance and the investments which the company held would not, in the normal course of business, be converted into cash and, therefore, should not be regarded as current in nature. In computing owners' equity, Woods subtracted leasehold improvements and goodwill from total assets to arrive at tangible assets. She stated that this was justified because she believed leasehold improvements would revert to the lessor upon default by the lessee. The item, goodwill, which was carried on the balance sheet at $901,000, represented the excess of the purchase price of the business paid by the current owners in 1974 over the book value of the assets acquired. She considered that in the event of liquidation, goodwill would have little or no realizable value and was not a residual asset of the business. Woods also included as a liability for the purpose of computing owners' equity and total debt, the amount due on the company's lease, which was written in 1976 for a period of 10 years and called for an annual rental of $150,000 plus a property tax commitment of an additional $75,000 per annum. She stated that this item represented a legal, long-term responsibility of the company and should be included as a liability.

Dickenson disagreed with Woods on the computation of working capital and said, "If you're going to include notes payable secured by life insurance as a current liability, you should consider the security for that loan -- the cash surrender value of the life insurance -- as a current asset." It was his contention also that all accounts receivable should be included as current assets, even if they were more than one year old. The accounts receivable represented obligations of some of the wealthier and more prominent Chicago citizens of unquestioned credit standing. He said that in the normal expectation of business the company could collect on these receivables any time it desired by simply requesting payment. In his view it was probably a policy of the company not to push collections because such customers might become indignant over having their reliability for credit questioned and take their business elsewhere.

Dickenson recommended renewal of the line of credit for another year. While he considered the current ratio of 1.73 somewhat weak, he believed it to be quite adequate in view of working capital being more than double current bank borrowings. He pointed out that "quick assets" equaled nearly 90 percent of total liabilities, and he considered this a strong position. With a current debt to equity ratio of only 0.19, which would increase to only about 0.5 with a maximum use of the credit line, Dickenson believed the equity cushion was sufficient to justify the line. Despite the company's spotty earnings record, he argued that the accounts receivable and cash surrender value of the life insurance policy were prime security. Finally, Dickenson pointed out that because the bank had been loaning to the company since the new owners purchased the assets in 1974, it had an obligation to the management to continue to make credit available. The company had always met its financial obligations fully and promptly, and Dickenson believed such a record merited a further extension. He summed up his position with "Where else could the bank get as secure loans at these interest rates?"

Woods was adamant in her belief that the line of credit should be terminated. She considered the company's cash position precarious because cash on hand was less than 13 percent of accrued expenses and accounts payable. According to her calculations, working capital was barely equal to total bank borrowings with a current ratio of only 1.27. She emphasized that these figures as of January 31 were probably far more favorable than had they been calculated during the period of heaviest borrowing. She said that she did not see how the bank could consider loaning to a company which had experienced a net operating loss of nearly $500,000 over a relatively prosperous period in the economy. She questioned the advisability of bank credit in the face of debt and lease requirements of more than five times the company's owners' equity. She contended that the bank had been extending equity-type capital to the company for years to the extent that the loan against the cash surrender value of life insurance, while evidenced by 90-day notes, had remained continually on the books. She questioned the ability of the company's management, not only because of the losses in the face of widespread economic prosperity, but also because of laxity in the collection of its accounts receivable. Some 5 percent were at least one year overdue, although all credit sales were on nominal terms of full payment due end of the month. She argued that loan demand currently was in excess of the bank's resources and that this was an opportune time to withdraw to make funds available for more dynamic, growing companies.

Bowers believed that the differences of opinion in this situation highlighted some basic problems of credit analysis. He considered these as: Which items should be included or excluded in such computations as working capital and debt to equity and current ratios? How significant and useful are these ratios? In evaluating a loan opportunity, should the bank look primarily at the company's earnings record or at the quality of the security offered? To what extent can the performance of company's management be judged by analysis of the income statements and balance sheets? If a company does not get out of debt to the bank at least once a year, is the bank furnishing, in effect, equity funds at a fixed, low rate of return? If so, is this proper use of depositors' funds? As Bowers considered these questions, he knew that Woods and Dickenson would look to him for specific answers as to which of them, if either, had made the computations correctly. Furthermore, for training purposes, he wished to make his position on this loan request clear and explain fully the reasoning back of his decision.

EXHIBIT 1

MICHIGAN AVENUE FURRIERS
Balance Sheets as of January 31
(000 omitted)

	1977	1978	1979	1980	1981	1982	1983
Assets							
Cash......................................	$ 63	$ 95	$ 98	$ 39	$ 56	$ 50	$ 93
Accounts receivable (gross)*.............	602	905	776	813	864	972	923
Inventories..............................	626	632	650	857	612	677	816
Total Current Assets..................	1,291	1,632	1,524	1,709	1,532	1,699	1,832
Unexpired insurance......................	26	20	22	28	26	27	27
Other prepaid expenses...................	15	9	9	7	7	7	6
Cash surrender value of life insurance..	83	87	93	98	104	108	113
Investments (at cost)**.................	30	1	1	1	1	1	1
Furniture and fixtures (gross)..........	132	142	153	176	182	186	200
Leasehold improvements (gross)..........	147	150	151	151	153	155	159
Goodwill.................................	901	901	901	901	901	901	901
Total Assets (Gross)..............	2,625	2,942	2,854	3,071	2,906	3,084	3,239
Reserve for doubtful accounts...........	31	33	31	33	38	41	38
Reserve for depreciation................	17	36	54	75	95	114	131
Leasehold improvement amortization......	66	75	82	92	100	110	118
Total.................................	114	144	167	200	233	265	287
Total Assets (Net).............	$2,511	$2,798	$2,687	$2,871	$2,673	$2,819	$2,952
Liabilities and Owners´ Equity							
Notes payable (secured by life insur.)..	$ 81	$ 81	$ 81	$ 81	$ 96	$ 96	$ 108
Notes payable (secured by accts. rcvbl.)		111	120	243	261	297	237
Accounts payable........................	500	651	608	647	554	590	686
Customers´ credits......................	18	19	15	15	18	14	11
Accrued expenses........................	106	56	54	45	43	50	54
Provision for federal income taxes......	48	26					
Total Liabilities....................	753	944	878	1,031	972	1,047	1,146
Common stock...........................	2,003	2,003	2,003	2,003	2,003	2,003	2,003
Retained earnings......................	(245)	(149)	(194)	(163)	(302)	(231)	(197)
Total Owners´ Equity..............	1,758	1,854	1,809	1,840	1,701	1,772	1,806
Total Liabilities and Owners´ Equity...............	$2,511	$2,798	$2,687	$2,871	$2,673	$2,819	$2,952

*See Exhibit 3 for aging of receivables.
**Common stock of Fur Storage Warehouse (1978-1983, 100 shares).

EXHIBIT 2

MICHIGAN AVENUE FURRIERS
Income Statements for years ending January 31
(000 omitted)

	1977	1978	1979	1980	1981	1982	1983
Net sales.................................	$3,821	$4,274	$4,344	$4,320	$4,214	$4,412	$4,519
Cost of sales............................	2,687	2,804	2,900	2,819	2,829	2,882	2,925
	1,134	1,470	1,444	1,501	1,385	1,530	1,594
Operating expenses.......................	1,439	1,296	1,428	1,405	1,452	1,391	1,489
	(305)	174	16	96	(67)	139	105
Depreciation and amortization...........	27	28	27	28	30	28	26
Interest expense.........................	7	50	34	36	41	40	43
	34	78	61	64	71	68	69
Income..................................	(339)	96	(45)	32	(138)	71	36
Nonrecurring expense....................	201						
Net Income (Loss)........................	$ (540)	$ 96	$ (45)	$ 32	$ (138)	$ 71	$ 36

EXHIBIT 3

MICHIGAN AVENUE FURRIERS
Age Distribution of Accounts Receivable
(000 omitted)

	1977	1978	1979	1980	1981	1982	1983
Outstanding less than 1 year..............	$585	$862	$730	$765	$802	$912	$867
Outstanding 1 to 2 years.................	11	32	37	37	50	49	38
Outstanding 2 to 3 years.................	4	8	5	6	8	6	11
Outstanding 3 to 4 years.................	2	3	2	3	2	3	5
Outstanding over 4 years.................			2	2	2	2	2
Total.................................	$602	$905	$776	$813	$864	$972	$923

EXHIBIT 4

MICHIGAN AVENUE FURRIERS
Selected Financial Data
(000 omitted)

	1977	1978	1979	1980	1981	1982	1983
"Quick Assets"--Woods	$ 648	$ 957	$ 828	$ 804	$ 858	$ 962	$ 960
--Dickenson	665	1,000	874	852	920	1,022	1,016
Current Assets--Woods	1,243	1,556	1,447	1,628	1,432	1,598	1,738
--Dickenson	1,445	1,749	1,649	1,843	1,670	1,842	1,979
Current Liabilities--Woods	978	1,169	1,103	1,256	1,197	1,272	1,371
--Dickenson	753	944	878	1,031	972	1,047	1,146
Working Capital--Woods	265	387	344	372	235	326	367
--Dickenson	692	805	771	812	698	795	833
Total Debt--Woods	2,106	1,992	1,776	1,674	1,482	1,293	1,070
--Dickenson	81	192	201	324	357	393	395
Shareholders' Equity--Woods	(1,249)*	(922)*	(736)*	(470)*	(378)*	(74)*	189
--Dickenson	1,872	1,998	1,976	2,040	1,934	2,037	2,093
"Quick Assets" to Current Liabilities							
--Woods	.66	.82	.75	.64	.72	.76	.70
--Dickenson	.88	1.06	1.00	.83	.95	.98	.89
Current Ratio--Woods	1.27	1.33	1.31	1.30	1.20	1.26	1.27
--Dickenson	1.93	1.85	1.88	1.79	1.72	1.76	1.73
Debt to Equity Ratio--Woods	*	*	*	*	*	*	5.66
--Dickenson	.04	.10	.10	.16	.18	.19	.19

*By Ms. Woods' computations, Total Liabilities exceed Total Assets, 1977-1982 inclusive.

EXHIBIT 4(A)

MICHIGAN AVENUE FURRIERS
Derivation of Computations

By Roberta Woods:

"Quick" Assets--Cash plus Accounts Receivable less than 1 year outstanding.

Current Assets--"Quick" Assets plus Inventories

Current Liabilities--All Balance Sheet Liabilities plus $225,000 due on lease in current year

Net Working Capital--Current Assets less Current Liabilities

Total Debt--Total Notes Payable plus amount due on lease through 1986 ($225,000 per year)

Shareholders' Equity--Total Assets (Net) less Goodwill, Leasehold Improvements (Net) Balance Sheet Liabilities and amount due on leases through 1986 ($225,000 per year)

By William Dickenson:

"Quick" Assets--Cash plus Accounts Receivable (Gross)

Current Assets--"Quick" Assets plus Inventories, Unexpired Insurance, Other Prepaid Expenses, Cash Surrender Value of Life Insurance, and Investments

Current Liabilities--All Balance Sheet Liabilities

Net Working Capital--Current Assets less Current Liabilities

Total Debt--Total Notes Payable

Shareholders' Equity--Total Assets (Gross) less all Liabilities

---

Questions

1. What would do if you were Mr. Bowers?

2. How would you explain your decision?

* * * * *

Case 13-18: Bedford Manufacturing Company (C)

Using the actual 1982 and projected 1983 financial statements based on Bedford Manufacturing Company (A) (Case 6-17), calculate the following ratios for 1982 and 1983. (Use year-end balance sheet account amounts throughout.)

1. Return on assets.
2. Return on equity.
3. Gross margin percentage.
4. Return on sales.
5. Asset turnover.
6. Days' cash.
7. Days' receivables.
8. Days' inventories (finished goods only).
9. Inventory turnover (all inventories).
10. Current ratio.
11. Acid-test ratio.
12. Times interest earned.

Question

As an outside analyst, what questions would you want to ask Bedford's management, based on these ratios?

Chapter 14

Understanding Financial Statements

Key Terms

Auditors
Scope paragraph
Opinion paragraph
"Clean" opinion

Qualified opinion
Full disclosure
Form 10-K

Basic Concepts (Review)

Money measurement
Entity
Going concern
Cost
Dual aspect
Time period

Conservatism
Realization
Matching
Consistency
Materiality

Discussion Questions

1. How is the "scope" of an audit determined? What role should the auditors' fee play in setting the scope?

2. How can the auditors examine the financial statements and related records of a company without reconstructing every financial transaction of the period under examination?

3. In the auditors' opinion they state whether or not the financial statements are presented "fairly." What, if anything, does this opinion of "fairness" have to do with the accuracy of the statements?

4. If a company uses an accounting principle that is inconsistent with an FASB pronouncement, what must the auditors disclose?

5. There are two general types of qualified opinions. What are they and when are they used?

6. On March 15, 1983, Margaret Allen had completed her audit of the financial statements of one of her clients and had given a "clean" opinion for the year ended December 31, 1982. On March 25, 1983, Ms. Allen learned that the company had arranged a new loan that will change the company's debt/equity ratio from 1 to 1 to 3 to 1. What effect, if any, should this new information have on the opinion, the 1982 financial statements, or the notes to those financial statements?

7. What are the three basic accounting criteria? How do conflicts arise in satisfying the three criteria simultaneously, and what effect have these conflicts had on the"sensibility" and "rationality" of accounting concepts and principles?

8. What are some basic exceptions to the cost principle of accounting?

9. The Felton Company has decided that a change to the LIFO inventory method would match costs and revenues more closely and would result in substantial tax savings for the company. Are these reasons "sound" enough to justify a change in accounting method under the consistency principle?

10. The net property, plant and equipment of a company are shown on the books at $100,000. This figure represents historical cost of 10 to 15 years ago less accumulated depreciation. An independent appraiser has valued these assets at $250,000 based on current market prices. It seems reasonable to value these assets at a market price set by an independent, competent appraiser. What justification is there, then, for leaving these assets on the books at historical cost?

11. Financial accounting statements are limited to information that can be expressed in monetary terms. What are some factors that are vitally important in evaluating the health and prospects of a company which do not appear in these statements?

12. An account called "deferred income taxes" often appears on a company's balance sheet. The balance in this account is related to the difference between taxes based on the income statement prepared for shareholders using GAAP, and income taxes based on the tax return prepared for the IRS. What are some of the variations from GAAP used in preparing an income statement for tax purposes?

13. A company may prepare its financial statements in accordance with GAAP and still choose from various methods of reporting the same transactions. What are some basic alternatives within GAAP for accounting for inventories, depreciation, revenue on long-term contracts, and revenue on installment sales?

14. Many laypersons think of accounting as a science akin to mathematics. After some study of accounting principles, it becomes apparent that there is no universal agreement on one method for handling certain specific accounting transactions. Why don't accountants formulate specific rules and make accounting totally uniform?

15. With the great diversity of accounting practice, of what value is accounting?

16. What is the difference between "measurement" of income and "determination" of income? Which concept is used in accounting and why?

17. In a period of inflation, how can a company "break even" in an accounting sense and yet not "break even" in an economic sense? What does this indicate about dividend policy during a period of inflation?

18. In Exxon's 1973 income statement, the revenue amount included gasoline excise taxes. These are taxes collected from consumers by the company, and remitted to the government. Exxon also included these excise taxes as part of the tax expense reported on the income statement. Texaco did not include gasoline excise taxes as either revenue or expense in their 1973 income statement. Both companies received "clean" opinions from their auditors.

Which of the two treatments of excise taxes do you feel is more defensible? What effect will the different treatments have on the two companies' comparative gross margin percentages? What effect will the different treatments have on the companies' comparative return on sales percentages? Do you think that both treatments should be allowed under GAAP?

19. If a company acquires another company, APB Opinion No. 20 requires that the acquiring company restate financial data shown in the current annual report for previous years so as to include the acquired company. (See the example in the text under "Comparative Statements.") APB-20 also applies to financial summaries appearing in annual reports. These summaries show such selected data as revenues, net income, and earnings per share for the past five or ten years. Prior to APB-20, many companies did not restate financial summary data to include acquisitions on a retroactive basis; e.g., if Company A acquired Company X in 1968, the 1970 Company A annual report's ten-year financial summary would include Company X for the years 1968-1970, but not for 1961-1967. How might a person not familiar with accounting practices have been misled by these financial summaries prior to the issuance of APB-20?

20. The following excerpt is taken from a decision on a case argued before the Supreme Court of Rhode Island. The case involved whether or not an appraiser was correct in valuing a company's stock at book value per share. (See Chapter 9 if you have forgotten what book value per share is.)

"In some states, notably Delaware, the book value of stock is declared to be of little or no evidentiary value in appraising stock for the reason that book value is 'arbitrary' and not 'real.'

"This conclusion is difficult to understand and to adhere to. Officers and directors of corporations prepare books of account. In the absence of proof to the contrary it should be presumed that their accounts are true and accurate. Corporate officers are presumed to have acted in good faith."

Comment on the court's view of book value.

CASES

Case 14-21: Vandiver Equipment Sales, Inc.

Exhibits 1-3 are the 1982 financial statements for Vandiver Equipment Sales, Inc. Examine these statements before answering the questions below.

Questions

1. Was 1982 the first year of operations for Vandiver Equipment Sales? On what do you base your answer?

2. In the current assets section of the balance sheet, Accounts Receivable was reduced by $5,000 before it was added into total current assets. Why?

EXHIBIT 2

VANDIVER EQUIPMENT SALES, INC.
Income Statement
for the Year Ended December 31, 1982

Net Sales...................	$4,576,200
Cost of goods sold.........	3,814,400
Gross margin...............	761,800
Operating expenses:	
Salaries and commissions..	277,700
Advertising...............	18,000
Utilities and insurance...	30,000
Supplies used.............	3,300
Depreication.............	25,200
Bad debt expense..........	4,500
Other operating expenses..	92,500
Total operating expenses.............	451,200
Operating income............	310,600
Other revenue and expenses:	
Interest revenue..........	5,400
Gain on sale of of equipment............	2,000
Interest expense..........	(13,000)
Income before federal income tax...............	305,000
Provision for income txes...	120,700
Net Income.................	$ 184,300

EXHIBIT 1

VANDIVER EQUIPMENT SALES, INC.
Balance Sheet, December 31, 1982

Assets

Current Assets:	
Cash and certificates of deposit...................	$161,600
Accounts receivable........	129,000
Less: Allowance for doubtful accounts....	(5,000)
Net accounts receivable.....	124,000
Notes receivable...........	27,000
Interest receivable........	200
Merchandise inventory.......	334,000
Prepaid expenses...........	1,100
Total Current Assets.....	647,900
Property and Equipment:	
Land.......................	26,400
Building and equipment......	653,700
Less: Accumulated depreciation........	(358,000)
Net building and equipment..	295,700
Total Assets............	$970,000

Liabilities and shareholders' Equity

Current Liabilities:	
Accounts payable...........	$102,500
Taxes payable..............	29,000
Salaries payable...........	4,000
Interest payable...........	1,500
Dividends payable..........	30,000
Advances from customers.....	6,000
Total Current Liabilities	173,000
Other Liabilities:	
Mortgage Loan payable.......	120,000
Total Liabilities........	293,000
Shareholders' Equity:	
Capital stock (10,000 shares outstanding).......	500,000
Retained earnings..........	177,000
Total Liabilities and Shareholders' Equity.....	$970,000

EXHIBIT 3

VANDIVER EQUIPMENT ALES, INC.
Cash Flow Statement
for the Year Ended December 31, 1982

Sources of Cash
From operations:
Revenues....................$4,576,200
Increse in accounts
   receivable............... (19,150)
Increase in customer
   advances.................. 1,500
Cash generated from
   revenues................. 4,558,550
Cost of goods sold and
   operating expenses....... 4,265,600
Depreciation expense....... (25,200)
Increase in inventory...... 39,000
Increase in payables....... (16,500)
Cash disbursed for
   expenses................. 4,262,900
                           295,650
Cash from interest revenue
   and for interest expense. (7,800)
Net cash generated by
   operations............... 287,850
From other sources:
Proceeds from sale of
   equipment................ 29,000
Total sources of cash........ 316,850

Uses of Cash
Acquisition of new
   equipment................ 142,500
Cash dividends............. 95,000
Total uses of cash.......... 237,500
Net increase in cash........ 79,350
Beginning cash balance....... 82,250
Ending Cash Balance..........$ 161,600

---

3. Describe specific circumstances that could have resulted in the adjusting entry that gave rise to the Interest Receivable balance of $200 listed under curent assets.

4. Assume that the company uses the periodic inventory method in determining cost of goods sold. Merchanise Inventory is listed on the balance sheet at 334,000. How would this amount have been used in computing the Cost of Goods Sold amount shown on the income statement?

5. Mention at least two different items which might have been included in the $1,100 balance for Prepaid Expenses under current assets.

6. The three amounts below are included under the property and equipment classification on the balance sheet. In each case indicate the actual significance of the amount for the "informed" balance sheet reader.
  (a) $653,700
  (b) $358,000
  (c) $295,700

7. Why is the amount for land listed separately from the other property and equipment?

8. Under what circumstances could you expect that the accounts payable might be settled in full for less than $102,500?

9. Under current liabilities, Salaries Payable has a balance of $4,000. What relationship exists between this item on the balance sheet and the Salaries and Commissions expense listed on the income statement?

10. The $1,500 Interest Payable balance was not recorded on the books until the adjusting entries were made on 12/31/82. If the accountant had failed to make an adjusting entry recognizing this liability, how would the error have affected the shareholders' equity balance on the balance sheet?

11. Should the corporation's management be concerned about the fact that current liabilities total $173,000 while there is only $161,600 in cash and certificates of deposit available to pay them? Why?

12. One of the current liabilities is Advances from Customers listed at $6,000. How will the settlement of this liability differ from the settlement of the other current liabilities?

13. Two of the current liabilities listed are Interest Payable and Dividends Payable. How do the transactions giving rise to these accounts differ in their effects on the computation of net income and the shareholders' equity reported on the balance sheet?

14. Why is the mortgage loan payable classified separately from the other liabilities listed on the balance sheet?

15. Shareholders' Equity is divided into two balances on the balance sheet, Capital Stock and Retained Earnings. Briefly distinguish between these two accounts.

16. The first item on the income statement is Net Sales. What balances might have been deducted from gross sales to determine the net sales?

17. Was the amount listed under operating expenses for salaries and commissions, $277,700, all paid to the employees in 1982? Why?

18. Mention at least two expenses shown

18. Mention at least two expenses shown on the income statement which did not require a cash outlay or the incurrence of a liability in 1982.

19. Describe a specific transaction which could have resulted in the Gain on Sale of Equipment shown under other revenue and expenses.

20. When closing out the various revenue and expense accounts at the end of the accounting period, the amount of the net income for the period is eventually entered in the Retained Earnings account and thus included in Retained Earnings on the end-of-the-period balance sheet. Give a reason why the Retained Earnings balance on the 12/31/82 balance sheet is less than the net income for 1982.

21. What is the significance of the (25,200) shown for depreciation on the cash flow statement? Why are increases or decreases in some current balance sheet accounts shown in the "from operations" portion of the cash flow statement?

22. What was the amount of dividends declared by Vandiver in 1982?

23. Assume that you are the loan officer in a bank where Vandiver Equipment Sales, Inc. has applied for a $500,000 loan to be used for expanding the business and opening salesrooms in some new locations. The loan will be repaid in five annual installments of $100,000. Mention at lest three factors based on the financial statements which might influence you to recommend approval of the loan.

24. Assuming the same conditions as in Question 23 above, list at least three additional significant items you might want to know about before acting on the loan application. (List items which are not apparent from the three statements.)

25. Do you think the management of the corporation has effectively employed the available assets for the benefit of the shareholders during the year 1982? Why?

26. In addition to the corporation's management, what other parties might be interested in examining these financial statements? Mention at least three.

27. Why are parties outside of the business willing to rely more on a corporation's financial statements if they have been audited and certified by a reputable public accounting firm, even though they know the corporation's own accounting department is probably competent?

28. One of the shareholders of a large business corporation was heard saying the following: "As a shareholder, I have a right to more dividends. You have millions stashed away in Retained Earnings. It's about time that you let the true owners get their hands on that pot of gold." Comment on this quote.

29. Explain the computation of Cost of Goods Sold under the two different inventory methods, perpetual and periodic.

30. The costs of buildings and equipment are capitalized in asset accounts at the time of acquistion, although these costs constitute an expense of doing business. Explain what is included in the "cost" of an item of of buildings and equipment, and describe a method for channeling this amount into operating expense.

31. There is only one point in the history of a business enterprise when the true net earnings of the business can be determined. Yet, common practice demands that net income be computed at least annually. Discuss these seemingly conflicting statements.

* * * * *

Case 14-22: Wilkinson & Gould

"Don't tell me we lost money last year. We cut our draws and fired two draftspersons to save wages. I have never worked so hard, so many hours, in my entire life. I tell you I'm exhausted! How can you lose money when you don't even count the draws? I want a new accountant!"

The outburst came from Gerald Wilkinson, architect and senior partner of Wilkinson & Gould, Architects. The firm specialized in commercial and industrial developments. Many of its jobs lasted from two to three years, although some were of shorter duration. The work typically involved several phases on a single contract, and included design engineering, preparation of specifications, letting and supervision of contracts, and approval and monitoring of all subcontracts. In general, Wilkinson & Gould represented the client, who might be a bank or financial group, in all dealings with the construction contractors.

On December 31, 1978, Howard James left the partnership to work for a major land developer. At the time he left, each senior partner's equity was about $80,000, and James was paid this amount in cash. This payment, plus an imbalance between cash receipts and cash disbursements, gradually had pushed bank loans up to their present $143,000. As a result, the bank had insisted on audited financial statements, something the firm did not previously have. The outburst in the opening paragraph was Wilkinson telling off Charles Lawton, the auditor agreed on by both parties.

Lawton tried to smooth over the outburst: "This is only a trial balance (Exhibit 1) taken from your bookkeeper's ledger. I know there are some expenses not recorded because she doesn't enter the bills until you write the checks. My audit assistant is going through the supplier statements now trying to locate your accounts payable, and we found a whole drawer full of unpaid bills. (These later showed up in Exhibit 2A.) The thing I really can't understand is how your revenues could be less than a quarter of last year's, if you have really been that busy. For example, there is absolutely nothing for the past three months."

"That's because," answered Wilkinson, "we have been so busy we haven't booked any new business. Heaven knows it is out there. Do you mean to say we have to write new contracts and let people stand in line so we can have the sale on our books to make you happy?"

"No," said Lawton, "I don't mean that at all. What does signing a contract have to do with revenue? You earn revenue by doing the jobs, not by signing a contract."

"Well that's not the way Howard (James) did it. He recorded the sales as we made them, and it made sense. That way we had big accounts receivable and the bank never bothered us. Howard was the businessman among us, and he

EXHIBIT 1

Trial Balance
At December 31, 1979

	dr.	cr.
Cash....................	897	
Accounts receivable....	187,223	
Equipment..............	16,940	
Automobiles............	18,000	
Bank loan*.............		143,000
Accum. deprec., equipment...........		8,210
Accum. deprec., automobiles..........		6,000
G. Wilkinson...........		80,120
A. Gould...............		60,090
G. Wilkinson--drawing..	16,000	
A. Gould--drawing......	12,000	
Sales--architectural...		53,000
Sales--automobile to H. James.............		2,500
Salaries --draftspersons......	31,800	
--secretary/ bookkeeper.........	7,200	
Engineering consulting fees......	22,000	
Fringe benefits........	8,120	
Rent, office...........	7,500	
Supplies...............	1,763	
Travel and entertainment........	5,124	
Interest...............	12,125	
Miscellaneous..........	6,228	
	352,920	352,920

*Interest on the outstanding balance of the bank loan at one percent per month was automatically deducted by the bank from Wilkinson & Gould's checking account on the 15th day of the following month.

made all the big sales, too. I have always been on the product side."

Lawton was aghast. "That is just ridiculous! You anticipate all revenues? You don't even match expenses? Is that what those revenues this year are? New orders?"

"Of course they are new contracts, or additions to current contracts. I tell you we couldn't handle more! Howard really did a fantastic job of booking us solid before he moved on. I think maybe he could have got more money for some of them -- but that's another story."

"And every contract was taken into revenue before he left?"

- 152 -

"Sure, sales, that's revenue isn't it? Yes, we had more sales that last three months than in the entire previous year."

"And those sales, did they increase your equity accounts?"

"You bet they did! Why it cost us $80,120 to buy Howard out, but my account was $ 80,120 too!"

"And Howard took his $80,120 out in cash?"

EXHIBIT 2
ANALYSIS OF SUPPLIER INVOICES

A. Goods and services received by Wilkinson & Gould in 1979 which were not entered in the accounts, or paid, before January 1, 1980.

Salaries--draftspersons.....$	440
--secretary........	100
Engineering consulting fees.	3,900
Fringe benefits.............	620
Rent.......................	500
Supplies...................	225
Travel and entertainment....	4,193
Miscellaneous...............	1,002
Blueprint machine...........	4,280
Total..................	$15,260

B. Goods and services received by Wilkinson, James & Gould in 1978 which were entered in the accounts only when paid in 1979.

Salaries--draftspersons.....$	723
--secretary........	100
Engineering consulting fees.	12,400
Fringe benefits.............	1,832
Rent.......................	2,000
Supplies...................	165
Travel and entertainment....	3,290
Miscellaneous...............	920
Total..................	$21,430

"Yes, that was part of our partnership agreement. The bank came through with a loan on the receivables."

"And Howard kept all the records?"

"Yes, he always took care of the business end. Look, nothing could be wrong. The income tax people never questioned our statements."

"Yes," sighed Lawton, "but their job is to collect taxes, and this place must have been a bonanza. I have to talk to the bank. This situation is beyond belief.

"You hit it there," said Wilkinson. I really had to borrow a lot of money to pay mine. I had to put a mortgage on my house."

Later, Lawton came back to Wilkinson & Gould to look at some results of his audit assistant's work. "Have you ever heard of percentage completion?" he asked Wilkinson.

"No, never."

"Well it goes like this. There is no revenue earned when the contract is signed, but it is earned by doing the work. If you have finished, say, 25 percent of a job by December 31, you could record 25 percent of the contract price as earned. It is backward to normal matching, because we take the expenses as they happen and match the revenues instead."

"I don't get you completely, but if I'm on the same wavelength, that means we have earned money this year because we have a lot of completion," said Wilkinson hopefully.

"That's right, except you took it all into revenue in 1978, so you have negative revenue from your incomplete jobs in 1979."

EXHIBIT 3
ANALYSIS OF CONTRACTS WORKED ON IN 1979

		Hours			
	Contract Signed	Prior to 1979	1979	To Complete	Contract Price
Altman Plaza...............	1977	1,225	1,750	0	$ 42,500
Barington Bros.............	(Note)	0	4,520	500	87,000
Conforstate Ltd...........	1978	1,230	1,165	1,000	52,000
Delmar Ltd................	1978	3,932	623	0	63,500
Edston Prop...............	1979	0	784	2,400	43,000
		6,387	8,842	3,900	$288,000

Note: Barrington Bros. original contract for $77,000 signed in 1978; 1979 addition for $10,000.

EXHIBIT 4

Balance Sheet at December 31, 1978

Assets

Cash..		$ 1,423
Accounts receivable......................		215,902
Equipment*...............................$16,940		
Less accumulated depreciation........ 8,210		8,730
Automobiles**............................ 18,000		
Less accumulated depreciation........ 6,000		12,000
Total Assets......................		$238,055

Liabilities

Bank loan...............................		$ 17,725

Equities

	G. Wilkinson	H. James	A. Gould	Total
Opening Balance..............	$ 10,920	$ 10,920	$ 8,190	$ 30,030
Add 1978 income..............	93,200	93,200	69,900	256,300
	104,120	104,120	78,090	286,330
Less 1978 draws.............	24,000	24,000	28,000	66,000
	$ 80,120	$80,120	$60,090	$220,330

Total Liabilities and Equities..$238,055

---

*Equipment is depreciated on a 20 percent declining balance.

**Three identical Pontiacs -- to be depreciated straight-line over 4 years with a $2,000 per car salvage value.

"How can I have negative revenue?" revenue?"

"Well, it's not easy. Last year (1978), for example, you took $87,000 into revenue on the Barrington Brothers contract (Exhibit 3). Your firm spent 4,520 hours on that job this past year according to your time cards. How close to finished is it?"

It took a long time for Wilkinson to answer, and he was doing a lot of mental arithmetic. "Most of the detail is over. It should wind up in about three to six months."

"How many labor hours?"

After another thoughtful pause, Wilkinson supposed there might be another 500 hours to finish the job.

"OK, then." Lawton punched some numbers on a pocket calculator. "You are about 90 percent complete, so you have earned about $78,000 out of the $87,000 revenue you booked in 1978.

You have $9,000 left to earn, so I have to subtract $9,000 from this year's revenue, for that job."

"But there aren't even any revenues for 1979 on that job!"

"I know. The trouble is you started the year on the wrong foot, accountingwise. The bank has instructed me to recast both your 1978 and 1979 year-ends, so we can get a reasonable view of how well you did in 1979. I have had my assistant compiling all the hours worked on all the jobs that were open in 1979, so we can do that. Now all I need is your estimates of how many hours each job will take to complete. (The eventual estimates appear in Exhibit 3.) By the way, Howard James also booked expenses only when they were paid, and he didn't pay many the last few months he was here. This list (Exhibit 2B) is 1978 expenses paid in 1979. Another thing, you haven't been progress billing these jobs very well. There is a lot of cash tied up there.

- 154 -

"Now I want you to come with me and talk to your former partner. The bank feels there might be legal grounds for recovery of most of the $80,000 you paid him at dissolution and I have been instructed by them to pursue it."

In the interview, James had answers to all Lawton's questions. For example, when asked about how he recorded revenue, he said: "We always did it that way. Gerry wouldn't be in any trouble if he had kept on selling. Then he would have had revenue. After all, the real trick in this business is getting the contracts. Anyone can grind out the work. My method shows this clearly."

When asked about expenses, his answer was the same. "We always did it that way. One year balances out another and cash accounting is OK with the tax people. Besides it lets us get our income where it has to be for the bank."

Finally, when asked if he would reopen the dissolution agreement, James said: "No dice. A deal is a deal. Both Gerry and Abe (Abner Gould) signed the deal and both signed the balance sheets (Exhibit 4). Are you calling me a crook?"

Gould shared in the partnership income at 75 percent of the senior partner's shares. All income was allocated to the partners' equity accounts in the income sharing ratio.

Questions

1. Recast the December 31, 1978 balance sheet and equity accounts to agree with generally accepted accounting principles.

2. Prepare proper financial statements for the year ended December 31, 1979.

* * * * *

Case 14-23: Johnson Company

Johnson Company was incorporated on August 21, 1983, and began operations on September 1, 1983. The company's books consisted of a two-column general ledger, two special journals (the Sales Register and the Cash Receipts Register), and a general ledger. Accompanying this case is the general ledger posted to and including Tuesday, September 27, 1983, except for cash receipts, sales, and discounts on sales. These items will be posted to the general ledger at the end of the month in total form along with the September 28-29 transactions. All transactions for September 1-27 have been journalized, although the general journal is not reproduced here. The transactions for the remainder of September 1983 are listed on the following pages.

Required:

1. Prepare journal entries to record the transactions for September 28 and 29. Round off to the nearest whole dollar in all computations. The last entry in the general journal on September 8 was made on page 5, and the subsequent entries should start on page 6.

2. Post all entries to the ledger accounts. Note that there are two ledgers: a General Ledger and an Accounts Receivable Ledger (called a subsidiary ledger). The Accounts Receivable account in the General Ledger is called a control account. The balance of this account represents the total amount due from customers. It is necessary, also, to know how much is due from each customer. This is the purpose of the subsidiary ledger.

The columns in the Cash Receipts Register and the Sales Register for accounts receivable are posted to the General Ledger in total only. (This rule also applies to the other columns -- Sales, Discount on Sales, Freight-Out, and Cash.) Each individual entry in the accounts receivable column, however, is also posted to the subsidiary ledger. Any time an entry is made in the General Ledger that affects accounts receivable (e.g., a sales return), the entry must be posted to both the General Ledger -- Control Account and the Specific Accounts Receivable Ledger account affected.

Note also that Cash Sales are recorded in both the Cash Receipts Register and the Sales Register. This will result in a set of two entries. For example, a cash sale of $100 would be recorded thus:

Cash Receipts Register:

```
Cash..................100
      Cash Sales........      100
```

Sales Register:

```
Cash Sales...........100
      Sales.............      100
```

The net result, when posted to the General Ledger will be:

```
Cash..................100
      Sales.............      100
```

When used in this fashion, the Cash Sales account is called a clearing account.

3. Prepare a trial balance as of September 30, 1983, before adjustments are made.

4. Prepare journal entries recording the adjusting data.

5. Post the adjusting entries to the ledger.

6. Prepare closing entries and post them to the ledger. Close and rule the ledger.

7. Prepare a balance sheet as of September 30 and an income statement for the month of September 1983.

8. (If this case is not assigned prior to your studying Chapter 10): Prepare either a cash flow statement, a working capital statement, or both (as your instructor directs) for the month of September 1983.

Transactions for September 28, 1983

(1) A check for $9,765 was received from Benton Furniture Company, the 2 percent sales discount having been taken.

(2) The payroll of $986 for the week ended September 24 was paid, less employees' share of FICA taxes of $66, withholding taxes of $147, and withholding of $25 for Blue Cross. The company set up the accrued liability of $66 for its share of FICA taxes.

(3) Merchandise costing $37,000 was purchased from the Bendel Corporation, on terms 2/

10, n/30 (2 percent discount if paid within 10 days; net amount due within 30 days).

(4) The Himber Company returned some defective merchandise, which had been sold to them on September 21 for $1,040. Since the Himber Company had taken a 2 percent discount when it paid the invoide on September 27, only $1,019 was alllowed as a credit.

(5) Cash sales were $1,860.

(6) T. S. Jones paid his account in full, less $44 for freight paid by him on goods shipped f.o.b. destination.

(7) A telephone bill for $95 was received.

(8) A sale of $7,300 was made to James Pickney on terms 2/10, n/30.

(9) Purchase of September 21 from the Bendel Corporation for $21,933 on terms 2/10, n/30 were paid in full, the discount being taken.

Transactions for September 29, 1983

(1) Defective merchandise purchased from the Bendel Corporation on September 21 for $836 and paid in full on September 28, less 2 percent cash discount, was returned for full credit of $819 (i.e., 98 percent of the invoice amount).

(2) A cash settlement was made with the Himber Company for the faulty merchandise returned on September 28.

(3) Cash sales were $975.

(4) A sale on account for $7,910, terms 2/10, n/30, was made to the Freemont Company.

(5) The telephone bill received September 28 was paid in full.

(6) Supplies costing $328 were purchased for cash.

(7) An advance of $125 was made to one of the salespersons for travel expenses.

(8) An officer of the corporation was reimbursed $366 for travel expenses for which he had received no advance.

(9) James Pickney returned for full credit some merchandise purchased by him for $1,720 on September 27, and he paid the balance of his account, taking the 2 percent discount.

(10) Merchandise with a list

price of $1,230 less a 20 percent trade discount was sold to T. S. Jones on terms of 2/10, n/30.

(11) A sale on account was made to R. B. Brown for $19,248, terms 2/10, n/30.

(12) A delivery truck was purchased for $12,000 cash.

(13) Merchandise costing $16,400 was purchased from the Burton Manufacturing Company on account, 2/10, n/30.

(14) A repair bill for $256 for roof repairs on the building was received from the Hart Roofing Company.

(15) Merchandise purchased from the Bendel Corporation on September 28 for $680 was returned for full credit.

(16) Purchases of $12,400 on terms 2/10, n/30 on September 22 from the Burton Manufacturing Company were paid in full.

Information for Adjusting Entries

1. A physical inventory taken on September 30 disclosed the following facts:

Merchandise inventory
    on hand...............$238,506
Supplies on hand........   2,540

2. Allowance for bad debs, 1 1/2 percent of sales, net of returns and discounts.

3. The building is being depreciated over a 50-year period on a straight-line basis.

4. Equipment is being depreciated at 10 percent per annum. No September depreciation expense will be taken on equipment purchased after September 15.

5. Wages accrued but not paid, $179. Withholding taxes on these wages were $27, and accrued FICA taxes were $12 for employees' share and $12 for employer's share.

6. Sales force commissions earned but not paid, $10,240.

7. The directors agreed that the organization expense should be written off in equal monthly installments over the first 20 months of business.

8. Prepaid insurance represented the premium paid on a three-year policy on September 1, 1983.

9. The company's bonds had an interest rate of 12 percent.

SALES REGISTER

DATE 1983		ACCOUNT DEBITED	TERMS	LF	DEBITS ACCOUNTS RECEIVABLE	DEBITS CASH	CREDIT SALES
Sept	6	D. W. Barstow	2/10, n/30	1	2,060		2,060
	7	T. S. Jones	2/10, n/30	2	5,520		5,520
	8	James Pickney	2/10, n/30	2	16,530		16,530
	10	Finney + Company	2/10, n/30	1	12,548		12,548
	17	Freedont Company	2/10, n/30	1	21,262		21,262
	19	D. W. Barstow	2/10, n/30	1	7,450		7,450
	21	Benton Furniture Company	2/10, n/30	1	9,964		9,964
	21	Hinder + Company	2/10, n/30	2	21,182		21,182
	24	Finney + Company	2/10, n/30	1	15,800		15,800
	26	Wagner Company	2/10, n/30	2	18,574		18,574
	27	James Pickney	2/10, n/30	2	14,540		14,540
	27	Cash	Cash Sales 1-27	✓		32,414	32,414

CASH RECEIPTS REGISTER

DATE 1983	ACCOUNT CREDITED	EXPLANATION	LF	CREDITS			DEBITS		
				ACCOUNTS RECEIVABLE	SALES	DISCOUNT ON SALES	FREIGHT OUT		CASH
Sept 19	James Pickney	Payment of invoice	2	16,530		331			16,199
20	D. W. Barstow	"	1	2,060					2,060
22	Finney & Company	"	1	12,548		251			12,297
26	Freemont Company	"	1	20,332		407			19,945
26	O. W. Barstow	"	1	7,450		149			7,301
27	Hinder & Company	"	2	21,182		424			20,758
27	Sales	Cash sales 1-27	✓		32,414				32,414

General Ledger

Cash   Page 1

DATE	EXPLANATION	F.	DEBIT	DATE	EXPLANATION	F.	CREDIT
1983 Sept 1	Balance		29 1 6 0 0	1983 Total	thru Sept 27		9 2 0 2 0

Accounts Receivable

DATE	EXPLANATION	F.	DEBIT	DATE	EXPLANATION	F.	CREDIT
				1983 Sept 17	Sales Ret.+All 3		9 3 0

Allowance for Doubtful Accounts

DATE	EXPLANATION	F.	DEBIT	DATE	EXPLANATION	F.	CREDIT

Merchandise Inventory

DATE	EXPLANATION	F.	DEBIT	DATE	EXPLANATION	F.	CREDIT
1983 Sept 1	Balance	✓	20 2 4 2 0				

Supplies Inventory

DATE	EXPLANATION	F.	DEBIT	DATE	EXPLANATION	F.	CREDIT
1983 Sept 1	Balance	✓	5 3 0 0				
7	Cash	1	1 1 4				

Advances to Salesforce

DATE	EXPLANATION	F.	DEBIT	DATE	EXPLANATION	F.	CREDIT
1983 Sept 17	Cash - J. Smith 2		1 0 0				

Land

DATE	EXPLANATION	F.	DEBIT	DATE	EXPLANATION	F.	CREDIT
1983 Sept 1	Balance	✓	7 0 0 0 0				

Building

DATE	EXPLANATION	F.	DEBIT	DATE	EXPLANATION	F.	CREDIT
1983 Sept 1	Balance	✓	59 4 0 0				

Accumulated Depreciation on Building — Page 3

DATE	EXPLANATION	F.	DEBIT	DATE	EXPLANATION	F.	CREDIT

Equipment

DATE	EXPLANATION	F.	DEBIT	DATE	EXPLANATION	F.	CREDIT
1983 Sept 1	Balance	✓	5 7 5 0 0				
3	Cash	1	1 9 4 0				
4	Accts Payable	1	9 6 2				

Accumulated Depreciation on Equipment

DATE	EXPLANATION	F.	DEBIT	DATE	EXPLANATION	F.	CREDIT

Prepaid Insurance

DATE	EXPLANATION	F.	DEBIT	DATE	EXPLANATION	F.	CREDIT
1983 Sept 1	Balance	✓	2 5 2 0 0				

Organization Costs

DATE	EXPLANATION	F.	DEBIT	DATE	EXPLANATION	F.	CREDIT
1983 Sept 1	Balance	✓	6 4 0 0				

Accounts Payable

DATE		EXPLANATION	F.	DEBIT	DATE		EXPLANATION	F.	CREDIT
1983					1983				
Sept	7	Cash	1	5 2 4 2 0	Sept	1	Balance	✓	5 2 4 2 0
	17	Cash	3	9 6 2		5	Equipment	1	9 6 2
	21	Sundries	3	1 1 5 6 0		7	Blue Cross	2	2 5
	24	Cash	4	8 4 8		10	Purchases	2	1 1 5 6 0
	24	Pur. Ret. & Allow	4	5 9 2		12	Purchases	2	2 8 4 8 0
	26	Sundries	5	2 1 3 5 2		14	Blue Cross	2	2 5
						21	Electricity Expense	3	5 9 2
						21	Telephone Expense	3	2 5 6
						21	Blue Cross	4	2 5
						21	Purchases	4	2 1 9 4 4
						21	Purchases	4	1 2 4 0 0
						26	Purchases	5	3 5 7 1 2
						27	Purchases	5	3 9 5 0 0

Accrued Wages

DATE	EXPLANATION	F.	DEBIT	DATE	EXPLANATION	F.	CREDIT

Accrued F I C A Taxes

DATE		EXPLANATION	F.	DEBIT	DATE		EXPLANATION	F.	CREDIT
					1983				
					Sept	7	Sundries	2	6 6
						7	Soc. Sec. Tax Exp.	2	6 6
						14	Sundry	2	6 6
						14	Soc. Sec. Tax Exp.	2	6 6
						21	Sundry	4	6 6
						21	Soc. Sec. Tax Exp.	4	6 6

DATE	EXPLANATION	F.	DEBIT	DATE		EXPLANATION	F.	CREDIT
				Sept 1983 7		Sundry	2	1 47
				14		Sundry	2	1 47
				21		Sundry	4	1 47

Accrued Salesforce Commissions

DATE	EXPLANATION	F.	DEBIT	DATE	EXPLANATION	F.	CREDIT

Interest Payable Accrued

DATE	EXPLANATION	F.	DEBIT	DATE	EXPLANATION	F.	CREDIT

Mortgage Bonds Payable

DATE	EXPLANATION	F.	DEBIT	DATE		EXPLANATION	F.	CREDIT
				Sept 1983 1		Balance	✓	40 00 00

Capital Stock

DATE	EXPLANATION	F.	DEBIT	DATE		EXPLANATION	F.	CREDIT
				Sept 1983 1		Balance	✓	80 00 00

General Ledger
Retained Earnings

DATE	EXPLANATION	F.	DEBIT	DATE	EXPLANATION	F.	CREDIT

Sales

DATE	EXPLANATION	F.	DEBIT	DATE	EXPLANATION	F.	CREDIT

Sales Returns and Allowances

DATE	EXPLANATION	F.	DEBIT	DATE	EXPLANATION	F.	CREDIT
1983 Sept 19	A. R. Freemont Co	3	9 30				

Sales Discounts

DATE	EXPLANATION	F.	DEBIT	DATE	EXPLANATION	F.	CREDIT

Purchases

DATE		EXPLANATION	F.	DEBIT	DATE	EXPLANATION	F.	CREDIT
1983 Sept	10	Accts Payable	2	1 1 5 6 0				
	11	Accts Payable	2	2 8 4 8 0				
	21	Accts Payable	4	2 1 9 4 4				
	21	Accts Payable	4	1 2 4 0 0				
	26	Accts Payable	5	3 5 7 1 2				
	27	Accts Payable	5	3 9 5 0 0				

Purchase Returns and Allowances

DATE	EXPLANATION	F.	DEBIT	DATE		EXPLANATION	F.	CREDIT
				1983 Sept	24	Accts Payable	4	5 9 2

Purchase Discounts · Page 8

DATE	EXPLANATION	F.	DEBIT	DATE	EXPLANATION	F.	CREDIT
				1983 Sept 22	Accts Payable	3	2 3 1
				26	Accts Payable	5	4 2 7

Wages

DATE	EXPLANATION	F.	DEBIT	DATE	EXPLANATION	F.	CREDIT
1983 Sept 7	Sundry	2	9 8 6				
14	Sundry	2	9 8 6				
21	Sundry	4	9 8 6				

Social Security Tax Expense

DATE	EXPLANATION	F.	DEBIT	DATE	EXPLANATION	F.	CREDIT
1983 Sept 7	Sundry	2	6 6				
14	Sundry	2	6 6				
21	Sundry	4	6 6				

Repairs

DATE	EXPLANATION	F.	DEBIT	DATE	EXPLANATION	F.	CREDIT
1983 Sept 12	Cash	2	3 5 6				
26	Cash	5	5 8 0				

Supplies Expense

DATE	EXPLANATION	F.	DEBIT	DATE	EXPLANATION	F.	CREDIT

Salesforce Commissions

DATE	EXPLANATION	F.	DEBIT	DATE	EXPLANATION	F.	CREDIT

Travel Expense

DATE	EXPLANATION	F.	DEBIT	DATE	EXPLANATION	F.	CREDIT
1983 Sept 24	Cash	4	2 0 2				

Telephone and Telegraph Expense

DATE	EXPLANATION	F.	DEBIT	DATE	EXPLANATION	F.	CREDIT
1983 Sept 21	Accts Payable	3	2 5 6				

Depreciation Expense

DATE	EXPLANATION	F.	DEBIT	DATE	EXPLANATION	F.	CREDIT

Insurance Expense

DATE	EXPLANATION	F.	DEBIT	DATE	EXPLANATION	F.	CREDIT

Electricity Expense

DATE	EXPLANATION	F.	DEBIT	DATE	EXPLANATION	F	CREDIT
1983 Sept 21	Accts Payable	3	5 9 2				

Bad Debt Expense

DATE	EXPLANATION	F.	DEBIT	DATE	EXPLANATION	F.	CREDIT

Interest Expense

DATE	EXPLANATION	F.	DEBIT	DATE	EXPLANATION	F.	CREDIT

Freight-Out

DATE	EXPLANATION	F.	DEBIT	DATE	EXPLANATION	F.	CREDIT

General Ledger
Organization Cost Amortization

DATE	EXPLANATION	F.	DEBIT	DATE	EXPLANATION	F.	CREDIT

Cost of Goods Sold

DATE	EXPLANATION	F.	DEBIT	DATE	EXPLANATION	F.	CREDIT

Cash Sales

DATE	EXPLANATION	F.	DEBIT	DATE	EXPLANATION	F.	CREDIT

DATE	EXPLANATION	F.	DEBIT	DATE	EXPLANATION	F.	CREDIT

D. W. Barstow   Page 1

DATE	EXPLANATION	F.	DEBIT	DATE	EXPLANATION	F.	CREDIT
1983 Sept 6	Sales.	S.R.1	20 60	1983 Sept 20	Cash	CR1	20 60
19	Sales	SR1	74 50	26	Sundries	CR1	74 50

Benton Furniture Company

DATE	EXPLANATION	F.	DEBIT	DATE	EXPLANATION	F	CREDIT
1983 Sept 21	Sales	SR1	99 64				

R. B. Brown

DATE	EXPLANATION	F.	DEBIT	DATE	EXPLANATION	F.	CREDIT

Finney & Co.

DATE	EXPLANATION	F.	DEBIT	DATE	EXPLANATION	F.	CREDIT
1983 Sept 10	Sales	SR1	1 25 48	1983 Sept 22	Sundries	CR1	1 25 48
24	Sales	SR1	1 58 00				

Freemont Company

DATE	EXPLANATION	F.	DEBIT	DATE	EXPLANATION	F.	CREDIT
1983 Sept 17	Sales	SR1	2 12 62	1983 Sept 19	Sales Ret. & Allow	3	9 30
				26	Sundries	CR1	2 03 32

Himber & Co.

DATE	EXPLANATION	F.	DEBIT	DATE	EXPLANATION	F.	CREDIT
1983 Sept 21	Sales	SR1	2 1 1 8 2	1983 Sept 26	Sundries	CR1	2 1 1 8 2

T. S. Jones

DATE	EXPLANATION	F.	DEBIT	DATE	EXPLANATION	F.	CREDIT
1983 Sept 7	Sales	SR1	5 5 2 0				

James Pickney

DATE	EXPLANATION	F.	DEBIT	DATE	EXPLANATION	F.	CREDIT
1983 Sept 8	Sales	SR1	1 6 5 3 0	1983 Sept 19	Sundries	CR1	1 6 5 3 0
27	Sales	SR1	1 4 5 4 0				

Wagner Co.

DATE	EXPLANATION	F.	DEBIT	DATE	EXPLANATION	F.	CREDIT
1983 Sept 26	Sales	SR1	1 8 5 7 4				

DATE	ACCOUNT TITLES AND EXPLANATION	FO-LIO	DEBIT	CREDIT

DATE	ACCOUNT TITLES AND EXPLANATION	FO-LIO	DEBIT	CREDIT

DATE	ACCOUNT TITLES AND EXPLANATION	FO-LIO	DEBIT	CREDIT

DATE	ACCOUNT TITLES AND EXPLANATION	FO-LIO	DEBIT	CREDIT

Chapter 15

Basic Management Accounting Concepts

Key Terms

Management accounting
Information
Operating information
Full cost accounting

Differential accounting
Responsibility center
Responsibility accounting

Discussion Questions

1. What is the difference between numbers and information?

2. Does a newspaper contain information? Is it management information?

3. What is the relationship between management accounting information and operating information?

4. For what uses is full cost accounting especially valuable?

5. For what uses is differential accounting especially valuable?

6. For what uses is responsibility accounting especially valuable?

7. Contrast management accounting with financial accounting.

8. Why is there less need for precision of information in management accounting than in financial accounting?

9. Explain the statement, "Accounting evidence is only partial evidence."

10. Why do generally accepted accounting principles affect management accounting even though there is no requirement that management accounting adhere to such principles?

11. What is the basic, pragmatic question in management accounting?

12. Contrast the contributions of management accounting's two source disciplines: economics and social psychology.

Problems

15-1. Below is a list of selected management positions in Baker Corporation and a list of various ledger accounts.

Required: Choose the accounts which reflect the area for which each member of management would be responsible.

Mnagement Position	Accounts
Treasurer	Cash
Controller	Salaries and Wages--Accounting
Credit manager	Salaries and Wages--Sales Force
Marketing manager	Equipment--Delivery
Purchasing manager	Equipment--Bookkeeping Machines
Production manager	Depreciation--Receiving Department Equipment
	Inventory--Finished Goods
	Inventory--Raw Materials
	Machinery and Equipment--Factory
	Salaries and Wages--Factory
	Accounts Receivable

15-2. Following is a management accounting report for the Morgan Ford Company. You are asked to contrast this report with a financial accounting report, according to the list of differences given in the text.

MORGAN FORD COMPANY
Service Department Report
September

	Planned	Actual	Difference*
Number of jobs completed..............	200	183	(17)
Number of employee days...............	370	368	2
Expenses:			
Employees wages.....................	$11,000	$11,386	$ (386)
Parts used..........................	8,000	6,287	1,713
Supplies used.......................	2,500	2,412	88
Other expenses......................	3,000	3,312	(312)
Total Expenses..................	24,500	23,397	1,103
Revenue................................	30,000	27,234	(2,766)
Profit..........................	$ 5,500	$ 3,837	$(1,663)

*( ) means unfavorable.

15-3. The purpose of some management accounting is "attention directing." What questions can be raised about the performance of the service department from the information given in the report shown in Problem 15-2?

15-4. As controller of American Steel, you have been asked to provide information to management that would be helpful in answering a variety of questions.

Required:

a. For each of the questions below, classify the needed information as being an example of either full cost accounting, differential accouting, or responsibility accounting.

1. Should the company own and operate its own iron ore mines or buy the ore from another firm?
2. As a result of a new labor contract with the United Steel Workers Union, what will be the profit margin on a ton of steel at current prices?
3. Is the supervisor of the maintenance shop doing a good job?
4. How much money does the company have invested in finished goods inventory?
5. Should the company consider replacing its old open-hearth furnaces with new ones?
6. Which district sales manager is doing the best job?

b. In addition to management accounting information, what other types of information might be useful in attempting to answer each of the questions above?

15-5. As controller of the city of Maple Heights, you have been asked to provide information to the mayor and city council which would be helpful in answering a variety of questions.

Required:

    a. For each of the questions below, classify the needed information as an example of either full cost accounting, differential accounting, or responsibility accounting.

        1. As a result of a recent wage increase for airport workers, what does it now cost to operate the municipal airport?
        2. Should the city continue to own and operate its own garbage trucks or contract with a private firm?
        3. What does it cost to prepare and mail annual tax notices to property owners?
        4. Is the new police chief doing a better job than the former one?
        5. Should the city close its jail and contract with the county for detention of prisoners?
        6. Which department head is doing the best job of staying within his or her budget?

    b. In addition to management accounting information, what other types of information might be useful in attempting to answer each of the questions above?

15-6. Following is a monthly report for a new branch office which the Second National Bank recently opened in a rapidly developing section of the city.

SECOND NATIONAL BANK
Westside Branch Office Report
July 1

	Planned	Actual	Difference*
Number of new accounts opened...............	150	120	(30)
Number of prospect calls made...............	75	56	(19)
Increase in deposit volume...................	$100,000	$80,000	$(20,000)
Increase in loan volume.....................	80,000	90,000	10,000
Expenses:			
Wages and salaries........................	$ 6,000	$ 4,800	$ 1,200
Utilities.................................	450	420	30
Rent on building..........................	675	675	0
Supplies.................................	225	230	(5)
Advertising...............................	300	225	75
Other expenses...........................	75	76	(1)
Total expenses.......................	7,725	6,426	1,299
Revenue from interest and service charges...	7,500	7,000	(500)
Profit (loss)................................	$ (225)	$ 574	$ 799

*( ) = unfavorable.

The branch manager is pleased that the report shows a $574 profit instead of the expected loss of $225.

Required: What questions can be raised about the performance of the Westside Branch and its manager based on information in the report?

CASES

Case 15-7: Bates Boat Yard

Upon returning to civilian life after several years in the Navy, Sarah Bates sought a small business that she might buy. Being a thrifty person with no dependents, she had built up a fair amount of capital, the accumulation of which had been aided by the fact that she had seen considerable duty in areas where there had been nothing to buy.

Bates finally located a small boat yard for sale in a town on trhe coast of Maine where she had spent many summers. The proprietor was getting along in years and wished to retire. He was offering the yard for sale at what Bates believed to be a fair starting price that could probably be worked down to a very reasonable figure through negotiation.

It is not necessary here to go into the details of investigation and negotiation. Bates bought the yard. The business being somewhat larger than she could finance alone, she had borrowed the additional funds required from a friend, giving a mortgage on the property as security.

Bates realized the need of adequate accounting records if she was to manage the business successfully. The records on hand were for cash receipts and disbursements only. Actual balance sheets and profit and loss statements which had been prepared for the former owner for tax purposes were also available. A person who was a reasonably capable bookkeeper and general office factotum had been inherited with the business.

Having had a course in accounting in college, Bates felt capable of using cost and financial information with some intelligence, but did not feel capable of initiating a suitable accounting system. Knowing that you, an old friend of hers, have been studying such matters, she has asked your advice as to what kind of accounting records should be kept and what kind of financial and cost information should be developed to control operations and to make proper charges to customers for service rendered. In addition to the information above she has told you the following facts about the business.

One of the properties of the business was a large shed for the winter storage of boats. Being the most suitable building in the locality for such storage, there was great demand for space in it on the part of owners of expensive boats among the summer people.

There was plenty of empty land on the shore front for outdoor storage. In most cases where space was rented for this purpose, the yard was also hired to haul the boats in on equipment that it had for the purpose.

In the spring, and from time to time during other seasons, there was a goodly amount of business available in painting and repair work on boats.

There was a large-sized work shed containing woodworking tools and space in which to construct at one time about six boats up to 40 feet in length. Larger boats could be built outside when the weather was suitable, but Bates did not expect to get many, if any, orders for such craft. She did, however, expect to have from one to six boats up to 40 feet in length in construction at all times, some for local fishermen and some for summer people.

The property included a good-sized wharf and float, a store for the sale of marine hardware and supplies, and gasoline pumps. There being no yacht club in the town, the summer people who were boating-minded tended to gather around the wharf and store. Bates intended to encourage this and to add fishing tackle, sporting goods, and refreshments to the items handled by the store.

Question

What would you tell Bates concerning her accounting needs?

* * * * *

Case 15-8: Conan Company

The Conan Company manufactured an inexpensive grade of men's clothing which it sold through house-to-house salesmen. A salesman took the measurements of the customer and entered them on the order blank, which the company used as a cutting order. Since the company found from experience that the measurements were usually of approximately regular sizes, it cut the garments from regular-sized patterns with only slight changes. The wool worsted goods used by the Conan Company cost approximately $9.00 per yard.

In order to insure very quick delivery the company made out cutting tickets for each garment as fast as orders were received and distributed them to the cutters together with a record of the standard yardage allowance for cutting that size of that style garment. It was expected that cutters would try to cut garments out of the least amount of cloth possible in order to keep down costs. They were, of course, also expected to cut as many garments as possible in a day. Each cutter earned $5.40 per hour and worked eight hours per day.

A careful record was kept of the garments cut each day. A transcript of the cutting record for one day is shown in Exhibit 1* on the next page. Yardage figures are given to the hundredth of a yard for ease in computation.

---

*The sample used in this case is too small to be adequate. A small sample is used, however, to bring out certain points without requiring the reader to spend time on more mechanical handling of a large number of figures. For purposes of class discussion, you may assume that this record is representative.

Questions

1. What conclusions can you draw from a crossclassification of yardage lost or saved according to cutters and styles? (By crossclassification is meant an orderly arrangement of the figures, grouped in column and row according to cutter, or style, or some other factor.) Who is apparently the fastest cutter? The most careful cutter? The best cutter?

2. Comment on the reliability and adequacy of the standards used to measure performance.

3. Should the most careful cutter specialize on the style for which losses are most frequent?

4. Before taking any action, what additional information would be needed?

EXHIBIT 1

CUTTING RECORD

Cutting Ticket Number	Cutter	Style	Cloth	Color	Size	Yards Saved	Yards Lost
1..........A		102	1073	Grey	37	....	0.10
2..........B		101	1116	Blue	39	....	0.02
3..........C		104	1178	Blue	37	....	0.10
4..........D		103	1241	Brown	38	0.04	....
5..........A		102	1073	Brown	40	....	0.14
6..........B		101	1116	Brown	38	0.04	....
7..........C		104	1178	Blue	38	....	0.06
8..........A		103	1241	Brown	36	0.08	....
9..........D		103	1241	Grey	35	0.10	....
10..........B		104	1178	Grey	37	0.06	....
11..........C		101	1116	Blue	36	....	0.06
12..........A		101	1116	Grey	40	0.02	....
13..........B		104	1178	Brown	37	0.00	0.00
14..........D		104	1178	Blue	39	0.06	....
15..........C		101	1116	Blue	36	....	0.08
16..........A		103	1241	Brown	38	0.04	....
17..........C		102	1073	Brown	40	....	0.18
18..........D		103	1241	Blue	42	0.02	....
19..........B		103	1241	Grey	36	....	0.04
20..........A		102	1073	Brown	37	....	0.08
21..........C		102	1073	Grey	37	....	0.16
22..........B		102	1073	Brown	36	....	0.10
23..........C		103	1241	Brown	38	0.02	....
24..........A		104	1178	Grey	38	0.06	....
25..........D		101	1116	Brown	36	0.04	....
26..........B		104	1178	Brown	37	0.08	....
27..........C		104	1178	Blue	39	0.02	....
28..........A		101	1116	Grey	37	....	0.06
29..........D		104	1116	Blue	42	0.08	....
30..........B		104	1178	Grey	38	0.04	....
31..........C		103	1241	Blue	37	....	0.12
32..........A		103	1241	Grey	40	....	0.02
33..........B		103	1241	Blue	38	0.02	....
34..........C		101	1116	Blue	36	....	0.04
35..........D		102	1073	Brown	39	....	0.06
36..........B		101	1116	Grey	35	0.06	....
37..........C		104	1178	Blue	44	....	0.06
38..........A		102	1073	Grey	37	....	0.18
39..........D		103	1241	Brown	40	0.02	....
40..........C		103	1241	Brown	38	....	0.04

Chapter 16

The Behavior of Costs

Key Terms

Variable costs
Fixed costs
Semivariable costs
Cost-volume diagram
Linear assumption
Relevant range
High-low method

Linear regression
Profitgraph
Break-even volume
Unit contribution margin
Margin of safety
Learning curve

Discussion Questions

1. Describe the appearance of the graph of an item of (a) variable cost, (b) fixed cost, and (c) semivariable cost, where the x-axis is volume and the y-axis is total cost.

2. Repeat question 1, but where the y-axis is cost per unit.

3. "My records show that gasoline costs me 6 cents a mile, regardless of how many miles I drive my car, whereas my insurance cost obviously varies with the number of miles I drive. Therefore, gasoline is a fixed cost and insurance is a variable cost." Comment.

4. Identify and discuss the validity of the two assumptions implicit in Illustration 16-2

5. The cost-volume diagram, Illustration 16-5, does not identify semivariable costs. Why?

6. "The cost-volume diagram shows the relationship between costs and volume under the conditions prevailing at a certain time." How would Illustration 16-5 be affected: (a) if there were an increase in wage and salary rates? (b) if the company added a safety engineer? (c) if direct material costs per unit decreased? (d) if the company purchased an automatic machine to perform certain operations that currently are done manually?

7. Describe methods for estimating the fixed cost per period and the variable cost per unit of volume.

8. A plant manager tells a cost analyst that a certain overhead cost item is fixed. Yet when the analyst runs a regression analysis of the annual amount of that item over the past ten years, the regression results indicate that the cost item is mostly variable. How can this be?

9. Identify the numbered components on the profitgraph in Illustration 16-13, on the next page.

Illustration 16-13

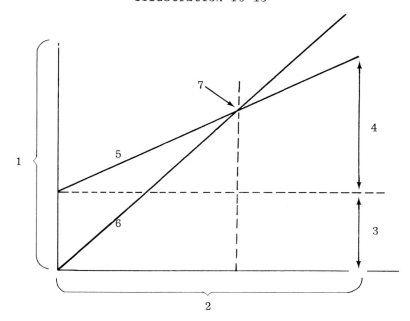

10. What are the four basic ways that the profit of a single-product business can be increased? How would each affect Illustration 16-13?

11. Under what circumstances could machine-hours appropriately be used as a measure of volume on a profitgraph?

12. Under what circumstances can a profitgraph such as that shown in Illustration 16-9 be used if a company makes several products? Why is it invalid under other circumstances?

13. Why might the costs in a cost-volume diagram for one period be different from those in a diagram for another period?

14. What does it mean to say that a certain cost element is subject to a 90 percent learning curve?

15. A cost analyst was told by an industrial engineer that a certain cost item should be subject to the learning curve. Yet when the analyst calculated the historical cost per unit of this item over the past few years, the cost per unit had increased from year to year. How can this be so?

Problems

16-1 The following are data on the behavior of costs in four departments:

Department	Fixed costs	Variable cost per unit	Volume units	Total costs
A.........	$30,000	$ 3	1,000	$?
B.........	?	6	200	3,000
C.........	5,000	10	?	7,000
C.........	80,000	?	2,000	110,000

Required: Calculate the missing number in each line.

16-2. The graphs in Illustration 16-14, on the following page, relate to the behavior of certain costs involved in the operation of a mechanical arts course offered by a local corporation in a program of adult education.

Illustration 18-12

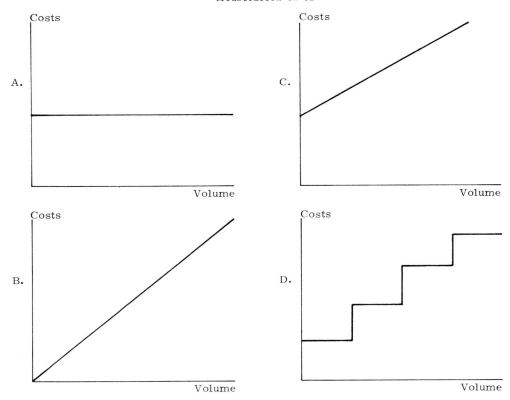

Required:

a. Title each graph to show the type of cost it describes (fixed, variable, semivariable, etc.)
b. From the list of costs described below select those which each graph
   describes:

Costs
(1) Cost of raw materials used by students.
(2) Depreciation of machinery and equipment used.
(3) Cost of blueprints and manuals. Extra copies must be acquired for
    every six students who enroll over the minimum number of 24.
(4) Utilities and maintenance. Utilities remain constant each month,
    but maintenance tends to vary with the usage of machinery and
    equipment.

16-3. Using the formula TC = TFC + (UVC)(X) for the cost at any volume, and the
formula (UR)(X) = TFC + (UVC)(X) for the break-even volume, answer the
questions below, using the data following:

```
Fixed costs per period...........................$55,500
Variable costs per unit...........................$     25
Standard sales volume per period (units)........  30,000
Selling price per unit............................$     55
```

Required:

a. Calculate the total cost at standard volume.
b. Calculate the break-even point in units.
c. Calculate the profit or loss at standard volume.
d. What is the marginal income
e. Compute the income which would result at the standard volume if both
   the variable cost per unit and the selling price per unit increased by
   20 percent.

16-4. Listed below are the expected costs of several items at the upper and lower levels of the Baxter Company's relevant range of activity.

	Lower level	Upper level
Production (units)................	10,000	20,000
Materials........................	$100,000	$200,000
Direct labor.....................	150,000	300,000
Depreciation (machinery).........	50,000	50,000
Indirect labor...................	80,000	140,000
Supervisory salaries.............	72,000	72,000
Maintenance......................	50,000	90,000

Required:

  a. For each item, calculate the cost per unit at both levels of activity.
  b. For each item, does the behavior of cost per unit over the relevant range of activity indicate the general type of cost (fixed, variable, or semivariable)? Explain your answer.

16-5. What are the equations of the various lines shown in Illustration 16-11? What are the new break-even volumes in parts A, B, and C?

16-6. Bolter Company sells two products, A and B. In 1982, it sold 2,000 units of A at $100 per unit. It had purchased those 2,000 units at a cost of $60 per unit, and had repackaged them at an additional cost of $10 per unit. It sold 2,000 units of Product B at $50 per unit. The purchase cost of these units was $35 per unit, and there were no repackaging costs. All other costs of Bolter Company were fixed; in 1982 they amounted to $60,000, and were allocated to Products A and B in proportion to sales revenue.

Required:

  a. Prepare an income statement for 1982 in which all costs are assigned to each product.
  b. Prepare an income statement for 1982 that shows the contribution of each product and for the company as a whole. Discuss the differences between this income statement and the income statement prepared in (a).
  c. In 1983, it is expected that the sales price of Product B must be decreased to $40 per unit in order to meet competition, other conditions remaining as in 1982. Prepare an estimated income statement for 1983.
  d. Under the circumstances given in (c), should Product B be discontinued?

16-7. Production costs in Department B for the preceding six months were as follows:

Month	July	Aug.	Sept.	Oct.	Nov.	Dec.
Units of production..	1,000	1,200	1,400	1,100	900	800
Total cost..........	$6,200	$7,000	$7,200	$6,200	$5,800	$5,200

Required:

a. Estimate fixed and variable costs by the high-low method.
b. Estimate fixed and variable costs by drawing a scatter diagram.
c. If production in a certain month is estimated to be 1,200 units, what is your estimate of total cost?

16-8. The 1983 budget for the College Soda Shop contains the following data:

Liabilities......................................	$ 40,000
Capital stock...................................	42,500
Retained earnings..............................	7,500
Sales..	100,000
Fixed expenses.................................	20,000
Variable expenses..............................	60,000

Required:

    a. What is the formula for estimating the income at various volumes under these circumstances?
    b. What is the break-even volume in 1983?
    c. If the maximum capacity of this firm is $150,000 of sales utilizing the current level of assets, what is the maximum potential rate of return on these assets?
    d. If the budgeted variable expenses can be reduced by $5,000 by changing suppliers, what is the dollar effect on (1) income, and (2) break-even point?

16-9. (C.M.A. adapted.) All-Day Candy Company is a wholesale distributor of candy. The company services grocery, convenience and drug stores in a large metropolitan area. Small but steady growth in sales has been achieved over the past few years while candy prices have been increasing. The compnay is formulating its plans for the coming fiscal year. Presented below are the data used to project the current year's after-tax net income of $165,600.

Average selling price.........................$6.00 per box

Average variable costs:
  Candy production............................$3.00 per box
  Selling expense............................. .60 per box
    Total...................................$3.60 per box

Annual fixed costs:
  Selling.....................................$240,000
  Administrative.............................. 420,000
    Total...................................$660,000

Expected annual sales volume................. 390,000 boxes
Tax rate..................................... 40%

Manufacturers of candy have announced that they will increase prices of their products an average 15 percent in the coming year due to increases in raw materials (sugar, cocoa, peanuts, etc.) and labor costs. All-Day Candy Company expects that all other costs will remain at the same rates or levels as the current year.

Required:

    a. What is All-Day Candy Company's break-even point in boxes of candy for the current year?
    b. What selling price per box must All-Day Candy Company charge to cover the 15 percent increase in variable production costs of candy and still maintain the current contribution margin percentage?
    c. What volume of sales in dollars must the All-Day Candy Company achieve in the coming year to maintain the same net income after taxes as projected for the current year if the selling price of candy remains at $6.00 per box and the variable production costs of candy increase 15 percent?

16-10. (C.M.A. adapted.) Tony Calderone started a pizzeria in 1980. For this purpose a building was rented for $1,200 per month. Two persons were hired to work full time at the restaurant and six college students were hired to work 30 hours per week delivering pizza. An outside accountant was hired for tax and bookkeeping purposes. For this service, Mr. Calderone pays $900 per month. The necessary restaurant equipment and delivery cars were purchased with cash. Mr. Calderone has noticed that expenses for utilities and supplies have been rather constant.

Mr. Calderone increased his business between 1980 and 1983. Profits have more than doubled since 1980. Mr. Calderone does not understand why his profits have increased faster than his volume.

A projected income statement for 1984 has been prepared by the accountant and is shown below:

Projected Income Statement
For the Year Ended December 31, 1984

Sales..		$285,000
Cost of food sold.......................................$85,500		
Wages & fringe benefits of restaurant help........... 24,450		
Wages & fringe benefits of delivery persons.......... 51,900		
Rent... 14,400		
Accounting services.................................. 10,800		
Depreciation of delivery equipment................... 15,000		
Depreciation of restaurant equipment................. 9,000		
Utilities... 6,975		
Supplies (soap, floor wax, etc.)..................... <u>3,600</u>		<u>221,625</u>
Income before taxes.................................		63,375
Income taxes...		<u>19,014</u>
Net Income...		<u>$44,361</u>

<u>Note</u>: The average pizza sells for $7.50. Assume that Mr. Calderone pays out
30% of his income in income taxes.

Required:

    a. What is the break-even point in number of pizzas that must be sold?

    b. What is the cash flow break-even point in number of pizzas that must be sold?

    c. If Mr. Calderone withdraws $14,400 for personal use, how much cash will be left from the 1984 income producing activities?

    d. Mr. Calderone would like an after-tax net income of $60,000. What volume must be reached in number of pizzas in order to obtain the desired income?

    e. Briefly explain to Mr. Calderone why his profits have increased at a faster rate than his sales.

    f. Briefly explain to Mr. Calderone why his cash flow for 1984 will exceed his profits.

16-11. (C.M.A. adapted.) R. A. Ro and Company, maker of quality smoking pipes, has experienced a steady growth in sales for the past five years. However, incresed competition has led Mr. Ro, the president, to believe that an aggressive advertising campaign will be necessary next year to maintain the company's present growth.

To prepare for next year's advertising campaign, the company's accountant has prepared and presented Mr. Ro with the following data for the current year, 1982.

<u>Cost Schedule</u>

Variable Costs:
    Direct Labor..........................$ 8.00/pipe
    Direct Materials...................... 3.25/pipe
    Variable Overhead..................... <u>2.50/pipe</u>
        Total Variable Costs............$13.75/pipe

Fixed Costs:
    Manufcturing..........................$ 25,000
    Selling............................... 40,000
    Administrative........................ <u>70,000</u>
        Total Fixed Costs...............$135,000

Selling Price, per pipe...............$ 25.00
Expected Sales, 1982 (20,000 units)....$500,000
Tax rate.............................. 40%

Mr. Ro has set the sales target for 1983 at a level of $550,000 (or 22,000 pipes).

Required:

a. What is the projected after-tax net income for 1982?
b. What is the break-even point in units for 1982?
c. Mr. Ro believes an additional selling expense of $11,250 for advertising in 1983, with all other costs remaining constant, will be necessary to attain the 1983 sales target. What will be the after-tax net income for 1983 if the additional $11,250 is spent?
d. What will be the break-even point in dollar sales for 1983 if the additional $11,250 is spent for advertising?
e. If the additional $11,250 is spent for advertising in 1983, what is the required sales level in dollar sales to equal 1982's after-tax net income?
f. At a sales level of 22,000 units, what is the maximum amount which can be spent on advertising if an after-tax net income of $60,000 is desired?

16-12. Two competing food vendors were located side by side at a state fair. Both occupied buildings of the same size, paid the same rent, $1,250, and charged similar prices for their food. Vendor A employed three times as many employees as B and had twice as much income as B even though B had more than half the sales of A. Other data:

	Vendor A	Vendor B
Sales	$8,000	$4,500
Cost of goods sold	50% of sales	50% of sales
Wages	$2,250	$750

Required:

a. Present the data given in the form of a marginal income analysis statement.
b. Explain why Vendor A is twice as profitable as Vendor B.
c. By how much would Vendor B's sales have to increase in order to justify the doubling of the number of employees at the same rate of pay if his desired net income is $350?

16-13. The condensed income statement for the past year for a line of antique bottles, one of several products manufactured by Reproductions, Inc., follows:

Sales	$70,000
Cost of goods sold	50,000
Gross margin	20,000
Selling and administrative expense	28,000
Loss	$(8,000)

The costs include certain allocations of fixed costs which would be incurred whether the line of bottles was made or not. Fixed product costs included in cost of goods sold amount to $26,000, and other fixed costs amount to $20,000.

Required:

a. Restate the results of operations for the antique bottle line in a form which management would find more useful in making a decision as to whether to continue to make antique bottles.
b. Which is more profitable, to continue or discontinue the bottle line?
c. What factors would become relevant to management's decision if there is an offer to buy the bottle operations?

16-14. (C.M.A. adapted.) The Metropolitan News, a daily newspaper, services a community of 100,000. The paper has a circulation of 40,000, with 32,000 copies delivered directly to weekly subscribers. The rate schedule for the paper is:

```
                                              Daily      Sunday
        Newstand price....................$0.45       $0.90
        Weekly subscription...............            $3.00
```

The paper has experienced profitable operations, as can be seen from the income statement for the year ended September 30, 1982 (000 omitted):

```
        Revenue:
          Newspaper sales..................$6,600
          Advertising sales................ 5,400      $12,000
        Costs and expenses:
          Personnel costs:
            Commissions:
              Carriers.....................   876
              Newsstands...................   219
              Advertising..................   144
            Salaries:
              Administration...............   750
              Advertising..................   300
              Equipment operators......... 1,500
              Newsroom.................... 1,200
            Employee benefits............    585        5,574
          Newsprint........................            2,502
          Other supplies...................            1,251
          Repairs..........................               75
          Depreciation.....................              540
          Property taxes...................              360
          Building rental..................              240
          Automobile leases................               30
          Other............................              270
              Total costs and expenses.....           10,842
        Income before income taxes........            1,158
        Income taxes......................              462
        Net Income........................           $    696
```

The Sunday edition usually has twice as many pages as the daily editions. Analysis of direct edition variable costs for 1982-83 is shown in the schedule below.

```
                                         Cost per Issue
                                        Daily      Sunday

        Newsprint........................$0.150     $0.300
        Other supplies................... 0.075      0.150
        Carrier and newsstand commissions. 0.075     0.075
                                         $0.300     $0.525
```

Several changes in operations are scheduled for the next year, in addition to the need to recognize increasing costs:

1. The building lease expired on September 30, 1983 and has been renewed with a change in the rental fee provisions from a straight fee to a fixed fee of $180,000 plus 1 percent of newspaper sales.

2. The advertising department will eliminate the payment of a 4 percent advertising commission on contracts sold by four of its employees. An average of two-thirds of the advertising has been sold on a contract basis in the past. The salaries of the four who solicited advertising will be raised from $22,500 each to $42,000 each.

3. Automobiles will no longer be leased. Employees whose jobs require automobiles will use their own and be reimbuirsed at $0.45 per mile. The leased cars were driven 80,000 miles in 1982-83, and it is estimated that the employees will drive some 84,000 miles next year on company business.

4. Cost increases estimated for next year:

a. Newsprint: $0.03 per daily issue and $0.06 for the Sunday paper.
b. Salaries: (1) Equipment operations   8%
           (2) Other employees   6%
c. Employee benefits (From 15% of   5%
   personnel costs, excluding carrier
   and newsstand commissions, to 20%)

5. Circulation increases of 5 percent in newsstand and home delivery are anticipated.

6. Advertising revenue is estimated at $5,670,000 with $3,780,000 from employee solicited contracts.

Required:

a. Prepare a projected income statement for the Metropolitan News for the 1983-84 fiscal year using a format that shows the total variable costs and total fixed costs for the newspaper (round calculations to the nearest thousand dollars).
b. The management of Metropolitan News is contemplating one additional proposal for the 1983-84 fiscal year -- raising the rates for its newspaper to the following amounts:

	Daily	Sunday
Single issue price	$0.60	$1.20
Weekly subscription (includes daily and Sunday)	$3.75	

It is estimated that the newspaper's circulation would decline to 90 percent of the currently anticipated 1983-84 level for both newsstand and home delivery sales if this change is initiated. Calculate the effect on the projected 1983-84 income if this proposed rate change is implemented. (Try to calculate this effect without preparing a second projected income statement, but instead using data in the statement you prepared above.)

16-15. (C.M.A. adapted.) Justa Corporation produces three products, A, B, and C, which Justa sells in a local market and in a regional market. At the end of the first quarter of the current year the following income statement has been prepared:

	Total	Local	Regional
Sales	$1,300,000	$1,000,000	$300,000
Cost of goods sold	1,010,000	775,000	235,000
Gross margin	290,000	225,000	65,000
Selling expenses	105,000	60,000	45,000
Administrative expenses	52,000	40,000	12,000
	157,000	100,000	57,000
Income	$ 133,000	$ 125,000	$ 8,000

Management has expressed special concern with the regional market because of the extremely poor return on sales. This market was entered a year ago because of excess capacity. It was originally believed that the return on sales would improve with time, but after a year no noticeable improvement can be seen from the results as reported in the above quarterly statement.

In attempting to decide whether to eliminate the regional market, the following information has been gathered:

	Products		
	A	B	C
Sales............................	$500,000	$400,000	$400,000
Variable manufacturing expenses as a percentage of sales........	60%	70%	60%
Variable selling expenses as a percentage of sales.............	3%	2%	2%

Sales by Markets

Product	Local	Regional
A	$400,000	$100,000
B	300,000	100,000
C	300,000	100,000

All administrative expenses and fixed manufacturing expenses are joint to the three products and the two markets and are fixed for the period. Remaining selling expenses are fixed for the period and separable by market. All fixed expenses are based upon a prorated yearly amount.

Required:

a. Prepare the quarterly income statement showing contribution margins by markets.

b. Assuming there are no alternative uses for the Justa Corporation's present capacity, would you recommend dropping the regional market? Why or why not?

c. Prepare the quarterly income statement showing contribution margins by products.

d. It is believed that a new product can be ready for sale next year if the Justa Corporation decides to go ahead with continued research. The new product can be produced by simply converting equipment presently used in producing Product C. This conversion will increase fixed costs by $10,000 per quarter. What must be the minimum contribution margin per quarter for the new product to make the changeover financially feasible?

16-16. Assume a company introduced a product this year for which the total costs to manufacture 5,000 units were $25,000. Construct a table showing cumulative quantity, cumulative unit cost, unit cost for incremental units, and average annual unit decrease for 1, 2, 4, and 8 years after introduction if annual production is 5,000 units. (Round results to the nearest cent.)

a. Assume an 80 percent learning rate.
b. Assume a 92 percent learning rate.

CASES

Case 16-17: Chris Collins

Chris Collins was supervisor of an assembly department in Dexter Electronics Company. In recent weeks, Collins had become convinced that a certain component, number S-36, could be produced more efficiently if certain assembly methods changes were made. Collins had described this proposal to the company's industrial engineer, but the engineer had quickly dismissed Collins' ideas -- mainly Collins thought, because the engineer had not thought of them first.

Collins had frequently thought of starting a business, and felt that the ability to produce the S-36 component at a lower cost might provide this opportunity. Dexter's purchasing agent assured Collins that Dexter would be willing to buy S-36s from Collins if the price were 10-15 percent below Dexter's current cost of $1.65 per unit. Working at home, Collins experimented with the new methods, which were bsed on the use of a new fixture to aid in assembling each S-36. This experimentation seemed successful, so Collins proceeded to prepare some estimates for large-scale S-36 production. Collins determined the following:

1. A local toolmaker would make the new fixtures for a price of $500 each. One fixture would be needed for each assembly worker.
2. Assembly workers were readily available, on either a full-time or part-time basis, at a wage of $3.75 per hour. Collins felt that another 20 percent of wages would be necessary for fringe benefits. Collins estimated that on the average (including restbreaks), a worker could assemble, test, and pack 15 units of the S-36 per hour.
3. Purchased components for the S-36 should cost about $.85 per unit over the next year. Shipping materials and delivery costs would amount to approximately $.05 per unit.
4. Suitable space was available for assembly operations at a rental of $600 per month. A twelve-month lease was required.
5. Assembly tables, stools, and other necessary equipment would cost about $300 per assembly worker.
6. Collins, as general manager, would receive a salary of $2,000 per month.
7. A combination office manager-bookkeeper was available for a salary of $900 per month.
8. Miscellaneous costs, including maintenance, supplies, and utilities, were expected to average about $325 per month.
9. Dexter Electronics would purchase between 400,000 and 525,000 units of S-36 a year, with 450,000 being Dexter's purchasing agent's "best guess." However, Collins would have to commit to a price of $1.40 per unit for the next twelve months.

Collins showed these estimates to a friend who was a cost analyst in another electronics firm. This friend said that all of the estimates appeared reasonable, but told Collins that in addition to the required investment in fixtures and equipment, about $70,000 would be needed to finance accounts receivable and inventories. The friend also advised buying enough fixtures and other equipment to enable producing the maximum estimated volume (525,000 units per year) on a one-shift basis (assuming 2,000 labor hours per assembler per year). Collins thought this was good advice.

Questions

1. What are Collins' expected variable costs per unit? Fixed costs per month? What would the total costs per year of Collins' business be if volume was 400,000 units? 450,000 units? 525,000 units? (Limit yourself to cash costs; ignore depreciation of fixtures and equipment. Also, disregard any interest costs Collins might incur on borrowed funds.)

2. What is the average cost per unit of S-36 at each of these three volumes?

3. Reanswer Questions 1 and 2, assuming that: (1) Collins wanted to guarantee assembly workers 2,000 hours of pay per year; (2) enough workers would be hired to assemble 450,000 units a year; (3) these workers could work overtime at a cost (including fringes) of $6.75 per hour; and (4) no additional fixed costs would be incurred if overtime were needed. (Do not use these assumptions for Question 4.)

4. Reanswer Questions 1 and 2, now including depreciation as an expense. Assume the fixtures and other equipment have a useful life of 6 years, and that straight-line depreciation will be used.

5. Do you think Chris Collins should resign from Dexter Electronics and form the proposed enterprise?

* * * * *

Case 16-18: Hill Associates, Inc.

Dr. Edgar Hill was introduced to the concept of the break-even chart while attending an executive training program during the fall of 1982. Dr. Hill was president and treasurer of Hill Associates, Inc. The company had been founded by Dr. Hill in 1967 to manufacture a product he had invented. Sales had grown to about $800,000 in 1982, and the company's plant had been expanded several times since it was built to accommodate the growing demand.

When Dr. Hill returned to his office in January 1983, he called in his accountant, Paula O'Leary. Together they discussed the problem of constructing a break-even chart for Hill Associates. The critical problem seemed to be to determine the relationship between cost and volume. Ms.

O'Leary agreed to see what she could do in this respect with data available in the company records.

As the first step, Ms. O'Leary consulted the records for the calendar year 1982 and assembled the information given in Exhibit 1. For each month of the year, this information consisted of: (a) the total amount of production during the month, valued at the selling price of the product;* and (b) the total amount of costs incurred during the month.

While she was assembling the data on 1982, it occurred to Ms. O'Leary that Hill Associates' cost-volume relationship might have changed over time. To check this possibility, she decided to look at data over the entire 10-year period from 1973 through 1982 inclusive. It was not possible to get monthly figures for this entire period, but Ms. O'Leary was able to obtain figures on annual production and annual costs. O'Leary recognized that the prices and wage rates paid by Hill Associates for goods and services had risen over the years and that Hill Associates had raised its own prices to customers in compensation. She felt that she ought to adjust for these price changes before trying to analyze the data and compare them with those given in Exhibit 1. Accordingly, for each year, she multiplied both production at sales value and costs by the ratio of Hill Associates' 1982 price to its price in the year in question. The adjusted figures, which Ms. O'Leary considered to be stated in 1982 dollars, are given in Exhibit 2.

Questions

1. Plot the data given in Exhibit 1 as points on graph paper and draw in a straight line which appears to give the "best fit" to the data. From

---

*This amount was not necessarily equal amount of sales during the month, because sales were made from inventory; new production during the month was used to replenish inventory.

EXHIBIT 1

Production Volume and Cost
by Month, 1982

Month	Production (At Sales Value)	Costs
January	$51,000	$51,000
February	57,000	52,000
March	71,000	58,000
April	76,000	59,000
May	75,000	58,000
June	95,000	64,000
July	45,000	51,000
August	51,000	52,000
September	66,000	54,000
October	73,000	59,000
November	78,000	62,000
December	77,000	63,000

EXHIBIT 2

Production Volume and Cost
by Year, 1973-1982
(In 1982 dollars)

Year	Production (At Sales Value)	Costs
1973	$289,000	$255,000
1974	391,000	381,000
1975	421,000	320,000
1976	489,000	436,000
1977	600,000	455,000
1978	573,000	491,000
1979	691,000	517,000
1980	687,000	551,000
1981	699,000	599,000
1982	815,000	683,000

this line, estimate the ratio of variable cost to production volume.

2. Repeat the above with the data of Exhibit 2.

3. (Optional.) Use the method of least squares to determine equations for the "best fit" lines for the data in Exhibits 1 and 2.

4. Has Hill Associates' cost-volume relationship changed over time?

Chapter 17

Full Costs and Their Uses

Key Terms

Cost
Cost objective
Direct costs
Indirect costs
Full cost
CASB
Prime cost

Overhead cost
Inventory cost
Selling cost
General and administrative cost
Normal pricing
Time and material pricing
Billing rate

Discussion Questions

1. Explain, with an example, why not all items of cost can be classified as direct costs.

2. Distinguish between direct labor cost and indirect labor cost, giving an example of each.

3. Distinguish between direct material cost and indirect material cost, giving an example of each.

4. Distinguish among materials costs, supplies costs, and services costs.

5. Distinguish among prime cost, inventory cost, and full cost.

6. Distinguish between order-getting costs and logistics costs.

7. What is the rationale for saying that indirect costs, which cannot be traced to an individual cost objective, are nevertheless part of the cost of that cost objective?

8. Which of the following are part of the full cost of building a certain house? Explain why.

    (a) Depreciation expense on the builder's trucks that haul material to the house.
    (b) Lumber originally delivered to the site but later removed because it was in excess of that needed.
    (c) Cost of the architect's plans that were used to build this and five other identical houses.
    (d) Fees paid to the municipality because of inspections required to see that the house conformed to building codes.
    (e) Advertising expenses incurred to sell the house.

9. Under what circumstances is job-order costing rather than process costing appropriate?

10. Consider that the course you are now taking is one cost objective. List as specifically as you can the items of direct costs to the school (not to you as an individual) of that cost objective and give examples of indirect costs of

that cost objective.

11. Distribution costs are not included as part of the inventory cost of a product. Why?

12. In an account flowchart for a cost accounting system, the flow is usually from the credit side of one account to the debit side of another account. Why is the flow in this direction, rather than the reverse?

13. How should the cost accounting system of a profit-seeking hospital differ from that of a not-for-profit hospital?

14. What are the primary uses for full cost information?

15. If you were asked to calculate the full cost of undergraduate education in a certain college or university, what items of cost would you include?

16. Would you expect the normal profit margin percentage that a retailer uses for setting the selling price of fine watches to be higher than that used by a supermarket in setting the selling price for cornflakes? List the factors that could explain a difference.

17. In time and material pricing, a profit is included both in the time component and also in the material component. Does this mean that profits are double counted? Explain?

Problems

17-1. Brown's Cabinet Shop makes a popular 30-inch wide bathroom vanity cabinet. Cost data are as follows:

```
Depreciation.....................$  600 per month
Rent on building................   450 per month
Cabinetmaker wages..............    30 per cabinet
Office expense..................   900 per month
Utilities.......................   300 per month
Cabinet material................    50 per cabinet
Insurance.......................   150 per month
Shop supervisor................. 1,200 per month
```

Normal production volume is 200 cabinets per month. Brown assigns indirect costs equally to each cabinet.

Required:

a. Classify Brown's costs a either direct or indirect assuming the individual cabinet is the cost objective.
b. What is the full cost of a cabinet?
c. Brown's next-door neighbor, Green, had considered making a 30-inch bathroom cabinet and had priced the necessary materials. Green asked if Brown would sell a finished cabinet at cost, and Brown agreed. Would you expect there to be any difference of opinion between the two people about the amount that Green should pay? Why?

17-2. The following data pertain to the Bolton Company for July:

```
Raw materials inventory, July 1..........$ 80,000
Work in process inventory, July 1........ 100,000
Finished goods inventory, July 1......... 60,000
Raw material purchases................... 45,000
Raw material issued...................... 75,000
Direct labor costs incurred.............. 35,000
Overhead costs incurred.................. 42,000
Costs of goods completed and transferred. 190,000
Cost of sales............................ 185,000
```

Required:

  a. Prepare T-accounts for the three inventory accounts and cost of sales.
  b. Record the beginning balances and post the transactions for the month.
  c. Draw arrows to show the transfers between accounts.
  d. Calculate the inventory balances as of July 31.

17-3. Prepare jounal entries for the transactions of the Bolton Company in Problem 17-2.

17-4. Sales revenue was $220,000 in July for the Bolton Company in Problem 17-2.

  Required: Prepare a partial income statement (one that ends with the gross margin line).

17-5. The following data pertain to Carter Company for September:

Raw material inventory, September 1	$ 65,000
Work in process inventory, September 1	80,000
Finished goods inventory, September 1	50,000
Raw material purchases	40,000
Raw material issued	85,000
Direct labor costs incurred	45,000
Overhead costs incurred	60,000
Cost of goods completed and transferred	175,000
Cost of sales	200,000

Required:

  a. Prepare T-accounts for the three inventory accounts and cost of sales.
  b. Record the beginning balances and post the transactions for the month.
  c. Draw arrows to show the transfers between accounts.
  d. Calculate the inventory balances as of September 30.

17-6. Prepare journal entries for the transactions of the Carter Company in Problem 17-5.

17-7. Assume that sales revenue was $240,000 in September for Carter Company in Problem 17-5.

  Required: Prepare a partial income statement.

17-8. Apex Assembly Company began business on January 1. Its employees earn $7 per hour. It incurred materials costs as indicated below. It purchased and received $20,000 of raw material on January 1. It had no other costs. During January it worked on three jobs, as follows:

	Job No. 1	Job No. 2	Job No. 3
Materials issued	$3,200	$6,000	$4,000
Labor	100 hours	200 hours	50 hours
Status, January 31	Complete	Complete	Incomplete
	Sold for $6,750	Not sold	

Required:

  a. What are the balances in the inventory accounts as of January 31?
  b. Prepare a partial income statement (to the gross margin line) for January.

17-9. Following are partial data for the Carol Company for February:

Direct material used	$ 70,000
Direct labor cost	80,000
Total manufacturing cost	200,000
Beginning work in process inventory	60,000
Ending work in process inventory	90,000

Required:

     a. What was the factory overhead cost for February?

     b. What was the cost of goods manufactured (i.e., transferred to Finished Goods Inventory)?

17-10. A partial summary of the Ferac Company's operations for March is given below:

Materials purchased...........................	$25,000
Beginning balance--raw material..............	10,000
Ending balance--raw material.................	2,000
Direct labor cost............................	14,000
Beginning balance--work in process...........	3,000
Ending balance--work in process..............	25,000
Beginning balance--finished goods............	20,000
Ending balance--finished goods...............	10,000
Cost of goods sold...........................	50,000
Revenue......................................	80,000

Required:

     a. Give the journal entry for the transfer from Raw Material Inventory to Work in Process Inventory.

     b. Give the journal entry for the transfer from Work in Process Inventory to Finished Goods Inventory. (Hint: This amount can be determined by analysis of the Finished Goods Inventory transactions; use a T-account.)

     c. What was the amount of factory overhead cost for March? (Hint: Use a T-account for Work in Process Inventory.)

     d. Prepare an income statement for March.

17-11. Refer to the situation illustrated in Illustrations 17-2 and 17-3 of the text. Assume each of the following events occurred instead of the related events shown in Illustration 17-2:

(1) No raw materials were purchased during the month.

(2) Costs were incurred as indicated, but only $60,000 worth of pens were completed during the month.

(3) The factory was shut down during the month. Factory overhead costs continued at $27,000 and were charged as an expense on the income statement. Sales were $100,000, and cost of goods sold was $60,000. No direct labor or direct material costs were incurred, and no raw materials purchases were made.

Required: Consider each of the three events separately.

     a. What changes would be required in Illustration 17-2 and the related journal entries?

     b. What would be the effect on the income statement, Illustration 17-3?

17-12. Complete the postings to the partial flowchart on the next page and use arrows to reflect the flow of costs from raw material through the cost of goods sold. Prepare journal entries for all of the data. Other data pertinent to operations for the month of April for Simplex Manufacturing Corp. follow (000s omitted):

Raw material purchases.....	$230	Repairs to factory...................	$ 10
Freight-in on purchases....	10	Factory rent.........................	50
Factory supplies used......	15	Rental of retail store...............	20
Indirect labor.............	80	Office heat, light, power............	8
Direct labor...............	400	Raw material used in production......	200
Depreciation of		Cost of goods completed during April.	700
factory machinery........	75	Finished goods ending inventory......	150
Factory heat, light, power.	12		

| Raw Materials Inventory | | | Work in Process Inventory | | |
| | | | | | |

Raw Materials Inventory

```
3/31
Inventory      50 | 200
            230  |
             10  |
```

Work in Process Inventory

```
3/31
Inventory      60 | 700
               15 |
              400 |
              200 |
              227 |
             ─────
              202 |
```

Wages Payable

```
               | 400
               |  80
```

Finished Goods Inventory

```
3/31
Inventory     200 | 750
              700 |
             ──── |
              150 |
```

Factory Overhead

```
   80 |
   75 |
   12 |
   10 |
   50 |
```

Cost of Goods Sold

```
  750 |
```

17-13. Overhill Bicycle Company had the following account balances as of May 1:

```
Cash.............................$115,000 dr.
Accounts receivable...............150,000 dr.
Raw materials inventory........... 80,000 dr.
Work in process inventory......... 75,000 dr.
Finished goods inventory.......... 50,000 cr.
Accounts payable.................. 42,000 cr.
Wages payable.....................  7,000 cr.
Various asset and liability
    accounts...................... 35,000 dr.
```

During the month of May, the following transactions occurred:

1. Raw materials of $50,000 were purchased on open account.
2. Various other assets in the amount of $19,000 were purchased for cash, and $57,000 of accounts payable were paid.
3. Raw materials costing $50,000 (mainly frames, wheels, tires, handlebars, seats, pedals, chains, gears, and brakes) were issued and sent to the factory for assembly into bicycles.
4. Direct labor costs of $18,000 were incurred.
5. The following items of overhead costs were incurred but not paid:
    Utilities...............$10,000
    Indirect labor.......... 11,000
    Depreciation............ 4,000
6. Employees were paid $30,000 cash.
7. Overhead costs for the month were charged to Work in Process Inventory.
8. Bicycles costing $104,000 were completed and transferred to Finished Goods Inventory.
9. Bicycles costing $113,000 were sold for $175,000 on account.
10. Accounts receivable of $145,000 were collected.
11. Selling and general and administrative expenses in the amount of $29,000 were incurred, $17,000 of which represented credits to accounts payable.

Required:

    a. Prepare an account flowchart for May using the above information.
       Include arrows to indicate flows between accounts.
    b. Prepare journal entries for the May transactions.
    c. Prepare an income statement for May. (Ignore income taxes.)

17-14. Taylor Company produces a number of products. In 19x1 the selling price of Product A, whose sales are normally 10,000 units per year, was calculated as follows:

	Unit costs
Direct material cost....................	$ 3.00
Direct labor cost......................	6.00
Overhead cost.........................	4.50
Selling and administrative cost........	3.00
Full cost.........................	16.50
Profit (10% of full cost).............	1.65
Selling price.....................	$18.15

In 19x2 the company estimates that direct material cost and direct labor cost will increase by 10 percent. It also estimates that overhead cost will increase by a total of $5,000 and that selling and administrative cost and sales volume will remain unchanged.

Required: What is the normal selling price for Product A in 19x2?

17-15. Freda Jones is a young attorney who has decided to leave her current employer and set up her own law practice. She has prepared the following monthly cost estimates:

Salary of legal secretary...............	$2,000
Office rent and utilities...............	1,000
Other costs............................	1,200
Total cost........................	$4,200

Freda would like to earn $3,000 a month and feels that she will be able to bill 160 hours of her time per month to clients.

Required:

    a. Assuming that Freda is correct in her estimates, what fee per hour
       should Freda charge her clients?
    b. At the fee calculated in (a), what would Freda earn in a month in
       which her time charged to clients was only 100 hours? Assume that all
       costs are fixed.

17-16. The owner of Morgan Television Repair Shop wants to use the time and material approach to pricing television repair services. The owner compiled the following data for a typical month:

Invoice cost of repair parts....................	$ 3,000
Cost of handling and storing parts.............	600
Salary and fringe benefits of repair personnel..	6,000
Other indirect costs (all related to repair personnel).......................................	2,400
Total monthly cost........................	$12,000
Hours of labor expected to be charged to repair work..................................	500

Based on assets employed in the business, a monthly profit of $3,000 is considered satisfactory.

Required:

   a. Assuming that the company uses the same profit margin (as a percentage of costs) for both labor and parts costs, what amount should be charged for (1) an hour of labor and (2) each dollar invoice cost of parts? What should be charged for a job that requires four hours of labor and parts with an invoice cost of $25?
   b. If only 420 hours of labor time were expected to be charged to customers each month instead of 500, but costs and total target profit were as above, what should be the charge to th customer for an hour of labor?

17-17. Foster Company produces two products, A and B. Estimated costs are presented below for a year in which 10,000 units of each product are expected to be sold:

	Total	Product A	Product B
Direct production cost	$500,000	$300,000	$200,000
Overhead cost	200,000	120,000	80,000
Selling and administrative cost	100,000	60,000	40,000

An annual profit of $160,000 for the whole company is considered satisfactory. The company uses the same profit margin (as a percentage of costs) to arr at the price for both products.

Required:

   a. Calculate normal selling prices for Products A and B.
   b. Using the prices calculated above, how much profit would result if the sales were 5,000 units of A and 15,000 units of B instead of 10,000 units of each?
   c. Comment on the effect of changes in the product mix on total profit when the same profit margin percentage is used.

CASES

Case 17-18: Zephyr Research Company

Zephyr Research Company, located in a university community, was a publishing company specializing in research aid books such as comprehensive indices and bibliographies. Each of Zephyr's publications was worked on in the editorial department by a group of about four editors, most of whom had graduate degrees in English or Library Science. Each publication took about a year to do, and there was frequently a period of several months before editorial staff members were assigned to new projects. Each publication was treated as a cost objective.

Since editorial staff members were salaried employees, they continued to draw pay for those periods when they had no publication to work on. The company did not wish to lay them off when there was no work, since the security of their positions was one of the reasons why these people were willing to accept the low rates of pay in the publishing industry. (The typical editor's salary was $12,000 per year.) Last year, when Zephyr replaced

some of their old keypunch data-entry machines with new key-to-disc machines, the company laid off some of its keypunch operators, and began assigning idle editorial employees to do data-entry work with the new machines.

Data-entry operations were part of the production department. The typical employee in this department was a high school graduate and was paid about $4 per hour. The head of the production department strenuously objected to being charged with the editors' salaries while they were doing production work. She maintained that her department should be charged no more than the average clerical rate, and certainly should not be charged the much higher editorial rate. In fact, she felt a lower-than-average clerical rate was justified, since the editors worked more slowly than those clerks who regularly did data-entry work. The vice president for operations replied that the editors would be paid the higher salaries whether they did data entry work or editorial work, and that

Production should be charged for the actual costs incurred in doing their work.

Question

How would you account for the editors' salaries while they are doing data-entry work in the production department?

* * * * *

Case 17-19: Conrad Taxi

Conrad owns a taxicab which he recently purchased for $8,000 cash. He operates it himself for 60 hours a week and rents it to Werner who also operates it 60 hours a week. Conrad pays all the bills. During the first year Conrad drove the taxicab 30,000 miles, of which 20,000 miles were "revenue miles" (i.e., miles for which fares were collected), and Werner drove 20,000 miles of which 10,000 miles were revenue miles. Costs for the year were:

Registration and insurance.......$1,800
Depreciation of the taxicab...... 1,600
Gasoline and oil................. 4,500
Tires (changed every
   25,000 miles)................. 400
Routine maintenance
   (every month)................. 1,500

The taxicab was garaged in a space leased by Conrad at $1,200 per year. Conrad would pay this amount whether or not the taxicab was used by Werner.

During the year Werner paid $50 for his operator's license and a $10 fine for a parking violation. Conrad paid $50 for his operator's license and a $20 fine for a second parking violation. (Parking fines were $10 for the first offense in a given year, $20 for the second offense, $30 for the third offense, and so on.)

Werner paid Conrad $75 per week ($3,900 per year) on account, and they agreed to settle up at the end of the year on an equitable basis. They could not agree on what this basis was, and they ask your help as an impartial outsider.

Question

How much more should Werner pay Conrad?

* * * * *

Case 17-20: Government Contracts

Many federal government contracts cannot be at a fixed price because the costs cannot be estimated closely in advance. Until 1976 the typical practice was to reimburse the contractor for its full cost plus a profit which was a certain percentage of cost (cost-based pricing). Beginning in 1976, some contractors were reimbursed at full cost plus a profit which was a certain percentage of assets employed (asset-based pricing).

For the purposes of discussion, assume that when the profit is based on cost the rate is 7 percent, and that when profit is based on assets employed, the rate is 14 percent. Assume three contracts, each with a cost of $1,000,000. Contractor A has assets of $1,000,000, Contractor B has assets of $500,000, and Contractor C has assets of $250,000. In other words, the asset turnovers (based on cost rather than revenue) are 1, 2, and 4 respectively.

Questions

1. Calculate the profit which each contractor would earn under (1) cost-based pricing and (2) asset-based pricing.

2. Assume that Contractor A owns fixed assets (plant and equipment) costing $500,000 and that depreciation on these assets is a contract cost of $100,000 per year. Suppose, instead, Contractor A had leased these fixed assets from another company, paying that company $110,000 per year. What would Contractor A's profit have been under (1) cost-based pricing and (2) asset-based pricing? Which pricing policy encourages contractors to lease assets?

3. Assume that under cost-based pricing (with a 7 percent rate) the aggregate profit of government contrac-

tors is satisfactory. What should be the average industry asset turnover (based on cost) to warrant a profit of 14 percent of assets employed?

4. As a taxpayer, do you favor cost-based pricing or asset-based pricing?

Chapter 18

Additional Aspects of Product Costing Systems

Key Terms

Job-order costing
Process costing
Equivalent production
Allocation
Cost center
Production cost center
Service cost center

Allocation basis
Step-down order
Overhead rate
Flexible overhead budget
Standard volume
Underabsorbed or overabsorbed
  overhead

Discussion Questions

1. Give examples of situations where job-order costing is appropriate; where process costing is appropriate.

2. Explain what is meant by "traceability" and "causal relationship" as bases for assigning costs to cost objectives.

3. Distinguish between variable costs and direct costs; between fixed costs and indirect costs. Why are these terms often used imprecisely in practice?

4. Give three reasons why costs might not be traced directly to a cost objective.

5. What are the similarities and differences between a cost center and a responsibility center?

6. Below are listed certain service cost centers and the five bases for allocation that are used in a certain factory. Which basis of allocation is most appropriate for each cost center? Explain your answer.

Service Cost Center	Basis for Allocation
a. Medical department	1. Direct labor cost
b. Employee pensions	2. Number of employees
c. Purchasing department	3. Direct material cost
d. Building maintenance	4. Square feet of space
e. Machine maintenance	5. Direct material plus direct labor cost
f. Employee cafeteria	
g. Telephone switchboard	
h. Factory superintendent	

7. Service center costs are first reassigned to production cost centers and then become part of the overhead rate that assigns them to products. Why not skip the step of assigning service center costs to production cost centers, and instead immediately assign service center costs to products?

8. Why, in all fairness, should one product have a higher overhead cost than another product?

9. Why are annual predetermined overhead rates better than monthly overhead rates determined after the fact?

10. Give several reasons why production overhead costs would be overabsorbed in a given month.

11. The text gives the journal entry for unabsorbed overhead costs. Give the corresponding entry for overabsorbed, assuming any numbers that you wish.

Very important-yes 12. Is it true that unabsorbed overhead is always reflected by a debit to the Overhead Variance account and overabsorbed overhead is always reflected as a credit?

13. "The Delia Company set selling prices on each job that are equal to cost plus 10 percent. Its total profit will therefore be 10 percent of cost, no matter how the costs are allocated to each job. It therefore makes no difference how the costs are allocated." Comment.

14. "It is absolutely impossible to measure the true cost of any cost objective if indirect costs are present." Comment.

Problems

18-1. Stevens Company uses a process cost system. Beginning work in process was valued at $4,500. Total production costs for May were $90,000. Production data for the month were as follows:

                                                    Units

        Beginning work in process..............1,100
        Transferred to finished goods..........8,500
        Ending work in process.................1,900

Required:

   a. Assuming that the partially completed units were 50 percent complete, calculate equivalent production in units for May.
   b. What is the unit cost and total cost of the units transferred to finished goods and the units remaining in work in process inventory?

18-2. Following is a summary of transactions for June for the Teetor Company:

                                    Transactions

(1) Raw materials purchased on account, $28,900
(2) Sales made on account were billed at $51,000 and cost of goods sold was $32,300.
(3) Paid bills in cash, as follows:

        Machine repairs...................................$ 3,400
        Direct labor (all for hours worked in June)....... 12,920
        Indirect labor (all for hours worked in June)..... 2,550
        Administrative costs..............................   850
        Salespersons' salaries............................ 2,550
        Miscellaneous indirect factory costs.............   850
        Accounts payable................................. 30,600

(4) Received $54,400 from customers on account.
(5) Raw material withdrawn from warehouse and put into production, $25,500.
(6) Overhead rate, 60 percent of direct labor cost.
(7) Cost of units of production completed during June, $52,700.
(8) Any overabsorbed or unabsorbed overhead is charged to the month's cost of goods sold.

Required:

   a. Journalize these transactions, and any necessary adjusting entries. Post to T-accounts.
   b. Prepare an income statement for June. (Ignore income taxes.)

18-3. Handy Tool Company manufactures various tools and parts for small gasoline engines, some for special order and some for stock. At the end of April a a summary of job-cost sheets reflects the following data:

Job No.	Customer or Stock No.	Total
1,002......................	Part No. 32	$4,500
1,100......................	Customer No. 45	7,800
1,205......................	Customer No. 69	7,200

During May two new jobs were started: 1,206 for stock Part No. 18, and 1,207 for Customer No. 70. Job Nos. 1,002, 1,100, and 1,206 were completed during May. Customer No. 45 paid $20,000 in full for his order. None of the stock parts were sold. Total costs incurred in May are shown below by job number:

Job No.	Amount
1,002................	$4,900
1,100................	8,000
1,205................	600
1,206................	5,000
1,207................	3,100

Required:

a. Produce a summary job cost sheet to show the jobs still in process May 31.
b. Compute the cost of goods completed (manufactured) for May.
c. Compute the gross margin for May.

18-4. Complete a job order cost record to show the accumulation of costs for Job No. 786, for a special-order refrigeration unit. Data pertinent to the costs of the job are as follows:

January
1   100 pounds of raw material C costing $10 per pound were requisitioned from the storeroom and used on the job.
7   Direct labor incurred on the job amounted to 10 hours at $6 per hour.
10 Raw material D was purchased at a cost of $1,500 for 100 pounds. This material will be used on Job No. 786 and on other future jobs requiring the same material.
11 Five pounds of raw material D were requisitioned from the storeroom and used on the job.
14 Direct labor cost incurred on the job amounted to 200 hours at $6 per hour and 10 hours at $9 per hour.
15 Factory indirect cost is assigned to the job on the basis of 150 percent of direct labor.
16 The job is completed.

18-5. Diversified Products, Inc., manufactures a product in four processes. Below are data relating to the final process, Process 4, for the month of March:

(1) Work in Process 4 on March 1 was 600 units shown at a cost of $3,600. Of this amount, $1,800 was the cost as transferred from Process 3, and $1,800 was direct labor and overhead of Process 4. These units were assumed to be 50 percent complete as to labor and overhead.

(2) During March $18,000 of direct labor cost and $19,800 of overhead cost were incurred in Process 4.

(3) During March 4,400 units, at $3 each, were transferred from Process 3, and 4,000 units were completed and transferred to finished goods inventory.

(4) Units in process at the end of March were assumed to be 50 percent complete as to direct labor and overhead. (No direct material was added in Process 4.)

Required

    a. What was the work in process inventory in units on March 31?
    b. What were the equivalent units of production in March?
    c. What was the direct labor and overhead cost per equivalent unit in March?
    d. What was the balance in work in process inventory as of April 1?
    e. What was the dollar amount transferred to finished goods inventory?

18-6. Drake Company allocates production overhead costs to jobs on the basis of direct labor hours. Its estimated average <u>monthly</u> production costs for the year are as follows:

	Average Monthly Costs
Direct material.....................................	$ 50,000
Direct labor (other than items below)...............	80,000
Overtime payments to direct workers.................	10,000
Fringe benefits on direct labor (including payroll taxes), 20 percent of direct labor..............	16,000
Other production overhead costs.....................	100,000

Drake's estimated average monthly production volume is 20,000 direct labor hours.

Among the jobs worked on in November were two jobs, G and H, for which the following information was collected:

	Job G	Job H
Direct material cost...........................	$5,000	$ 5,000
Direct labor cost (other than overtime and fringe benefits)...........................	8,000	10,000
Overtime cost..................................	1,000	-0-
Direct labor hours.............................	2,000	2,000

Assume that no fringe benefits were paid on overtime work.

Required:

    a. Compute the overhead rate and the total production costs of Jobs G and H on each of the following assumptions:

        (1) Overtime and fringe benefits are classified as production overhead cost.
        (2) Fringe benefits are classified as production overhead cost and overtime as direct labor cost.
        (3) Both overtime and fringe benefits are classified as direct labor cost.

    b. Discuss which of the above methods is preferable.

18-7. Smith Company estimated that costs of production for the coming year would be:

Raw materials....................	$50,000
Direct labor.....................	60,000
Production overhead..............	90,000

Required:

    a. Calculate the overhead rate for the next year, assuming that it is based on direct labor dollars.
    b. Journalize the entry necessary to show the total cost of production for the month of April if the raw materials put into production totaled $4,000 and direct labor was $5,100.
    c. If actual production overhead costs incurred in April were $7,500, calculate the overabsorbed overhead for the month.

18-8. Tempo Company has three production departments, A, B, and C, for which expected average montly overhead cost and direct labor hours are as follows:

	Total	A	B	C
Overhead cost	$300,000	$210,000	$50,000	$40,000
Direct labor hours	60,000	30,000	10,000	20,000

Among the jobs worked on in January were the following, together with the direct hours of labor each:

		Direct Labor Hours		
Job	Total	A	B	C
150	600	200	100	300
151	600	300	100	200
152	600	100	100	400

The company considered the whole plant as one cost center (i.e., it used a plantwide overhead rate). The rate was based on direct labor hours.

Required:

    a. Compute the overhead cost allocated to each job in January.
    b. Suppose that instead of having a single cost center, each department was treated as a separate cost center. What would the production overhead costs of the three jobs have been?
    c. Discuss whether the single cost center is preferable to having three cost centers.

18-9. The Cable Company estimates that production costs for the operations of the coming year will be $920,000 for materials, $1,380,000 for labor, and $1,932,000 for production overhead. Overhead is charged to cost objectives on the basis of percentage of direct labor cost.

Required:

    a. Calculate the overhead rate for the estimated production for the coming year.
    b. Compute the debits to Work in Process for the month of January, assuming actual costs were $57,500 for direct materials, $80,500 for direct labor, and $149,500 for production overhead.
    c. Calculate the overabsorbed and unabsorbed overhead for January.
    d. Assume that no changes are made in estimated production for the whole year. What disposition should be made of the overabsorbed or unabsorbed overhead?

18-10. The adjusted trial balance of Troy Corporation includes the following overhead costs which are to be distributed before the books are closed to its three cost centers, A, B, and C.

	Total	Building	Furniture and Fixtures	Machinery and Equipment
Heat, light, power	$40,000			
Depreciation	23,800	$3,000	$800	$20,000
Insurance:				
Inventories	200			
Other	2,210	1,300	60	850
Repairs	5,900	4,000		1,900
Telephone expense	1,800			
	$73,910			

Data used for cost distribution follow:

	Cost Center		
	A	B	C
Cubic feet.........................700,000		200,000	100,000
Square feet of floor space........ 48,000		9,000	3,000
Number of telephone extensions.... 6		30	9

Three fourths of the furniture and fixtures are in Cost Center B and one fourth are in Cost Center C. Half of the inventory is in Cost Center A and half is in Cost Center B. Assume that all building costs except utilities are allocated on the basis of floor space. Utilities are allocated based on cubic feet. All machinery and equipment is in Cost Center A.

Required: Calculate the amount of cost to be allocated to each cost center.

18-11. Mid-City College is organized into three instruction centers and two service centers. The instruction centers are Arts and Sciences, Education, and Business Administration. The service centers are Buildings and Grounds and Central Administration. The president wants to know the cost per student in each of the three instruction centers. As a part of the task, you have been asked to assist with the reassignment of overhead costs from the service centers to the instruction centers. The following data represent estimates for the current school year:

	Total	Arts and Sciences	Education	Business Adminis- tration	Building and Grounds	Central Adminis- tration
Overhead costs (000)	$6,500	$2,000	$1,500	$1,500	$1,000	$500
Percent of space occupied.........	100	30	25	20	10	15
Number of employees.	250	65	50	35	60	40
Number of students..	8,000	4,000	2,500	1,500	--	--

Required:

a. Reassign the overhead costs from the service centers to the instructions centers, beginning with buildings and grounds. (Round results to the nearest whole dollar.)
b. Calculate the overhead cost for each instruction center on a number-of-students basis. (Round results to the nearest cent.)

18-12. Northwest Company calculated expected indirect costs for the coming year as shown in Exhibit A on the next page of this workbook.

Required:

a. Allocate the indirect costs of the service centers to the production centers using the step-down procedure as follows:
    Personnel--on basis of employees.
    General factory--on basis of square feet of area.
    Stores--on basis of requisitions.

b. Compute the overhead rate per direct labor dollar for each product center.
c. Calculate the overabsorbed or unabsorbed overhead for each product center for January.

18-13. Middy Company uses a job-order cost system. The following data relate to the month of March:

Order No.	Raw Materials Issued	Direct Labor Hours	Direct Labor Dollars
11...................	$ 2,000	1,000	$ 4,000
12...................	6,100	2,000	8,000
13...................	7,000	5,000	19,000
14...................	5,300	2,000	9,000
15...................	6,200	3,000	12,000
Total..........	$26,600	13,000	$52,000

Exhibit A

Departmental Expected Cost Distribution

| | | Production Centers | | | Service Centers | | |
Expense	Basis for Distribution	Stamping	Grinding	Assembly	Stores	Personnel	General Factory
Indirect wages	Payroll dollars	50,000	95,000	10,000	4,000	29,000	15,000
Rent	Square feet	1,200	1,200	600	1,200	240	360
Depreciation--							
Buildings	Square feet	2,400	2,400	1,200	2,400	480	720
Machinery	Value	89,750	8,650	1,785	10	15	820
Insurance	Value	300	280	150	15	15	60
Taxes--building	Square feet	600	600	300	600	120	180
Heat	Radiators	400	400	200	250	50	70
Power	Direct meter	450	450	175	25	80	40
Total		145,100	108,980	14,410	8,500	30,000	17,250

Additional data pertaining to the departments above:

		Stamping	Grinding	Assembly	Stores	Personnel	General Factory
Area in square feet		10,000	10,000	5,000	10,000	2,000	3,000
Number of employees		10	15	2	1	5	2
Expected raw materials issued		11,000	3,000	1,000			
Expected direct labor		114,400	110,400	14,400			
Actual direct labor--January		15,000	16,000	4,000			
Raw material--January		40,000					
Actual indirect costs--January		23,000	19,000	6,000			

Production overhead cost is applied to production on the basis of $4 per direct labor hour. Product overhead cost for the month was $55,000. Production orders 11, 13, 14, and 15 were completed during the month. Production orders 11 and 14 were shipped and invoiced to customers during the month at a price double the total production cost.

Required:

    a. Prepare the following journal entries:

        (1) Transferring raw material to work in process.
        (2) Transferring direct labor to work in process.
        (3) Transferring factory overhead cost to work in process.
        (4) Transferring from work in process to finished goods inventory.
        (5) Recording sales revenue and cost of goods sold.

    b. Prepare a job cost record for Order No. 12.
    c. What was the gross margin for the month?

18-14. Wendell Canning Company has a busy season lasting six months from September through February and a slack season lasting from March through August. Typical data for these seasons are as follows:

	Busy Season	Slack Season
Average monthly direct labor hours..........	12,000	4,000
Average monthly factory overhead costs.......	$120,000	$60,000

Factory overhead cost is allocated to cases of canned goods on the basis of direct labor hours. The typical case requires one direct labor hour. The same type of products is packed in all months. On December 31, the company has 20,000 cases in finished goods inventory.

Required:

    a. If the company allocated each month's factory overhead costs to the products made in that month, what would be the factory overhead cost per case in the busy season and in the slack season, respectively? What would be the factory overhead cost component of finished goods inventory?
    b. If, instead, the company used a predetermined annual overhead rate, what would be its cost per case? What would be the factory overhead cost component of finished goods inventory?
    c. Discuss which method of overhead allocation is preferable.

CASES

Case 18-15: Mason Automotive Company

Sandy Gund, a recent business school graduate who had recently been employed by Mason Automotive Company, was asked by Mason's president to review the company's present cost accounting procedures. In outlining this project to Gund, the president had expressed three concerns about the present system: (1) its adequacy for purposes of cost control; (2) its accuracy in arriving at the true cost of products; and (3) its usefulness in providing data to judge supervisors' performance.

Mason Automotive was a relatively small supplier of selected automobile parts to the large automobile compan-

ies. Mason competed on a price basis with larger suppliers that were long-established in the market. Mason had competed successfully in the past by focusing on parts that, relative to the auto industry, were of small volume and hence did not permit Mason's competitors to take advantage of economies of scale. For example, Mason produced certain parts usable only in four-wheel-drive vehicles.

Gund began the cost accounting study in Mason's carburetor division, which accounted for about 40 percent of Mason's sales. This division contained five production departments: casting and stamping, grinding, machining, custom work, and assembly. The casting and stamping department produced carburetor cases, butterfly valves, and certain other carburetor parts. The grinding department prepared these parts for further machining, and precision ground those parts requiring close tolerances. The machining department performed all necessary machining operations on standard carburetors; whereas the custom work department performed these operations (and certain others) on custom carburetors, which usually were replacement carburetors for antique cars or other highly specialized applications. The assembly department assembled and tested all carburetors, both standard and custom.

Thus custom carburetors passed through all five departments and standard carburetors passed through all departments except custom work. Carburetor spare parts produced for inventory went through only the first three departments. Both standard and custom carburetors were produced to order; there were no inventories of completed carburetors.

Gund's investigation showed that, with the exception of materials costs, all carburetor costing was done based on a single, plant-wide direct-labor hourly rate. This rate included both direct labor and factory overhead costs. Each batch of carburetors was assigned its labor and overhead cost by having workers charge their time to the job number assigned the batch, and then multiplying the total hours charged to the job number by the hourly rate. Exhibit 1 shows how the July hourly rate of $17.61 was calculated.

It seemed to Gund that, because the average skill level varied from department to department, each department should have its own hourly costing rate. With this approach, time would be charged to each batch <u>by department</u>; then the hours charged by a department would be multiplied by that department's costing rate to arrive at a departmental labor and overhead cost for the batch; and finally these departmental costs would be added (along with materials cost) to obtain the cost of a batch.

Gund decided to see what impact this approach would have on product costs. The division's accountant pointed out to Gund that labor hours and payroll costs were already traceable to departments. Also, some overhead items, such as departmental supervisors' salaries and equipment depreciation, could be charged directly to the

EXHIBIT 1

CALCULATION OF PLANT-WIDE LABOR AND
OVERHEAD HOURLY RATE
Month of July

	Dollars	Hours
Labor:		
Casting/Stamping...	$ 17,064	2,528
Grinding...........	11,984	2,140
Machining..........	61,400	7,675
Custom Work........	25,984	3,712
Assembly...........	92,142	15,357
Total labor.....	208,574	31,412
Overhead...........	344,589	
Total labor		
and overhead.......$553,163		

Hourly rate = $553,163/31,412
= $17.61 per hour

(= $6.64 labor
+ $10.97 overhead)

relevant department. However, many other overhead items, including heat, electricity, property taxes and insurance, would need to be allocated to each department if the new approach were implemented. Accordingly, Gund determined a reasonable allocation basis for each of these joint costs (e.g., cubic feet of space occupied as the basis of allocating heating costs), and then used these bases to recast July's costs on a departmental basis. Gund then calculated hourly rates for each department, as shown in Exhibit 2.

EXHIBIT 2

PROPOSED DEPARTMENTAL LABOR AND
OVERHEAD HOURLY RATES

Department	Labor Rate per Hour	Overhead per Hour	Total Cost per Hour
Casting/			
Stamping..	$6.75	$ 9.83	$16.58
Grinding....	5.60	9.42	15.02
Machining...	8.00	19.58	27.58
Custom Work.	7.00	12.71	19.71
Assembly....	6.00	6.65	12.65

In order to have some concrete number to show the president, Gund decided to apply the proposed approach to three carburetor division activities:

production of model CS-29 carburetors (Mason's best-selling carburetor), production of spare parts for inventory, and work done by the division for other divisions in Mason. Exhibit 3 summarizes the hourly requirements of these activities by department. Gund then costed these three activities using both the July plant-wide rate and the pro forma July department rates.

Upon seeing Gund's numbers, the president noted that there was a large difference in the indicated cost of CS-29 carburetors as calculated under the present and proposed methods. The present method was therefore probably leading to incorrect inferences about the profitability of each product, the president surmised. The impact of the proposed method on spare parts inventory valuation was similarly noted. The president therefore was leaning toward adopting the new method, but told Gund that the supervisors should be consulted before any change was made.

Gund's explanation of the proposal to some of the supervisors prompted strong opposition. The supervisors of the outside departments for which the carburetor division did work each month felt it would be unfair to increase their costs by increasing charges from the carburetor division. One of them stated:

The carburetor division handles our department's overflow machining work when we're at capacity. I can't control costs in the carburetor division, but if they increase their charges, I'll never be able to meet my department's cost budget. They're already charging us more than we can do the work for in our own department, if we had enough capacity, and

you're proposing to charge us still more!

Also opposed was the production manager of the carburetor division:

I've got enough to do getting good quality output to our customers on time, without getting involved in more paperwork! What's more my department supervisors haven't got time to become bookkeepers, either. We're already charging all of the divisions' production costs to products and work for other departments; why do we need this extra complication?

The company's sales manager also did not favor the proposal, telling Gund:

We already have trouble being competitive with the big companies in our industry. If we start playing games with our costing system, then we'll have to start changing our prices. You're new here, so perhaps you don't realize that we have to carry some low-profit -- or even loss -- items in order to sell the more profitable ones. As far as I'm concerned, if a product line is showing an adequate profit, I'm not hung up about cost variations among items within the line.

When Gund reported this opposition to the president, the president replied:

You're not telling me anything that I haven't already heard from unsolicited phone calls from several supervisors the last few days. I don't want to cram anything down their throats -- but I'm still not satisfied our current system is adequate. Sandy, what do you think we should do?

EXHIBIT 3

DIRECT LABOR HOUR DISTRIBUTION FOR THREE CARBURETOR DIVISION ACTIVITIES

Department	CS-29 Carburetors (per batch of 100)	Spare Parts for Inventory (per typical month)	Work for Other Divisions (per typical month)
Casting/Stamping.........	21 hrs.	304 hrs.	674 hrs.
Grinding.................	12	270	540
Machining................	58	1,115	2,158
Custom Work..............	--	--	--
Assembly.................	35	--	--
Total................	126 hrs.	1,689 hrs.	3,372 hrs.

Questions

1. Using the data in the exhibits, determine the cost of a 100-unit batch CS-29 carburetors, spare parts, and work done for other divisions under both the present and proposed methods.

2. Are the cost differences between the two methods significant? What causes these differences?

3. Suppose that Mason purchased a new machine costing $400,000 for the custom work department. Its expected useful life is 5 years. This machine would reduce machining time and result in higher quality custom carburetors. As a result, the department's direct labor hours would be reduced by 30 percent, and this extra labor would be transferred to departments outside the carburetor division. About 10 percent of the custom work department's overhead is variable with respect to direct labor hours. Using July's data:

   a. Calculate the plant-wide hourly rate (present method) if the new machine were acquired. Then calculate indicated costs for the custom work department in July, using both this new plant-wide rate and the former $17.61 rate.
   b. Calculate the hourly rate for the custom work department only (proposed method), assuming the machine were acquired and the proposed costing procedure were adopted. Then calculate indicated costs for the custom work department in July, using both this new rate and the former $19.71 rate.
   c. Under the present costing procedures, what is the impact on indicated custom carburetor costs if the new machine is acquired? What is this impact if the proposed costing procedures are

used? What inferences do you then draw concerning the usefulness of the present and proposed methods?

4. Assume that producing a batch of 100 model CS-29 carburetors requires 126 hours, distributed by department as shown in Exhibit 3, and $875 worth of materials. Mason sells these carburetors for $32 each. Should the price of a CS-29 carburetor be increased? Should the CS-29 be dropped from the product line? (Answer using both the present and the proposed costing methods.)

5. Assume that Mason also offers a model CS-30 carburetor that is identical to a CS-29 in all important aspects, including price, but is preferred for some applications because of certain design features. Because of the CS-30's relatively low sales volume, Mason buys certain major components for the CS-30 rather than making them in-house. The total cost of purchased parts for 100 units of model CS-30 is $1,800; the labor required per 100 units is 12, 7, 17, and 35 hours respectively in the casting/stamping, grinding, machining, and assembly departments. If a customer ordered 100 carburetors and said that either model CS-29 or CS-30 would be acceptable, which model should Mason ship? Why? (Answer using only the proposed costing method.)

6. What benefits, if any, do you see to Mason if the proposed costing method is adopted? Consider this question from the standpoint of (a) product pricing, (b) cost control, (c) inventory valuation, (d) charges to outside departments, (e) judging departmental performance, and (f) diagnostic uses of cost data. What do you conclude Mason should do regarding the proposal?

* * * * *

Case 18-16: Sylvan Pools, Inc.

Sylvan Pools was born in 1947, when the company's president, Herman Silverman, who at the time was operating a small landscaping business in Pennsylvania, was asked by a customer to convert a mudhole into a concrete pond. Silverman fulfilled the request by lining the mudhole with wire and hand-cementing over the wire. As a result of this venture, Herman wondered why residential swimming pools could

not be built as economically. That same year he experimented by building two such pools; the following year he built eight. Extending the simple methods used in the mudhole, Herman perfected the Unipour method of swimming pool construction, which produced a pool with no seams or joints, and employed no forms in pouring the concrete. The result was a lifetime pool impervious to all weather conditions, and even recommended for use in the winter as an ice skating rink.

In 1953, Herman was joined in the business by his brother Ira, who became Executive Vice President. The company continued to grow, building sixty pools in 1953 and eighty in 1954. The increased demand was kept manageable by keeping prices up, but in spite of the premium pricing policy the company reported losses regularly.

The reported results puzzled Herman and Ira. They knew that they were succeeding in producing a quality product, prices were at least in line with what the competition was charging, their employees seemed to be working efficiently, and yet their financial statements reported that they were losing money. Every manager in the company had his own explanation of the reasons, often based on his personal "back pocket slip" on costs. Everyone was sure that the company's problems were someone else's fault. In particular, interminable arguments resulted from the allocation procedures. No one could agree on whether labor hours, labor dollars, sales, or any other base was appropriate for allocating particular overhead items.

The U.S. Swimming Pool Industry. Formerly confined primarily to building large pools for institutions, the U.S. swimming pool industry was undergoing a major transformation in the late 1950s. Rising consumer affluence was permitting more individuals to own a private pool, resulting in an industry divided into two segments: commercial and residential. Almost all commercial pools were constructed by a few big companies. Residential pools, on the other hand, were marketed both by a few large companies, each putting in hundreds of pools per year, and by a large number of small companies, each putting in a few pools per year. There were few barriers to entry into the business -- all that one needed was a bulldozer and a truck -- resulting in many small firms being formed every year. Many of these firms were under-financed and run by people who did not have the expertise required; as a result, there was a high rate of turnover.

Residential pools were constructed of various materials. One of the advantages of gunnite or poured concrete was that every pool could be unique in size and shape. In the colder parts of the country, pool construction was necessarily a seasonal business. When winter came, instllations stopped. Sales also dropped off in the winter,

and peaked on the hottest summer days. Even though residential pools cost $8,000-$15,000, they were often purchased on impulse.

Company Background. In the early years of Sylvan Pools, Herman Silverman sold pools by night and worked with the construction crews by day. Sylvan gradually developed consumer confidence, and was able to develop strong relationships with several prominent architects and builders. These architects often required construction to Sylvan's specifications. As a result, Sylvan usually received the contract to build the pool since the Unipour process was patented. Sylvan's economical and dependable method of construction broke the barrier with the middle-to-upper income resident, and enabled the company to capture a large market share in Pennsylvania.

Sylvan's construction employees worked about nine months during the year although, due to bad weather, they did not always work a five-day week. However, they worked so hard and such long hours during the days that they did work, and Sylvan paid them such a high hourly rate, that employee turnover was practically nil and there was a very high sense of company loyalty. The office and sales staffs worked a twelve-month year.

During the slow winter season, the equipment and rolling stock were repaired and repaintd in order to have them appear spanking new for the commencement of work in the spring. Only repairs absolutely necessary to keep the equipment operating were made during the summer. Herman and Ira felt that a good-looking fleet of vehicles was important in enhancing Sylvan's quality image. Also, all of the construction workers wore uniforms in order to achieve this end.

The Construction of a Sylvan Pool. In addition to the pool shell itself, there were many subsidiary parts needed for a pool. Plumbing was required for filling and draining the pool. A filter was needed to clean the water, and often a heater was added to lengthen the swimming season. Lighting was usually installed, sometimes both underwater and above ground. A ladder and diving board were virtually standard equipment. While skimmers (water surface level outlets) were used to keep the water free of surface debris, an underwater vacuum cleaner was required to remove dirt which had settled on the bottom of the pool. A terrace was often installed around the pool and a fence was usually a legal requirement for safety reasons. Sometimes an alarm sensitive to waves in the pool was installed to detect uninvited swimmers. Some manufacturers offered covers for pools which could be locked above the water surface for safety. In inclement climates, pool enclosures, either rigid or supported by internal air pressure, were used to lengthen the swimming season.

Every pool Sylvan installed was unique in size, shape, the amount of materials required (ready-mix concrete was the predominant material), the amount of labor required, the distance from the main plant, and in the accessories desired by the owner. Every night, employees at the warehouse asembled on pallets the materials needed for each crew for the next day's work. Given the diversity in the pools, a different quantity and/or variety of material had to be "picked" for each pallet.

After plans had been approved by both Sylvan and the customer, a three-person excavation crew arrived with a bulldozer and trucks and made the excavation, adding finishing touches by hand, and laying down a crushed stone base to relieve hydrostatic pressure. Then a reinforcing crew of two workers arrived and assembled half-inch steel reinforcing rods into an electrically bonded mesh. Later, the pouring crew, which usually consisted of eight workers, using the Unipour method poured the pool shell. The coping and tiling crew of three people installed the concrete coping and tiling around the edge of the pool. Terracing followed if required. Then the completion crew sanded and painted the pool, installed accessories, and cleaned up the site. Finally, fencing was installed if ordered.

Unexpected problems sometimes developed, especially in the excavation step. While items such as stumps could be observed and charged for accordingly, rocks or hardpan might appear after excavation had begun, blasting might be required, or the customer might exercise his privilege under the sales contract either to change the pool location, requiring new plans, or simply to have the hole refilled. In the contract, Sylvan protected itself by trying to assure that it would break even on the extra work required if unexpected problems occurred.

There were many crews of constant membership in each trade. Each step was completed in one day and it was im-portant that excavation be followed promptly by reinforcing and pouring, lest rain cause wall collapse. Sylvan subscribed to a weather service and all trucks carried plastic tarpaulins to minimize rain damage. If rain was expected, the crews did not leave the home office, thus disrupting the schedule which had been established.

Actual Cost System. When a job was started, it received a code number, and all costs relevant to this job were identified by this number. When materials such as plumbing supplies, reinforcing rods, and accessories were requisitioned from the warehouse, a record of the quantity issued and the job code number was made on the requisition form. The quantity of material was multiplied by the purchase cost per unit (on a FIFO basis) to arrive at the actual cost of material used. Leftover materials returned to the warehouse were credited to the appropriate job. Invoices from ready-mix concrete companies were also recorded by code number. By summarizing all these items, it was easy to arrive at the total material cost for a given pool.

Similarly, labor costs were accumulated from employees' time cards which indicated how many hours had been spent at how much per hour on which pools. Finally, Sylvan's overhead costs which could not be directly identified with a particular pool were allocated among all pools on a basis proportional to the number of hours of labor devoted to each job. For example, if 5 percent of the hours worked during a calendar quarter were spent on pool A, then pool A would bear 5 percent of the allocated overhead incurred in that quarter.

Under this system, management knew toward the end of a quarter how much each pool built in the preceding quarter had cost. Income statements were prepared quarterly recognizing all costs recorded by the cost system and recognizing revenue for each pool as it was completed. Customer progress payments on pools were used as a much-needed source of cash, but were not recognized as revenue.

Salespersons, construction supervisors, and management all had individual "back pocket slips" concerning costs. There were endless arguments about overhead allocations. According to Ira, "nobody really knew what the costs were" and the whole situation was "chaotic." The financial statements, which used a fiscal year end of March 31, appeared late and showed steady losses. Though their accountant urged them to file a petition in bankruptcy, the Silverman brothers pushed on, obtaining the cash they needed through good relations with their bankers. Sylvan just kept growing larger and larger.

Questions

1. What kind of information should a cost system provide to management?

2. How well does Sylvan's system fulfill your idea of what a good system should be?

3. What recommendations for improvement would you make to Herman and Ira?

Chapter 19

Standard Costs, Joint Costs, and Variable Costing Systems

Key Terms

Standard cost system
Variance account
Joint products
By-products

Split-off point
Absorption costing
Variable costing

Discussion Questions

1. What is the essential difference between an actual cost system and a standard cost system?

2. What does it mean if it is necessary to debit a variance account? To credit one?

3. Explain the nature of both debit entries and credit entries to the Overhead clearing account.

4. Why is the estimate of normal volume of great importance in the calculation of overhead rates in a standard cost system?

5. Does overabsorbed overhead mean that overhead costs charged to Work In Process Inventory were more than actual overhead costs, or does it mean the opposite?

6. For what purposes are standard cost systems used?

7. A furniture company using an actual job cost accounting system has separate job cost records for each of two dining room tables. The recorded costs of each table are identical except in one respect; namely, the direct labor cost of assembly and finishing was $64 for one table and $72 for the other. This operation required eight hours for each table, but for one table it was performed by an employee who earned $8 per hour, while for the other it was performed by an employee who, because of seniority, earned $9 per hour. Did the cost of the two tables differ? Should they be sold at different prices?

8. Explain how a standard cost accounting system can reduce recordkeeping costs. Give some examples of companies in which such a system would be more expensive than an actual cost system.

9. If someone says, "raw materials are debited to Work in Process at standard," is it clear how the entry is calculated? Explain.

10. Distinguish between joint products and by-products.

11. In the text's example of the sales-value method for allocating joint costs, what would happen to the profit on Product B if the price of A were increased to $10.50 per unit?

12. How can two equally competent accountants arrive at different costs for the same product?

13. Explain the difference between variable costing and absorption costing.

14. What is the rationale of not permitting variable costing to be used in shareholder reports (i.e., reports prepared under GAAP)?

15. What are the advantages claimed for variable costing by its proponents? Given all of these advantages, why do most companies use only absorption costing?

16. What are some of the choices that must be made in designing a costing system?

Problems

19-1. Standard unit material and labor costs for the single product manufactured by Zimmer Company are as follows:

```
Direct material, 10 pounds at $3 per pound.......... $30
Direct labor, 5 hours at $7 per hour...............   35
```

During June the following transactions occurred:

(1) Purchased 1,000 pounds of direct material at $3.10 per pound.
(2) Issued 4,100 pounds of material from raw material inventory to manufacture 400 units of product.
(3) Incurred direct labor costs of $13,500 in manufacturing these 400 units. (There was neither a beginning nor an ending balance in Work in Process Inventory.)

Required: Journalize these transactions.

19-2. Drake Company allocates overhead costs to jobs on the basis of direct labor-hours. Its estimated average monthly factory costs for 1983 are as follows:

	Average montly costs
Direct material cost............	$ 50,000
Direct labor cost..............	240,000
Overhead cost..................	160,000

Its estimated average monthly direct labor-hours are 20,000. Among the jobs worked on in November 1983 were two jobs, G and H, for which the following information was collected:

	Job G	Job H
Direct material cost............	$ 5,000	$ 5,000
Direct labor cost..............	24,000	30,000
Direct labor-hours.............	2,000	2,500

Required:

a. Compute the overhead rate for Drake Company.
b. Compute the total production costs of jobs G and H.
c. At what amounts would customers be billed if the company's practice was to charge 180 percent of the production cost of each job?

19-3. A partial income statement for May Pex Company is as follows:

Sales revenue..		$437,000
Standard cost of goods sold:		
Beginning inventory...............................	$ 41,400	
Cost of goods manufactured.......................	253,000	
Ending inventory.................................	(36,800)	257,600
Standard gross margin...............................		$179,400

Variances for this accounting period, which were not included in costs of goods manufactured, were:

Favorable direct labor variance of $11,500.
Favorable overhead variance of $8,970.
Unfavorable material usage variance of $6,900.

Required: Compute the gross margin assuming actual costs were used instead of standard costs.

19-4. Following are standard and actual unit costs of product B-9 taken from the books of Matice Company for the month of May:

	Standard Unit Costs	Actual Unit Costs
Raw materials...............	10 pounds @ $0.75	11 pounds @ $0.78
Direct labor.................	4 hours @ $7.50	5 hours @ $7.65
Factory overhead............	4 hours @ $9.00	4 hours @ $8.85
Units produced..............		70,000
Units sold..................		68,000

Required:

a. Compute the toal actual and standard costs and the variances for each of the three elements of production cost for the 70,000 units produced.
b. (1) Give an analysis of the elements of cost comprising the finished goods ending inventory at standard cost. There were no beginning inventories, and no ending inventory of work in process.
   (2) Compute the amount of the finished goods ending inventory at actual cost.

19-5. At the end of the fiscal year of Multi-Products, Inc., the following data appeared in accounts in the general ledger:

	Debits	Credits
Materials inventory.............................	$22,500	$18,000
Finished goods inventory.......................	52,500	45,000
Factory overhead costs.........................	18,750	18,750
Wages payable..................................		40,500
Materials usage variance.......................	2,100	
Direct labor variance..........................		1,050
Factory overhead variance......................	675	

There were no inventories at the beginning of the year. The Materials Inventory, Wages Payable, and Factory Overhead Cost accounts were debited at actual cost.

Required:

a. Reconstruct the journal entries needed to record the accumulation of standard costs in work in process and the standard cost of goods sold for the year.
b. Compute the cost of goods sold using actual costs.

19-6. Ellis Enterprises produces two joint products, L and M. Joint costs are $21,000 for a batch of material that will be made into 1,000 units of L and 500 units of M. Processing costs beyond the split-off point are $16,000 for L and $4,000 for M. Selling prices are $40 per unit for L and $20 per unit for M. Each product has the same weight per unit.

Required:

a. Calculate the amount of joint cost per batch to be allocated to each product using the weight basis of allocation.
b. Calculate the amount of joint cost per batch to be allocated to each product using sales-value basis of allocation.
c. Calculate the gross margin for each product which would result from

the two different methods of allocating joint costs. Which method
would you recommend? Why?
d. Repeat Requirements (b) and (c) assuming that Ellis raises the price
of L to $50 per unit.

19-7. The standard costs for one unit of product 470 are determined to be as follows:

<pre>
Direct materials--3 sq. ft. @ $6.............$18.00
Direct labor--4 hours @ 6.................... 24,00
Overhead--$7.50 per hour of direct labor..... 30.00
Standard cost per unit.......................$72.00
</pre>

Operating results for March:

<pre>
Purchases of raw materials...................$106,200
Actual cost of raw materials used............ 108,360
Standard cost of raw materials used.......... 108,000
Actual direct labor cost..................... 161,940
Actual factory overhead cost................. 156,900
Units completed in March..................... 6,000
Units sold in March.......................... 5,000
</pre>

Inventories: Work in process, March 1 and 31, zero
Raw materials, March 1: 4,500 sq. ft. @ $6
Finished goods, March 1: 800 units @ $72

Required: Prepare a flowchart that will reflect the accumulation of costs in
the inventory accounts for March operations, assuming the use of a
standard cost system in which all differences between actual and
standard are removed prior to debits to Work in Process.

19-8. Mayfair Company uses a standard cost system. Debits to the factory overhead
account for Mayfair for the month of September resulted from the posting of
the following entry:

<pre>
September 30   Factory Overhead...................113,100
                 Cash..........................   44,850
                 Depreciation Expense.........   58,500
                 Prepaid Insurance............   1,950
                 Property Taxes...............   7,800
</pre>

Overhead is assigned to product on the basis of $4.875 per direct labor hour.
Four hours of work are normal for one unit of product, and 5,000 units were
completed during September. Raw materials bought during September for
$224,250 and having a standard cost of $220,350 were transferred to production. At the beginning of September there was a raw material inventory of
$4,290. The payroll for September totaled $111,150 for 19,000 hours at $5.85
per hour. The planned payroll for the units produced was 20,000 hours at
$5.85. All work started during the month was completed by the end of the
month.

Required:

a. Construct a flowchart to show computation of the standard cost of
goods manufactured and transferred to finished goods inventory
assuming the use of only one manufacturing variance account where all
production cost variances are isolated when the goods are transferred
to finished goods inventory.
b. Show what parts of the total manufcturing variance are attributable to
differences between actual and standard costs for material, labor, and
overhead.

19-9. The following information relates to the operations of the Forest Woodworking
Corporation for the month of April.

<pre>
Materials purchased..........................$ 9,800
Materials used............................... 9,000
Labor.. 15,000
</pre>

```
Heat, light, and power (direct costs)....... 1,129
Supplies used................................  500
General factory overhead.....................1,200
Machine shop (direct costs)..................  800
Inventories, April 1:
  Process I..................................    0
  Process II.................................    0
  Process III................................    0
  Finished goods.............................1,500
```

All materials enter Process I at actual cost, and production flows from Process I, to II, to III. All supplies were used by the machine shop. Labor is used by all three processes equally. General factory overhead costs are allocated on the same basis as labor. Utility costs are allocated 20 percent to the machine shop, 60 percent to Process I, and 10 percent each to Processes II and III. The machine shop services only Processes I and II with 75 percent of the work being done for Process I. Six thousand units of product were started and finished during April. There were no units left unfinished at the end of the month, and 5,800 units with a standard cost of $4.50 per unit were sold.

Required:

  a. On a sheet of paper, set up the following eight T-accounts: Machine Shop; Heat, Light, Power; Process I; Process II; Process III; Manufacturing Variances; Finished Goods; and Cost of Goods Sold. Then make postings to these accounts to show the accumulation of costs for Forest Woodworking Corporation's process cost system. Assume the use of only one manufacturing variance account, where variances are isolated when goods are transferred to Finished Goods.
  b. Compute the actual manufacturing cost per unit in April.

19-10. The Nutrient Company manufactures soybean oil and soybean meal. The company pays $64 per ton (2,000 pounds) for soybeans and incurs processing costs of $36 per ton. The average output from a ton of soybeans is 800 pounds of soybean oil and 1,200 pounds of soybean meal. Soybean oil is sold for $12 per cwt. (100 pounds), and soybean meal is sold for $3 per cwt.

Required:

  a. Calculate the cost per cwt. of each product if:

    (1) Joint costs are allocated on the basis of weight.
    (2) Joint costs are allocated on the basis of market value.
    (3) Soybean meal is treated as a by-product rather than as a joint product.

  b. Which method of costing is preferable?
  c. If output were 800 pounds of soybean oil, 1,100 pounds of soybean meal, and 100 pounds of chaff which had no market value, how, if at all, would your answer to Question (a) be different?

19-11. The production processes involved in making maple syrup can also produce maple sugar. Vermont Sugar Enterprises wishes to produce only syrup, but on occasion some sugaring takes place. Production for March produced the following results:

	Syrup	Sugar	Total
Units produced................	10,000	500	10,500
Unit selling price............	$7.50	$1.00	
Total process costs:			
After split-off.............	$6,000	$155	$ 6,155
Joint costs.................			55,000

Required:

  a. Calculate the cost of the syrup if the sugar is considered a by-product and the gross margin from its sale is considered to be a reduction of syrup cost.

    b. Calculate product costs asduming this company decided to make and sell as much maple sugar as possible after filling all syrup orders (i.e., it regarded syrup and sugar as joint products). Use the sales value method.

19-12. Smith Company estimated that costs of production for the following year would be:

        Direct material cost..........$500,000
        Direct labor cost............. 600,000
        Overhead cost................. 900,000

Required:

    a. Calculate the overhead rate for the next year assuming that it is based on direct labor dollars.
    b. Journalize the entry necessary to show the total cost of production for the month of April if the raw materials put into production totaled $40,000 and direct labor was $51,000.
    c. If actual factory overhead costs incurred in April were $75,000, calculate the overabsorbed or underabsorbed overhead for the month.
    d. What disposition should be made of the overabsorbed or underabsorbed overhead for April? Why?

19-13. Shuman Corporation uses variable costing for internal reporting purposes. Its preadjusting trial balance for the year ended December 31 shows:

        Cost of goods sold (at variable cost)................$500,000
        Finished goods inventory (at variable cost).......... 50,000
        Nonvariable production costs........................ 275,000

An analysis shows that cost of goods sold represents 25,000 direct labor hours, and finished goods inventory 2,500 direct labor hours. Shuman feels that the best way of allocating a fair share of nonvariable production costs to products is on the basis of direct labor hours.

Required:

    a. Prepare an adjusting entry which will put cost of goods sold and finished goods inventory on an absorption costing basis.
    b. What will be the difference between pretax income on a variable costing basis and on an absorption costing basis (assume zero beginning-of-year finished goods inventory)?
    c. What will be the December 31 amount of finished goods inventory on an absorption costing basis?

19-14. The following data pertain to the year's activities of the Lewis Company:

        Sales revenue..$1,300,000
        Variable manufacturing costs........................ 600,000
        Fixed manufacturing costs........................... 300,000
        Variable selling and administrative costs......... 100,000
        Fixed selling and administrative costs............. 200,000
        Production (units).................................. 200
        Beginning finished goods inventory (units)........ 0
        Ending finished goods inventory (units)........... 40

Required:

    a. Prepare an income statement using absorption costing.
    b. Prepare an income statement using variable costing.
    c. Explain why net income was different on the two statements.

CASES

Case 19-15: Bennett Body Company

Ralph Kern, controller of Bennett Body Company, received a memorandum from Paul Bennett, the company's president, suggesting that Kern review an attached magazine article and comment on it at the next executive committee meeting. The article described the Conley Automotive Corporation's cost accounting system. Bennett Body was a custom manufacturer of truck bodies. Occasionally a customer would reorder an exact duplicate of an earlier body, but most of the time some modifications caused changes in design and hence in cost.

The Conley System. Kern learned from the article that Conley also manufactured truck bodies but that these were of standard design. Conley had 12 models that it produced in quantities based upon management's estimates of demand. In December of each year, a plan, or budget, for the following year's operations was agreed upon, which included estimates of costs and profits as well as of sales volume.

Included in this budget were estimated costs for each of the 12 models of truck bodies. These costs were determined by totaling estimated labor at an expected wage rate, estimated materials at an expected cost per unit, and an allocation for overhead that was based on the proportion of estimated total overhead costs to estimated total direct labor dollars. This estimate for each model became the standard cost of the model.

No attempt was made in Conley's accounts to record the actual costs of each model. Costs were accumulated for each of the four direct production departments and for several service departments. Labor costs were easily obtainable from payroll records, since all employees assigned to a production department were classified as direct labor for that department. Material sent to the department was charged to it on the basis of signed issue slips. Overhead costs were charged to the department on the basis of the same percentage of direct labor as that used in determining the standard cost.

Since Conley's management also knew how many truck bodies of each model were worked on by each department monthly, the total standard costs for each department could easily be calculated by multiplying the quantity of that model produced by its standard cost. Management watched closely the difference between the actual cost and the standard cost as the year progressed.

As each truck body was completed, its cost was added to Finished Goods Inventory at the standard cost figure. When the truck body was sold, the standard cost became the Cost of Goods Sold figure. This system of cost recording avoided the necessity of accumulating detailed actual costs on each specific body that was built; yet the company could estimate, reasonably well, the costs of its products. Moreover, management believed that the differences between actual and standard cost provided a revealing insight into cost fluctuations that eventually should lead to better cost control. An illustrative tabulation of the costs for Department 4 is shown in Exhibit 1. No incomplete work remained in this department either at the beginning or at the end of the month.

EXHIBIT 1

SUMMARY OF COSTS, DEPARTMENT 4, NOVEMBER

Standard	Number of Bodies	Material Per Unit	Material Total	Labor Per Unit	Labor Total	Overhead Per Unit	Overhead Total
Model 101	10	$ 945	$ 9,450	$1,386	$13,860	$1,386	$13,860
109	8	1,260	10,080	1,104	8,832	1,104	8,832
113	11	1,923	21,153	1,323	14,553	1,323	14,553
154	20	597	11,940	1,221	24,420	1,221	24,420
Total	49		$52,623		$61,665		$61,665
Actual costs			57,456		63,189		63,189
Variances			$-4,833		$-1,524		$-1,524

The Bennett System. Because almost every truck body that Bennet built was in some respect unique, costs were accumulated by individual jobs. When a job was started it received a code number, and costs for the job were collected weekly under that code number. When materials used for a particular job were issued to the workers, a record of the quantities issued was obtained on a requisition form. The quantity of a given material -- so many units, board feet, linear feet, pounds, and so on -- was multiplied by its purchase cost per unit to arrive at the actual cost of material used. Maintenance of cumulative records of these withdrawals by code number made the total material cost of each job easy to determine.

Likewise, all labor costs of making a particular truck body were recorded. If a worker moved from job to job, a record was made of the worker's time spent on each job, and the worker's weekly wages were divided among these jobs in proportion to the amount of time spent on each. Throughout the shop, the time of any person working on anything directly related to an order -- Job No. 1375J, for example -- was ultimately converted to a dollar cost and charged to that job.

Finally, Bennett's overhead costs that could not be directly associated with a particular job were allocated among all jobs on the proportional basis of direct labor hours involved. Thus, if in some month 135 direct labor hours were spent on Job No. 1375J, and this was 5 percent of the 2,700 direct labor hours spent on all jobs at Bennett that month, then Job No. 1375J received 5 percent of all the overhead cost -- supplies, salaries, depreciation, and so forth -- for that month.

Under this system Bennett's management knew at the end of each month what each body job in process

cost to date. They could also determine total factory cost and therefore gross profit at the completion of each job.

The note that Mr. Bennett attached to the magazine article read:

Ralph:

Please review the system of cost accounting described in this article with the view of possible applications to our company. Aside from the overall comparison, I am interested particularly in your opinion on--

1. Costs of paper work and recordkeeping, as compared with our system.
2. Possible reasons for cost differences between the actual and standard costs under Conley's system.
3. How you think Conley develops the standard cost of factory overhead for a particular model for the purpose of preparing the budget.
4. Whether you think that we should change our period for determining the overhead allocation rate from monthly to annually. If so, why?
5. Which system is better from the standpoint of controlling costs?

These are just a few questions which might be helpful in your overall analysis. I would like to discuss this question at the next executive committee meeting.

Thank you.

Paul Bennett

Question

As Mr. Kern, what would you be prepared to say in response to Mr. Bennett's memorandum? How, if at all, should Bennett Body modify its present system?

* * * * *

Case 19-16: Black Meter Company

Refer to the description of Black Meter's cost accounting system in the Appendix, and consider the following:

1. Trace through the cost accounting procedures described so that you are able to show how the numbers in each illustration are derived from, and/or help derive, the other illustrations.

2. Try to imagine what an actual cost system for Black Meter would look like. How would it compare with the standard cost system in terms of:
   a. Recordkeeping effort required?
   b. Usefulness of cost information to Black Meter's management?

3. Develop a flowchart for Black Meter's system similar to the one in Illustration 19-1. Do not use dollar amounts, but indicate flows between

accounts and show whether entries are at standard or actual costs. In what respects, if any, do these two flow-charts differ?

4. Suppose that the direct labor rate for Department 120A was increased to $7.75 per hour, and that for Department 131 was increased to $6.25 per hour. What effect would these changes have on the succeeding illustrations and on the total standard cost of 100 5/8-inch HF meters?

5. As a consultant to Black Meter Company's controller, what would be your evaluation of the present system?

* * * *

Case 19-17: Pilbeam Company

Pilbeam Company made radio antennas, which were sold through retail stores and mail-order catalogs. These antennas were used by vehicle owners to replace antennas that had been vandalized or had otherwise become ineffective. Pilbeam made two models: the F-100 was used for fender mounting, and the S-100 was used for side mounting (e.g., on truck cabs).

Pilbeam used a standard cost system, which included these standards per dozen antennas:

	F-100	S-100
Materials:		
Chrome-plated tubing..	$ 8.25	$ 7.50
Cable and plug........	7.20	7.20
Mounting device.......	4.42	5.62
	19.87	20.32
Direct labor (@ $6 per hr.)........	9.00	9.00
Overhead (@ 125% of direct labor)......	11.25	11.25
Total cost per dozen.........	$40.12	$40.57

Materials were debited to Materials Inventory at standard cost upon receipt, any difference between the standard amount and actual invoice price being entered in the Material Price Variance account. Credits to Materials Inventory reflected the actual quantities issued, costed at standard cost per unit. All debits to Work in Process Inventory were based on standard quantities and standard prices or rates. Credits to Work in Process Inventory, debits to Finished Goods Inventory, and credits to Cost of Sales were all based on the $40.12 and $40.57 full standard costs shown above. Variance accounts were closed to the Income Summary account at the end of the month.

The following descriptions relate to April operations:

1. On April 1, balance sheet account balances were as follows:

	Dr.	Cr.
Materials Inventory......	$ 50,250	
Work in Process Inventory.....	75,600	
Finished Goods Inventory......	155,400	
All other assets.	325,500	
Accounts Payable		$104,700
Wages Payable....		6,150
All other liabilities....		47,250
Shareholders Equity.........		448,650
Total........	$606,750	$606,750

2. During April, Pilbeam received materials for 2,500 dozen F-100 antennas and 1,000 dozen S-100 antennas. The invoice amounts totaled $68,550.

3. During April, Pilbeam paid $102,300 worth of accounts payable. It collected $192,000 due from its customers. (Both Cash and Accounts Receivable are included in "All other assets" in the above account list.)

4. The stockroom issued materials during April for 3,200 dozen F-100 antennas and 700 dozen S-100 antennas, consistent with the planned production for the month. Stockroom requisition also included issues of materials in excess of quantities needed to produce these 3,900 dozen antennas. These issues were to replace parts that had been bent or broken during the production process, and were as follows: 100 dozen F-100 tubes; 20 dozen S-100 tubes; 45 dozen cables and plugs; 20 dozen F-100 mounting devices; and 4 dozen S-100 mounting devices. The original parts issued that these extra issues replaced were all thrown into the trash bin, because they had no significant scrap value.

5. Direct labor expense incurred in April was $36,150. Indirect labor

expense was $20,250. Wages paid were $58,350. (Ignore social security taxes and fringe benefits.)

6. Actual production overhead costs (excluding indirect labor) in April totaled $27,900. Of this amount, $18,750 was credited to Accounts Payable and the rest to various asset accounts (included above in "All other assets").

7. Selling and administrative expenses in Arpil were $39,375; this same amount was credited to various asset accounts.

8. April's standard cost sheets showed the following standard costs for antennas worked on during the Month: direct labor, $39,600; overhead, $49,500.

9. During April, 3,000 dozen F-100 antennas and 800 dozen S-100 antennas were delivered to the finished goods storage area; work on some of these goods had been started during March.

10. April sales were $154,800 for 2,400 dozen F-100 antennas and $59,400 for 900 dozen S-100 antennas. The offsetting entries were to Accounts Receivable (included in "All other assets").

Questions

1. Set up T-accounts, post beginning balances, and then record the above transactions. Adjust and close the accounts, determine April's income (ignore income taxes), and close this income to Shareholders' Equity. Do not create any balance sheet T-accounts not listed above.

2. Prepare the April income statement (again, disregarding income taxes). Why is your number for April income only an approximation?

3. Prepare a balance sheet as of April 30.

Chapter 20

Production Cost Variances

Key Terms

Material usage variance

Material price variance

Labor efficiency variance

Labor rate variance

Joint variance

Budgeted overhead cost

Absorbed overhead cost

Variable budget

Overhead production volume variance

Overhead spending variance

Favorable variance

Unfavorable variance

Discussion Questions

1. How is the standard direct labor cost <u>per unit</u> of product determined? How is the total standard labor cost for an <u>accounting period</u> determined?

2. Why are the total material and labor variances decomposed into quantity and price components?

3. Comment on this statement: "The material usage variance is always caused by actions of production personnel, whereas the material price variance is always the responsibility of the purchasing people."

4. A possible treatment of a joint material or labor variance would be to allocate it in some way between the price and quantity variances. Suggest some reasons why this is seldom done in practice.

5. Assume that a company pays its direct workers on a <u>piece-rate basis</u>. Why would one then expect there to be no labor rate or efficiency variance? Under what conditions could there be labor variances under a piece-rate system?

6. An instructor put on the board a diagram like the one in Illustration 20-5, except that she labeled the budget line "the real world" and labeled the absorption line "the accountant's world." What was she trying to convey to the class with these labels?

7. Discuss this comment, made by a plant manager: "I can help the company make more money this quarter by increasing production and thus absorbing more of our fixed overhead costs."

8. Explain in your own words why if a variable costing system is used there is no overhead volume variance.

9. Why might it happen that a company's actual annual production volume turns out to be exactly the same as the standard volume used in calculating the predetermined overhead rate, and hence there is zero overhead volume variance for the year, and yet the company reports an overhead volume variance every month during the year?

10. Why is the overhead spending variance based on actual volume, rather than on the standard volume?

11. How can one tell without doing any calculations whether the overhead volume variance for a period will be zero, favorable, or unfavorable?

12. In a given year, Lehman Company's standard production volume was 10,000 units; its sales volume was 11,000 units; and its actual production volume was 10,000 units. What can be said about its overhead volume variance that year?

13. In the following year, Lehman's standard production volume was again 10,000 units; but 10,500 units were actually produced. Raw materials were purchased at standard prices and consumed in standard quantities throughout the year. What can be said about Lehman's raw materials variances for the year?

14. What is the justification for treating production cost variances in a month as period costs, rather than allocating them among Work in Process, Finished Goods, and Cost of Goods Sold (as would be dictated by the matching principle)?

15. Why is it useful to think of the overhead rate as the sum of (1) the variable overhead per unit of volume, and (2) the fixed overhead per unit at standard volume ("fixed cost absorption rate")?

16. In a three-part overhead variance analysis, why is the term "overhead efficiency variance" potentially misleading?

Problems

20-1. Alpha Company calculates prime cost variances monthly. For May, the following data apply to its two products:

	Standard Material per Unit	Standard Labor per Unit	Units Produced in May
Product 1...............	9 lbs.	7.5 hrs.	500
Product 2...............	11 lbs.	9.0 hrs.	800

Actual usage in May was 14,000 lbs. of materials and 10,000 labor hours.

Required:

a. Calculate the material usage variance in pounds and the labor efficiency variance in hours.
b. If the standard materials price is $24 per lb. and the standard labor rate is $7.50 per hr., restate the variances in monetary terms.

20.2. Beta Company produces two products, A and B, each of which uses materials X and Y. The following unit standard costs apply:

	Material X	Material Y	Direct Labor
Product A............2 lbs. @ $5		1 lb. @ $4	1/5 hr. @ $6
Product B............3 lbs. @ $5		2 lbs. @ $4	1/3 hr. @ $6

During November, 4,200 units of A and 3,600 units of B were produced. Also, 19,000 lbs. of X were purchased @ $4.90, and 11,500 lbs. of Y were purchased @ $4.05; all of these materials (but no other materials) were used for the month's production. This production required 2,050 direct labor hours @ $5.80.

Required:

a. Calculate the material price and usage variances for the month.
b. Calculate the labor rate and efficiency variances for the month.
c. How would your answers to Questions a and b change if you had been told that November's planned production activity was 4,000 units of A and 4,000 units of B?
d. How would your answers to Questions a and b change if you had been told that November's sales were 4,000 units of A and 3,500 units of B?

20-3. Powers Company uses a standard cost system in which raw materials inventories are recorded at actual cost and the material price variance is based on quantities used. The following data refer to production of Product 822 during the month of August:

Standard material cost, $4 per pound
Standard labor rate, $10 per hour
Standard quantity of material per unit of product, 4 pounds
Standard labor hours per unit of product, 6
Quantity of material actually used, 8,500 pounds
Actual material cost, $3.80 per pound
Actual labor cost, 11,500 hours, $116,150
Units of product produced, 2,000

Required:

a. Calculate the price, usage, and net variances for direct materials and direct labor.
b. Comment on the possible causes of the variances you calculated.

20-4. Gamma Company makes one product, which passes through two production operations. Under normal conditions, 150 lbs. of raw material are required to make 100 units of product; all of the materials for a unit are issued to and used in Operation 1. In Operation 1, standard output is 8 partially completed units per direct labor hour, with a standard wage rate of $6 per hour. In Operation 2, standard labor time is 12.5 hours per 100 units, at a standard wage rate of $6.60. Normal volume is 550,000 units per month. In March, output was 479,000 units, and 732,864 lbs. of raw material were consumed. No spoilage occurred in Operation 2. Since the production cycle is very short, there was no beginning or ending work in process inventory. March direct labor hours and costs were as follows:

| | Direct Labor | |
	Hours	Costs
Operation 1............	60,354	$365,142
Operation 2............	58,438	383,938

Required:

a. Prepare an analysis of direct labor in March for Gamma's two operations.
b. Suppose that in Operation 1, standard labor performance was expressed as 12 lbs. of raw material processed per direct labor hour (rather than 8 partially completed units per direct labor hour). Assume that the off-standard raw material yield in March was caused by the purchasing agent's buying raw materials of an off-standard quality. How, if at all, would this change your analysis of direct labor costs for March?

20-5. (C.M.A. adapted.) Felton Company manufactures a complete line of radios. Because a large number of models have plastic cases, the company has its own molding department for producing the cases. The month of April was devoted to the production of the plastic case for one of the portable radios -- Model SX76.

The molding department has two operations -- molding and trimming. There is no interaction of labor in these two operations. The standard labor cost for producing ten plastic cases for Model SX76 is as follows:

Molders......... 0.50 hrs. @ $6.00 = $3.00
Trimmers........ 0.25 hrs. @ $4.00 = 1.00
                                     $4.00

During April, 70,000 plastic cases were produced in the molding department. However, 10 percent of these cases had to be discarded because they were found to be defective at final inspection. The purchasing department had changed to a new plastic supplier to take advantage of a lower price for

Direct labor hours worked and direct labor costs charged to the molding department are shown below.

Direct Labor Charged to the Molding Department

Molders...........3,800 hrs. @ $6.25 = $23,750
Trimmers..........1,600 hrs. @ $4.15 =   6,640
Total labor charges $30,390

As a result of poor scheduling by the production scheduling department, the supervisor of the molding department had to shift molders to the trimming operation for 200 hours during April. The company paid the molding workers their regular hourly rate even though they were performing a lower rated task. There was no significant loss of efficiency caused by the shift. In addition, the department supervisor indicated that 75 hours and 35 hours of idle time occurred in the molding and trimming operations respectively as a result of unexpected machinery repairs required during the month.

Required:

    a. The monthly report which compares actual costs with standard cost of output for the month of April shows the following labor variance for the molding department:

        Actual labor costs for April............... $30,390
        Standard labor cost of output
          (63,000 x $4.00/10)...................... 25,200
        Unfavorable labor variance................ $ 5,190

    This variance is significantly higher than normal and management would like an explanation. Prepare a detailed analysis of the unfavorable labor variance for the molding department which shows the variance resulting from (1) labor rates; (2) labor substitution; (3) material substitution; (4) operating efficiency; and (5) idle time.

    b. The molding department supervisor is concerned with the large variances charged to the department. The supervisor feels that the variances due to labor substitution and change in raw materials should not be charged to the department. Does the supervisor have a valid argument? Briefly justify your position.

20-6. Jay and Kay Enterprises had a production overhead budget of $450,000 fixed costs and $300,000 variable costs for a standard monthly volume of 100,000 units of production. Actual overhead costs for the month of February amounted to $727,500, and the company operated at 90 percent of capacity.

    Required:

        a. Compute the overhead rate.
        b. Analyze the net overhead variance.

20-7. Sundry Products, Inc., had the following data for Production Department 20:

    Standard hours for production completed........................$39,800
    Unfavorable overhead volume variance........................... 1,000
    Unfavorable overhead spending variance.........................   600
    Overhead absorption rate: $8 per standard direct labor hour
    Variable costs per standard direct labor hour.................$ 3

    Required: From these data reconstruct the postings to the factory overhead cost account to show the actual overhead debited and the absorbed overhead credited.

20-8. Delta Company's flexible budget formula for overhead costs is $85,000 per month fixed costs plus $20.40 per unit variable costs. Standard volume is 5,000 units a month. Actual overhead costs for May were $229,500, and output was 6,000 units.

Required: Determine the following:

   a. Budgeted overhead at standard volume.
   b. Overhead absorption rate.
   c. overhead costs absorbed in May.
   d. May's overhead production volume variance.
   e. May's overhead spending variance.
   f. May's net overhead variance.

20-9. Epsilon Company's expected volume for the year was 360,000 units. At this
       volume, planned annual overhead costs were $216,000 variable overhead and
       $72,000 nonvariable overhead. In March, output was 25,000 units, and actual
       overhead expense was $19,200.

       Required: Determine for March:

   a. The overhead flexible budget formula.
   b. Standard overhead per unit of output.
   c. The overhead vairances.

20-10. Zeta Company absorbed overhead at the rate of 75 cents per direct labor dol-
       lar. According to Zeta's flexible budget for overhead, for a direct labor
       payroll of $8,000, overhead should be $5,600; and overhead should be $6,800
       for a payroll of $10,000.

       Required:

   a. What is the budget formula?
   b. If actual overhead costs turned out to be $6,000 and $7,000, respec-
      tively, at these two volumes, what would be the overhead variance?
   c. What is Zeta's standard volume?

20-11. In June, Eta Company's overhead volume variance was $0 and its spending vari-
       ance was a debit of $600; actual overhead expense was $7,000 for an output of
       800 tons. In July, overhead expense was $5,600, and output was 600 tons;
       spending variance was $0. In August, output was 900 tons and actual overhead
       expense was $7,100.

       Required:

   a. What was July's volume variance?
   b. What was the budget amount for August?
   c. How much overhead was absorbed in August?
   d. What were the August overhead variances?

20-12. Department 12 of the Theta Company manufactured rivets and no other products.
       All rivets were identical. The company used a standard cost system plus a
       variable budget for overhead expense. Standard unit overhead cost was deter-
       mined by dividing budgeted costs at an expected average volume by the number
       of rivets (in thousands) which that volume level represented.

       Certain cost information is shown in the following table, and you are re-
       quested to fill in the blank spaces. The clue to determining the expected
       average volume can be found by a close analysis of the relationships among
       the figures given for allocated service and general overhead.

	Actual Cost, August	Standard Charge per 1,000 Rivets	Total Standard Cost, August	Overhead Budget, August	Overhead Budget Formula
Direct labor.........	$10,500	$3.00	$ _____	Not used	
Direct material.......	22,000	5.00	20,000	Not used	
Department direct overhead expense....	9,500	_____	_____	$ 9,200	$6,000 per month plus $0.80 per thous. rivets

- 235 -

	Actual Cost, August	Standard Charge per 1,000 Rivets	Total Standard Cost, August	Overhead Budget, August	Overhead Budget Formula
Allocated service and general overhead...........	$ 5,000	1.00	4,000	5,000	$5,000 per month
Total..........	$47,000	$ ___	$ ___	$14,200	

Required:

    a. How many rivets were produed in August?
    b. What was the expected average volume (in terms of rivet output) at which the standard unit overhead charge was determined?
    c. Fill in the blanks.
    d. Explain as much of the difference between total actual costs and total standard costs as you can on the basis of the information given.

20-13. Brown Company uses a standard cost system in which factory overhead is allocated on the basis of direct labor hours. Results for the month of July appear below:

```
Actual units of raw materials purchased.....................    900
Actual units of raw materials put into process.............    750
Actual direct labor hours used in production...............    425
Standard direct labor hours used in production.............    375
Actual factory overhead costs..............................$3,750
Standard price of one unit of raw material.................$ 6.00
Variances:
    Raw materials price...................................$225.00 cr.
    Labor efficiency......................................  175.00 dr.
    Factory overhead, total...............................  150.00 cr.
    Materials usage.......................................  150.00 dr.
    Labor rate............................................  215.50 dr.
```

Required: Use the data above to compute the following:

    a. Standard units of material put into process.
    b. Standard labor rate per hour.
    c. Actual labor rate per hour.
    d. Standard factory overhead rate.
    c. Factory overhead absorbed into product.
    f. Actual cost per unit of materials purchased.

20-14. Below are details of entries to selected T-accounts taken from the records of Midlands Corporation for the month of January. The company uses a standard cost system which removes the raw materials variance due to price upon purchase, the labor rate variance when labor is charged to goods in process, and carries finished goods at standard cost.

	Debits	Credits
Accounts Payable.....................	--	55,000
Factory Payroll Payable.............	--	72,600
Various Accounts....................	--	50,600
Factory Overheads...................	50,600	49,060
		1,540
Raw Materials Inventory.............	53,680	30,800
Goods in Process Inventory..........	30,800	121,000
	74,800	
	49,060	
Finished Goods Inventory............	121,440	88,000
Cost of Goods Sold..................	88,000	
Material Price Variance.............	1,320	
Material Usage Variance.............		880
Labor Rate Variance.................		2,200
Labor Quantity Variance.............	440	
Factory Overhead Variance...........	1,540	

Required:

    a. Journalize the entries which resulted in the postings to the accounts above.

    b. Compute the actual cost of goods sold which would appear on the January income statement after closing all variances to the cost of goods sold.

20-15. The standard cost of Product X is as follows:

Material	3 ft. at $1.00/ft.	$3.00
Direct labor	1/2 hr. at $9.00/hr.	4.50
Variable overhead	1/2 hr. at $8.00/hr.	4.00
Fixed overhead	1/2 hr. at $10.00/hr.	5.00

Standard volume is 2,000 direct labor hours per month (factory overhead is allocated on the basis of direct labor hours). Selling expenses are $40,000 per month plus $1.00 per unit sold. Administrative expenses are $20,000 per month. There were no beginning or ending inventories.

Other information:

    1,000 feet of material were purchased for $8,400.
    240 hours were worked at a cost of $22,200.
    Actual variable overhead incurred, $18,840.
    Actual fixed overhead incurred, $24,720.

Required: Calculate all possible variances.

20-16. Iota Company uses a standard cost system. One month's data for one of the company's products are given below:

    (1) Standard pounds of material in finished product: 3 lbs./unit.
    (2) Standard direct material cost: $3.00/lb.
    (3) Standard hours of direct labor time: 1 hr./unit.
    (4) Standard direct labor cost: $5/hr.
    (5) Materials purchased (12,000 lbs.): $35,400.
    (6) Materials used: 11,000 lbs.
    (7) Direct labor cost incurred (3,475 hours): $17,722.
    (8) Actual production: 3,500 units.
    (9) Overhead budget formula: $14,000 per month plus $2.50 per direct labor hour.
    (10) Overhead incurred: $21,385.
    (11) Standard volume: 4,000 units.

Required:

    a. Compute the material usage and price variances.
    b. Compute the labor efficiency and rate variances.
    c. Compute the overhead volume and spending variances.

20-17. As part of its development activity, Vista Land Company had built a road. Its financial vice president was reviewing a report his construction superintendent had sent him:

Cost Report
Wordsworth Drive

	Budget			
	Price	Quantity	Total	Actual Cost
Grading.............$60/hr.	250 hrs.	$ 15,000	$ 15,120
Paving.............$18/yd.	10,000 yrd.	180,000	277,200
Labor.............$15/hr.	800 hrs.	12,000	11,520
Supervision......... --	--	6,000	6,000
Overhead............ --	--	12,000	12,000
		$225,000	$321,840

Notes:

(1) Budget based on a 1,000-yard long road. Actual length was 1,200 yards.
(2) Grading budget based on efficiency factor of 4 yards per hour. Actual performance was 5 yards per hour.
(3) Paving budget based on 10 yards of asphalt per yard of road length. Actually needed 11 yards of asphalt per yard of road length.
(4) Labor based on 4/5 hour per yard of road length. Actual efficiency was same as budget.

Required: The financial vice president wanted to evaluate the performance of the work on Wordsworth Drive. Specifically, he desired to know the reasons why the actual cost of the road exceeded the budget by $96,840. He has asked you to prepare a variance analysis for the Wordsworth Drive project and identify the reasons why cost exceeded budget.

20-18. Kodol Company prepared its income statements for the current year on three alternative cost accounting systems as follows:

	A	B	C
Sales revenue	$100,000	$100,000	$100,000
Cost of goods sold	33,000	40,000	43,000
	67,000	60,000	57,000
Variances:			
Direct material	--	(2,000)	--
Direct labor	--	(1,000)	--
Factory overhead	--	(5,000)	(5,000)
Gross margin	67,000	52,000	52,000
Other operating expenses	55,000	40,000	40,000
Operating Income	$ 12,000	$ 12,000	$ 12,000

Required: Explain your answers to the following questions:

a. Match the following cost systems with alternatives A, B, and C: (1) standard full cost system; (2) actual absorption cost system; and (3) actual variable cost system.
b. How much much, if any, of the factory overhead cost was variable?
c. What was the actual factory overhead cost incurred for the year?
d. What were the nonfactory costs incurred for the year?
e. What percentage was actual factory volume for the year to normal factory volume?
f. Which of the alternative statements was not prepared in accordance with generally accepted accounting principles?
g. How did actual direct material cost compare with planned direct material cost?

CASES

Case 20-19: SunAir Boat Builders, Inc.

Located in New Hampshire, SunAir Boat Builders served boaters with a small, light-weight fiberglass sailboat capable of being carried on a car roof. While the firm could hardly be considered as one of the nation's industrial giants, its burgeoning business had required it to institute a formal system of cost control. Jan Larson, SunAir's president, explained, "Our seasonal demand, as opposed to a need for regular, level production, means that we must keep a good line of credit at the bank. Modern cost control and inventory valuation procedures enhance our credibility with the bankers and, more importantly, have enabled us to improve our operations. Our supervisors have realized the value of good cost accounting and the main office has, in turn, become much more aware of problems in the barn."

SunAir's manufacturing and warehouse facilities consisted of three historic barns converted to make 11-

foot "Silver Streak" sailboats. The company's plans included the addition of 15- and 18-foot sailboats to its present line. Longer-term plans called for adding additional sizes and styles in the hope of becoming a major factor in the regional boat market.

The "Silver Streak" was an open--cockpit, day sailer sporting a main-sail and small jib on a 17-foot, tele-scoping, aluminum mast. It was ideally suited to the many small lakes and ponds of the region and after three years it had become quite popular. It was priced at $1,012 complete.

Manufacturing consisted basically of three processes: molding, finishing, and assembly. The molding department mixed all ingredients to make the fiberglass hull, performed the actual molding, and removed the hull from the mold. Finishing included hand addi-tions to the hull for running and standing rigging, reinforcement of the mast and tiller steps, and general sanding of rough spots. Assembly consisted of the attachment of cleats, turnbuckles, drain plugs, tiller, and so forth, and the inspection of the boat with mast, halyards, and sails in place. The asembly department also prepared the boat for storage or shipment.

Mixing and molding fiberglass hulls, while manually simple, required a great deal of expertise, or "eye-ball," as it was known in the trade. Addition of too much or too little catalyst, use of too much or too little heat, or failure to allow proper time for curing could cause a hull to be discarded. Conversely, spending too much time on adjustments to mixing or molding equipment or on "personalized" supervision of each hull could cause severe underproduction problems. Once a batch of fiberglass was mixed there was no time to waste being overcautious or it was likely to "freeze" in its kettle.

With such a situation, and the company's announced intent of expanding its product line, it became obvious that a standard cost system would be necessary to help control costs and to provide some reference for supervisors' performance.

Randy Kern, the molding department supervisor, and Bill Schmidt, SunAir's accountant, agreed after lengthy dis-cussion to the following standard costs:

Glass cloth		
--120 sq. ft. @ $0.90	=	$108.00
Glass mix		
--40 lbs. @ $1.65	=	66.00
Direct labor, mixing		
--0.5 hr. @ $9.00	=	4.50
Direct labor, molding		
--1.0 hr. @ $9.00	=	9.00
Indirect costs		
--absorb at $10.80		
per hull*	=	10.80
Total cost to mold hull	=	$198.30

*The normal volume of operations for overhead derivation purposes was as-sumed to be 450 hulls per month. The estimated monthly indirect cost equa-tion was: Budget = $4.32 x hulls + $2,916.

Analysis of Operations. After several additional months of opera-tions, Schmidt expressed disappointment about the apparent lack of attention being paid to the standard costs. Molders tended to have a cautious out-look toward mixing too little or "cook-ing" too long. No one wanted to end up throwing away a partial hull because of too little glass mix.

In reviewing the most recent month's production results, Schmidt noted the following actual costs for production of 430 hulls:

Materials:
Purchased   60,000 sq. ft. glass
                      cloth @ $0.825
                20,000 lbs. glass mix
                      @ $1.785
Used   54,000 sq. ft. glass cloth
                19,000 lbs. glass mix
Direct labor:
                Mixing, 210 hrs. @ $9.375
                Molding, 480 hrs. @ $9.00
Overhead:
                Incurred, $4,950

Before proceeding with further an-alysis, Schmidt called Kern to arrange a discussion of variances. He also told Jan Larson, "Maybe we should look into an automated molding operation. Although I haven't finished my analy-sis, it looks like there will be unfav-orable variances again. Kern insists that the standards are reasonable, then never meets them!"

Larson seemed disturbed and an-swered, "Well, some variances are inev-itable. Why don't you analyze them in some meaningful manner and discuss your ideas with Kern, who is an expert in molding, and whose opinion I respect. Then the two of you meet with me to discuss the whole matter."

1. Determine the molding department's direct cost and overhead variances. Why do you think they occurred?

2. Do you think SunAir's standards are meaningful? How would you improve them?

3. Assume that the month's actual and standard production costs for items other than molding hulls amounted to $409.20 per boat, and that 430 boats were sold. Prepare a statement of budgeted and actual gross margin for the month, assuming planned sales of 450 boats.

* * * * *

Case 20-20: Cotter Company, Inc.

In preparing its annual profit plan, the management of Cotter Company, realized that its sales were subject to monthly seasonal variations, but expected that for the year as a whole the profit before taxes would total $240,000, as shown below:

	Annual Budget	
	Amount	Percent of Sales
Sales...............	$2,400,000	100
Standard cost of goods sold:		
Prime costs......	960,000	40
Production overhead.......	840,000	35
Total standard costs..........	1,800,000	75
Gross margin.......	600,000	25
Selling and General expense..	360,000	15
Income before taxes...........	$ 240,000	10

Management defined "prime costs" as those costs for labor and materials that were strictly variable with the quantity of production. The production overhead included both fixed and variable costs; management's estimate was that, within a range around planned sales volume of plus or minus $1,000,000 per year, variable production overhead would be equal to 25 percent of prime costs. Thus the total production overhead budgeted for the year consisted of $240,000 of variable costs (25 percent of $960,000) and $600,000 of fixed costs. All of the selling and general expenses were fixed, except for commissions on sales equal to 5 percent of the selling price.

Sal Cotter, the president of the company, approved the budget, stating that, "A profit of $20,000 a month isn't bad for a little company in this business." During January, however, sales suffered the normal seasonal dips and production was also cut back. The result, which came as some surprise to the president, was that January showed a loss of $7,000.

Operating Statement
January

Sales.............		$140,000
Standard cost of goods sold......		105,000
Standard gross margin..........		35,000
Manufacturing variances.......		
	Favorable or (Unfavorable)	
Prime cost variance......	$ (3,500)	
Production overhead:		
Spending variance....	1,000	
Volume variance....	(12,500)	(15,000)
Actual gross margin..........		20,000
Selling and general expenses...		27,000
Loss before taxes.		$ (7,000)

Questions

1. Explain, as best you can with the data available, why the January profit was $27,000 less than the average monthly profit expected by the president.

2. At what level of monthly volume does Cotter expect to earn exactly zero profit? (Hint: For simplicity, assume that Cotter makes only one product, which has a selling price of $1 per unit.)

3. What was Cotter's January production volume? (Use the hint from Question 2.)

4. How much did finished goods inventory change in January?

5. What were actual production overhead costs in January?

6. Continuing to use the assumption in Question 2's hint, assume further that Cotter's standard prime production costs per unit are as follows:

materials, 2.5 pounds at 10 cents; labor, 1.0 minute at $9.00 per hour. In January, 390,000 pounds of material were used, at a cost of 9 cents per pound. Total direct labor costs were $28,400 for 2,500 hours. Calculate the four detailed prime cost variances.

Chapter 21

Differential Accounting: Short-Run Decisions

Key Terms

Differential costs
Differential revenues
Contribution margin
Alternative choice problem
Base case
Opportunity cost
Sunk cost
Make-or-buy problem

Differential income
Contribution pricing
Economic order quantity
Expected value
Sensitivity analysis
Decision tree
Linear programming

Discussion Questions

1. Explain in your own words the differences between full costs and differential costs.

2. The accounts contain an item, "Wages earned, $1,000." Describe, so as to distinguish between them, situations in which this $1,000 would be (a) a product cost, (b) a direct cost, (c) a variable cost, (d) a differential cost, (e) an indirect cost, and (f) a fixed cost.

3. Why are differential costs not labeled as such in an accounting system?

4. A company has heard that a new machine has been developed that might be better than a machine it now uses for a certain production operation. List the steps it should go through in investigating this matter.

5. In connection with the new machine referred to in Question 4, give examples of quantitative and nonquantitative factors that should be considered, and distinguish between these two types of factors.

6. In an alternative choice problem it is said that a manager chooses the "best" decision. What is "best"?

7. What is the advantage of using numbers to express the importance of factors in an alternative choice problem?

8. "Overhead costs are allocated to products at 200 percent of direct labor costs. This means that if direct labor costs increase, overhead costs also increase. Therefore, if direct labor costs are differential, so are overhead costs." Do you agree?

9. "In the very long run, all costs are differential." Explain what this means.

10. Opportunity costs, as such, are not recorded in accounting records. Why?

11. Historical costs are irrelevant in alternative choice problems, but the numbers used in many such problems are in fact historical costs. Explain this apparent paradox.

12. The book value of a machine on the balance sheet is genuinely an asset, but in

alternative choice problems this asset is disregarded. Why?

13. The book value of a machine is a sunk cost. However, if the same machine is rented rather than owned, the rental payments are _not_ a sunk cost. Explain this apparent paradox.

14. Under some circumstances, a reduction of two hours of labor time required to make a product reduces differential costs and in other circumstances it does not. Distinguish between these circumstances, with examples.

15. "A company must recover its full costs or eventually go out of business." Do you agree? Why?

16. Airlines sometimes have special lkow rates for families who fly on certain days. Explain why they do this, using concepts described in this chapter. Under what circumstances should airlines have low rates for students?

17. Selling an item at a price less than its full cost will result in negative gross margin on the sale. How, then, can such a sale ever be justified?

18. What conditions must prevail for linear programming to be an appropriate analytical technique for solving alternative choice problems?

Problems

21-1. Wepner Construction Company wants to establish a decision rule on when to rent a house trailer for an on-site construction office, and when to build an on-site office. Trailers of the kind which Wepner uses can be rented for $200 per month, with a minimum rental of eight months. Construction of an on-site office generally costs Wepner $1,800 for materials, 20 percent of which are salvagable upon dismantling, and $2,400 in labor. Other costs would be unaffected.

  Required: In terms of length of construction project, when should Wepner rent a trailer and when should it construct its own on-site office?

21-1. Mo-Go Cycle Company has been operating at 80 percent of palnt capacity. In order to utilize more capacity the plant manager is considering making a headlight which had previously been purchased for $6.10 per unit. The plant has the equipment and labor force necessary to manufacture this light, which the design engineer estimates would cost $1.40 for raw materials and $2 for direct labor. The plant overhead rate is $2 per direct labor dollar of which $1.20 is variable cost.

  Required: Should the company make the light or continue to buy it from an outside supplier? Support your answer with appropriate computations and reasons.

21-3. Porter Rubber Company had been offered a contract to supply 500,000 premium automobile tires to a large automobile manufacturer at a price of $29.75 per tire. Porter's full cost of producing the tire is $37. The normal sales price for the tire is $52.50 to both distributors and some selected retailers. Variable costs per tire amount to $24.50; however, in order to meet the needs of the auto manufacturer, Porter will have to cut its sales to regular customers by 100,000 tires annually. The auto maker has clearly indicated that it will enter into the agreement only if Porter will agree to supply all 500,000 of the tires requested.

  Required: Should Porter accept the offer?

21-4. Delta Venus Swimsuit Company is considering dropping its line of women's beach robes. A recent product income statement for the robe line follows:

```
Revenue...............................$792,300
Cost of goods sold....................  718,200
Gross margin..........................   74,100
Selling and administrative expenses....  114,000
Net Loss..............................$(39,900)
```

Factory overhead accounts for 26 percent of the cost of the goods sold and is one third fixed. These data are believed to reflect conditions in the immediate future.

21-5. Johnson's Health Club sponsors boxing matches twice a week for 25 weeks during fall and winter. The charge per ticket has been $3.50 with an average attendance of 900 spectators at each match. In an effort to increase attendance, the club managerr is considering decreasing the ticket price. There are 1,000 seats available now, but for an added $15,000 per year, capacity can be tripled. Yearly fixed costs are now $90,000 and variable costs are $0.25 per spectator. Expected ticket sales and attendance are as follows:

| Price per ticket | $3.50 | $3.00 | $2.50 | $2.00 |
| Estimated attendance | 900 | 1,250 | 1,750 | 2,000 |

Required:

   a. Prepare an analysis showing which of the four ticket prices should be adopted.
   b. Calculate the difference in pretax income that would result if the price were changed from $3.50 to the amount you recommended in (a) above.

21-6. Bracy Enterprises can produce 10,000 snow blowers a month at capacity operations. Average normal production and sales have been 8,000 per month, but an economic slump in the area has caused the sales manager to believe he can only sell 4,000 units through usual outlets during the coming month. Bracy has received an offer from a large mail-order company requesting a total of 5,000 units of production. Bracy would receive $300 per unit. Indentical snow blowers are sold through regular wholesale channels for $320 each, the amount that the company feels allows for a satisfactory return on investment. Monthly fixed costs are $800,000; the variable costs of production, distribution, and administration are $120 per unit.

Required:

   a. Compute the cost of a snow blower that would need to be recovered if a profit of $90 per unit was desired on the mail-order contract.
   b. How much does it cost Bracy to produce and sell a snow blower? Why do you feel this is the most reasonable cost?
   c. What should Bracy do: use regular channels only or sell to the mail-order firm?

21-7. (C.M.A. adapted.) George Jackson operates a small machine shop. He manufactures one standard product available from other similar businesses, and he also manufactures products to customer order. His accountant prepared the annual income statement shown below:

	Custom Sales	Standard Sales	Total
Sales	$100,000	$50,000	$150,000
Material	20,000	16,000	36,000
Labor	40,000	18,000	58,000
Depreciation	12,600	7,200	19,800
Power	1,400	800	2,200
Rent	12,000	2,000	14,000
Heat and light	1,200	200	1,400
Other	800	1,800	2,600
	88,000	46,000	134,000
	$ 12,000	$ 4,000	$$16,000

The depreciation charges are for machines. The power charge is apportioned based on estimated power consumed. The rent is for the building space that has been leased for 10 years at $14,000 per year. The rent, and heat and light are apportioned to the product lines based on amount of floor space occupied. All other costs are current expenses identified with the product line causing them.

A valued custom parts customer has asked Mr. Jackson if he would manufacture 5,000 special units for him. Mr. Jackson is working at capacity and would have to give up some other business in order to take this business. He can't renege on custom orders already agreed to, but he could reduce the output of his standard product by about one half for one year while producing the specially requested custom part. The customer is willing to pay $14.00 for each part. The material cost will be about $4.00 per unit and the labor will be $7.20 per unit. Mr. Jackson will have to spend $4,000 for a special device that will be discarded when the job is done.

Required:

     a. Calculate the following costs related to the 5,000-unit custom order:
        (1) The differential cost of the order;
        (2) The full cost of the order;
        (3) The opportunity cost of taking the order;
        (4) The sunk costs related to the order.
     b. Should Mr. Jackson take the order? Explain your answer.

21-8. Ace Fastener Company, a manufactuer of nails, has received a request from Sunshine Builders for Ace to supply Sunshine with ten 100 pound kegs of nails per week for a one-year period, at a price of $10.30 per keg. Ace is presently working at 100 percent capacity for one eight-hour shift and would have to incur overtime expense in order to meet Sunshine's request. Ace's normal sales price for nails is $11.30 per 100-pound keg.

The steel used for manufactur of nails is purchased by Ace at a cost of $160 per ton. Ace experiences a 5 percent material waste factor in production. Labor costs per 100 pounds of output are $1.00; however, overtime production would increase labor costs by 50 percent. Overhead, which is currently 18 percent variable and 82 percent fixed, is allocated on a 100 percent-of-direct-labor-dollar basis.

Required: Should Ace Fastener Company accept Sunshine's order at the $10.30 per keg price?

21-9. (C.M.A. adapted.) Vernom Corporation, which produces and sells to wholesalers a highly successful line of summer lotions and insect repellents, has decided to diversify in order to stabilize sales throughout the year. A natural area for the company to consider is the production of winter lotions and creams to prevent dry and chapped skin.

After considerable research, a winter products line has been developed. However, because of the conservative nature of the company management, Vernom's president has decided to introduce only one of the new products for this coming winter. If the product is a success, further expansion in future years will be initiated.

The product selected (called Chap-Off) is a lip balm that will be sold in a lipstick type tube. The product will be sold to wholesalers in boxes of 24 tubes for $8.00 per box. Because of available capacity, no additional fixed charges will be incurred to produce the product. However, a $100,000 fixed charge will be absorbed by the product to allocate a fair share of the company's present fixed costs to the new product.

Using the estimated sales and production of 100,000 boxes of Chap-Off as the standard volume, the accounting department has developed the following costs per box:

                    Direct labor....................$2.00
                    Direct materials................. 3.00
                    Total overhead................... 1.50
                    Total cost per box..............$6.50

Vernom has approached a cosmetics manufacturer to discuss the possibility of purchasing the tubes for Chap-Off. The purchase price of the empty tubes from the cosmetics manufacturer would be $.90 per 24 tubes. If Vernom accepts the purchase proposal, it is estimated that direct labor and variable overhead costs would be reduced by 10 percent and direct material costs would be reduced by 20 percent.

Required:

    a. Should Vernom Corporation make or buy the tubes?

    b. What would be the maximum purchase price acceptable to Vernom for the tubes?

    c. Instead of sales of 100,000 boxes, revised estimates show sales volume of 125,000 boxes. At this new volume additional equipment, at an annual rental of $10,000, must be acquired to manufacture the tubes. However, this incremental cost would be the only additional fixed cost required even if sales increased to 300,000 boxes. (The 300,000 level is the goal for the third year of production.) Under these circumstances, should Vernom make or buy the tubes?

    d. The company has the option of making and buying the tubes at the same time. What would be your answer to part (c) if this alternative were considered?

    e. What nonquantifiable factors should Vernon consider in determining whether they should make or buy the lipstick tubes?

21-10. (C.M.A. adapted.) Gosset Chemical Company annually evaluates pricing policies, production decisions, and unit costs for its various products. One particular product group, which involves two joint products and two by-products, is separately analyzed each year.

The two joint products, ALCHEM-X and CHEM-P, emerge at the end of processing in Department 20. Both chemicals can be sold at this split-off point, ALCHEM-X for $2.50 per unit, and CHEM-P for $3.00 per unit. By-product BY-D20 also emerges at this split-off point, and is salable without further processing for $0.50 per unit. Unit costs of preparing this by-product for market are $0.03 for freight and $0.12 for packaging.

CHEM-P is sold without further processing, but ALCHEM-X is transferred to Department 22 for additional processing into a refined chemical, ALCHEM-XF. No additional raw materials are added in Department 22. ALCHEM-XF has been sold in the past for $5.00 per unit. By-product BY-D22 is created by the additional procesing in Department 22, and it can be sold for $0.70 per unit. Unit marketing costs for BY-D22 are $0.05 for freight and $0.15 for packaging.

Gossett accounts for by-product production by crediting the net realizable value of by-products produced to production costs of the main products. The relative sales value method is used to allocate net joint production costs for inventory valuation purposes.

A portion of the 1984 profit plan established in September 1983 is presented on the next page. Shortly after this budget was compiled the company learned that a chemical that would compete with ALCHEM-XF was to be introduced. The marketing department estimated that this would require a permanent price reduction to $3.50 a unit for the ALCHEM-XF to be sold in present quantities. Gossett must now reevaluate the decision to further process ALCHEM-X. The market for ALCHEM-X will not be affected by the introduction of this new chemical. Consequently, the quantities of ALCHEM-X that are usually processed into ALCHEM-XF can be sold at the regular price of $2.50 per unit. The costs for marketing ALCHEM-X are estimated to be $105,000. If the further processing is terminated, Department 22 will be dismantled and all costs except equipment depreciation, $18,400, supervisory salaries, $21,200, and general overhead, $35,200, will be eliminated.

Required:

    a. Verify that $225,000 is the correct charge to Department 22 for costs incurred in Department 20. (Review the section of Chapter 19 on joint products and by-products, if necessary.)

    b. Should Gossett sell ALCHEM-X at the split-off point or continue to process it further in Department 22? Prepare a schedule of differential costs and revenues to support your answer.

    c. During discussions of the possible dropping of ALCHEM-XF, one person

Units of Production

	CHEM-P	ALCHEM-XF
Estimated sales......	400,000	210,000
Planned inventory change.............	(8,000)	(6,000)
Required production..	392,000	204,000
Minimum production based upon joint output ratio......	392,000	210,000
By-product output:		
BY-D20.............		90,000
BY-D22.............		60,000

Budgeted Costs

Production costs:	Department 20	Department 22
Raw materials.......	$160,000	---
Costs transferred from Dept. 20.....	---	$225,000
Hourly direct labor.	170,000	120,000
Variable overhead...	180,000	140,800
Fixed overhead......	247,500	188,000
	$757,500	$673,800

	CHEM-P	ALCHEM-XF
Marketing costs.....	$196,000	$105,000

noted that the manufacturing margin for ALCHEM-X would be 57.2 percent [(2.50 - 1.07)/2.50] and 57.3 percent for CHEM-P. The normal mark-up for products sold in the market with ALCHEM-X is 72 percent. For the CHEM-P portion of the line the mark-up is 47 percent. This person argues that the company's unit costs must be incorrect because the margins differ from the typical rates. Briefly explain why Gossett's rates for the two products are almost identical when "normal" rates are not.

21-11. (C.M.A. adapted.) Anchor Company manufactures several styles of jewelry cases. Management estimates that during the third quarter of 1983 the company will be operating at 80 percent of normal capacity. Because the company desires a higher utilization of plant capacity, the company will consider a special order.

Anchor has received a special order inquiry from JCP Inc., which would like to market a jewelry case similar to one of Anchor's cases. The JCP case would be marketed under JCP's own label. JCP has offered Anchor $5.75 per case for 20,000 cases to be shipped by October 1, 1983. The cost data for the Anchor case, which would be similar to the specifications of the JCP special order, are as follows:

```
Regular selling price per unit...................$9.00
Costs per unit:
    Raw materials................................ 2.50
    Direct labor (.5 hrs. @ $6.00)............... 3.00
    Overhead (.25 machine hrs. @ $4.00).......... 1.00
    Total costs..................................$6.50
```

According to the specifications provided by JCP, the special order case requires less-expensive raw materials costing only $2.25 per case. Management has estimated that the remaining costs, labor time, and machine time will be the same as the Anchor jewelry case.

A second special order has been submitted by the Kraye Co. for 7,500 jewelry cases at $7.50 per case. These jewelry cases would be marketed under the Kraye label and have to be shipped by October 1, 1983. However, the Kraye jewelry case is different from any jewelry case in the Anchor line. The estimated per unit costs of this case are as follows:

```
Raw materials...................................$3.25
Direct labor (.5 hrs. @ $6.00)................... 3.00
Overhead (.5 machine hrs. @ $4.00).............. 2.00
Total costs.....................................$8.25
```

In addition, Anchor will incur $1.500 in additional set-up costs and will have to purchase a $2,500 special device to manufacture these cases: this device will be discarded once the special order is completed.

Anchor's manufacturing capabilities are limited to 90,000 machine hours per year or 7,500 machine hours per month. The budgeted fixed overhead for 1983 amounts to $216,000. All manufacturing overhead costs are applied to production on the basis of machine hours at $4.00 per hour.

Anchor will have the entire third quarter to work on the special orders. Management does not expect any repeat sales to be generated from either special order. Company practice precludes Anchor from subcontracting any portion of an order when special orders are not expected to generate repeat sales.

Required: Should Anchor Company accept either special order? Justify your answer and show your calculations.

21-12. Canterbury, Inc., makes several different products. Each product may be produced several different times a year. As part of an effort to control costs, the controller wants to determine the economic lot size of a production run of Product M. The factory cost per unit is $10.30, set-up costs are $300, the inventory carrying charge is $0.23 per dollar of factory cost, and there are expected to be 15,000 units of M produced annually.

Required: What is the most economical number of units of Product M to produce in one production run?

21-13. Fine Foods, Inc., a regional supermarket chain, orders 400,000 cans of frozen orange juice per year from a California distributor. A 24-can case of frozen juice delivered to the Fine Foods central warehouse costs $24.00, including freight charges. Fine Foods borrows funds at a 12 percent interest rate to finance its inventories.

The Fine Foods purchasing agent has calculated that it costs $200 to place an order for frozen juice, and that the annual storage expenses for one can of juice (electricity, insurance, handling) amount to $0.10 per can.

Required:

a. How many cans of frozen juice should Fine Foods request in each order?
b. If the California distributor offers Fine Foods a 12 percent discount off the delivery price for minimum orders of 80,000 cans, what should Fine Foods do?

21-14. When questioned by the district sales manager, a salesperson provided the following sales prediction. "I think there will be two chances in ten that sales will be $50,000, three in ten that they will be $55,000, four in ten that they will be $60,000, and one chance in ten that they will be $70,000."

Required:

a. What is the expected value of this forecast?
b. What would the single value estimate be?

21-15. ABC Food Company is trying to decide whether or not to further develop "Tastee," a new product. If they do not further develop the product, they will not introduce it to consumers. If they proceed with development and the results are favorable, they will introduce the product and differential income (excluding the development costs) is forecast as follows:

Amount.................$47,000 $50,000 $60,000
Probability.......... 0.2   0.5   0.3

If development results are unfavorable, ABC will drop the product. The probability of favorable results is 70 percent and the additional development will cost $20,000.

Required:

a. Based on decision-tree analysis using expected value, should ABC undertake further development?
b. Is ABC guaranteed this expected value?

21-16. Beta Company makes two radio models, Y and Z. They are both manufactured totally in two departmens: A, which has a total capacity of 240 labor hours per week; and B, which has a capacity of 480 labor hours per week. The labor requirements (hours per unit) for each model are:

	Model Y	Model Z
Department A	1.0	0.8
Department B	0.5	2.0

The unit contribution of Model Y is $4.00 and for Model Z it is $5.00. The total production of Y can be sold, but only a weekly maximum of 200 units of Model Z can be sold.

Required: How many of each radio should be manufactured? (Construct the basic equations and solve graphically.)

CASES

Case 21-17: Import Distributors, Inc.

Import Distributors, Inc. (IDI) imported appliances and distributed them to retail appliance stores in the Rocky Mountain states. IDI carried three broad lines of merchandise: audio equipment (tuners, turntables, CB radios, etc.), television equipment (including videotape recorders), and kitchen appliances (refrigerators, freezers, and stoves that were more compact than U.S. models). Each line accounted for about one third of total IDI sales revenues. Although each line was referred to by IDI managers as a "department," until 1983 the company did not prepare departmental income statements.

In late 1982, departmental accounts were set up in anticipation of preparing quarterly income statements by department starting in 1983. In early April 1983, the first such statements were distributed to the management group. Although in the first quarter of 1983 IDI had earned net income amounting to 4.3 percent of sales, the television department had shown a gross margin that was much too small to cover the department's operating expenses (see Exhibit 1).

The television department's poor showing prompted the company's accountant to suggest that perhaps the department should be discontinued. "This is exactly why I proposed that we prepare departmental statements -- to see if each department is carrying its fair share of the load," the accountant explained. This suggestion led to much discussion among the management group, particularly concerning two issues: first, was the first quarter of the year representative enough of longer term results to consider discontinuing

the television department? and second, would discontinuing television equipment cause a drop in sales in the other two departments? One manager, however, stated that "even if the quarter was typical and other sales wouldn't be hurt, I'm still not convinced we'd be better off dropping our television line."

Question

What action should be taken with regard to the television department?

EXHIBIT 1

Television Department Income Statement
For the first 3 months of 1983

		Percent
Net sales revenues....	$930,233	100.0
Cost of goods sold....	820,658	88.2
Gross margin.........	109,575	11.8
Operating expenses:		
Personnel expenses (Note 1)..........	5,850	
Department manager's office..	7,078	
Rent (Note 2).......	28,908	
Inventory taxes and insurance.....	21,094	
Utilities (Note 3)..	1,734	
Delivery costs (Note 4)..........	19,272	
Sales Commission (Note 5)..........	37,209	
Administrative costs (Note 6)....	19,403	
Inventory financing charge (Note 7)...	13,678	
Total operating expenses.......	154,226	16.6
Income taxes (credit).	(21,395)	(2.3)
Net income (loss).....	$(23,256)	(2.5)

1. These were warehouse personnel. Although merchandise in the warehouse was arranged by department, these personnel performed tasks for all three departments on any given day.
2. Allocated to departments on the basis of square footage utilized. IDI had a 5-year noncancellable lease for the facilities.
3. Allocted to departments on the basis of square footage utilized.
4. Allocated on the basis of sales dollars. A delivery from IDI to a retail store typically included merchandise from all three departments.
5. Salespersons were paid on a straight commission basis; each one sold all three lines.
6. Allocated on the basis of sales dollars.
7. An accounting entry that was not directly related to the cost of financing inventory; assessed on average inventory, in order to motivate department managers not to carry excessive stocks. This charge tended to be about three times the company's actual out of-pocket interest costs.

* * * * *

Case 21-18: Bob Mogielnicki

In June 1982, Bob Mogielnicki went to work for the Brandywine Corporation, a medium-sized manufacturer of electrical controls and electronic devices. What particularly attracted Bob to the job offer from Brandywine was the fact that it presented an opportunity to assume line responsibilities after a brief training period. The position in question was that of supervisor of the parts fabrication shop at the company's San Jose plant.

At that time, the staff of the parts fabrication shop consisted of ten machine operators and two clerks in addition to the supervisor. The shop was producing five parts that were used by other departments of the San Jose plant in the assembly of final products. A statement of costs incurred by the parts fabrication shop during the first week of Bob's supervision is shown in Exhibit 1.

When he took over the parts fabrication shop, Bob was told by the plant manager, Kelley Wallis, that it was Bob's responsibility to see that the five parts being produced by the shop were acquired at the lowest possible cost to the company. For this reason, he had the authority to buy all or any of these parts from outside sources if he found this to be more advantageous to the company.

In order to carry out his responsibility for "make-or-buy" decisions, Bob felt he needed more cost information than was supplied by the weekly cost statement (Exhibit 1). He discussed his need with the plant accountant, Dana Dreyfus, and together they agreed on a format for a second weekly report, which would show the actual cost of producing 100 of each of the

EXHIBIT 1

Cost Statement For Week of
September 13, 1982

Prime Cost
Labor.........................$ 4,193
Materials...................... 9,350
  Total Prime Cost........... 13,543

Departmental Overhead
Departmental supervision
  and services................ 3,006
Depreciation.................. 3,600
  Total Departmental
    Overhead................. 6,606

General Overhead................. 4,500
  Total Costs................$24,649

parts during the week in question. The first such report, corresponding to the cost statement of Exhibit 1 is shown in Exhibit 2.

The figures in Exhibit 2 were obtained as follows:

1. Direct labor/hundred. Each machine operator kept a time sheet indicating the time (in hours and tenths of an hour) spent on each part. These times were accumulated for each part and costed at the direct labor rate of $10.50/hour. The total cost for each part was then divided by the amount of production.
2. Direct materials/hundred. When materials were drawn from the storeroom, an issue slip was prepared indicating the amount drawn and the part on which the materials were to be used. The amounts were totalled for each part and the totals divided by the amount of production.

EXHIBIT 2

Product Cost Report for week of September 13, 1982

| | Cost per 100 Units of Part No. | | | | |
Cost Element	101	102	103	104	105
Labor....................	$ 25.44	$ 39.90	$ 15.75	$ 21.99	$ 12.93
Materials................	55.20	72.00	44.40	51.60	40.80
Total Prime Cost.........	80.64	111.90	60.15	73.59	53.73
Overhead.................	67.26	105.45	41.64	58.14	34.17
Total Cost...............	$147.90	$217.35	$101.79	$131.73	$ 87.90
Production (100 units)	33	40	32	42	26

EXHIBIT 3

Product Cost Report for Week of April 11, 1983

| | Cost per 100 Units of Part No. | | | | |
Cost Element	101	102	103	104	105
Labor....................	$ 27.06	$ 42.00	$ 16.80	$ 23.46	$ 12.99
Material.................	55.29	72.03	44.34	51.60	40.97
Total Prime Cost.........	82.35	114.03	61.14	75.06	53.76
Overhead.................	92.76	144.00	57.60	80.40	44.58
Total Cost...............	$175.11	$258.03	$118.74	$155.46	$ 98.34
Production (100 unit)....	26	32	20	30	21

3. <u>Overhead/hundred</u>. The total of all departmental and general overhead costs was divided by the number of direct labor hours to produce a cost per hour. This figure was multiplied by the number of direct labor hours charged to each part and the result was then divided by the amount of production.

After receiving the information in Exhibit 2 from Dana Dreyfus, Bob Mogielnicki solicited bids on each of the five parts from several small shops in the San Jose area. The lowest bid received on each part was as follows:

Part No.	Lowest Bid
101...........	$195.00
102...........	270.00
103...........	112.50
104...........	180.00
105...........	103.50

After studying these bids, Bob concluded that the company should continue to make each part in its own shop.

In the spring of 1983, demand for Brandywine's products fell sharply. This decline was reflected in the workload in the parts fabrication shop. Because of the reduced workload, Bob Mogielnicki had laid off one ma-chine operator and had transferred another to performing maintenance of equipment which had been deferred during the period of higher production.

When Bob received his product cost report for the week of April 11, 1983, shown in Exhibit 3, he discovered that costs were up on all five parts, and that part 103, in particular, now cost more to make than the bid of $112.50 per hundred he had received in the fall. Bob called up the owner of the shop who had made that bid and asked him for an updated bid. The owner responded with a bid of $108.00 per hundred, saying that his business was off and so he was willing to shave his earlier price a bit if it would help to keep his shop busy. Bob promptly accepted the reduced offer and asked the purchasing agent of the San Jose plant to issue a purchase order to the outside source for 4,000 units (about a two-week supply at the current usage wage). Bob estimated that his decision would save Brandywine about $420.

The cost reports for the week of April 25, 1983 (Exhibit 4) showed a further rise. Once again Bob checked with the sources of earlier bids, this time on parts 102 and 105, and learned that in both cases the bidders were sticking by their earlier quotes.

EXHIBIT 4

Product Cost Report for Week of April 25, 1983

| Cost Element | \multicolumn{5}{c}{Cost per 100 Units of Part No.} |
	101	102	103	104	105
Labor....................	$ 26.04	$ 39.99	--	$ 22.50	$ 13.50
Material.................	55.29	72.00	--	51.60	40.65
Total Prime Cost.........	81.33	111.99	--	74.10	54.15
Overhead.................	112,80	174.00	--	96.42	54.00
Total Cost...............	$ 94.13	$285.99	--	$170.52	$108.15
Production (100 unit)....	25	30		28	20

Questions

1. What was the total overhead expense in Bob Mogielnicki's department for the week of April 11, 1983? What reasons can you give for the change from the week of September 13, 1982?

2. What should Bob Mogielnicki do with regard to parts 102 and 105?

* * * * *

Case 21-19: Sheridan Carpet Company

Sheridan Carpet Company produced high-grade carpeting materials for use in automobiles and recreational vans. Sheridan's products were sold to finishers, who cut and bound the material so as to fit perfectly in the passenger compartment or cargo area (e.g., automobile trunk) of a specific model automobile or van. Some of these finishers were captive operations of major automobile assembly divisions, particularly those that assembled the "top of the line" cars that included high-grade carpeting; other finishers concentrated on the replacement and van customizing markets.

Late in 1982, the marketing manager and the chief accountant of Sheridan met to decide on the list price for carpet number 104. It was industry practice to announce prices just prior to the January-June and July-December "seasons." Over the years, companies in the industry had adhered to their announced prices throughout a six-month season unless significant unexpected changes in costs occurred. Sales of carpet 104 were not affected by seasonal factors during the two six-month seasons. Sheridan was the largest company in its segment of the automobile carpet industry; its 1981 sales had been over $40 million. Sheridan's salespersons were on a salary basis, and each one sold the entire product line. Most of Sheridan's competitors were smaller than Sheridan; accordingly, they usually awaited Sheridan's price announcement before setting their own selling prices.

Carpet 104 had an especially dense nap; as a result, making it required a special machine, and it was produced in a department whose equipment could not be used to produce Sheridan's other carpets. Effective January 1, 1982, Sheridan had raised its price on this carpet from $3.90 to $5.20 per square yard. This had been done in order to bring 104's margin up to that of the other carpets in the line. Although Sheridan was financially sound, it expected a large funds need in the next few years for equipment replacement and plant expansion. The 1982 price increase was one of several decisions made in order to provide funds for these plans.

Sheridan's competitors, however, had held their 1982 prices at $3.90 on carpets competitive with 104. As shown in Exhibit 1, which includes estimates of industry volume on these carpets, Sheridan's price increase had apparently resulted in a loss of market share. The marketing manager, Mel Walters, estimated that the industry would sell about 630,000 square yards of these carpets in the first half of 1983. Walters was sure Sheridan could sell 150,000 yards if it dropped 104's price back to $3.90. But if Sheridan held its price at $5.20, Walters feared a further erosion in Sheridan's share. However, because some customers felt that 104 was superior to competitive products, Walters felt that Sheridan

EXHIBIT 1
CARPET 104:   PRICES AND PRODUCTION, 1980-1982

| | Production Volume (square yards) | | Price (per square yard) | |
Season*	Industry Total	Sheridan Carpet	Most Competitors	Sheridan Carpet
1980-1..................	549,000	192,000	$5.20	$5.20
1980-2..................	517,500	181,000	5.20	5.20
1981-1..................	387,000	135,500	3.90	3.90
1981-2..................	427,500	149,500	3.90	3.90
1982-1..................	450,000	135,000	3.90	5.20
1982-2..................	562,500	112,500	3.90	5.20

*198x-1 means the first 6 months of 198x; 198x-2 means the second six months of 198x.

EXHIBIT 2
ESTIMATED COST OF CARPET 104 AT VARIOUS VOLUMES
First Six Months of 1983

Volume (square yards):	65,000	87,500	110,000	150,000	185,000	220,000
Raw materials	$ .520	$ .520	$ .520	$ .520	$ .520	$ .520
Materials spoilage.	.052	.051	.049	.049	.051	.052
Direct labor......	1.026	.989	.979	.962	.975	.997
Departmental overhead:						
Direct(1)..........	.142	.136	.131	.130	.130	.130
Indirect (2).....	1.200	.891	.709	.520	.422	.355
General overhead(3)...	.308	.297	.294	.289	.293	.299
Factory cost........	3.248	2.884	2.682	2.470	2.391	2.353
Selling and administration (4)	2.111	1.875	1.743	1.606	1.554	1.529
Total cost.....	$5.359	$4.759	$4.425	$4.076	$3.945	$3.882

(1) Materials handlers, supplies, repairs, power, fringe benefits.
(2) Supervision, equipment depreciation, heat and light.
(3) 30 percent of direct labor.
(4) 65 percent of factory cost.

could sell at least 65,000 yards at the $5.20 price.

During their discussion, Walters and the chief accountant, Terry Rosen, identified two other aspects of the pricing decision. Rosen wondered whether competitors would announce a further price decrease if Sheridan dropped back to $3.90. Walters felt it was unlikely that competitors would price below $3.90, because none of them was more efficient than Sheridan, and there were rumors that several of them were in poor financial condition. Rosen's other concern was whether a decision relating to carpet 104 would have any impact on the sales of Sheridan's other carpets. Walters was convinced that, since 104 was a specialized item, there was no interdependence between its sales and those of other carpets in the line.

Exhibit 2 contains cost estimates that Rosen had prepared for various volumes of 104. These estimates represented Rosen's best guesses as to costs during the first six months of 1983, based on past cost experience and anticipated inflation.

Questions

1. What was the relationship (if any) between the 104 pricing decision and the company's future need for capital funds?

2. Assuming no intermediate prices are to be considered, should Sheridan price 104 at $3.90 or $5.20?

3. If Sheridan's competitors hold their prices at $3.90, how many square yards of 104 would Sheridan need to sell at a price of $5.20 in order to earn the same profit as selling

150,000 square yards at a price of $3.90?

4. What additional information would you wish to have before making this pricing decision? (Despite the absence of this information, still answer Question 2!)

5. With hindsight, was the decision to raise the price in 1982 a good one?

* * * * *

Case 21-20: Liquid Chemical Company

Liquid Chemical Company manufactured and sold a range of high grade products throughout Great Britain. Many of these products required careful packing, and the company had always made a feature of the special properties of the containers used. They had a special patented lining, made from a material known as GHL, and the firm operated a department especially to maintain its containers in good condition and to make new ones to replace those that were past repair.

Dale Walsh, the general manager, had for some time suspected that the firm might save money, and get equally good service, by buying its containers from an outside source. After careful inquiries, he approached a firm specializing in container production, Packages, Ltd., and asked for a quotation from it. At the same time he asked Paul Dyer, his chief accountant, to let him have an up-to-date statement of the cost of operating the container department.

Within a few days, the quotation from Packages, Ltd., came in. The firm was prepared to supply all the new containers required -- at that time running at the rate of 3,000 a year -- for £87,500* a year, the contract to run for a guaranteed term of five years and thereafter to be renewable from year to year. If the required number of containers increased, the contract price would be increased proportionally. Additionally, and irrespective of whether the above contract was concluded or not, Packages, Ltd., would undertake to carry out purely maintenance work on containers, short of replacement, for a sum of £26,250 a year, on the same contract terms.

Walsh compared these figures with the cost figures prepared by Dyer, covering a year's operations of the container department, which were as follows:

	£	£
Materials................		49,000
Labour...................		35,000
Department overhead:		
Manager's salary......	5,600	
Rent..................	3,150	
Depreciation of machinery...........	10,500	
Maintenance of machinery..........	2,520	
Other expenses........	11,025	
		32,795
		116,795
Proportion of general administrative overhead.............		15,750
Total Cost of Department for Year..............		132,545

Walsh's conclusion was that no time should be lost in closing the department and in entering into the contracts offered by Packages, Ltd. However, he felt bound to give the manager of the department, Sean Duffy, an opportunity to question this conclusion before he acted on it. He therefore called him in and put the facts before him, at the same time making it clear that Duffy's own position was not in jeopardy; for even if his department were closed, there was another managerial position shortly becoming vacant to which he could be moved without loss of pay or prospects.

Duffy asked for time to think the matter over. The next morning, he asked to speak to Walsh again, and said he thought there were a number of considerations that ought to be borne in mind before his department was closed. "For instance," he said, "what will you do with the machinery? It cost £84,000 four years ago, but you'd be lucky if you got £14,000 for it now, even though it's good for another five years or so. And then there's the stock of GHL we bought a year ago. That cost us £70,000, and at the rate we're using it now, it'll last us another four years or so. We used up about one fifth of it last year. Dyer's figure of £49,000 for materials probably includes about £14,000 for GHL. But it'll be tricky stuff to

---

*At the time of this case, one British pound (£) was worth about $2.00.

handle if we don't use it up. We bought it for £350 a ton, and you couldn't buy it today for less than £420. But you wouldn't have more than £280 a ton left if you sold it, after you'd covered all the handling expenses."

Walsh thought that Dyer ought to be present during this discussion. He called him in and put Duffy's points to him. "I don't much like all this conjecture," Dyer said. "I think my figures are pretty conclusive. Besides, if we are going to have all this talk about 'what will happen if,' don't forget the problem of space we're faced with. We're paying £5,950 a year in rent for a small warehouse a couple of miles away. If we closed Duffy's department, we'd have all the warehouse space we need without renting."

"That's a good point," said Walsh. "But I'm a bit worried about the workers if we close the department. I don't think we can find room for any of them elsewhere in the firm. I could see whether Packages can take any of them. But some of them are getting on. There are Walters and Hines, for example. They've been with us since they left school 40 years ago. I'd feel bound to give them a small pension -- £1,050 a year each, say."

Duffy showed some relief at this. "But I still don't like Dyer's figure," he said. "What about this £15,750 for general administrative overhead? You surely don't expect to sack anyone in the general office if I'm closed, do you?" "Probably not," said Dyer, "but someone has to pay for these costs. We can't ignore them when we look at an individual department, because if we do that with each department in turn, we shall finish up by convincing ourselves

that directors, accountants, typists, stationery, and the like don't have to be paid for. And they do, believe me."

"Well, I think we've thrashed this out pretty fully," said Walsh, "but I've been turning over in my mind the possibility of perhaps keeping on the maintenance work ourselves. What are your views on that, Duffy?"

"I don't know," said Duffy, "but it's worth looking into. We shouldn't need any machinery for that, and I could hand the supervision over to a foreman. You'd save £2,100 a year there, say. You'd only need about one fifth of the workers, but you could keep on the oldest. You wouldn't save any space here or at the rented warehouse, so I suppose the rent would be the same. I shouldn't think the other expenses would be more than £4,550 a year." "What about materials?" asked Walsh. "We use about 10 percent of the total on maintenance," Duffy replied.

"Well, I've told Packages, Ltd., that I'd let them know my decision within a week," said Walsh. "I'll let you kow what I decide to do before I write to them."

Questions

1. Identify the four alternatives implicit in the case.

2. Using cash flow as the criterion, which alternative is the most attractive?

3. What, if any, additional information do you think is necessary in order to make a sound decision?

Chapter 22

Longer-Run Decisions: Capital Budgeting

Key Terms

Capital investment problem
Present value
Discounting
Net present value
Required rate of return
Cost of capital
Economic life
Tax shield

Residual value
Internal rate of return method
Payback method
Discounted payback method
Unadjusted return on investment method
Screening problem
Preference problem
Profitability index

Discussion Questions

1. In general, under what circumstances should an investment proposal be accepted?

2. In a "Christmas Club" plan, a person deposits a specified amount weekly in a bank savings acccount and the total amount accumulated is paid back just before Christmas. No interest, or very little interest, is paid on these deposits. Is a Christmas Club member acting irrationally by depositing money under these conditions? Would a business be acting irrationally if it joined a Christmas Club?

3. Would you prefer cash inflows of $600 a year for four years or cash inflows of $400 a year for six years, assuming your required rate of return is 18 percent? Explain. Is there any required rate of return that would change your answer?

4. Companies are said to expect higher profits on investments in underdeveloped countries than in Western European countries with stable economic conditions, and this is said to be an example of exploitation of underdeveloped countries. Is there another explanation for this?

5. For each of the following types of investment projects, state how estimates should be made of the investment, the economic life, and the cash inflows:

   (a) Building a new plant.
   (b) Replacing existing equipment with more efficient equipment.
   (c) Buying a machine to perform an operation now done manually.
   (d) Adding a new product.

6. Table B is used to find the present value of a stream of equal annual cash inflows. Suppose that payments were $250 a year in each of years 2, 3, 4, and 5, and $300 in year 1. Without making calculations, explain two ways in which Table B could be used in such a situation.

7. It is said that investors basically have a choice between eating well and sleeping well. Explain what is meant by this statement, using differences in required rates of return in your explanation.

8. In analyzing an investment proposal, why is depreciation excluded from the calculation of pretax cash inflows but included in the calculation of the income

tax effect?

9. A company has invested $100,000 to develop a new item of electronic equipment, but it doesn't operate properly. It then decides to invest $50,000 additional, but the equipment still doesn't work. Under what circumstances would the company be well advised to spend yet another $50,000?

10. Is the relevant income tax rate for analyzing investment proposals (a) an average of rates over the past several years, (b) the current rate, or (c) the rate anticipated in the future?

11. Supposing the Congress made the following changes in income taxes, what effect would each probably have on the total amount of capital investments made in the United States? Why?

(a) Reduction in the income tax rate from 46 percent to 40 percent.
(b) Elimination of the investment tax credit.
(c) Permit only straight-line depreciation for tax purposes; forbid the use of accelerated depreciation.
(d) Permit an investment to be fully depreciated over one half its economic life.

12. Can there be an acceptable proposal to acquire a machine for the purpose of reducing direct labor costs in which the depreciation completely shielded the pre-tax cash inflow; that is, so that no additional income tax payments would be required? Explain.

13. Explain the difference between the internal rate of return and the net present value methods.

14. In a preference problem, two or more proposals are ranked in order of their desirability. If each of the proposals is acceptable, why does anyone want to know how they rank; that is, why aren't they all accepted?

15. What are some of the nonquantitative considerations that are important in a capital investment problem? Can you think of any practical, important problem that does not require the use of judgment?

16. Discuss issues involved in deciding between the following investment opportunities, only one of which can be undertaken. Assume a 10 percent required rate of return.

Case No. 1. Provides a 17 percent return, with moderate risk, for a 13-year period.
Case No. 2. Provides a 25 percent return, with moderate risk, for a five-year period.

Problems

Note: Disregard income taxes in Problems 22-1 through 22-7.

22-1. A bank makes the following offer: If you will deposit $45,000 cash, the bank will immediately give you a brand-new automobile worth $11,400 and it will also return your $45,000 at the end of five years.

Required:

a. What earnings rate is implicit in this offer?
b. If you had $45,000 to invest, would you accept this proposition?

22-2. You have won the grand prize in a drawing held by Reader's Digest. You may choose either (1) $2,000 a month for one year, (2) $100 a month for life, or (3) $24,000 cash immediately. Which would you choose? Would your choice be different if you were 20 years older than you actually are?

22-3. What is the maximum investment a company would make in an asset expected to produce annual cash inflow of $5,000 a year for 8 years if its required rate of return is 15 percent?

22-4. The Bowman Company is considering three proposed investments, A, B, and C. Each requires an investment of $4,900, and each has an economic life of three years and total cash inflow over that period of $6,000. The pattern of cash inflows for each proposal differs, however, as indicated below:

Year	A	B	C
1...............	$1,000	$2,000	$3,000
2...............	2,000	2,000	2,000
3...............	3,000	2,000	1,000
	$6,000	$6,000	$6,000

Required:

a. Calculate the net present value of each proposal if the required rate of return is 18 percent.
b. Calculate the net present value of each proposal if the required rate of return is 14 percent.
c. Explain why the results differ.

22-5. Last year Main Line Company installed a machine with the expectation of substantial labor cost savings. The expected results for the first year of operations follow:

Cost of machine, installed..........................$15,000
Useful life..5 years
Labor savings......................................$ 6,000
Increased power costs..............................   450
Increased insurance and property taxes.............   550

The company actually paid $15,500 for the machine as installation costs were greater than expected. Actual labor savings were only $5,700. Increased maintenance costs (unanticipated) were $600. All other costs were as expected.

Required:

a. Assuming the company has a required earnings rate of 15 percent, should the proposal have been accepted, based on expected results? Show all computations.
b. If all other costs remain the same as the actual results of the first year of operations, do you feel this company made a sound investment decision? Comment.

22-6. "Old Faithful" was a plastics extruder, long since fully depreciated, which Kupper Plastics Company had owned since its inception in 1959. It was judged to be able to run indefinitely at its present rate of 75 percent of capacity. It had zero residual value.

Company engineers informed Mr. Kupper, the president, that a new, more efficient extruder was on the market which could save the company $6,750 per year in reduced labor costs and increased output, 60 percent due to the former and 40 percent due to the latter. The new extruder would cost the company $42,750 delivered and installed. The engineers claimed that its economic life was 20 years. Kupper's required earnings rate was 15 percent.

Required:

a. If the engineers are correct, should the plastic extruder be purchased?
b. Mr. Kupper thought the estimate of economic life was unrealistic. What minimum economic life is necessary in order to justify the investment?

22-7. Bill Coyne is considering opening a self-service laundromat which would require an investment of $54,000 for washers, dryers, and related equipment. Bill estimates that the equipment will have a seven-year life, and seeks a return of 25 percent without regard to tax considerations, which he recognizes will reduce his actual return.

Bill plans to charge $0.50 for the use of a washing machine and $0.25 for the use of a dryer for 25 minutes. He has estimated that he will gross $450 and $225 from the washers and dryers, respectively, each week. Variable costs would amount to $0.04 per wash for water and electricity and $0.03 per 25-minute dryer cycle for gas and electricity. Bill has estimated that his monthly fixed expenses will consist of rent of $450 and maintenance and cleanup labor of $200.

Required: Can Bill Coyne obtain the return he desires, given the revenue and expense estimates?

Note: In Problems 22-8 through 22-15, unless otherwise specified, use the following assumptions:

Tax rate: 51 percent
Depreciation method: straight line
Aftertax required rate of return: 10 percent

22-8. A company owned a plot of land that appeared in its fixed assets at its acquisition cost in 1910, which was $10,000. The land was not used. In 1983 the local boys club asked the company to donate the land as the site for a new recreation bulding. The donation would be a taxable deduction of $110,000, which was the current appraised value. The company's tax rate was 51 percent. Some argued that the company would be better off to donate the land than to keep it or to sell it for $110,000. Assume that, other than the land, the company's taxable income as well as its accounting income before taxes was $10,000,000.

Required: How would the company's aftertax cash inflow be affected if (a) it donated the land of (b) it sold the land for $110,000? How would its net income be affected?

22-9. Re-Cycle Company is just starting operations with new equipment costing $30,000 and a useful life of four years. At the end of four years the equipment probably can be sold for $6,000. The company is concerned with its cash flow and wants a comparison of straight-line and sum-of-the-years'-digits depreciation to help management decide which depreciation method to use for financial statements and for its income tax return.

Required:

a. Calculate the difference in taxable income and cash inflow under each method.
b. Which depreciation method is preferable for tax purposes? Why?

22-10. Thomas Company owns a warehouse which it no longer needs in its own operations. The warehouse was built at a cost of $270,000 ten years ago, at which time its estimated useful life was 15 years. There are two proposals for the use of the warehouse:

(1) Rent it at $72,000 per year, which includes estimated costs of $27,000 per year for maintenance, heat, and utilities.
(2) Sell it outright to a prospective buyer who has offered $225,000. Any capital gain would be taxed at the 30 percent rate.

Required:

a. Calculate the aftertax income if (1) Thomas Company keeps the warehouse and (2) if Thomas Company sells the warehouse.
b. Which proposal should the company accept? Why?

22-11. Bonnie Vaughn, head of Stonewell Company's typing activities, was trying to decide whether a new electronic word-processing machine should be purchased or leased. The purchase price was $7,500; the machine had an estimated useful life of 8 years and residual value of $2,000. The machine could be leased for $100 per month. In either case, any repair or other servicing costs would be in addition to the purchase cost or rental fee.

Required: Should the word-processing machine be purchased or leased?

22-12. (Disregard income taxes in this problem.) Compute the following:

a. An investment of $12,000 has an investment/inflow ratio of 6.2 and a useful life of 12 years. What is the annual cash inflow and internal rate of return?

b. The internal rate of return for an investment expected to yield an annual cash inflow of $1,500 is 14 percent. How much is the investment if the investment/inflow ratio is 6.14?

c. What is the maximum investment a company would make in an asset expected to produce annual cash inflow of $5,000 a year for 8 years if its required rate of return is 18 percent?

d. How much investment per dollar of expected annual operating savings can a company afford if the investment has an expected life of 7 years and its required rate of return is 15 percent?

22-13. Wentworth Corporation estimates that it will have $500,000 available for capital investments next year. Half of this will be reserved for emergency projects and half will be invested in the most desirable projects from the following list. None of the investments has a residual value.

Project Number	Added Investment	Expected Aftertax Cash Inflow	Estimated Life of Project
1	$100,000	$25,000	6 years
2	100,000	30,000	4
3	40,000	5,000	15
4	20,000	10,000	2
5	50,000	12,500	3

Required: Rank the projects in order of their desirability.

22-14. Brant Company is considering the replacement of a machine with a newer more efficient model. The old machine currently has a book value of $10,000, present resale value of $7,000, and expected residual value of $2,000 after the remaining four years of its economic life. Data on the new machine and the estimated effect on annual operating costs are as follows:

```
Cost.....................................$50,000
Delivery and installation...............  4,000
Residual value..........................  5,000
Additional working capital required.....  6,000
Reduction in labor costs................  8,000
Reduction in maintenance costs..........  3,000
Increase in utility costs...............  1,000
```

The reduction in maintenance costs applies only to the first five years, after which maintenance costs of the new are expected to be the same a for the old. Brant's required rate of return is 14 percent. The economic life is 10 years. Disregard income taxes.

Required:

a. Diagram the cash flows and calculate the net present value of the proposed investment in the machine using the format in Illustration 22-2.

b. Do you recommend purchase of the new machine? Why?

c. The cost analyst who prepared the data above just called to say she has discovered a couple of errors in her computations. The cost of the new machine should be $56,000 instead of $50,000, but the savings in labor costs should be $10,000 per year instead of $8,000. Using the new data, recalculate the net present value and reassess your recommendation on possible purchase of the new machine.

22-15. Manuel Varga is considering the purchase of 62 acres of land, presently owned

owned by Talcott and leased from Talcott by Weeden. Weeden uses the land as a golf driving range and pays $1,500 per month rental.

The purchase price of the land is $400,000; however, Varga has knowledge of state plans to build a highway that will run adjacent to the property. Varga is convinced that once the highway is built he will be able to sell the land for $650,000. Varga plans to finance the purchase with $100,000 of his own funds, plus a $300,000, five-year, 9.5 percent bank note secured by the land, with interest payable on a quarterly basis.

The plans for the new highway call for its completion in four and a half years, and Varga has been informed by Weeden that a five-year lease on the land at the present rental rate would be agreeable to him. Varga is aware of some of the risks involved in his plan and as a result wishes to evaluate the proposal using a 15 percent aftertax required rate of return.

Required: Assuming the following tax rates -- ordinary income, 51%; capital gains, 30% -- should Varga undertake this venture?

22-16. (C.M.A. adapted.) Baxter Company manufactures short-lived, fad-type items. The research and development department came up with an item that would make a good promotional gift for office equipment dealers. Aggressive effort by Baxter's sales personnel has resulted in almost firm commitments for this product for the next three years. It is expected that the product's novelty will be exhausted after three years.

In order to produce the quantity demanded, Baxter will need to buy additional machinery and rent some additional space. About 25,000 square feet will be needed; 12,500 square feet of presently unused, but leased, space is available now. (Baxter's present lease with 10 years to run costs $3.00 a square foot.) There is another 12,500 square feet adjoining the Baxter facility that Baxter will rent for 3 years at $4.00 per square foot per year if it decides to make this product.

The equipment will be purchased for $900,000. It will require $30,000 in modifications, $60,000 for installation, and $90,000 for testing. All of the expenditures will be paid for on January 1, 1984. The equipment should have a salvage value of about $180,000 at the end of the third year. No additional general overhead costs are expected to be incurred.

The following estimates of revenues and expenses for this product for the three years have been developed:

	1984	1985	1986
Sales.....................................	$1,000,000	$1,600,000	$800,000
Material, labor and direct overhead......	400,000	750,000	350,000
Allocated general overhead..............	40,000	75,000	35,000
Rent.....................................	87,500	87,500	87,500
Depreciation.............................	450,000	300,000	150,000
	977,500	1,212,500	622,500
Income before taxes.....................	22,500	387,500	177,500
Income taxes (40%)......................	9,000	155,000	71,000
Net Income..............................	$ 13,500	$ 232,500	$106,500

Required:

  a. Prepare a schedule that shows the differential after-tax cash flows for this project.
  b. If the company requires a two-year payback period for its investment, would it undertake this project?
  c. Calculate the after-tax accounting rate of return for the project.
  d. A newly hired business school graduate recommends that the company use net present value analysis to study this project. If the company sets a required rate of return of 20 percent after taxes, will this project be accepted? (Assume all operating revenues an expenses occur at the end of the year.)
  e. What is the internal rate of return of the proposed project?

CASES

Case 22-17: Gallup Company

A. Equipment Replacement

Gallup Company is considering the purchase of new equipment to perform operations currently being performed on different, less efficient equipment. The purchase price is $150,000, delivered and installed.

A Gallup production engineer estimates that the new equpment will produce savings of $30,000 in labor and other direct costs annually, as compared with the present equipment. He estimates the proposed equipment's economic life at 10 years, with zero salvage value. The present equipment is in good working order and will last, physically, for at least 20 more years.

The company can borrow money at 12 percent, although it would not plan to negotiate a loan specifically for the purchase of this equipment. The company requires a return of at least 20 percent before taxes on an investment of this type. Taxes are to be disregarded.

Questions

1. Assuming the present equipment has zero book value and zero salvage value, should the company buy the proposed equipment?

2. Assuming the present equipment is being depreciated at a straight-line rate of 10 percent, that it has a book value of $72,000 (cost, $120,000; accumulated depreciation, $48,000), and has zero net salvage value today, should the company buy the proposed equipment?

3. Assuming the present equipment has a book value of $72,000 and a salvage value today of $45,000, and that if retained for 10 more years its salvage value will be zero, should the company buy the proposed equipment?

4. Assume the new equipment will save only $15,000 a year, but that its economic life is expected to be 20 years. If other conditions are as described in (1) above, should the company buy the proposed equipment?

B. Replacement Following Earlier Replacement

Gallup Company decided to purchase the equipment described in Part A (hereafter called "Model A" equipment). Two years later, even better equipment (called "Model B") comes on the market and makes the other equipment completely obsolete, with no resale value. The Model B equipment costs $300,000 delivered and installed, but it is expected to result in annual savings of $75,000 over the cost of operating the Model A equipment. The economic life of Model B is estimated to be 10 years. Taxes are to be disregarded.

Questions

1. What action should the company take?

2. If the company decides to purchase the Model B equipment, a mistake has been made somewhere, because good equipment, bought only two years previously, is being scrapped. How did this mistake come about?

C. Effect of Income Taxes

Assume that Gallup Company expects to pay income taxes of 46 percent and that a loss on the sale or disposal of equipment is treated as a capital loss, resulting in a tax saving of 28 percent. Gallup Company uses a 10 percent discount rate for analyses performed on an after-tax basis. Depreciation of the new equipment for tax purposes is computed on the sum-of-years'-digits basis. (Note: the present value of the sum-of years'-digits depreciation stream per $1 of depreciable investment, using a 10 year life and 10 percent discount rate, is 0.701.) The new equipment qualifies for an 8 percent investment tax credit, which will not reduce the cost basis of the asset for calculating depreciation for tax purposes.

Questions

1. Should the company buy the equipment if the facts are otherwise as described in Part A(1)?

2. If the facts are otherwise as described in Part A(2)?

3. If the facts are otherwise as described in Part B?

D. Change in Earnings Pattern

Assume that the savings are expected to be $37,500 in each of the first five years and $22,500 in each of the next five years, other conditions remaining as described in Part A(1).

Questions

1. What action should the company take?

2. Why is the result here different from that in Part A(1)?

3. What effect would the inclusion of income taxes, as in Part C, have on your recommendation?

* * * * *

Case 22-18: Thurber Company

Thurber Company was a manufacturing firm owned by the Thurber family. The executive committee of Thurber Company was considering the addition of a new super-widget to its product line. It had before it an unfavorable report from the assistant treasurer which read as follows:

1. It is recommended that we <u>not</u> add the super-widget to the current product line. This is largely based on a consideration of the quantity we can sell annually versus that required to break even. According to our market research department, we can anticipate sales of about 45,000 units per year. My calculations show the break-even sales volume is 50,000 units per year, as shown in Item 2.

2. The marketing department has indicated that the best selling price would be $40.00 per unit. The cost department has prepared the following per-unit estimate of costs:

```
Materials.....................$12.00
Direct labor:  1 hour
   @ $8.00 per hour...........  8.00
Variable overhead
   @ 25% of direct labor.......  2.00
Other factory overhead
   @ 25% of direct labor.......  2.00
Selling and administrative
   @ 20% of selling price......  8.00
      Total cost per unit.....$32.00
```

Apart from the overhead costs specified above, it is expected that the new super-widget department will incur fixed costs of $400,000 per year. This includes $200,000 per year for depreciation and the remainder for supervision, indirect labor, and light and power.

The sales volume at which the unit contribution of $8.00 ($40.00 selling price less $32.00 unit cost) will just cover the $400,000 fixed departmental expenses is 50,000 units per year.

3. The rates used for determining the unit charges for variable overhead,

other factory overhead, and selling and administrative expense are standard for all of the company's product lines.

4. The estimated depreciation expense is based on $2,000,000 of new equipment and an economic life of 10 years. Straight-line depreciation will be used on this investment.

5. A total of $1,200,000 was spent last year on product development and market research for the super-widget. This has already been expensed for tax purposes, but we still have this on our books as an asset. It was planned to write this off over the first five years of super-widget sales. An additional $80,000 will be required to clean up the factory area in which the new super-widget department will go. This can probably be expensed for tax purposes. Since the $80,000 represents a one-shot expenditure, it has been excluded from the break-even analysis.

6. Our working capital needs will be about 25% of the expected annual sales volume or $450,000 (25% of 45,000 units times $40.00 per unit). Since this will be recovered any time we want to drop super-widgets from our product line, this has not been included in the break-even analysis.

7. I doubt that the company will want to incur a loss on the super-widget even though the marketing people say it would be a desirable addition to the company product line and can be handled without any increase in the sales force.

8. Setting up the new department for the manufacture of super-widgets would also provide some administrative problems for the factory management. This would be the only department at Thurber whose personnel cannot be used in other departments or vice versa. In effect, the "direct labor" would become a fixed cost for the company, raising the break-even point still higher than

- 264 -

that calculated in this memorandum.

9. Certainly this project will not earn the 10 percent return after taxes that you have specified as desirable for investments in new product introduction.

Questions

1. Evaluate the assistant treasurer's report and suggest ways, if any, in which it might be improved. (Assume a 55 percent tax rate in any calculations you perform.)

2. What will the company's accounting net income after taxes be if the new super-widget is introduced?

3. What volume of new super-widgets would be required to make this a desirable investment?

4. On the basis of the information provided, what should Thurber Company do? What additional information is required, if any?

Chapter 23

Responsibility Accounting:
The Management Control Structure

Key Terms

Management control
Strategic planning
Task control
Responsibility center
Responsibility accounting
Expense center

Revenue center
Profit center
Transfer price
Investment center
Residual income

Discussion Questions

1. Distinguish between line units and staff units, and give examples of each.

2. What are the differences among the planning activities that take place in the strategic planning process, the management control process, and the task control process, respectively? Give examples.

3. Distinguish carefully between a "cost center" and an "expense center." Can one department in a company be both?

4. Distinguish between an engineered expense center and a discretionary expense center.

5. What actions could a profit center manager take that would improve the center's reported performance but would be against the long-run best interest of the company?

6. Under what circumstances should a transfer price be a cost-based price?

7. Suggest some inefficiencies or unwise actions that would be revealed on performance reports if a responsibility center were a profit center, that would not be revealed if it were an expense center. Similarly, suggest some inefficiencies or unwise actions that would be revealed if a responsibility center were an investment center, that would not be revealed if it were a profit center.

8. A certain company has a typing and secretarial pool which various offices may call on for additional assistance when their own staffs are too busy to handle the work load. What factors should be considered in deciding whether or not to make this pool a profit center? If it is made a profit center, how should the transfer price of typing be arrived at? If the typing pool is a profit center, should other departments be permitted to hire temporary outside help to handle their overflow work load?

9. Distinguish between a profit center and an investment center.

10. What are the differences between full cost accounting and responsibility accounting?

11. What method of charging maintenance costs to responsibility centers is appropriate under each of the following circumstances?

a. Top management wants line managers to have complete responsibility for the operation of their responsibility centers.
b. The responsibility centers are research and development departments. Top management wants them to devote all their energies to research projects.
c. Top management wants the maintenance department to be responsible for the normal painting and other upkeep work of buildings but wants the responsibility centers to be responsible for the cost of alterations, such as new partitions.

12. Under what circumstances should a responsibility center not be organized as a profit center?

13. Contrast the cost construction used to transfer products from one department to another in a product cost accounting system and the amount used to transfer products from one profit center to another.

14. What is the difference between the way return on investment and residual income are calculated?

Problems

23-1. Bountiful Bread Company delivers bread and pastries daily to retail stores. It has six driver-salespersons assigned to different routes. Each salesperson is paid a weekly salary plus a commission based on sales. Route lengths are from 50 to 175 miles, some in densely settled areas, some in rural areas. All but one route have been operated for several years and are well established. Each salesperson may advertise if he or she wishes, and the cost is paid by him or her. Because of complaints from drivers about the mileage differential, and route density differences, the question of developing varying commission rates has arisen.

Required: Discuss the possibilities of considering each driver-salesperson as a profit center for measuring performance.

23-2. The Box Division of Maple Company manufactures cardboard boxes that are used by other divisions of Maple Company and which are also sold to external customers. The Hardware Division of Maple Company has requested the Box Division to supply a certain box, Style K, and the Box Division has computed a proposed transfer price per thousand boxes on this box, as follows:

Variable cost.	$180
Fixed cost.	40
Total cost.	220
Profit (to provide normal return on assets employed).	30
Transfer price.	$250

The Hardware Division is unwilling to accept this transfer price because Style K boxes are regularly sold to outside customers for $240 per thousand. The Box Division points out, however, that competition for this box is unusually keen, and that this is why it cannot price the box to external customers so as to earn a normal return. Both divisions are profit centers.

Required: What should the transfer price be? (Explain your answer.)

23-3. Six months after the Box Division of Maple Company started to supply Style K boxes to the Hardware Division (see Problem 23-2), Eastern Company offered to supply boxes to the Hardware Division for $235 per thousand. The Hardware Division thereupon informed the Box Division that the transfer price should be reduced to $235 because this was now the market price.

Required (explain your answers):

a. Should the transfer price be reduced to $235 per thousand?
b. Under what circumstances should the Box Division refuse to supply boxes to the Hardware Division?
c. If the Box Division refused to supply boxes at $235 per thousand, should the Hardware Division be permitted by top management to buy boxes from the Eastern Company?

d. If outside market prices continued to decrease, and eventually reached $210 per thousand, would this change your answer to any of the preceding questions?

23-4. (C.M.A. adapted.) Texon Company is organized into autonomous divisions along regional market lines. Each division manager is responsible for sales, cost of operations, acquisition and financing of divisional assets, and working capital management.

Texon's vice president of operations will retire in September 1983. A review of the performance, attitudes, and skills of several managers has been undertaken in trying to choose the next vice president. Interviews with qualified outside candidates also have been held.

The selection committee has narrowed the choice to the managers of Divisions A and F. Both candidates were appointed division managers in late 1979. The Division A manager had been the assistant manager of that division for the prior five years. The Division F manager had served as assistant division manager of Division B before being appointed to his present post. He took over Division F, a division newly formed in 1978, when its first manager left to join a competitor. The financial results of their performance in the past three years are reported below. (All dollar amounts are thousands.)

| | Division A | | | Division F | | |
	1980	1981	1982	1980	1981	1982
Estimated industry sales --market area......	$10,000	$12,000	$13,000	$5,000	$6,000	$6,500
Division sales.......	$ 1,000	$ 1,100	$ 1,210	$ 450	$ 600	$ 750
Variable costs.......	300	320	345	135	175	210
Managed costs........	400	405	420	170	200	230
Committed costs......	275	325	350	140	200	250
Total costs......	975	1,050	1,115	445	575	690
Income..........	$ 25	$ 50	$ 95	$ 5	$ 25	$ 60
Assets employed......	$ 330	$ 340	$ 360	$ 170	$ 240	$ 300
Liabilities incurred.	103	105	115	47	100	130
Net investment.......	227	235	245	123	140	170
Return on investment.	11%	21%	39%	4%	18%	35%

Required:

a. Texon Company measures the performance of the divisions and the division managers on the basis of their return on investment (ROI). Is this an appropriate measurement for the division managers? Explain.
b. Many people believe that a single measure, such as ROI, is inadequate to fully evaluate performance. What additional measure(s) could be used for performance evaluation? Give reasons for each measure listed.
c. On the basis of the information given, which manager would you recommend for vice president of operations? Present reasons to support your answer.

23-5. Department 12 of the Minow Company manufactures a variety of components for products, one of which is Part No. 16. Data on this part are as follows:

Item of Cost	Monthly Planned Cost Per Unit	Actual Cost, June Per Unit	Total
Direct material and direct labor.......	$21.60	$21.06	$21,060
Fixed costs, Department 12.............	5.40	5.94	5,940
Costs allocated to Department 12.......	8.10	8.91	8,910
Total......................	$35.10	$35.91	$35,910

Part No. 106 can be purchased from an outside vendor for $22.

Required: What costs are relevant for each of the following purposes:

    a. For preparing financial statements for June?
    b. For deciding whether to make or buy Part No. 106?
    c. For assessing the performance of the manager of Department 12?

23-6. Kentow Company manufactures three products, A, B, and C. It has three marketing managers, one for each product. During the first year of operations, the company allocated its $30,000 of actual advertising expense to products on the basis of the relative net sales of each product. In the second year, the advertising budget was increased to $50,000. Half was spent on general institutional advertising in the belief the company image would be enhanced. The other half was spent $8,000 on Product A, $12,000 on Product B, and $5,000 on Product C. For purposes of income measurement, all advertising expenses continued to be allocated on the basis of sales. Certain data in the second year were as follows:

	Total	Product A	Product B	Product C
Net sales................	$450,000	$193,500	$126,000	$130,500
Advertising expense......	50,000	21,500	14,000	14,500
Income..................	55,000	25,500	12,000	17,500

When the marketing manager of Product A received these figures, he complained that his department was charged with an unfair portion of advertising, and that he should be held responsible only for the actual amount spent to advertise Product A.

Required:

    a. Comment on the sales manager's complaint.
    b. In Kentow's responsibility accounting system, how much advertising expense should be charged to the department responsible for marketing Product A?

23-7. Jersey Company, a distributor of hardware items, offers a cash discount of 2 percent for customers paying their accounts within 10 days of sale, but charges 1.5 percent per month on all accounts not paid within 30 days of sale. Each department decides which of its customers will be allowed to buy on credit. The net sales of each department are computed by subtracting the cash discount actually taken on department sales. Revenue from finance charges is allocated to the departments on the basis of credit sales made during the current month. A summary of these monthly transactions follows:

	Total	Department 1	Department 2	Department 3
Cash sales............$	740,000	$180,000	$260,000	$300,000
Cash discounts........	9,400	3,600	5,200	600
Total sales..........	1,340,000	280,000	560,000	500,000
Finance charges collected..........	31,200	5,200	15,600	10,400

Required:

    a. Comment on the method of allocating cash discounts and the revenue from finance charges for responsibility accounting purposes.
    b. Compute the net revenue due to credit sales, assigning the discounts and finance revenue in a manner which you believe would produce more useful results for management use.

23-8. The Lane Confectionery Company is a wholesaler of candies and tobacco products. At the end of each month the controller prepares statements for each of the three branch managers and the company president. The statement for the current month is as follows:

	Branch 1	Branch 2	Branch 3
Sales.......................................	$300,000	$200,000	$400,000
Direct costs:			
Cost of sales.............................	180,000	124,000	220,000
Salespersons' salaries.....................	34,000	26,000	38,000
Supplies...................................	400	300	450
Utilities..................................	1,100	900	1,200
Delivery expense...........................	5,000	3,800	6,200
Depreciation--branch assets................	20,000	19,200	22,500
Branch contribution........................	59,500	25,800	111,650
Allocated costs:			
Advertising expense........................	12,000	8,000	16,000
Administrative salaries and other			
administrative expense	32,000	32,000	32,000
Income before Taxes........................	$ 15,000	$(14,200)	$ 63,650

Required:

    a. Comment on the strengths and weaknesses of this statement.
    b. Comment on the basis of allocation of the overheads.
    c. Should Branch 2 be discontinued? Support your answer.

23-9. The city of Burham operates an extended care facility called Burham Community Care. Patients who are not sick enough to stay the the County Hospital but too sick to go home are admitted to this facility.

When Burham Community Care was founded, it was expected that its cost per patient day would be only 65-75 percent of those at the County Hospital because of the lower level of care required. A recent analysis of Burham Community Care costs revealed that they were 88 percent of County Hospital costs. The escalating costs of Burham as compared to County General became a major concern for Burham's board of trustees. They hired a consulting firm which specialized in nonprofit health care facilities to study the problem.

The consultants recommended that the Burham administrator be given complete control over all expenditures at the institution and that financial management information systems be developed by her. They pointed out that currently the administrator was primarily involved in day-to-day operating problems, and paid relatively little attention to the control of costs.

When this recommendation was discussed with the administrator, she questioned its practicality. She felt that she could not actually control expenditures. Among the reasons she gave were: (a) the level of nursing care furnished a patient was set by the patient's physician; (b) some patients had special diets, also prescribed by the physician, and these affected food costs; and (c) the number of patients fluctuated, and the fixed costs per patient fluctuated correspondingly. The administrator continued to believe that responsibility accounting in the Burham facility is only a theoretical concept, and that in reality it is just not practical.

Required:

    a. As chairperson of the Burham board of trustees, how do you view the consultant's report in light of the administrator's response?
    b. If the recommendation were adopted, what do you think would happen to the quality of service and professional morale?

23-10. First National Bank has branches in several communities. They are under the supervision of the bank's branch division, headed by Nancy Shea. The bank has just received permission from the state banking commission to do business in Plymouth, a city in which it had not previously operated. Investigation of possible branch locations resulted in five possible investment projects, some involving several locations, and some only one. The estimated gross investment required for each project was as follows:

Project	Gross investment	Estimated annual income
A...............$	500,000	$125,000
B.............	1,000,000	200,000
C.............	1,500,000	250,000
D.............	2,000,000	360,000
E.............	2,500,000	420,000

Only one of these projects would be implemented:

Required:

    a. Assuming that Ms. Shea's performance is judged on the basis of return on investment, which project should she recommend to top management?

    b. Assuming that Ms. Shea's performance is judged on the basis of residual income, after a capital charge of 8 percent of gross investment, which project should she recommend to top management?

    c. Assuming that Ms. Shea's performance is judged on the basis of residual income, after a capital charge of 15 percent of gross investment, which project should she recommend to top management?

    d. Discuss which basis of performance measurement provides the soundest basis for motivating Ms. Shea.

23-11. Mogul Truck Company has a division that produces batteries. It sells them to its assembly division and also to outsiders through regular market channels. Operating details are as follows:

	To Assembly Division	To Outsiders	Total
Sales 100,000 units @ $70*....	$7,000,000	50,000 @ $100....$5,000,000	$12,000,000
Variable costs: 100,000 units @ $50.........	5,000,000	50,000 @ $50..... 2,500,000	7,500,000
Fixed costs.......	1,500,000	750,000	2,250,000
Total costs....	6,500,000	3,250,000	9,750,000
Operating income..	$ 500,000	$1,750,000	$ 2,250,000

*The $70 price is established by corporate headquarters.

The Assembly division manager has a chance to get a firm contract with an outside supplier at $65 for the ensuing period. The Battery Division manager says that he cannot sell at $65 because no operating income can be earned. Assume that fixed costs would be unaffected no matter what is done.

Required:

    a. What would be the impact on operating income for the Battery Division if the Assembly division manager bought outside?

    b. What would be the impact on operating income for the Mogul Truck Company if the Assembly Division manager bought outside?

    c. What do you expect the Assembly Division manager to do? Explain.

    d. Does the transfer price of $70 motivate the managers to act in the corporation's best interest? Explain.

    e. What would be your advice to the Battery Division manager?

    f. As Battery Division manager, what is the minimum price you would set in bargaining with the Assembly Division manager?

23-12. Physician Services, Inc., a management consulting group, is in its fourth year of operation. It consists of three independent groups: (1) legal services, (2) accounting services, and (3) portfolio management. All its revenue comes from physicians and dentists. It has no plans to expand its services outside these markets. Clients are billed at hourly rates for services rendered to them.

One group often performs services for another group. For example, after the accounting services group has decided that a client physician needs to shelter some of his or her income, it requests the portfolio management group to match the needs of the client with the best shelter possible for this client.

Corporate policy allows each group manager to operate his or her group as if it were a separate company. The following is representative of the pricing and cost information for each group:

Per consulting hour:

Group	Billing rate	Variable cost	Total fixed cost
Legal services.................	$70	$21.00	$240,000
Accounting services...........	84	28.00	280,000
Portfolio management.........	63	34.65	200,000

Required:

    a. The staff of the portfolio management group is working at capacity with its own outside clients. If the legal services group wants to buy consulting services from the portfolio management group, at what price per hour should the portfolio management group bill the legal services group?

    b. Are there any conditions under which the portfolio management group should bill the legal services group at less than this price?

    c. The accounting services group has been using about 1,400 hours per quarter of legal services group time at a rate of $70. If the legal services group manager decides to raise the rate to $77, should the accounting services group be forced by corporate management to pay the new rate in order to keep the business in the firm?

23-13. The Transistor Division of Mador Company produces components used in radio transmitters that the Electronics Division sells to the Air Force. Cost per transmitter data used in negotiating a selling price are as follows:

	Transistor Division components	Complete transmitter
Components from Transistor Division.......	--	$ 220
Other direct material.....................	$ 20	480
Direct labor..............................	80	100
Indirect cost.............................	100	200
Total cost............................	200	1,000
Profit margin.............................	20	100
Price.................................	$220	$1,100

The Air Force representative argued that the $1,100 price was too high because profit on the transistors was double counted.

Required:

    a. If Mador Company calculated its profit margin on the basis of assets employed, is the Air Force position correct?

    b. If Mador Company calculated its profit on the basis of a percentage of cost, is the Air Force position correct?

    c. From the data given above, which method of calculating profit did the Mador Company probably use?

23-14. Dwight Company makes two products, A and B, each of which is worked on in factory departments 1 and 2. A third factory department provides various services to the two production departments. A recent month's production cost report for Dwight Company showed the following:

```
Direct materials....................................$ 75,000
Direct labor........................................ 120,000
Other costs direct to Departments 1 and 2........ 50,000
Production support costs (Department 3).......... 80,000
    Total production costs.........................$325,000
```

Forty percent of the total direct materials cost and 50 percent of the total direct labor cost were attributable to Product A. Eighty percent of the total direct materials cost and thirty percent of the total direct labor cost were incurred in Department 1. Of the other direct department costs, 35 percent was attributable to Department 1. Production support costs were allocated to the two production departments in proportion to their direct labor costs. Departments 1 and 2 each charged Products A and B with overhead in proportion to the direct labor incurred by each product in the respective departments. Half of Department 1's direct labor cost was attributable to Product A, whereas 60 percent of Department 2's direct labor cost was attributable to Product A. Sixty percent of Department 1's direct material cost was attributable to Product A; 30 percent of Department 2's direct material cost was attributable to Product A.

Required: Using the cost element production data given above, develop a matrix like the one in Part C of Illustration 23-4. (Hint: develop responsibility center data first. The sum of all the numbers in your matrix should be $325,000.)

CASES

Case 23-15: Shuman Automobiles Inc.

Clark Shuman, owner and general manager of an automobile dealership, was nearing retirement, and wanted to begin relinquishing his personal control over the business's operations. (See Exhibit 1 for current financial

EXHIBIT 1

SHUMAN AUTOMOBILES, INC.
Income Statement
For the Year Ended December 31

Sales of new cars.....................		$3,821,873
Cost of new car sales*...............	$3,456,401	
Sales remuneration...................	76,372	3,532,773
		289,100
Allowances on trade**................		86,112
New cars gross profit................		202,988
Sales of used cars...................	1,695,696	
Cost of used car sales*.............. $1,457,277		
Sales remuneration................... 51,564		
	1,508,841	
	186,855	
Allowances on trade**................	31,118	
Used cars gross profit...............		155,737
		358,725
Service sales to customers...........	547,511	
Cost of work*........................	404,884	
	142,627	
Service work on reconditioning		
Charge.............................	236,580	
Cost*..............................	244,312	(7,732)
Service work gross profit...........		134,895
		493,620
General and administrative expenses..		191,710
Income before taxes.................		$ 301,910

*These amounts include all costs assignable directly to the department, but exclude allocated general dealership overhead.
**Allowances on trade represent the excess of amounts allowed on cars taken in trade over their appraised value.

statements.) The reputation he had established in the community led him to believe that the recent growth in this business would continue. His long-standing policy of emphasizing new car sales as the principal business of the dealerhsip had paid off, in Shuman's opinion. This, combined with close attention to customer relations so that a substantial amount of repeat business was generated, had increased the company's sales to a new high level. Therefore, he wanted to make organizational changes to cope with the new situation, especially given his desire to withdraw from any day-to-day managerial responsibilities. Shuman's three "silent partners" agreed to this decision.

Accordingly, Shuman divided up the business into three departments: new car sales, used car sales, and the service department. He then appointed three of his most trusted employees managers of the new departments: Janet Moyer, new car sales; Paul Fiedler, used car sales; and Nate Bianci, service department. All of these people had been with the dealership for several years.

Each manager was told to run his or her department as if it were an independent business. In order to give the new managers an incentive, their remuneration was to be calculated as a straight percentage of their department's gross profit.

Soon after taking over as manager of new car sales, Janet Moyer had to settle upon the amount to offer a particular customer who wanted to trade his old car as a part of the purchase price of a new one with a list price of $9,600. Before closing the sale, Moyer had to decide the amount she would offer the customer for the trade-in value of the old car. She knew that if no trade-in were involved, she would deduct about 8 percent from the list price of this model new car to be competitive with several other dealers in the area. However, she also wanted to make sure that she did not lose out on the sale by offering too low a trade-in allowance.

During her conversation with the customer, it had become apparent that the customer had an inflated view of the worth of his old car, a far from uncommon event. In this case, it probably meant that Moyer had to be prepared to make some sacrifices to close the sale. The new car had been in stock for some time, and the model was not selling very well, so she was

rather anxious to make the sale if this could be done profitably.

In order to establish the trade-in value of the car, the used-car manager, Fiedler, accompanied Moyer and the customer out to the parking lot to examine the car. In the course of his appraisal, Fiedler estimated the car would require reconditioning work costing about $525, after which the car would retail for about $3,700. On a wholesale basis, he could either buy or sell such a car, after reconditioning, for about $3,200. The wholesale price of a car was subject to much greater fluctuation than the retail price, depending on color, trim, model, and so forth. Fortunately, the car being traded in was a very popular shade. The retail automobile dealer's handbook of used car prices, the "Blue Book," gave a cash buying price range of $2,750 to $2,930 for the trade-in model in good condition. This range represented the distribution of cash prices paid by automobile dealers for that model of car in the area in the past week. Fiedler estimated that he could get about $2,400 for the car "as is" (that is, without any work being done to it) at next week's auction.

The new-car department manager had the right to buy any trade-in at any price she thought appropriate, but then it was her responsibility to dispose of the car. She had the alternative of either trying to persuade the used car manager to take over the car and accepting the used-car manager's appraisal price, or she herself could sell the car through wholesale channels or at auction. Whatever course Moyer adopted, it was her primary responsibility to make a profit for the dealership on the new cars she sold, without affecting her performance through excessive allowances on trade-ins. This primary goal, Moyer said, had to be "balanced against the need to satisfy the customers and move the new cars out of inventory -- and there was only a narrow line between allowing enough on a used car and allowing too much."

After weighing all these factors, with particular emphasis on the personality of the customer, Moyer decided she would allow $3,250 for the used car, provided the customer agreed to pay the list price for the new car. After a certain amount of haggling, during which the customer came down from a higher figure and Moyer came up from a lower one, the $3,250 allowance was agreed upon. The necessary papers were signed, and the customer drove off.

Moyer returned to the office and explained the situation to Joanne Brunner, who had recently joined the dealership as accountant. After listening with interest to Moyer's explanation of the sale, Brunner set about recording the sale in the accounting records of the business. As soon as she saw the new car had been purchased from the manufacturer for $8,160, she was uncertain as to the value she should place on the trade-in vehicle. Since the new car's list price was $9,600 and it had cost $8,160, Brunner reasoned the gross margin on the new car sale was $1,440. Yet Moyer had allowed $3,250 for the old car, which needed $525 repairs and could be sold retail for $3,700 or wholesale for $3,200. Did this mean that the new car sale involved a loss? Brunner was not at all sure she knew the answer to this question. Also, she was uncertain about the value she should place on the used car for inventory valuation purposes. Brunner decided that she would put down a valuation of $3,250, and then await instructions from her superiors.

When Fiedler, the used-car manager, found out what Brunner had done, he stated forcefully that he would not accept $3,250 as the valuation of the used car. His comment went as follows:

My used car department has to get rid of that used car, unless Janet (Moyer) agrees to take it over herself. I would certainly never have allowed the customer $3,250 for that old tub. I would never have given any more than $2,675, which is the wholesale price less the cost of repairs. My department has to make a profit too, you know. My own income is dependent on the gross profit I show on the sale of used cars, and I will not stand for having my income hurt because Janet is too generous towards her customers.

Brunner replied that she had not meant to cause trouble, but had simply recorded the car at what seemed to be its cost of acquisition, because she had been taught that this was the best accounting practice. Whatever response Fiedler was about to make to this comment was cut off by the arrival of Clark Shuman, the general manager, and Nate Bianci, the service department manager. Shuman picked up the phone and called Janet Moyer, asking her to come over right away.

"All right, Nate," said Shuman, "now that we are all here, would you tell them what you just told me?"

Bianci said: "Clark, the trouble is with this trade-in. Janet and Paul were right in thinking that the repairs they thought necessary would cost about $525. Unfortunately, they failed to notice that the rear axle is cracked; it will have to be replaced before we can retail the car. This will probably use up parts and labor costing about $400."

"Besides this," Bianci continued, "there is another thing which is bothering me a good deal more. Under the accounting system we've been using, I can't charge as much on an internal job as I would for the same job performed for an outside customer. As you can see from my department statement (Exhibit 2), I lost almost 8,000 bucks on internal work last year. On a reconditioning job like this which costs out at $925, I don't even break even. If I did work costing $925 for an outside customer, I would be able to charge about $1,250 for the job. The Blue Book gives a range of $1,225 to $1,275 for the work this car needs, and I have always aimed for about the middle of the Blue Book range.* That would give my department a gross profit of $325, and my own income is based on that gross profit. Since looks like a large proportion of the work of my department is going to be the reconditioning of trade-ins for resale, I figure that I should be able to make the same charge for repairing a trade-in as I would get for an outside repair job."

Fiedler and Moyer both started to talk at once at this point. Fiedler managed to edge out Moyer: "This axle business is unfortunate, all right; but it is very hard to spot a cracked axle. Nate is likely to be just as lucky the other way next time. He has to take the rough with the smooth. It is up to him to get the cars ready for me to sell."

Moyer, after agreeing that the failure to spot the axle was unfortunate, added: "This error is hardly my fault, however. Anyway, it is ridiculous that the service department should make a profit on jobs it does for the rest of the dealership. The company can't make money when its left hand sells to its right."

*In addition to the Blue Book for used car prices, there was a Blue Book which gave the range of charges for various classes of repair work. Like the used car book, it was issued weekly, and was based on the actual charges made and reported by vehicle repair shops in the area.

At this point Clark Shuman was getting a little confused about the situation. He thought there was a little truth in everything that had been said, but he was not sure how much. It was evident to him that some action was called for, both to sort out the present problem and to prevent its recurrence. He instructed Ms. Brunner, the accountant, to "work out how much we are really going to make on this whole deal," and then retired to his office to consider how best to get his managers to make a profit for the company.

A week after the events described above Clark Shuman was still far from sure what action to take to motivate his managers to make a profit for the business. During the week, Bianci had reported to him that the repairs to the used car had cost $996, of which $463 represented the cost of those repairs which had been spotted at the time of purchase, and the remaining $533 the cost of supplying and fitting a replacement for the cracked axle. To support his own case for a higher allowance on reconditioning jobs, Bianci had looked through the duplicate invoices over the last few months, and had found examples of similar (but not identical) work to that which had been done on the trade-in car. The amounts of these invoices averaged $1,276, which the customers had paid without question, and the average of the costs assigned to these jobs was $945. (General overhead was not assigned to individual jobs.) In addition, Bianci had obtained from Ms. Brunner the cost analysis shown in Exhibit 2. Bianci told Shuman that this was a fairly typical distribution of the service department expense.

Questions

1. Suppose the new car deal is consummated, with the repaired used car being retailed for $3,700, the repairs costing Shuman $996. Assume that all sales personnel are on salary (no commissions), and that general overhead costs are fixed. What is the dealership incremental gross profit on the total transaction (i.e., new and repaired-used cars sold)?

2. Assume each department (new, used, service) is treated as a profit center, as described in the case. Also assume in a-c that it is known with certainty beforehand that the repairs will cost $996.

   a. In your opinion, at what value should this trade-in (unrepaired) be transferred from the new car department to the used car department? Why?
   b. In your opinion, how much should the service department be able to charge the used car department for the repairs on this trade-in car? Why?
   c. Given your responses to a and b, what will be each department's incremental gross profit on this deal?

3. Is there a strategy in this instance that would give the dealership more profit than the one assumed above (i.e., repairing and retailing this trade-in used car)? Explain. In answering this question, assume the service department operates at capacity.

4. Do you feel the three profit center

EXHIBIT 2

Analysis of Service Department Expenses
For the Year Ended December 31

	Customer Jobs	Reconditioning Jobs	Total
Number of jobs........................	3,780	751	4,531
Direct labor...........................	$168,471	$ 98,820	$267,291
Supplies...............................	58,392	32,755	91,147
Department overhead (fixed)..........	49,720	26,067	75,787
	276,583	157,642	434,225
Parts..................................	128,301	86,670	214,971
	404,884	244,312	649,196
Charges made for jobs to customers or other departments.................	547,511	236,580	784,091
Gross profit (loss)...................	142,627	(7,732)	134,895
General overhead proportion..........			77,080
Departmental profit for the year......			$ 57,815

approach is appropriate for Shuman? If so, explain why, including an explanation of how this is better than other specific alternatives. If not, propose a better alternative and explain why it is better than three profit centers and any other alternatives you have considered.

* * * * *

Case 23-16: South American Coffee Company

South American Coffee Company sold its own brands of coffee throughout the Midwest. Stock of the company, which was founded in 1903, was closely held by members of the family of the founder. The president and secretary-treasurer were members of the stock-owning family; other management personnel had no stock interest.

Sales policies and direction of the company were handled from the home office in Cincinnati, and all salespersons reported to the sales manager through two assistants. The sales manager and the president assumed responsibility for advertising and promotion work. Roasting, grinding, and packaging of coffee was under the direction of the vice president of manufacturing, whose office was in Cincinnati.

The company operated three roasting plants in the Midwest. Each plant had profit and loss responsibility and the plant manager was paid a bonus on the basis of a percent of his plant's gross margin. Monthly gross margin statements were prepared for each plant by the home office (see Exhibit 1). Exhibit 2 shows gross margin for the entire company. Each month the plant manager was given a production schedule for the current month and a tentative schedule for the next succeeding month. Deliveries were made as directed by the home office.

All financial statements were prepared in the home office and billing, credit, and collection were done there. Each plant had a small accounting office at which all manufacturing costs were recorded. Plant payrolls were prepared at the plant. Green coffee costs were suppplied each plant on a lot basis, as described below.

The procurement of green coffee for the roasting operations was handled by a separate purchasing unit of the company, which reported to the secretary-treasurer in Cincinnati. Because of the specialized problems and the need for constant contact with coffee brokers, the unit was located in the section of New York City where the green coffee business was concentrated. The purchasing unit operated on an autonomous basis, keeping all records and handling all financial transactions pertaining to purchasing, sales to outsiders, and transfer to the three company-operated roasting plants.

The primary function of the purchasing unit was to have available for the roasting plants the variety of green coffees necessary to produce the blends which were to be roasted, packed, and sold to customers. This necessitated dealing in 40 types and grades of coffee, which came from tropical countries all over the world.

Based on estimated sales budgets, purchase commitments were made that would provide for delivery in from 3 to 15 months from the date that contracts for purchase were made. While it was possible to purchase from local brokers for immediate delivery, such purchases usually were more costly than purchases made for delivery in the country of origin and hence these "spot" purchases

EXHIBIT 1

Operating Statement
Plant No. 1, April

Net sales (shipments at billing prices).....		$744,620
Less:		
Cost of sales		
Green cofee--at contract cost.....		373,660
Roasting and grinding:		
Labor............	$38,220	
Fuel.............	24,780	
Manufacturing expenses........	33,620	96,620
Packaging:		
Container........	84,620	
Packing carton...	9,140	
Labor...........	12,160	
Manufacturing expenses........	25,440	131,460
Total manufacturing cost...		601,740
Gross Margin on Sales...........		$142,880

EXHIBIT 2

Income Statement
April

	Plants*			Green Coffee	Total
	1	2	3		
Net sales............................	$744,620			$123,740	$2,856,400
Cost of sales					
Green coffee......................	373,660			111,270	1,421,680
Roasting and grinding.............	96,620				299,440
Packaging.........................	131,460				600,410
Purchasing department.............					78,400
	601,740				2,399,930
Gross Margin........................	$142,880			$ 12,470	$ 456,470

*Detailed amounts for Plants 2 and 3 omitted here; total amounts include all three plants plus green coffee.

---

were kept to a minimum. A most important factor was the market "know-how" of the purchasing agent, who must judge whether the market trend was apt to be up or down and make commitments accordingly.

The result was that the green coffee purchasing unit was buying a range of coffees for advance delivery at various dates. At the time of actual delivery, the sales of the company's coffees might not be going as anticipated when the purchase commitment was made. The difference between actual deliveries and current requirements was handled through "spot" sales or purchase transactions in green coffee with outside brokers or other coffee roasters.

As an example, the commitments of the company for Santos No. 4 (a grade of Brazilian coffee) might call for deliveries in May of 20,000 bags. These deliveries would be made under 50 contracts executed at varying prices from 3 to 12 months before the month of delivery. An unseasonal hot spell at the end of April had brought a slump in coffee sales, and it developed that the company plants required only 16,000 bags in May. The green coffee purchasing unit therefore had to decide whether to store the surplus in rented storage facilities (which would increase the cost) or to sell it on the open market. This example was typical of the normal operation.

Generally speaking, the large volume of the company permitted it to buy favorably and to realize a normal brokerage and trading profit when selling

in smaller lots to small roasting companies. Hence, the usual policy was to make purchase commitments on a basis of maximum requirements; the usual result was that there was a surplus to be sold on a "spot" basis.

In accounting for coffee purchases, a separate cost record was maintained for each purchase contract. This record was charged with payments for coffee purchased, with shipping charges, import expenses and similar items, with the result that net cost per bag was developed for each purchase. Thus, the 50 deliveries of Santos 4 coffee cited in the example would come into inventory at 50 separate costs. The established policy was to treat each contract on an individual basis. When green coffee was shipped to a plant, a charge was made for the cost represented by the contracts which covered that particular shipment of coffee, with no element of profit or loss. When green coffee was sold to outsiders, the sales were likewise costed on a specific contract basis with a resulting profit or loss on these transactions.

The operating cost of running the purchasing unit was transferred in total to the central office, where it was recorded as an element in the company's general and administrative expenses.

For the past several years there had been some dissatisfaction on the part of plant managers with the method of computing gross margin subject to bonuses. This had finally led to a request from the president to the controller to study the whole method of reporting on results of plant operations and the purchasing operation.

Question

What changes, if any, would you propose in the present reporting and control system? Explain. (Consider the purchasing and marketing functions, as well as the plants.)

Chapter 24

Responsibility Accounting: The Management Control Process

Key Terms

Programming
Budgeting
Controllable cost
Engineered cost
Discretionary cost

Committed cost
Extrinsic and intrinsic needs
Expectancy theory
Rewards and punishment
Goal congruence

Discussion Questions

1. What are the differences between programming and budgeting?

2. Give some examples of programming decisions that might be made in a college or univerity.

3. What are the differences between a controllable cost and a noncontrollable cost cost?

4. Why is it incorrect to define a controllable cost as an item of cost over which a manager has complete control?

5. Why are allocated costs not controllable by the responsibility center to which they are allocated?

6. Contrast controllable costs with direct costs. With variable costs.

7. The cost of processing sales invoices in an accounting department is an engineered cost, but the cost of operating the whole accounting department is a discretionary cost. Explain the difference.

8. "The controller presumably knows more about the nature and meaning of responsibility accounting information than anyone else. He or she therefore should be the principal person who discusses this information with line managers." Comment on this assertion.

9. Why is an understanding of the behavioral aspects of the members of an organization important in developing a workable management control system?

10. Why do a participant's personal goals differ from those of the organization of which he or she is a part? Give some examples.

11. Why are both cooperation and conflict desirable in an organization?

12. A school wants its students to (a) work diligently on their studies, and (b) to learn as much as they are capable of learning. What motivational devices might it use for each of these purposes? Might some of these devices conflict with one another?

13. Give examples of costs that are typically (1) engineered, (2) discretionary, and (3) committed.

14. What is the effect of a short-run increase in volume on most engineered costs? On most discretionary costs? On committed costs?

15. What are the two important questions to ask when evaluating any practice used in a management control system?

Problems

24-1. Eastern Aluminum Corporation produces five different consumer and industrial products. Each product is produced in a separate department, with the department head having authority in the following areas: (1) hiring of production workers, (2) requisition of any maintenance services for their department's machinery from the corporate maintenance pool, and (3) purchase supplies.

The factory overhead cost report for Department 5 (aluminum lawn chairs) for the month is as follows:

```
Depreciation, factory..........................$10,000
Liability insurance, factory...................  1,200
Indirect labor, Department 5...................    500
Supplies.......................................  2,200
Factory heat, light, and power.................  1,100
Depreciation, Department 5 equipment...........  7,400
Factory general management.....................  4,000
Maintenance costs (chargeable from
   maintenance pool)...........................    995
Supervisors' salaries..........................  1,100
       Total cost..............................$28,495
```

Required:

a. List and total the Department 5 manager's controllable costs.
b. List and total the direct department costs.
c. List and total the costs that have been allocated to Department 5.

24-2. Chester Mills, vice president of Farragut Manufacturing Company, was reviewing the performance report for the equipment maintenance department for the month just ended. He was particularly interested in this month's report because he was considering Russ Olive, the department supervisor, for promotion. He recalled having praised Olive for spending less than the budgeted amount in the previous month and was looking to see whether that month was a fluke or if Olive was as good at reducing maintenance costs as the earlier report suggested.

Olive knew he was being considered for promotion and let it be known that he was working hard at cutting costs and that he had ambitions to move up the ladder to a more responsible, higher paying job. He had been head of the equipment maintenance department for only four months, taking over from a department manager who was notorious for spending more than the budget allowed for monthly equipment maintenance. Mills was quite hopeful that Olive would be the person who could take over supervision of one or two of the stamping or drilling departments which have been experiencing cost overruns lately.

Partial information taken from the current monthly performance report showed the following:

	Budget	Actual
Maintenance labor-hours worked...............	1,000	700
Oils and lubricants...........................	$ 3,500	$ 2,200
Maintenance labor.............................	5,000	4,000
Depreciation.................................	2,000	2,000
Department head salary........................	1,800	1,800
Other materials and supplies.................	1,500	500
Total costs.............................	$13,800	$10,500

Required:

   a. Discuss the pros and cons of Olive's potential for promotion.
   b. What equipment maintenance department cost data should be examined in order to evaluate Olive?
   c. What other data shuld be considered?

24-3. Budgeted costs for the glass products department of Fisher Kitchen Products Corporation, headed by Kathy Kane, are given below for two different levels of production. One budget shows the costs expected at the normal level of production, the other at 80 percent of the normal. The figures include Kane's salary of $34,000. The remainder of the supervisory salaries consists of allocated costs of plant supervisors. Kane hires all labor personnel and requisitions all materials used in the department. The entire amount of power and electricity costs and all repairs and maintenance costs are measured at the plant level and are distributed to the departments. Equipment acquisitions are decided at the division level.

	Budgets	
Glass Products Department	60,000 hours	48,000 hours
Direct materials...........................	$210,000	$168,000
Direct labor..............................	63,700	50,960
Indirect labor -- glass products.........	21,000	16,800
Supplies used............................	28,500	22,800
Supervisory salaries.....................	62,000	62,000
Power and light -- fixed.................	9,000	9,000
Power and light -- variable..............	2,000	1,600
Depreciation -- equipment................	4,000	4,000
Depreciation -- building.................	1,100	1,000
Repairs and maintenance -- fixed.........	4,200	4,200
Repairs and maintenance -- variable......	500	400
Property taxes...........................	4,500	4,500
Insurance................................	3,400	3,400
	$413,900	$348,760

Required:

   a. Show the total costs controllable by Kane.
   b. Show the costs traceable to the glass products department.
   c. Explain why costs that are not controllable by Kane are shown as part of the glass products department costs.

24-4. Bonnie Syrup Company produces chocolate syrup which it sells to fast-food chains. Recently it received a proposal from a fast-food chain that, if accepted, would require additional capacity to be built. However, management does not know how long this additional demand will continue and thus has decided not to build additional plant capacity.

As an alternative to increasing capacity, the controller proposed an incentive program that hopefully would lead to increased productivity within the present capacity (15,000 direct labor-hours per month) within present production supervision. Normally 40,000 gallons of syrup can be produced operating at a level of 15,000 direct labor-hours per month. Direct labor earns $3.50 per hour. To encourage more production in the same amount of time, the proposed incentive pay plan would pay a bonus equal to the regular hourly rate for each hour saved in syrup production.

Based upon 15,000 direct labor-hours the following additional costs are projected:

   Cost of direct materials used per gallon.......... $1.75

Variable overhead per direct labor-hour:

Supplies..	$0.24
Indirect materials..............................	0.40
Repairs...	0.21
Lubrication.....................................	0.09
Energy..	0.06
Variable overhead per hour......................	$1.00

Fixed overhead per month:

Supervision.....................................	$ 2,000
Indirect labor..................................	6,000
Depreciation....................................	5,900
Insurance.......................................	5,100
Energy..	4,900
	$23,900

The controller believes that with the incentive plan direct labor will work faster and less wastefully and that 40,000 gallons of syrup will be produced with only 11,250 direct labor-hours. This would allow additional syrup production in the hours saved.

Required:

a. Compute the expected cost to produce 40,000 gallons of chocolate syrup in the regular time.
b. Compute the expected cost to produce 40,000 gallons of chocolate syrup in 11,250 direct labor-hours assuming that actual costs will conform to the budgeted amounts.
c. If you were a production worker in Bonnie Syrup Company, would you want to participate in this plan?
d. How is the production supervisor likely to view this incentive plan?
e. What are the dangers of this incentive plan?

24-5. Brownie Baker Company produces snack cakes that are sold to vending machine companies, schools, and supermarkets. Management is concerned about the firm's declining percentage of gross margin on sales. The chief financial officer has called for a review of all three production departments. The following information is available for this review:

Departments	Mixing	Baking	Packaging	Total
Budgeted overhead:				
Factory supervision...........	$ 36,000	$ 40,000	$ 42,000	$118,000
Indirect labor................	54,400	57,800	69,800	182,000
Composite depreciation........	14,800	16,800	15,200	46,800
Equipment maintenance parts...	11,600	12,600	14,200	38,400
Equipment repairs.............	7,400	9,200	6,600	23,200
Lubrication of equipment......	5,200	1,400	4,800	11,400
Factory insurance.............	6,600	6,600	6,600	19,800
Heat and light allocated......	5,000	4,800	4,600	14,400
Power.........................	6,600	7,600	4,800	19,000
Total.....................	$147,600	$156,800	$168,600	$473,000

Departments	Mixing	Baking	Packaging	Total
Actual overhead:				
Factory supervision...........	$ 36,000	$ 40,000	$ 42,000	$118,000
Indirect labor................	61 800	58,800	68,800	189,400
Composite depreciation........	15,000	17,200	16,400	48,600
Equipment maintenance parts...	18,000	12,000	15,800	45,800
Equipment repairs.............	12,800	9,400	6,200	28,400
Lubrication of equipment......	6,600	2,200	7,800	16,600
Factory insurance.............	6,600	6,600	6,600	19,800
Heat and light allocated......	5,800	5,600	5,400	16,800
Power.........................	9,600	9,000	8,000	26,600
Total.....................	$172,200	$160,800	$177,000	$510,000

Brownie Bakery usually works at its normal operating capacity and thus has based its budgeted overhead on this normal operating capacity.

Overhead costs are assigned to each snack cake on the basis of machine-hours, which have been estimated at normal operating capacity as follows:

Machine hours

Mixing.....................	40,000
Baking.....................	70,000
Packaging.................	80,000

Required:

a. Prepare a statement showing budgeted controllable costs for each of the three production departments and the actual costs compared with these amounts.
b. Evaluate the declining percentage of gross margin caused by the increasing percentage of the cost of goods sold, using results calculated in requirement (a). Be specific.
c. What would be possible explanations of the deviation from budget for costs across all departments?
d. If you were the manager of one of the three producing departments, what would you do with respect to those items of cost that exceed budget in all three departments

24-6. Rapid Cab Company owns a fleet of 20 taxicabs, each of which has two or three drivers per 24-hour day. Drivers are paid $3 per hour and may keep all tips. Maintenance of cabs is done by the company at its own garage. Profits have been declining, and part of the problem is believed caused by such practices as withholding fares, use of the cabs for personal use, and not trying hard enough to solicit business. In an effort to reduce such activities, the company is considering doing away with the hourly wages and paying each driver 60 percent of the total fares as shown on the meter, less the actual cost of gasoline, oil, tires, and maintenance.

Required: Discuss the proposed compensation plan.

24-7. (C.M.A. adapted.) Parsons Company compensates its field sales force on a commission and yearend bonus basis. The commission is 20% of standard gross margin (planned selling price less standard cost of goods sold on a full absorption basis) contingent upon collection of the account. Customer's credit is approved by the company's credit department. Price concessions are granted on occasion by the top sales management, but sales commissions are not reduced by the discount. A year-end bonus of 15% of commissions earned is paid to salespersons who equal or exceed their annual sales target. The annual sales target is usually established by applying approximately a 5% increase to the prior year's sales.

Required:

a. What features of this compensation plan would seem to be effective in motivating the sales force to accomplish company goals of higher profits and return on investment? Explain why.
b. What features of this compensation plan would seem to be counter-effective in motivating the sales force to accomplish the company goals of higher profits and return on investment? Explain why.

24-8. (C.M.A. adapted.) Harden Company has experienced increased production costs. The primary area of concern identified by management is direct labor. The company is considering adopting a standard cost system to help control labor and other costs. Useful historical data are not available because detailed production records have not been maintained.

Harden has retained an engineering consulting firm to establish labor standards. After a complete study of the work process, the consultants recommended a labor standard of one unit of production every 30 minutes or 16 units per day for each worker. They further advised that Harden's wage rates were below the prevailing rate of $6 per hour.

Harden's production vice president thought this labor standard was too tight and the employees would be unable to attain it. From his experience with the labor force, he believed a labor standard of 40 minutes per unit or 12 units per day for each worker would be more reasonable. Harden's president believed the standard should be set at a high level to motivate the workers, but he also recognized the standard should be set at a level to provide adequate information for control and reasonable cost comparisons.

After much discussion, the management decided to use a dual standard. The labor standard recommended by the consultants would be employed in the plant as a motivation device, but a standard of 40 minutes per unit would be used in management reporting. The workers would not be informed of the standard used for reporting purposes. The production vice president conducted several sessions prior to implementation in the plant informing the workers of the new standard cost system and answering questions. The new standards were not related to incentive pay, but were introduced at the same time wages were increased to $6 per hour.

The new standard cost system was implemented on January 1, 1979. At the end of six months of operation, the following statistics on labor performance were presented to top management:

	Jan.	Feb.	Mar.	Apr.	May	June
Production (units)	5,100	5,000	4,700	4,500	4,300	4,400
Direct labor hours	3,000	2,900	2,900	3,000	3,000	3,100
Variance from labor standard	$2,700U	$2,400U	$3,300U	$4,500U	$5,100U	$5,400U
Variance from reporting standard	$2,400F	$2,600F	$1,400F	$ -0-	$ 800U	$1,000U

Raw material quality, labor mix, and plant facilities and conditions have not changed to any great extent during the six-month period.

Required:

    a. Discuss the impact of different types of standards on motivation, and specifically discuss the effect on motivation in Harden Company's plant of adopting the labor standard recommended by the consulting firm.
    b. Evaluate Harden Company's decision to employ dual standards in their standard cost system.

24-9. Farro Manufacturing Company has a printing and copying department that supplies all types of duplicating services to other departments. The demand for these services is always high but becomes even greater during certain peak periods of the year. Full capacity operations are estimated to be 7,000 operating hours per year, and budgeted costs are based on 7,000 operating hours.

For the year 19x1 the printing and copying department operated at 90 percent of its capacity. The department's performance report for 19x1 was as follows:

	Budget	Actual
Supplies	$ 20,000	$ 18,000
Direct labor	25,000	20,000
Energy costs	10,000	11,000
Equipment depreciation	120,000	120,000
Building depreciation	50,000	50,000
Building related costs	7,000	10,000
Maintenance and repairs	2,000	2,000
	$234,000	$231,000

Following is a breakdown of the printing and copying department's services rendered to the user departments:

Department	Budgeted operating hours	Actual operating hours
Accounting............................	1,800	1,700
Marketing.............................	2,000	1,800
Personnel.............................	500	450
Engineering and production..........	2,700	2,350
	7,000	6,300

Required:

a. Revise the performance report so that the budget is adjusted for the actual volume of activity. Show the items broken down by controllable and noncontrollable costs. Explain why you put a certain cost into either a controllable or a noncontrollable category.

b. How much of the actual cost of $231,000 will be charged to each user department if service costs are charged on the basis of actual operating hours?

c. Assume that the actual and budgeted operating hours were as given but that the actual cost for the printing and copying department was $233,000. How much cost will be absorbed by each department if costs are charged on the basis of actual operating hours?

d. The manager of the engineering and production department wants the department to have its own printing and copying capabilities rather than waiting for services from the printing and copying department. If allowed by top management to proceed with this possibility, discuss the implications that this decision would have on:

1. The printing and copying manager's performance evaluation.
2. The costs distributed to other user departments.

e. What basis of charging services of the printing and copying department would you recommend in order to motivate managers properly?

24-10. Holiday Ice Cream Incorporated sells its packaged ice cream products to supermarkets. For marketing and distribution purposes it divides its territory into six marketing regions. Over the past several years the northeast marketing region has had only a moderate increase in sales volume -- primarily as a result of heavy media advertisement by the major ice cream manufacturers in the northeast.

To counter this growing problem, the corporate vice president of marketing, in late 19x1, hired Neil Allen to take over the advertising manager's position in this region. Mr. Allen previously was a divisional advertising manager with a national ice cream manufacturer.

The following information represents partial data taken from the annual divisional performance reports:

	Actual 19x1	Actual 19x2	Budgeted 19x2
Sales.........................	$1,620,000	$1,860,000	$1,680,000
Cost of sales:			
Variable production costs....	1,080,000	1,302,000	1,120,000
Fixed production costs.......	400,000	400,000	400,000
Gross margin on sales..........	140,000	158,000	160,000
Selling and administrative (direct).....................	80,000	120,000	80,000
Selling and administrative operating allocated..........	30,000	30,000	30,000
Income........................	$ 30,000	$ 8,000	$ 50,000
Sales (units).................	26,000	31,000	28,000

Required:

a. Evaluate the divisional performance report for 19x2 under the leadership of Neil Allen.
b. With the information given in this problem and your solution of Requirement a, what suggestions would you give Neil Allen concerning the actions he should take in 19x3?

24-11. Puritan Cleaners has been operating a large clothes cleaning firm for a number of years and has a citywide reputation for doing high-quality work with a fast turnaround time to the customer. "Bring it by 9, wear it by 6" was its byline. Outlets in several neighborhoods serve as pickup and drop-off stations for the central cleaning facility. The company is always faced with fluctuations in volume over the months of the year. It has been company policy to lay off shirt press operators from the shirt pressing department as soon a there was an insufficient amount of work to keep them busy, and to rehire them when demand picked up again. Because of this policy the company has developed a poor reputation as a place to work and finds it difficult to hire good shirt press operators. As a result, the quality of the work has been declining.

The plant manager has proposed that shirt press operators who earn $6 per hour be retained during slow periods to do some general light-duty cleanup work which is usually performed by persons earning $3.75 per hour in the plant maintenance department.

Required:

a. Indicate which department or departments should be charged with wages paid to shirt press operators who do plant maintenance work.
b. Discuss the implications of your plan for the plant manager, department manager, and employee view.
c. Assume that the paid shirt presser workday is 8:00 a.m. to 3:00 p.m. and that there is plenty of shirt pressing work generally. However, the volume differences sometimes require the shirt press operators to work right up to 3:00 p.m. on busy days. On other days, the shirt press operators are finished at 1:30 p.m. and they are allowed to leave then; they receive pay to 3:00 p.m. Comment.

24-12. In a belt-tightening measure the Redwood Company is taking a close look at its four divisions with an eye toward closing any unprofitable ones.

Costs incurred at the corporate headquarters level have been distributed to each division in proportion to sales revenue. All costs incurred by each division except the allocated corporate headquarter costs are considered to be avoidable if a division is shut down. The corporate headquarter costs amount to $770,000.

The following data represents the seminannual results:

| | Total | Divisions ($000s) | | | |
		Norwich	Easton	Westgate	South Cove
Sales.................	$3,300	$495	$1,320	$ 495	$ 990
Costs.................	3,113	286	1,045	638	1,144
Profits (losses).........	$ 187	$209	$ 275	$(143)	$ (154)

Required:

a. Based upon the above information what recommendations would you make concerning possible division closings? Show all calculations.
b. Since the above data represents semiannual information, what other variables should be included in the decision to close down a division?

24-13. (C.M.A. adapted.) College Publications (CP) was established in 1969 by the president of Boyd College to improve the quality and effectiveness of the college's communications. CP provides professional editing and designing services to all academic and administrative units requesting help in the publication of catalogs, brochures, posters and other forms of printed material. CP is under the vice president for public affiars, employs 20 professional staff, and has an annual operating budget of $500,000.

To encourage the use of CP's services, the costs of operating CP have not been allocated to units requesting services. Instead, these operating costs are included in central administration overhead. However, to maintain as much uniformity as possible in the content and design of the college's publications, all items submitted to CP for publication are reviewed and approved by CP. Thus, CP can reject or require the complete revision of a unit's publication. The number of copies for each publication is determined jointly by CP and the unit requesting service.

During the last two years Boyd College ha experienced considerable financial pressure. During the spring of 1979 the president established a number of task forces to review various aspects of the college's operations. The task force on publications recommended the use of a charge-back system in which user units pay for services requested from CP. In the fall of 1979 the president issued a memorandum requiring the use of a charge-back system for CP services. The memorandum stated that the purpose of the new system was "to put control and responsibility for publication expenditures where the benefits were received and to make academic and administrative units more aware of the publication costs they were incurring." The memorandum suggested that the costs of operating CP be charge back to user units on the basis of actual hours used in servicing their publication needs.

The units that purchased publication services through CP were generally pleased with the president's memorandum, even though they had some reservations about how the charge-back rate would be calculated. They had not been happy about having to obtain CP's approval in purchasing publication services. Their major complaint had been that CP imposed excessively high standards that resulted in overly expensive publications.

The director of CP was very upset about the president's memorandum. She believed that the charge-back system was a political maneuver by the president to get the task force pressures off his back. She believed that the task force had paid too much attention to publication costs and that the new system would reduce the effectiveness of CP to the college as a whole. She also was upset that the president took unilateral action in establishing the new system. She believed that it was a big jump from the memorandum to the installation of the new system, and was concerned about whether the new system would achieve the desired results.

Required:

    a. What are the likely motivational and operational effects of the new system on
       (1) academic and administrative units requesting and using the services of CP?
       (2) College Publications?
       (3) Boyd College?
    b. Evaluate the president's methods for instituting an organization change with respect to College Publications.

24-14. (C.M.A. adapted.) A. R. Oma, Inc., manufactures a line of men's colognes and after-shave lotions. The manufacturing process is a series of mixing operations with the addition of aromatic and coloring ingredients. The finished product is packaged in a company-produced glass bottle and packed in cases containing 6 bottles. The company distributes its products to various wholesalers around the country.

A. R. Oma feels that the sales of its products are heavily infuenced by the appearance and appeal of the bottle and has, therefore, devoted considerable managerial effort to the bottle production process. This has resulted in the development of certain unique bottle production processes in which management takes considerable pride.

The two areas of responsibility (i.e., bottle manufacture, and cosmetics production and marketing) have evolved over the years in an almost independent manner. In fact, a rivalry has developed among management personnel as to "which operation is the more important" to A. R. Oma. This attitude is intensified because the bottle manufacturing operation was purchased as an ongoing entity 10 years ago and no real interchange of management personnel or ideas (except at the top corporate level) has taken place.

Since the acquisition, all bottle production has been absorbed by the cosmetic manufacturing plant. The bottle and cosmetics areas are considered as separate profit centers and are evaluated as such. As the new corporate controller, you are responsible for the determination of a proper transfer price for the bottles.

At your request, the bottle division general manager has asked certain other bottle manufacturers to quote a price for the quantity and sizes demanded by the cosmetics division. these competitive prices are:

Volume	Total Price	Price per Case
2,000,000 eq. cases*	$ 4,000,000	$2.00
4,000,000	7,000,000	1.75
6,000,000	10,000,000	1.67

*An "equivalent case" represents 6 bottles each.

A cost analysis of A. R. Oma's bottle operations indicates that they can produce bottles at these costs:

Volume	Total Price	Cost per Case
2,000,000 eq. case	$ 3,200,000	$1.60
4,000,000	5,200,000	1.30
6,000,000	7,200,000	1.20

(Your cost analyst points out that these costs represent fixed costs of $1,200,000 and variable costs of $1.00 per equivalent case.)

These figures have given rise to considerable corporate discussion as to the proper price to use in the transfer of bottles to the cosmetics division. This interest is heightened because a significant portion of a division manager's income is an incentive bonus based on the division's profit performance.

The cosmetics division has the following production, marketing, and administrative costs in addition to the bottle costs:

Volume	Total Cost	Cost per Case
2,000,000 cases	$16,400,000	$8.20
4,000,000	32,400,000	8.10
6,000,000	48,400,000	8.07

After considerable analysis, the cosmetics division's marketing research department has furnished you with the following price-demand relationship for the finished product:

Sales Volume	Total Sales Revenue	Sales Price per Case
2,000,000 cases	$25,000,000	$12.50
4,000,000	45,600,000	11.40
6,000,000	63,900,000	10.65

Required:

a. Assume that sales of cosmetics products will be either 2 million, 4 million, or 6 million cases, and that bottles will be transferred from the bottle division to the cosmetics division at the prices quoted by

outside bottle manufcturers. Analyze the goal congruence of the present profit center measurement scheme.
b. Discuss the pros and cons of the present profit center approach, and of any alternative approaches you feel should be considered. Reach a conclusion as to whether you prefer the status quo or some specific alternative.

CASES

Case 24-15: Tru-Fit Parts, Inc.

Tru-Fit Parts, Inc. manufactured a variety of parts for use in automobiles, trucks, buses, and farm equipment. these parts fell into three major groupings: ignition part, transmission parts, and engine parts. Tru-Fit's parts were sold both to original-equipment manufacturers (the "OEM" market), and to wholesalers, who constituted the first link in the channel of distribution for replacement parts (the "aftermarket" or "AM").

As shown in Exhibit 1, Tru-Fit had a manufacturing division for each of its three product groupings. Each of these divisions, which were treated as

investment centers for management control purposes, was responsible not only for manufacturing parts, but also for selling its parts in the OEM market. Also, each manufacturing division sold parts to the fourth division, AM Marketing. This division was solely responsible for marketing all Tru-Fit parts to AM wholesalers. It operated several company-owned warehouses in the U.S. and overseas. AM Marketing was also treated as an investment center.

Before elimination of intracompany sales, the sum of the four divisions' sales was about $500 million a year. Of this, approximately $130 million was

EXHIBIT 1

PARTIAL ORGANIZATION CHART

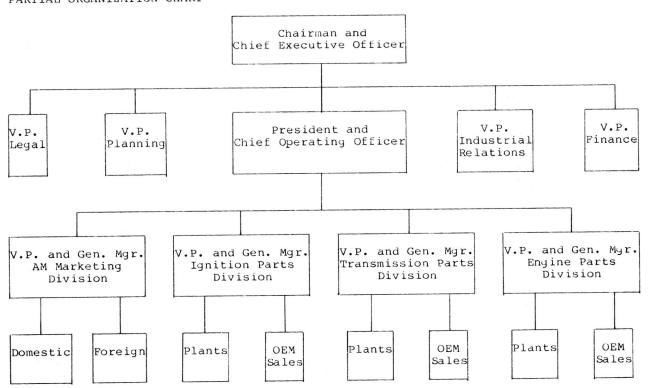

attributable to the Ignition Parts Division, $100 million to the Transmission Parts Division, $90 million to the Engine Parts Division, and $180 million to Am Marketing. After elimination of intracompany sales from the manufacturing divisions to AM Marketing, outside sales totalled about $400 million. Thus, intracompany sales constituted almost one third of the manufacturing divisions' volume. Top management's goal was to increase to 50 percent the AM portion of outside sales from the present level of 45 percent.

Within each manufacturing division, each plant was treated as an investment center. OEM sales were credited to the plants, which maintained finished goods inventories, shipments to OEM customers were made directly from the plants. A plant's ROI target was based on budgeted profit (including allocations of divisions and corporate overhead and on imputed income tax) divided by actual beginning-of-the-year net assets (defined to be total assets less current liabilities). Actual ROI was actual profit divided by actual beginning-of-the-year net assets. The reason that the profit figure included allocated overheads and taxes was so that the figure would correspond to the manner in which profit was calculated for shareholder reporting purposes. According to top management, this gave a plant manager a clearer perspective of the plant's contribution to the corporate "bottom line." Beginning-of-the-year net assets was used because, according to top management, added investment in a given year resulted in little incremental profit in that year, but rather increased later years' profits. Since the investment base for the year was "frozen" at the beginning-of-the-year level, during the year maximizing profits was equivalent to maximizing ROI. (AM Marketing's ROI was measured in the same manner as was the plants' ROI.)

The OEM sales department in each manufacturing division was responsible for working with OEM company engineers to develop innovative and cost-effective new parts, and for servicing customer accounts for parts already being supplied the OEM by Tru-Fit. Each of these OEM sales departments was treated as a revenue center. Because of the differing nature of OEM and AM marketing, it was not felt desirable by top management to consolidate AM and OEM marketing activities in a single organization. Even OEM marketing was not consolidated, because each division's OEM marketers tended to work with different people within a given customer's organization. Moreover, two of the three manufacturing divisions had been independent companies before being acquired by Tru-Fit, and so there was a tradition of their doing their own OEM marketing.

According to Tru-Fit executives, the factors critical to success in the OEM market were (1) the ability to design innovative and dependable parts that met the customers' performance and weight specifications; (2) meeting OEM delivery requirements so that the OEM company could minimize its own inventories; and (3) controlling costs, since the market was very price competitive. In the AM market, availability was by far the most important factor, followed by quality and price.

Approximately fifty Tru-Fit line managers and staff group heads participated in an incentive bonus plan, which worked as follows. First, the size of the corporate-wide bonus pool was established; its size was related by a formula to corporate earnings per share. Each participant in the bonus plan had a certain number of "standard bonus points;" the higher the participant was in the organizational hierarchy, the more standard points he or she had. The total of these points for all participants was divided into the bonus pool to arrive at a standard dollar award per point. Then this amount was multiplied by the participant's number of standard points to arrive at the participant's "standard bonus." This standard award could be varied upward or downward as much as 25 percent at the discretion of the participant's superiors.

In the case of a plant manager, the standard award was also adjusted by a formula that related percent of standard award to the plant's profit variance. For example, if the plant's actual profit for the year exceeded its budgeted profit by 5 percent, the plant manager's bonus was raised from 100 percent of standard to 110 percent of the standard. In making this bonus adjustment, the plant's actual profit was adjusted for any favorable or unfavorable gross margin variance caused by sales volume to the AM Marketing division being higher or lower than budgeted. For example, if all of a plant's favorable profit variance were attributable to a favorable gross margin volume variance on sales to AM Marketing, the plant manager's bonus would not be raised above 100 percent of standard. Similarly, the plant manager would not be penalized if AM Marketing actually purchased less from the plant than the amount that had been estimated by AM Marketing when the plant's annual profit budget had been prepared.

In general, top management was satisfied with the present performance measurement scheme. In discussions with the casewriter, however, they mentioned three areas of concern.

First, there always seemed to be a few disputes over transfer prices from the manufacturing division to AM Marketing. Whenever possible, transfers were made at outside OEM market prices. In the case of a part sold as an OEM part several years earlier, the former OEM market price was adjusted upward for inflation to arrive at the AM transfer price; this procedure caused virtually no disputes. The problems occurred when the part being transferred was strictly an AM part, i.e., one that had never been sold by Tru-Fit in the OEM market, and for which there was neither a current OEM outside market price nor a former OEM market price that could be adjusted upward for inflation. Usually, such transfer price issues were resolved by the two divisions involved, but occasionally the corporate controller was asked to arbitrate a dispute.

Second, top management felt that the manufacturing divisions too often tended to treat AM Marketing as a "captive customer." For example, it was felt that when AM Marketing and an outside OEM customer were placing competing demands on a plant, the plant usually favored the OEM customer, because the OEM customer could take its business elsewhere, whereas AM Marketing could not. (Management was not willing to let AM Marketing sell a competitor's product, feeling this would reflect adversely on the overall image of the company.)

Third, top management felt that both AM Marketing and the three manufacturing divisions carried excessive inventories most of the year. The controller said, "Thank goodness we have a generous Christmas vacation policy around here; at least the inventories get down to a reasonable level at year end, when our production volume is low because of employee holiday vacations."

Questions

1. What would you recommend to top management regarding the three problems they have identified?

2. Are there any matters not mentioned by top management that you feel are problematical?

Chapter 25

Programming and Budgeting

Key Terms

Zero-base review
Benefit/cost analysis
Long-range plan
Master budget
Operating budget
Program budget
Responsibility budget

Project budget
Variable budget
Management by objectives
Rolling budget
Incremental budgeting
Cash budget
Capital expenditure budget

Discussion Questions

1. Why is a zero-base review not a budgeting technique?

2. Why is benefit/cost analysis widely used in nonprofit organizations?

3. Why are budgets a better baseline for measuring performance than historical data?

4. Explain the relationship between a program budget and the program that results from the programming process.

5. Distinguish between program budgets and responsibility budgets.

6. Under what circumstances is a flexible budget appropriate?

7. What is "management by objectives"? Under what circumstances is this technique appropriately used?

8. Distinguish between the role of the line organization and the role of the staff in budget preparation. Does the budget director function in a line capacity when he or she prepares the budget for his or her own office?

9. Why is determining the planned sales volume an early step in preparing the operating budget?

10. What is the difference between a sales budget and a sales forecast?

11. The management team of a small printing shop consists of the president, the production manager, the sales manager, and the controller. They meet one afternoon, and at the end of the afternoon have prepared a budget for the coming year. Describe briefly, step by step, what probably happened that afternoon, identifying the part that each person played.

12. "Negotiation is the most critical stage of the budgetary process from a control standpoint." Comment.

13. Why is an imposed budget an unsatisfactory motivating device?

14. What is the distinction between a baseline budget and a current budget?

15. Suppose that a current budget is prepared as carefully as is humanly possible. Can management use such a budget in lieu of actual reports on performance?

16. Compare a cash budget with a cash-basis statement of changes in financial position.

Problems

25-1. (C.M.A. adapted.) Clarkson Company is a large multi-division firm with several plants in each division. A comprehensive budgeting system is used; the annual budgeting process commences in August, five months prior to the beginning of the fiscal year. At this time the division managers submit proposed budgets for sales, production and inventory levels, and expenses. Capital expenditure requests also are formalized at this time.

The expense budgets include direct labor and all overhead items, which are separated into fixed and variable components. Direct materials are budgeted separately in developing the production and inventory schedules. A division's expense budgets are developed from its plants' results, as measured by the percent variation from an adjusted budget in the first six months of the current year, and a target expense reduction percentage established by the corporation.

To determine plant percentages, the plant budget for the just completed half-year period is revised to recognize changes in operating procedures and costs outside the control of plant management (e.g., labor wage changes, product style changes, etc.). The difference between this revised budget and the actual expenses is the controllable variance, and is expressed as a percentage of the actual expenses. This percentage is added (if unfavorable) to the corporate target expense reduction percentage. A favorable plant variance percentage is subtracted from the corporate target. If a plant had a 2 percent unfavorable controllable variance and the corporate target reduction was 4 percent, the plant's budget for next year should reflect costs approximately 6 percent below this year's actual costs.

Next year's final budgets for the corporation, divisions, and plants are adopted after corporate analysis of the proposed budgets and a careful review with each division manager of the changes made by corporate management. Division profit budgets include allocated corporate costs, and plant profit budgets include allocated division and corporate costs.

Return on assets (ROA) is used to measure the performance of divisions and plants. The asset base for a division consists of all assets assigned to the division, including its working capital, and an allocated share of corporate assets. For plants, the asset base includes the assets assigned to the plant plus an allocated portion of the division and corporate assets. Recommendations for promotions and salary increases for the executives of the plants are influenced by how well actual ROA compares with budgeted ROA.

The plant managers exercise control only over the cost portion of the plant profit budget, because the divisions are responsible for sales. Only limited control over the plant assets is exercised at the plant level.

The manager of the Dexter Plant, a major plant in the Huron division, carefully controls his costs during the first six months so that any improvement appears after the target reduction of expenses is established. He accomplishes this by careful planning and timing of his discretionary expenditures.

During 1983 the property adjacent to the Dexter Plant was purchased by Clarkson. This expenditure was not included in the 1983 capital expenditure budget. Corporate management decided to divert funds from a project at another plant since the property appeared to be a better longterm investment.

Also during 1983, Clarkson experienced depressed sales. In an attempt to achieve budgeted profit, corporate management announced in August that all plants were to cut their annual expenses by 6 percent. In order to accomplish this expense reduction, the Dexter Plant manager reduced preventive maintenance and postponed needed major repairs. Employees who quit were not replaced unless absolutely necessary. Employee training was postponed whenever possible. The raw materials, supplies and finished goods inventories were reduced below normal levels.

Required:

    a. Evaluate the budget procedures of Clarkson Company with respect to their effectiveness for planning and controlling operations.
    b. Is the Clarkson Company's use of return on assets to evaluate the performance of the Dexter Plant appropriate?
    c. Analyze and explain the Dexter Plant Manager's behavior during 1983.

25-2. (C.M.A. adapted.) Melcher Company produces farm equipment at several plants. The business is both seasonal and cyclical in nature. The company has attempted to use budgeting for planning and controlling activities, but the fluctuating nature of the business has caused some company officials to be skeptical about the usefulness of budgeting. The accountant for the Adrian plant has been using a system she calls "flexible budgeting" to help her plant's management control the plant's operations.

The company president has asked he to explain what the term means, how she applies the system at the Adrian plant, and how it could be applied to the company as a whole. The accountant presented the following data as part of her explanation:

Budget data for 1984

Normal monthly capacity of the plant in direct labor hours....10,000 hours
Material costs (6 lbs. @ $3.00)................................$18.00 per unit
Labor costs (2 hours @ $6.00).................................$12.00 per unit

Overhead estimate at normal monthly capacity:
Variable (controllable):
    Indirect labor...$13,300
    Indirect materials... 1,200
    Repairs.. 1,500
        Total variable... 16,000
Fixed (noncontrollable):
    Depreciation... 6,500
    Supervision.. 6,000
        Total fixed.. 12,500
        Total Overhead..$28,000

Planned units for January 1984............................... 4,000
Planned units for February 1984.............................. 6,000

Actual data for January 1984

Hours worked... 8,400
Units produced... 3,800
Costs incurred:
    Material (24,000 lbs.)......................................$ 72,000
    Direct labor.. 50,400
    Indirect labor.. 12,000
    Indirect materials.. 1,200
    Repairs... 3,600
    Depreciation.. 6,500
    Supervision... 6,000
        Total Costs...$151,700

Required:

    a. Prepare a budget for January.
    b. Prepare a report for January comparing actual and budgeted costs for the actual activity for the month.

c. Can flexible budgeting be applied to the nonmanufacturing activities of the company? Explain.

25-3. (C.M.A. adapted.) Boyne University offers a continuing education program in many cities throughout the state. For the convenience of its faculty, and also to save costs, the university operates a motor pool. Until February the motor pool operated with 20 vehicles. However, an additional automobile was acquired in February. The motor pool furnishes gasoline, oil, and other supplies for the cars, and hires one mechanic who does routine maintenance and minor repairs. Major repairs are done at a commercial garage. A supervisor managers the motor pool.

Each year the supervisor prepares an operating budget for the motor pool. The budget informs university management of the funds needed to operate the pool. Depreciation on the automobiles is recorded in the budget in order to determine the costs per mile.

The schedule below presents the annual budget approved by the university. The actual costs for March are compared to one-twelfth of the annual budget.

The annual budget was constructed upon the following assumptions:
(1) 20 automobiles in the pool
(2) 30,000 miles per year per automobile
(3) 25 miles per gallon per automobile
(4) $1.20 per gallon of gas
(5) $0.012 per mile for oil, minor repairs, parts, and supplies
(6) $270 per automobile in outside repairs

The supervisor is unhappy with the monthly report comparing budget and actual costs for March, claiming it presents unfairly performance for March. The supervisor's previous employer used flexible budgeting.

UNIVERSITY MOTOR POOL
Budget Report For March

	Annual Budget	One Month Budget	March Acutal	Over* Under
Gasoline........................$	28,800	$ 2,400	$ 3,200	$ 800*
Oil, minor repairs, parts and supplies..........	7,200	600	700	100*
Outside repairs...............	5,400	450	150	300
Insurance.....................	18,000	1,500	1,600	100*
Salaries and benefits.........	90,000	7,500	7,500	--
Depreciation..................	66,000	5,500	6,000	500*
	$215,400	$17,950	$19,150	$1,200*
Total miles...................	600,000	50,000	63,000	
Cost per mile.................	$0.3590	$0.3590	$0.3040	
Number of automobiles.........	20	20	21	

Required:

a. Employing flexible budgeting techniques, prepare a report that shows budgeted amounts, actual costs, and monthly variation for March.
b. Explain briefly the basis of your budget figure for outside repairs.

25-4. Sandy Kinnear, personnel director for the Metropolitan Bank, had recently attended a two-day seminar on "Management by Objectives" at the City College. Currently, Metropolitan treated each of its 23 branch bank offices as profit centers, with heavy emphasis given to budgeted versus actual branch profit in evaluating the performance of the branch manager. Kinnear felt that many items affecting a branch's profitability, such as checking account service charges, time deposit interest rates, and rates on automobile loans and home mortgages, were not controllable by the branch manager.

Kinnear was therefore considering proposing to top management that an MBO system be established. While profit would still be used to evaluate the performance of a <u>branch</u>, the MBO system would be used in evaluating the performance of the <u>branch's</u> <u>manager</u>. Kinnear felt that the MBO system could focus on such factors as the following:

(1) Average deposits
(2) Average loans
(3) Number of new accounts
(4) Calls on existing commercial customers
(5) Calls on prospective customers
(6) Expenses clearly controllable by a branch manager

<u>Required</u>: Evaluate Sandy Kinnear's idea to establish an MBO system for the branches.

25-5. Exotic Gifts, Ltd., is preparing a budget for the second quarter of the current calendar year. The March ending inventory of merchandise was $106,000, which was higher than expected. The company prefers to carry ending inventory amounting to the expected sales of the next two months. Purchases of merchandise are paid for by the end of the next month, and the balance due on accounts payable at the end of March was $24,000. Budgeted sales follow:

April.............	$40,000	July.............	$72,000
May..............	48,000	August...........	56,000
June.............	60,000	September........	60,000

<u>Required</u>: Assuming a 25 percent gross margin is budgeted, prepare a budget showing the following amounts for the months of April, May, and June:

a. Cost of goods sold.
b. Purchases required.
c. Cash payments for merchandise purchases.

25-6. Home Equipment Center has been organized to sell a line of lawn and garden equipment. The company began operations on January 1 with the following assets:

Cash...............	$ 11,250	Buildings and equipment.....$200,000
Inventory..........	23,500	(useful life 20 years, and no residual
Land..............	25,000	value), of which $160,000 relates to selling and $40,000 to general and administrative activities.

Sales for January, February, and March (i.e., the first quarter) are expected to be $90,000; they are expected to be $180,000 for the next three months, and $270,000 for the three months after that. Certain expenses are expected to vary with sales as follows:

	Percent of Sales Dollars
Cost of goods sold.........................	70
Bad debts..................................	1
Variable selling expenses..................	12
Variable administrative expenses..........	3

Other expenses not expected to vary with sales:

Selling......................................	$12,000 per quarter
Administrative..............................	8,550 per quarter
Depreciation...............................	2,500 per quarter

<u>Required</u>: Prepare an operating budget for the first and second quarters of operations for Home Equipment Center

25-7. Wallace Box Company manufactures cardboard cartons that are used by other manufacturers to package a wide variety of consumer products. The sales vice president has gathered various items of information as a basis for top management's decision as to the sales budget for 1984, as follows:

(1) Sales revenue in 1983 is estimated to be $12,800,000, based on actual sales for the first 10 months. This is an estimated 5 percent of all cardboard cartons sold in Wallace's marketing territory. A trade association forecasts that industry sales, in units, will increse 4 percent in 1984 as compared to 1983.

(2) The sales staff estimates that selling prices will be at least 5 percent higher in 1984, and may well be 8 percent higher.

(3) Sales estimates for each territory, obtained from the salesperson responsible for that territory, add up to $1,520,000 for 1984. In the past such estimates have tended to be somewhat optimistic. Included in the $1,520,000 is a sizable increase in one territory that reflects an estimated $480,000 of sales to the Marvel Company, a possible new customer. Discussions with Marvel have been underway for several months, and the salesperson is "practically certain" that Marvel will give its carton business to Wallace in 1984.

The financial vice president, who keeps well informed on general business conditions, believes that the trade association forecast is too high. Her own estimate is that industry sales in units will not increase at all in 1984. The sales vice president, on the other hand, not only believes that the trade association forecast is reliable, but also believes that Wallace's market share (i.e., percentage of industry sales) will be 5.4 percent of industry sales in units.

Required:

    a. Set boundaries on the sales budget for 1984; that is, state the lowest amount and the highest amount of sales revenue that you believe top management should reasonably consider.

    b. Within this range, what number would you use as the sales budget for 1984?

25-8. Ripple Company is compiling a cash forecast for its second year of operations. Total sales have been estimated for the first four months of the year as follows: January, $67,000; February, $57,000; March, $37,500; and April, $46,800. The January 1 net accounts receivable amount is $13,000. During Ripple's first year, cash and credit sales have been approximately equal. Customers on the average have paid their bills on the following schedule:

    90 percent of net accounts receivable at the beginning of the month are collected that month.

    60 percent of gross credit sales during the month are collected that month.

    2 percent of gross credit sales become bad debts and are written off. (The bad debt expense each month thus is equal to 2 percent of that month's gross credit sales.)

Required: Prepare a budget of cash sales and collections on credit sales expected for the first four months of the year.

25-9. At the end of the first quarter, Soloman, Inc., had a cash balance of $12,600, accounts receivable of $80,000, and accounts payable of $53,400. All liabilities are paid in one month after they have been incurred. Customers pay for 80 percent of credit sales by the end of the next month, 15 percent by the end of the second month, and 3 percent by the end of the third month. Budgeted amounts for the second quarter follow:

	April	May	June
Cash sales......................	$24,000	$18,000	$32,000
Sales on account..............	65,000	42,000	60,000
Purchases on account..........	48,000	43,000	38,000
Cash payments:			
Salaries and wages..........	7,000	7,000	7,800
Delivery truck..............		18,000	
Dividends...................			8,000
Interest....................	2,400	2,400	2,400
Miscellaneous...............	3,600	4,600	4,200

Required: Prepare a cash budget which will show for each month:

    a. The beginning cash balance.
    b. Cash receipts.
    c. Cash disbursements.
    d. The cash balance at the end of the month.

25-10. Home Equipment Center, referred to in Problem 25-6, is also preparing a cash budget for the first two quarters. In addition to the data given in Problem 25-6, the following estimates are available:

Three fourths of the receivables will be paid in the quarter in which the sale is made and 24 percent in the following quarter. Sixty percent of merchandise purchased and two thirds of operating expenses will be paid for in the quarter in which the purchase is made, and the balance in the following quarter. The ending inventory of each quarter should be equal to one third of the amount of estimated cost of sales for the coming quarter. An additional $22,500 equipment investment will have to be made at the end of the second quarter to handle the increased sales volume expected in the third quarter.

Required:

    a. Prepare a cash budget for the first and second quarters.
    b. Assuming that a minimum cash balance of $5,000 is desired at all times, what steps would you advise Home Equipment Center to take at the end of each of the first two quarters?

25-11. Terry McVea, president of McVea Company, a wholesaling establishment, asks your assistance in preparing a budget of cash receipts and disbursements for the next two months, October and November. The company borrowed $90,000 on August 5, to help meet the peak seasonal cash needs, the note becoming due on November 30. There is some question in the president's mind about whether the cash position of the company will be strong enough to pay off the note on time.

The September 30 trial balance of the company shows, among other things, the following account balances:

Cash......................$ 14,200		Inventory..................$193,800
Accounts receivable......... 227,000		Accounts payable........... 86,000
Allowance for bad debts..... 9,100		Notes payable............. 124,000

McVea Company sells only one product. Sales price of the product is $100 per unit and terms are uniform to all customers: 2 percent discount if paid within the first 10 days of the month subsequent to purchase, otherwise due by the end of the month subsequent to purchase. Historically the company has experienced a 60 percent collection within the discount period, an 85 percent collection within the month subsequent to purchase, and a 98 percent collection within the second month subsequent to purchase. Uncollectibles average 2 percent of sales.

The company has projected annual sales for the current year ending December 31 of $1.5 million. Sales for recent months and estimates of sales for the remainder of the year follows:

            August.........................$180,000
            September...................... 200,000
            October (estimate)............. 220,000
            November (estimate)............ 280,000
            December (estimate)............ 150,000

All purchases of merchandise from suppliers are payable within 10 days. Accordingly, month-end balances in accounts payable represent approximately one third of the purchases of merchandise made in the month then ended. The unit purchase price is $68. Target ending inventory is set at 80 percent of next month's estimated sales in units.

Selling and administrative expenses for the year are estimated to total

$400,000, of which 40 percent is fixed (including depreciation of $32,000). Variable selling and administrative expenses vary directly with sales, and all selling and administrative expenses are paid as incurred.

Required:

    a. Prepare a cash budget for the McVea Company for the months of October and November.

    b. Will the company be able to meet the $90,000 note due at the end of November?

25-12. In early January, McCartney Sales, a medium-size retailing establishment, was considering a change in its credit policy, whereby customers previously refused charge accounts would be granted accounts with relatively low ($100-$200) credit limits. McCartney's president, Lou Harrison, estimated that the present monthly sales volume of $400,000 would increase by 50 percent with the change in policy, which can be put into effect by the end of the month.

Management of McCartney Sales recognized that as the new policy takes effect, not only would sales volume and the level of accounts receivable rise, but in addition, inventories and salaries would also unavoidably increase. Salaries, which currently were $60,000 per month, were expected to increase by 25 percent. Inventories, costing an average of 70 percent of selling price, were expected to increase in proportion to sles. Sales on account presently made up 75 percent of total sales and averaged a 45-day collection period. It was estimated that the additional sales obtained through the change in policy would be 90 percent on account and average a 60-day lag for collection.

McCARTNEY SALES
Pro Forma Balance Sheet as of January 31
(000 omitted)

Cash........................	$ 200	Liabilities.................	$ 700
Accounts receivable.........	450	Owners' equity..............	510
Inventory...................	560	Total Liabilities and	
Total Assets...............	$1,210	Owners' Equity.............	$1,210

Required: Assuming the following, prepare pro forma balance sheets and income statements for McCartney Sales for the months of February, March, April, and May.

(1) The new credit policy is put into effect at the end of January.

(2) Expenses other than cost of goods sold and salaries are fixed at $50,000 per month.

(3) A minimum cash balance of $100,000 must be maintained.

(4) Expansion of accounts receivable and inventory levels are to be financed with surplus cash and debt.

CASES

Case 25-13: Lake Erie Table Company

Following is a detailed description of the mechanics involved in preparing a budget. It is presented primarily to illustrate the relationships among the various parts. It should be emphasized that this example deals with mechanics only. It does not describe the judgmental process tha led to the assumptions on which the budget was based, nor the process of negotiation that led to approval of the estimates. In order to save space, only the data

for three months are shown. In actuality, the budget was prepared for the first three months and for each of the other three quarters of the year. The company involved is Lake Erie Table Company, Inc.

Lake Erie Table Company (LET) employes 128 people (21 in sales, 24 in administration, and 83 in production). Exhibit 1 is the company's organization chart. LET manufactures and sells directly to retailers (department stores, discount houses, furniture stores) two folding card tables, the Royal and Superior models. The Royal and Superior card tables have suggested retail prices of $24.95 and $18.95, respectively, and are sold to the retailers at $15.00 and $11.40, respectively, which is approximately 40 percent off of the retail price. Both tables have tubular steel frames with a baked enamel finish. Both tops are made of plywood covered with vinyl. Both tables come in forest green, desert tan, or fruitwood color. Each table requires the same amount of direct labor and factory overhead to manufacture. Although the Royal has only slightly more material in it, the company can sell the Royal to retailers for $3.60 more than the Superior.

Exhibit 2 shows the relationships among the various schedules that constitute the budget. The responsibility for the preparation of the various schedules parallels the responsibility structure of the organization as defined in the organization chart.

Exhibits 3 through 7 contain basic data and calculations that are part of the budget preparation.

The master budget is made up of the following schedules:

Schedule 1: The sales budget is the responsibility of the sales vice president. The sales budget is the foundation of all other budgets since they are related partially or completely to the budgeted sales volume. The sales budget is influenced by the planned unit sales prices and the planned advertising and selling expenses. The planned unit sales prices are decided by top management.

Schedule 2: The production budget and all of the budgets supporting it (Schedules 3 through 6) are the responsibility of the production vice president. The production budget is prepared after the sales budget and inventory budget (Schedule 7).

Schedule 3: The materials usage budget is prepared by the supervisors of the machining and assembly departments. The machining department supervisor prepares the estimates for materials A and B, and the assembly department supervisor prepares the estimates for materials C and D.

Schedule 4: The materials purchase budget is the responsiblity of the purchasing manager (who in this case is also the production vice presi-

dent), who provides the planned unit purchase price for raw materials.

Schedule 5: The direct labor budget is the responsibility of the managers of the machining and assembly departments. They prepare estimates of their departments' total direct labor hours. The budgeted rate per hour is prepared by the industrial relations department.

Schedule 6: The factory overhead budget is also the responsibility of the production department managers. The production and direct labor budgets provide the basis for projecting the planned volume of work for the machining and assembly departments, which in turn is used in planning the volume of work in the maintenance and general factory overhead departments.

Schedule 7: The inventory budget reflects the planned inventory policy of top management and is prepared by the budget director. The company uses first-in, first-out cost flow for all inventories.

Schedule 8: The budget director uses all of the preceding budgets to prepare the cost ofgoods sold budget.

Schedule 9: Each district sales manager prepares a selling expense budget concurrently with the district's sales budget. The sales vice president prepares the general sales overhead budget and approves the district sales managers' budgets.

Schedule 10: The controller and industrial relations manager prepare their departmental budgets and the administrative vice president prepares the general administrative budget and approves the accounting and industrial relations budgets.

Schedules 11, 11a, and 11b: The chief financial officer, in this case the controller, is responsible for preparing the cash budget. Note that some expenses such as insurance, taxes, and interest do not require an immediate cash outlay and some expenses such as depreciation and bad debts expense never require a cash outlay.

Schedules 12 and 13: The budgeted income statement and balance sheet are prepared by the budget director.

Capital budget. The capital budget is not illustrated. Note, however, that the company's planned capital expenditures have been included in the cash budget, Schedule 11. This $300,000 outlay represents that portion of the long-range capital spending budget that will materialize in March.

The completed budget is discussed with the company president; after the president approves it, it is presented to the board of directors for their approval.

Questions

1. Trace through each schedule of the case and be prepared to describe what is being done on each and their interrelationship. One good way of doing this is to start with the budgeted income statement and balance sheet (Schedules 12 and 13) and work backward to find the source of each number on these statements.

2. Budget amounts may represent a ceiling, a floor, or a guide. Which is appropriate for each of the items listed on Schedules 9 and 10? Why?

3. Give examples of cost items in the exhibits and schedules which are probably engineered, discretionary, and committed, respectively. Give examples of cost items that are controllable and of others that are noncontrollable. (By "controllable" is meant controllable in the short run by the responsibility center manager.)

* * * * *

Exhibit 1   Lake Erie Table Company organization chart*

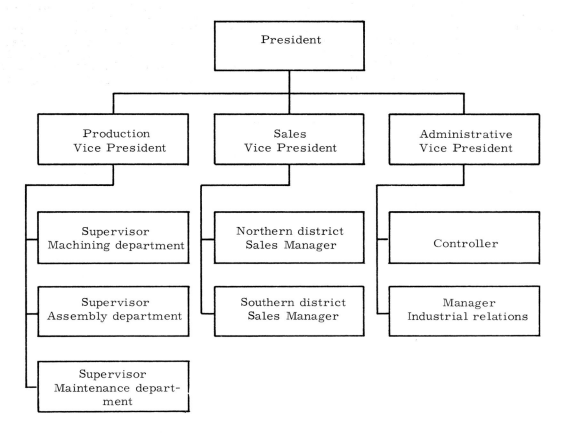

Exhibit 2   Lake Erie Table Company schematic of budget relationships*

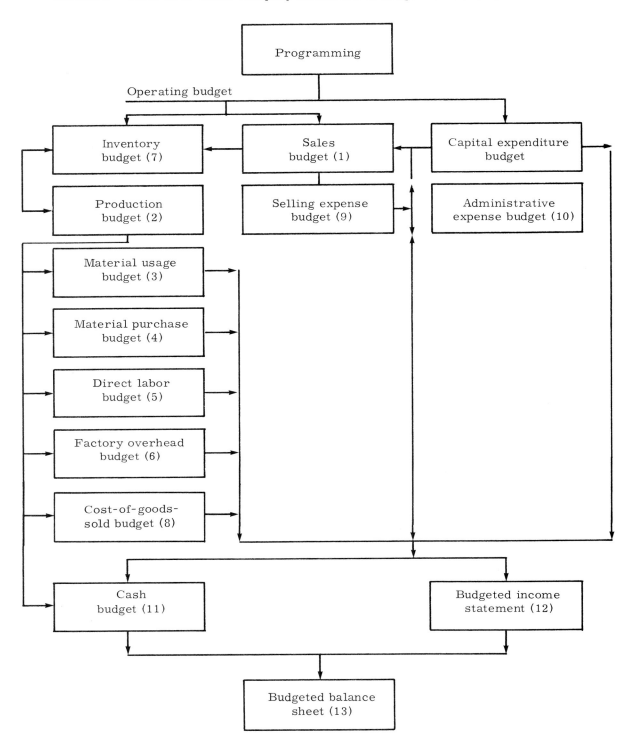

_____
*Figures in parentheses are schedule numbers.
Note: This exhibit should be examined carefully and then Schedules 1 through 13 should be examined also and integrated into this framework.

Exhibit 3

LAKE ERIE TABLE COMPANY
Bill of Material
Royal and Superior Folding Card Tables*

Part Identification	Description	Raw Material Required Royal	Superior
A	Tubular steel legs: 1 in. diameter × 30 in. length...	10 ft.	
	1 in. diameter × 27 in. length...		9 ft.
B	Plywood top: ½ in. × 41 in. diameter............	12 sq. ft.	
	½ in. × 3 sq. ft..................		9 sq. ft.
C	Vinyl top: 41 in. diameter......................	12 sq. ft.	
	3 sq. ft.............................		9 sq. ft.
D	Assembly kit (1 in. flat steel edging, bolts, hinges, cardboard packing).........................	1	1

* The *Royal* folding card table is a *round* table with a 41 in. diameter and is 30 in. high. The *Superior* folding card table is a 36 in. *square* table and is 27 in. high. Both tables use the same materials, but the Royal uses slightly more material. Both tables require the same amount of direct labor to manufacture.

Exhibit 4

LAKE ERIE TABLE COMPANY
Cost Sheet

			Estimated Cost per Table Royal	Superior
Machining Department	Quantity	Price		
Materials:				
A—Steel legs.................	10 ft.	$0.12	$1.20	
	9 ft.	0.12		$1.08
B—Plywood top..............	12 sq. ft.	0.10	1.20	
	9 sq. ft.	0.10		0.90
	Time	Rate		
Direct labor:				
Each table...................	9 min.	$6.00	0.90	0.90
	DLD	Budgeted Rate		
Budgeted factory overhead (see Exhibit 5):				
Variable rate per DLD*.......	0.90	0.51	0.46	0.46
Fixed rate per DLD..........	0.90	0.46	0.414	0.414
Machining cost per unit...			$4.194	$3.754
Assembly Department	Quantity	Price		
Materials:				
C—Vinyl top.................	12 sq. ft.	$0.02	$0.24	
Vinyl top...............	9 sq. ft.	0.02		$0.18
D—Assembly kit............	1	1.00	1.00	1.00
Direct labor:				
Each table...................	12 min.	$5.00	1.00	1.00
	DLD	Budgeted Rate		
Budgeted factory overhead (see Exhibit 6):				
Variable rate per DLD........	1.00	0.561	0.561	0.561
Fixed rate per DLD.........	1.00	0.472	0.472	0.472
Assembly cost per unit....			$3.273	$3.213
Total cost per unit to manufacture.....................			$7.447	$6.967

* Direct labor dollar.

Exhibit 5

LAKE ERIE TABLE COMPANY
Machining Department Cost Budget
For the Quarter Ending March 31, 1983

Volume: $77,670 direct labor dollars (DLD); 12,945 direct labor hours (DLH)
(Schedule 5)

	Royal	Superior
Material and labor estimates (Exhibit 4):		
Material....................................	$2.40	$1.98
Labor time.................................	9 min.	9 min.
Labor rate per hour.........................	$6.00	$6.00

	Fixed per Quarter	Variable per DLD
Variable budget for overhead costs (Schedule 6):		
Supervision..................................	$ 9,900	. . .
Wages.......................................	1,500	$0.13
Factory supplies.............................	. . .	0.11
Power.......................................	. . .	0.10
Depreciation................................	3,600	. . .
Insurance and taxes on employees.............	1,200	0.15
Maintenance (F = 240 hrs. $\times$ $6.442; V = 258 hrs. $\times$ $6.442 = $1,662 $\div$ $77,670 SDLD = $0.02) (see Exhibit 7)	1,546	0.02
General factory overhead, allocated (see Exhibit 7)	17,934	. . .
	$35,680	
($35,680 $\div$ $77,670 DLD = $0.46 per DLD).........	$0.46	$0.51
Overhead rate per DLD (= $0.46 + $0.51).............	$0.97	

Exhibit 6

LAKE ERIE TABLE COMPANY
Assembly Department Cost Budget
For the Quarter Ending March 31, 1983

Volume: $86,300 direct labor dollars (DLD); 17,260 direct labor hours (DLH)
(Schedule 5)

	Royal	Superior
Material and labor estimates (Exhibit 4):		
Material....................................	$1.24	$1.18
Labor time.................................	12 min.	12 min.
Labor rate per hour.........................	$5.00	$5.00

	Fixed per Quarter	Variable per DLD
Variable budget for overhead costs (Schedule 6):		
Supervision..................................	$14,400	. . .
Wages.......................................	2,100	$0.17
Factory supplies.............................	. . .	0.10
Power.......................................	. . .	0.12
Depreciation................................	3,000	. . .
Insurance and taxes on employees.............	1,800	0.15
Maintenance (F = 240 hrs. $\times$ $6.442; V = 286 $\times$ $6.442 = $1,842 $\div$ $86,300 SDLD = $0.021) (see Exhibit 7)	1,546	. . .
General factory overhead, allocated (see Exhibit 7)	17,934	. . .
	$40,780	
($40,780 $\div$ $86,300 DLD = $0.472 per DLD)........	$ 0.472	$0.561
Overhead rate per DLD (= $0.472 + $0.561)..........	$1.033	

Exhibit 7

LAKE ERIE TABLE COMPANY
Computation of Budget Factory Overhead Rate
For the Quarter Ending March 31, 1983

	Total	Service Departments		Producing Departments	
		Gen. Fact. Over-head	Mainte-nance	Ma-chining	As-sembly
Total factory overhead.......	$164,625	$36,600	$5,865	$54,258	$67,902
Allocations*:					
1. General factory over-head.................		36,600	732	17,934	17,934
2. Maintenance.........			$6,597	3,207	3,390
Total..............	$164,625			$75,399	$89,226
Direct labor dollars (DLD) from Schedule 5........				$77,670	$86,300
Budgeted factory overhead rate per DLD..........				$0.9708	$ 1.034
Variable and fixed portions of factory overhead rate:					
Variable.................				$ 0.51	$ 0.561
Fixed...................				0.46	0.472
Total.................				$ .97	$ 1.033

* Allocation bases:
1. Relative floor space: 2 percent for maintenance and 49 percent each for machining and assembly.
2. Planned direct repair hours:
   Machining: 80 hours per month (fixed) plus one hour for every 50 direct labor hours (from Schedule 5) equals 258 variable hours for a total of 498 repair hours.
   Assembly: 80 hours per month (fixed) plus one hour for every 50 direct labor hours (from Schedule 5) equals 286 variable hours for a total of 526 repair hours.

$$\frac{\$6,597}{1,024 \text{ hrs.}} = \$6.442 \text{ per planned repair hour.}$$

Schedule 1

LAKE ERIE TABLE COMPANY
Sales Budget
For the Quarter Ending March 31, 1983

District and Product	Unit Price	January Units	January Amount	February Units	February Amount	March Units	March Amount	Quarter Total Units	Quarter Total Amount
Northern:									
Royal........	$15.00	6,000	$ 90,000	6,000	$ 90,000	6,100	$ 91,500	18,100	$ 271,500
Sup..........	$11.40	10,000	114,000	10,000	114,000	10,300	117,420	30,300	345,420
Total			$204,000		$204,000		$208,920		$ 616,920
Southern:									
Royal........	$15.00	4,000	$ 60,000	4,000	$ 60,000	4,000	$ 60,000	12,000	$ 180,000
Sup..........	$11.40	8,000	91,200	8,000	91,200	8,200	93,480	24,200	275,880
Total			$151,200		$151,200		$153,480		$ 455,880
Totals:									
Royal........	$15.00	10,000	$150,000	10,000	$150,000	10,100	$151,500	30,100	$ 451,500
Sup..........	$11.40	18,000	205,200	18,000	205,200	18,500	210,900	54,500	621,300
		28,000	$355,200	28,000	$355,200	28,600	$362,400	84,600	$1,072.800

Estimated sales for April, which are necessary for the production budget, are:

	April Sales in Units Royal	April Sales in Units Superior
Northern district.........................	6,200	10,400
Southern district.........................	4,200	8,200
	10,400	18,600

Schedule 2

LAKE ERIE TABLE COMPANY
Production Budget (Units)
For the Quarter Ending March 31, 1983

Product	January	February	March	Quarter Total	April
Royal:					
Units to be sold*.................	10,000	10,000	10,100	30,100	10,400
Add: Planned ending inventory†...	10,000	10,100	10,400	30,500	10,400
Total.....................	20,000	20,100	20,500	60,600	20,800
Less: Planned beginning inventory‡...........................	9,800	10,000	10,100	29,900	10,400
Units to be produced.............	10,200	10,100	10,400	30,700	10,400
Superior:					
Units to be sold*.................	18,000	18,000	18,500	54,500	18,600
Add: Planned ending inventory† ..	18,000	18,500	18,600	55,100	18,600
Total.....................	36,000	36,500	37,100	109,600	37,200
Less: Planned beginning inventory‡...........................	17,500	18,000	18,500	54,000	18,600
Units to be produced.............	18,500	18,500	18,600	55,600	18,600
Quarter total.....................	28,700	28,600	29,000	86,300	29,000

* From Schedule 1.
† At the end of any month the company wishes to maintain a basic inventory of the next month's sales.
‡ From Schedule 7.

LAKE ERIE TABLE COMPANY
Materials Usage Budget (Units)
For the Quarter Ending March 31, 1983

| Material and Month | Royal | | | Superior | | | Total | | |
	Production Planned*	Units Required†	Units Needed for Production	Production Planned*	Units Required†	Units Needed for Production	Units Needed for Production	Unit Cost†	Total Material Cost
A									
January	10,200	10	102,000	18,500	9	166,500	268,500	$0.12	$32,220
February	10,100	10	101,000	18,500	9	166,500	267,500	0.12	32,100
March	10,400	10	104,000	18,600	9	167,400	271,400	0.12	32,568
Total	30,700		307,000	55,600		500,400	807,400		$96,888
B									
January	10,200	12	122,400	18,500	9	166,500	288,900	0.10	$28,890
February	10,100	12	121,200	18,500	9	166,500	287,700	0.10	28,770
March	10,400	12	124,800	18,600	9	167,400	292,200	0.10	29,220
Total	30,700		368,400	55,600		500,400	868,800		$86,880
C									
January	10,200	12	122,400	18,500	9	166,500	288,900	0.02	$ 5,778
February	10,100	12	121,200	18,500	9	166,500	287,700	0.02	5,754
March	10,400	12	124,800	18,600	9	167,400	292,200	0.02	5,844
Total	30,700		368,400	55,600		500,400	868,800		$17,376
D									
January	10,200	1	10,200	18,500	1	18,500	28,700	1.00	$28,700
February	10,100	1	10,100	18,500	1	18,500	28,600	1.00	28,600
March	10,400	1	10,400	18,600	1	18,600	29,000	1.00	29,000
Total	30,700		30,700	55,600		55,600	86,300		$86,300

Quarter Totals	A	B	C	D	Total
January	$32,220	$28,890	$ 5,778	$28,700	$ 95,588
February	32,100	28,770	5,754	28,600	95,224
March	32,568	29,220	5,844	29,000	96,632
Total	$96,888	$86,880	$17,376	$86,300	$287,444

* From Schedule 2.
† From Exhibit 3.

LAKE ERIE TABLE COMPANY
Materials Purchases Budget (Units)
For the Quarter Ending March 31, 1983

Material and Month	Units Needed for Production*	Add Ending Inventory†	Total Units Required	Less Beginning Inventory	Purchases Units	Unit Cost	Total Cost
A							
January.........	268,500	267,500	536,000	268,500	267,500	$0.12	$32,100
February........	267,500	271,400	538,900	267,500	271,400	0.12	32,568
March...........	271,400	271,400	542,800	271,400	271,400	0.12	32,568
Total...........	807,400	810,300	1,617,700	807,400	810,300		$97,236
B							
January.........	288,900	287,700	576,600	288,900	287,700	0.10	$28,770
February........	287,700	292,200	579,900	287,700	292,200	0.10	29,220
March...........	292,200	292,200	584,400	292,200	292,200	0.10	29,220
Total...........	868,800	872,100	1,740,900	868,800	872,100		$87,210
C							
January.........	288,900	287,700	576,600	288,900	287,700	0.02	$ 5,754
February........	287,700	292,200	579,900	287,700	292,200	0.02	5,844
March...........	292,200	292,200	584,400	292,200	292,200	0.02	5,844
Total...........	868,800	872,100	1,740,900	868,800	872,100		$17,442
D							
January.........	28,700	28,600	57,300	28,000	29,300	1.00	$29,300
February........	28,600	29,000	57,600	28,600	29,000	1.00	29,000
March...........	29,000	29,000	58,000	29,000	29,000	1.00	29,000
Total...........	86,300	86,600	172,900	85,600	87,300		$87,300

Quarter Totals	A	B	C	D	Total
January......	$32,100	$28,770	$ 5,754	$29,300	$ 95,924
February	32,568	29,220	5,844	29,000	96,632
March.......	32,568	29,220	5,844	29,000	96,632
	$97,236	$87,210	$17,442	$87,300	$289,188

* From Schedule 3.
† At the end of any month the company wishes to maintain a basic inventory of the next month's units needed for production.

LAKE ERIE TABLE COMPANY
Direct Labor Budget
For the Quarter Ending March 31, 1983

Month and Dept.	Royal			Superior			Total		
	Units to Be Produced	Hours per Unit	Total Hours	Units to Be Produced	Hours per Unit	Total Hours	Dept. Hours	Rate per Hour	Labor Cost
Jan.									
Machining........	10,200	0.15	1,530	18,500	0.15	2,775	4,305	$6.00	$ 25,830
Assembly.........	10,200	0.20	2,040	18,500	0.20	3,700	5,740	5.00	28,700
			3,570			6,475	10,045		$ 54,530
Feb.									
Machining.......	10,100	0.15	1,515	18,500	0.15	2,775	4,290	6.00	$ 25,740
Assembly........	10,100	0.20	2,020	18,500	0.20	3,700	5,720	5.00	28,600
			3,535			6,475	10,010		$ 54,340
Mar.									
Machining.......	10,400	0.15	1,560	18,600	0.15	2,790	4,350	6.00	$ 26,100
Assembly.........	10,400	0.20	2,080	18,600	0.20	3,720	5,800	5.00	29,000
			3,640			6,510	10,150		$ 55,100
Quarter Totals									
Machining.......	30,700	0.15	4,605	55,600	0.15	8,340	12,945	6.00	$ 77,670
Assembly........	30,700	0.20	6,140	55,600	0.20	11,120	17,260	5.00	86,300
			10,745			19,460	30,205		$163,970

Schedule 6

LAKE ERIE TABLE COMPANY
Factory Overhead Budget
For the Quarter Ending March 31, 1983

Department and Account	Variable Budget Formula	January	February	March	Total
		(DLD, $25,830)*	(DLD, $25,740)	(DLD, $26,100)	(DLD, $77,670)
Machining:					
Supervisory salaries	$3,300 + $ 0 per DLD	$ 3,300	$ 3,300	$ 3,300	$ 9,900
Indirect labor	500 + 0.13	3,858	3,846	3,893	11,597
Factory supplies	0 + 0.11	2,841	2,831	2,871	8,543
Power	0 + 0.10	2,583	2,574	2,610	7,767
Depreciation	1,200 + 0	1,200	1,200	1,200	3,600
Employee benefits	400 + 0.15	4,275	4,261	4,315	12,851
Total	$5,400 + $0.49 per DLD	$18,057	$18,012	$18,189	$ 54,258
		(DLD, $28,700)	(DLD, $28,600)	(DLD, $29,000)	(DLD, $86,300)
Assembly:					
Supervisory salaries	$4,800 + $ 0 per DLD	$ 4,800	$ 4,800	$ 4,800	$ 14,400
Indirect labor	700 + 0.17	5,579	5,562	5,630	16,771
Factory supplies	0 + 0.10	2,870	2,860	2,900	8,630
Power	0 + 0.12	3,444	3,432	3,480	10,356
Depreciation	1,000 + 0	1,000	1,000	1,000	3,000
Employee benefits	600 + 0.15	4,905	4,890	4,950	14,745
Total	$7,100 + $0.54 per DLD	$22,598	$22,544	$22,760	$67,902
		(DRH, 341)†	(DRH, 340)	(DRH, 343)	(DRH, 1,024)
Maintenance:					
Supervisory salaries	$1,100 + $ 0 per DRH	$ 1,100	$ 1,100	$ 1,100	$ 3,300
Indirect labor	400 + 0	400	400	400	1,200
Factory supplies	0 + 0.60	205	204	206	615
Depreciation	100 + 0	100	100	100	300
Employee benefits	150 + 0	150	150	150	450
Total	$1,750 + $0.60 per DRH	$ 1,955	$ 1,954	$ 1,956	$ 5,865
General factory overhead (all fixed):					
Salaries and wages		$ 6,000	$ 6,000	$ 6,000	$ 18,000
Employee benefits		600	600	600	1,800
Factory supplies		100	100	100	300
Power, water, fuel, and phone		550	550	550	1,650
Insurance and taxes		950	950	950	2,850
Depreciation		4,000	4,000	4,000	12,000
Total		$12,200	$12,200	$12,200	$ 36,600
Total factory overhead		$54,810	$54,710	$55,105	$164,625

* Direct labor dollars.
† Direct repair hours.

LAKE ERIE TABLE COMPANY
Inventory Budget
For the Quarter Ending March 31, 1983

Inventory	January 1, 1983 Beginning Inventory*			March 31, 1983 Ending Inventory†		
	Units	Unit Cost	Total Amount	Units	Unit Cost	Total Amount
Raw materials:						
Material A............	268,500	$0.12	$ 32,220	271,400	$0.12	$ 32,568
Material B............	288,900	0.10	28,890	292,200	0.10	29,220
Material C............	288,900	0.02	5,778	292,200	0.02	5,844
Material D............	28,000	1.00	28,000	29,000	1.00	29,000
Total..............			$ 94,888			$ 96,632
Finished goods:						
Royal...............	9,800	7.447	$ 72,981	10,400	7.447	$ 77,449
Standard.............	17,500	6.967	121,923	18,600	6.967	129,586
Total.............			$194,904			$207,035
Total inventory.........			$289,792			$303,667

* Estimated amount.
† From Schedules 2 and 4.

LAKE ERIE TABLE COMPANY
Cost of Goods Sold Budget*
For the Quarter Ending March 31, 1983

Schedule
Reference

	Raw materials used:		
7	Inventory, January 1, 1983..................	$ 94,888	
4	Purchases of raw materials..................	289,188	
	Total.................................	$384,076	
7	Less inventory, March 31, 1983................	96,632	
3	Cost of raw materials used.....................		$287,444
5	Direct labor................................		163,970
6	Factory expenses............................		164,625
	Total manufacturing cost..................		$616,039
7	Add beginning finished goods inventory..........		194,904
	Total cost of goods available for sale........		$810,943
7	Less ending finished goods inventory............		207,035
	Total cost of goods sold...................		$603,908†

* The company does not have any goods in process inventory at the beginning or end of any month. If the company did have goods in process inventories, the beginning goods in process would be added to the total manufacturing costs and the ending goods in process would be deducted from the total manufacturing costs.

† As a check,	*Royal*	*Superior*
Total sales for the quarter are...................................	30,100	54,500
Cost to manufacture, from Exhibit 5	$7.447	$6.967
Total cost of goods sold is $603,857.............................	$224,155	$379,702

The slight difference of $51 ($603,908–$603,857) is due to rounding.

Schedule 9

LAKE ERIE TABLE COMPANY
Selling Expense Budget
For the Quarter Ending March 31, 1983

Department and Account	Variable Budget Formula	January	February	March	Total
Northern district:		(Sales, $204,000)	(Sales, $204,000)	(Sales, $208,920)	(Sales, $616,920)
Salaries and wages	$ 3,300 F + $ 0 per $100 sales	$ 3,300	$ 3,300	$ 3,300	$ 9,900
Sales commissions	0 F + $5.00	10,200	10,200	10,446	30,846
Employee benefits	330 F + 0.50	1,350	1,350	1,375	4,075
Telephone	440 F + 0	400	400	400	1,200
Travel and entertainment	6,375 F + 0	6,375	6,375	6,375	19,125
Office rent and supplies	1,475 F + 0	1,475	1,475	1,475	4,425
Freight-out	120 F + 0.50	1,140	1,140	1,165	3,445
Total	$12,000 F + $6.00 per $100 sales	$24,240	$24,240	$24,536	$73,016
Southern district:		(Sales, $151,200)	(Sales, $151,200)	(Sales, $153,480)	(Sales, $455,880)
Salaries and wages	$ 3,100 F + $ 0 per $100 sales	$ 3,100	$ 3,100	$ 3,100	$ 9,300
Sales commissions	0 F + $5.00	7,560	7,560	7,674	22,794
Employee benefits	310 F + 0.50	1,066	1,066	1,077	3,209
Telephone	340 F + 0	340	340	340	1,020
Travel and entertainment	4,875 F + 0	4,875	4,875	4,875	14,625
Office rent and supplies	1,275 F + 0	1,275	1,275	1,275	3,825
Freight-out	100 F + 0.50	856	856	867	2,579
Total	$10,000 F + $6.00 per $100 sales	$19,072	$19,072	$19,208	$ 57,352
General sales overhead (all fixed):					
Salaries and wages		$ 4,600	$ 4,600	$ 4,600	$ 13,800
Employee benefits		460	460	460	1,380
Depreciation—office equipment		140	140	140	420
Advertising		6,000	6,000	6,000	18,000
Telephone		220	220	220	660
Travel and entertainment		400	400	400	1,200
Office supplies		180	180	180	540
Total		$12,000	$12,000	$12,000	$ 36,000
Total selling expenses		$55,312	$55,312	$55,744	$166,368

LAKE ERIE TABLE COMPANY
Administrative Expense Budget
For the Quarter Ending March 31, 1983

Department and Account	January	February	March	Total
Controller:				
Salaries and wages	$ 9,500	$ 9,500	$ 9,500	$ 28,500
Insurance and taxes on employees	950	950	950	2,850
Office supplies	330	330	330	990
Depreciation—office equipment	220	220	220	660
Loss on bad debts ($0.50 per $100 sales*)	1,776	1,776	1,812	5,364
Total	$12,776	$12,776	$12,812	$ 38,364
Industrial relations:				
Salaries and wages	$ 4,500	$ 4,500	$ 4,500	$ 13,500
Insurance and taxes on employees	450	450	450	1,350
Travel and entertainment	200	200	200	200
Office supplies	50	50	50	150
Depreciation—office equipment	100	100	100	300
Total	$ 5,300	$ 5,300	$ 5,300	$ 15,900
General administration:				
Salaries and wages	$10,400	$10,400	$10,400	$ 31,200
Insurance and taxes on employees	1,040	1,040	1,040	3,120
Office supplies	200	200	200	600
Depreciation—office equipment and building	2,060	2,060	2,060	6,280
Insurance and taxes—real estate and property	500	500	500	500
Power, fuel, water, and telephone	700	700	700	2,100
Interest expense	500	500	500	1,500
	$15,400	$15,400	$15,400	$ 46,200
Total administrative expenses	$33,476	$33,476	$33,512	$100,464

* This is the only expense that varies with sales, hence, no variable budget is needed for these three responsibility centers.

LAKE ERIE TABLE COMPANY
Cash Budget
For the Quarter Ending March 31, 1983

Schedule Reference	Item	January	February	March
Given	Beginning cash balance	$ 50,000	$118,527	$189,317
11a	Budgeted cash receipts	349,074	351,648	355,212
	Total cash available	$399,074	$470,175	$544,529
	Budgeted cash disbursements:			
11b	Operations	$280,547	$280,858	$282,445
	Capital expenditures*	0	0	300,000
	Total cash disbursements	$280,547	$280,858	$582,445
Given	Minimum cash balance desired	50,000	50,000	50,000
	Total cash needed	$330,547	$330,858	$632,445
	Excess (or deficiency)†	$ 68,527	$139,317	$(87,916)
	Financing:			
Given	Bank loan	0	0	90,000
	Bank repayments	0	0	0
	Ending cash balance	$118,527	$189,317	$ 52,084

* Estimated cost of new equipment to be purchased in March.
† Minimum cash balance desired plus any excess or less any deficiency and plus any loans less any repayments.

LAKE ERIE TABLE COMPANY
Schedule of Cash Receipts and Ending Balances in Accounts Receivable*
For the Quarter Ending March 31, 1983

Item		January	February	March
December, 1982 sales†	$350,000			
Collected in January	49½%	$173,250		
January, 1983 sales	355,200			
Collected in January: 50%	177,600			
Less 1% cash discount	1,776	175,824		
Collected in February	49½%		$175,824	
February, 1983 sales	$355,200			
Collected in February: 50%	177,600			
Less 1% cash discount	1,776		175,824	
Collected in March	49½%			$175,824
March, 1983 sales	$362,400			
Collected in March: 50%	181,200			
Less 1% cash discount	1,812			179,388
Total collections		$349,074	$351,648	$355,212
Add cash discounts		1,776	1,776	1,812
Total reduction of receivables		$350,850	$353,424	$357,024
Accounts receivable beginning balances (½ of previous month's sales)		$175,000	$177,600	$177,600
Add sales during the month		355,200	355,200	362,400
		$530,200	$532,800	$540,000
Less reductions from above		350,850	353,424	357,024
Accounts receivable ending balance		$179,350	$179,376	$182,976

* Collection schedule:
  1. 50 percent of month's sales are collected during the month and a 1 percent cash discount is taken.
  2. 49½ percent of month's receivables are collected the following month.
  3. One-half percent of month's receivables are never collected and are written off at the year-end.
† This is a given amount.

LAKE ERIE TABLE COMPANY
Schedule of Cash Disbursements
For the Quarter Ending March 31, 1983

Schedule Reference	Item	January		February		March	
4	Materials*................	$95,924		$96,632		$96,632	
	Less 1%, discount........	959	$ 94,965	966	$ 95,566	966	$ 95,566
5	Direct labor†..............		54,530		54,340		55,100
6	Factory overhead‡..........	$54,810		$54,710		$55,105	
	Less:						
	Depreciation...........	6,300		6,300		6,300	
	Insurance and taxes.....	950	47,560	950	47,460	950	47,855
9	Selling expenses...........	$55,312		$55,312		$55,744	
	Less: Depreciation........	140	55,172	140	55,172	140	55,604
10	Administrative expenses.....	$33,476		$33,476		$33,512	
	Less:						
	Depreciation...........	2,380		2,380		2,380	
	Insurance and taxes.....	500		500		500	
	Interest expense..........	500		500		500	
	Bad debts expense........	1,776	28,320	1,776	28,320	1,812	28,320
	Total disbursements........		$280,547		$280,858		$282,445

* All material expenditures are in the same month the purchase is made and a 1 percent cash discount is taken.

† Disbursements for labor assumed to be in the same month as incurred.

‡ Overhead disbursements are in the same month the expenditure is incurred except: (1) depreciation and bad debts expense do not require cash outlays; (2) insurance and taxes on real estate and personal property are paid in July of each year; (3) interest is paid on April 1 and October 1.

LAKE ERIE TABLE COMPANY
Budgeted Income Statement
For the Quarter Ending March 31, 1983

Schedule Reference			
1	Sales....................................		$1,072,800
8	Cost of goods sold......................		603,908
	Gross margin...........................		$ 468,892
	Less:		
9	Selling expenses.....................	$166,368	
10	Administrative expenses................	100,464	266,832
	Net income before taxes..................		$ 202,060
Given	Less federal income taxes (48%)..........		96,989
	Net Income............................		$ 105,071

LAKE ERIE TABLE COMPANY
Budgeted Balance Sheet
As of March 31, 1983

Assets

Current Assets:

Cash (Schedule 11).....................................		$ 52,084	
Accounts receivable (Schedule 11a).......................	$ 221,946		
Less: Allowance for uncollectible (Schedule 10)*..........	5,364	216,582	
Inventories (Schedule 7)		303,667	$ 572,333

Fixed Assets:

Land (given)...		$ 50,000	
Buildings (given).....................................	$1,000,000		
Less: Accumulated depreciation (given).................	100,000	900,000	
Equipment (given)....................................	1,000,000		
Less: Accumulated depreciation (given).................	425,000	575,000	1,025,000
Total Assets....................................			$1,597,333

Liabilities

Current Liabilities:

Accrued interest payable (Schedule 11b)..................		$ 1,500	
Accrued insurance and taxes on real estate personal property (Schedule 11b)..............................		4,350	$ 5,850

Long-Term Liabilities:

Notes payable—$100,000 due January 1, 1988; 6% interest payable on April 1 and October 1 (see Schedule 10).......			100,000

Shareholders' Equity

Common stock, $1 par value, 200,000 shares authorized; 100,000 shares outstanding (given).......................			100,000
Paid-in capital in excess of par (given).....................			400,000
Retained earnings:			
Beginning balance (given).............................		$876,412	
Plus estimated earnings (Schedule 12)....................		105,071	981,483
Total Liability and Shareholders' Equity..............			$1,597,333

    * The debit to bad debt expense each month is offset by a credit to allowance for uncollectible accounts which had a zero balance at January 1, 1975.

Case 25-14: Mammoth Manufacturing Company

Mammoth Manufacturing Company produced stampings, machined castings, and assemblies of stamped and machined parts for the automobile industry, the appliance industry, the tractors and implements business, and several other types of manufacturers and assemblers. The company produced few parts for direct sale to the consumer. Instead, the parts were included in the final assembly of a consumer product such as an automobile or a home appliance sold by Mammoth's customers. Mammoth had 41 manufacturing plants spread out over the country. Total sales were in excess of one-half billion dollars.

For many years, Mammoth had no cost control system worthy of the name. The plants had an historical cost system and reports were submitted monthly to the central office in Cleveland, Ohio. Nothing much was done with these reports and, as long as the plant managers met their production commitments, no one bothered much about costs. In the 1980s, however, competition became quite severe in the type of products Mammoth produced. As a consequence, profit margins were reduced drastically and management began looking around for means of improving their competitive position. Manufacturing cost control was an obvious area.

Several people with experience in standard costing and budgeting were hired to develop and install a cost control system in the manufacturing plants. Each manufacturing plant was considered to be a cost responsibility center, with the plant manager responsible for meeting his cost targets.

At each plant, an industrial engineering department was established and labor standards were set for each part. The accounting department at each plant was expanded to include a budgeting section. This section was responsible for developing flexible budgets to cover manufacturing overhead costs in accordance with instructions from the corporate controller's staff.*

Under the corporate controller, at the central staff in Cleveland, was the Budget Analysis Department. It was the responsibility of this department: to establish timetables for budget submission; to provide forms and instructions so that the budgets would be prepared in a uniform manner; and to analyze the budget proposals and recommend whether they should be accepted or not. This was to insure a uniform "task" in each budget. The Budget Analysis Department also had responsibility for prescribing the budget performance reports. Each month the direct labor and overhead cost performance of each plant was analyzed and the results summarized for management.

Almost from the beginning the effect of the new control system was to reduce manufacturing costs significantly. Part of these savings came from the industrial engineering studies required to set the labor standards. Part of the savings resulted from the analysis of overhead costs that was required to prepare the budgets. Often, it became evident on analysis that certain costs were seriously out of line. Much of the savings came because the system made the plant managers and the department supervisors conscious. The system, however, was not installed without problems; the purpose of this case is to describe three situations that occurred during the initial period of installation.

Situation 1: Definition of Fixed Expense

Several of the people in the Budget Analysis department came from a large automobile company where the flexible budget equation was calculated by using the budgeted costs at two volumes: zero and standard volume. The budgeted expense at zero volume was defined as the "level of costs that would be required with a six months' shut down." This resulted in a low fixed cost and, consequently, a high variable cost. Since the variable cost per unit was relatively high using this method, the reduction in budgeted cost for each unit below standard volume was also high. This meant that when a plant was operating below standard volume, the budget allowance was squeezed. On the other hand, when volume exceeded standard, the budget authorization would be relatively high. This relationship is shown in Exhibit 1.

The argument for using this method was that it forced costs down when volume fell and the company really needed the cost savings, whereas when volume was above standard, the company could afford to be a little more liberal about the expenditures because they were earning increased profits from the additional volume.

---

*Material costs were controlled by a different system and will not be considered in this case.

EXHIBIT 1

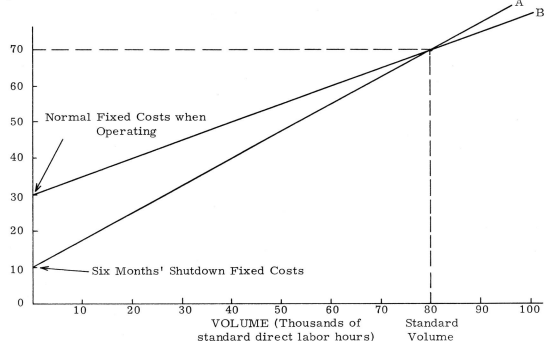

COST ($000)

Line A shows the relation of budgeted expenses to volume assuming that there is a
fixed cost at zero volume of $10,000. This is the estimated fixed cost that
would be incurred after a six months' shutdown.
Line B shows the relation of budgeted expenses to volume assuming that there is a
fixed cost at zero volume of $30,000. This is the estimated normal fixed
cost incurred when the plant is operating.

At a standard volume (SV) of 80,000 hours, the total budgeted expense is estimated to be $70,000. Note that at less than SV, Line B gives the greater
budget authorization. At more than SV, Line A provides the higher budget.

Questions

1. What do you think of the method of
determining the budget equation used
by the automobile company?

2. How do you think the budget equation
should be calculated at Mammoth?

Situation 2: Reasonable and Consistent
"Task"

The Budget Analysis Department was
responsible for analyzing the proposed
budget from each plant and recommending
to to management whether it should be
accepted as proposed, accepted with adjustment, or rejected. The ideal budget was one that could be attained if
plant management was consistently efficient. The variance from budget, then,
represented the extent of the plant's
inefficiency.

It was important not only that the
approved budget represent an efficient
"task," but that the degree of "task"
be consistent among the plants. Although each plant's budget performance
was analyzed individally, comparison
among the plants was inevitable. If
the budget levels did not represent a
consistent task, some managers would be
judged unfairly.

One of the principal problems
facing the Budget Analysis Deartment
was how to insure that the approved
budgets included a reasonable task and
that the degree of task was consistent
among the plants. This problem was
made particularly difficult because the
plants realized that it was to their
benefit to have a "loose" budget since
they were being evaluated against it.
Furthermore, no absolute standards

existed. Overhead rates differed because of differences in automation, in facilities, in location, and so forth. Also, it was not possible to compare plants directly. No two plants produced exactly the same product line. Even where roduction processes are similar, there were enough differences because of geographic location, type of equipment, and mix of products that direct comparisons were not meaningful.

Question

How would you solve the problem described above if you were the manager of the Budget Analysis Department? The constraints within which you must work are:

a. The Budget Analysis Department consists of thirty analysts, varying in experience from one to ten years.
b. Each Plant Budget Department consists of a supervisor and three to five analysts. The budeting people, however, tend to identify themselves with the plant rather than with the central controller's office.

Situation 3: The Oak Park Plant

The Oak Park Plant produced machined parts and assembles almost exclusively for the automobile industry. At the time that the budget system was first being introduced, a new plant manager, Lou Hart, was placed in charge of the Oak Park Plant. Hart came from one of the large automotive manufacturers where he had developed a reputation as a "cost cutter."

Hart went to work on cost cutting at Oak Park with vigor. His first budget proposal was 15 percent less than the previous year's actual expense, adjusted to a comparable colume of production. Although the budget represented substantial reduction in all areas of cost, Hart's proposal represented a 25 percent reduction in indirect labor.

The Oak Park Plant's actual costs for the first year of the budget system (also Hart's first year with the com-

pany) were 10 percent less than budget. In other words, Hart's actual overhead costs, for his first year as manager of the Oak Park Plant, were about 25 percent less than the preceding year's, at comparable volumes. Because of this performance, Hart was given a special award by the president of Mammoth.

Hart's proposed budget for his second year was 10 percent less than his first year's actual costs. The proposed indirect labor budget was now about one half of the amount being spent when Hart first took over the Oak Park Plant. Hart's actual costs continued to be better than budget until the autumn of the second year.

The Oak Park Plant had been producing the same parts, with only slight modifications, for the past several years. During Hart's second year at Oak Park, almost all of the automobile companies made drastic changes in the design of the parts that were being produced at Oak Park. Hart was faced with the necessity of changing over nearly every production line in the plant. This process was made particularly difficult because one of the automobile producers failed to finalize several designs until very close to the time that production on the parts was supposed to begin. Hart had reduced his staff so drastically that he did not have nearly enough manufacturing and industrial engineers to handle the changeover. Furthermore, his supervision was spread so thin that, even where the changeover was accomplished, trouble developed on several lines and production was severely curtailed. As a result, Hart failed to meet production schedules on several major parts and, consequently, the business was given to competitors. By the time the production had been straightened out, the Oak Park Plant had lost nearly half of its business. Needless to say, Hart was replaced.

Question

How do you make sure that a budget system does not motivate a manager to take too drastic cost-cutting action?

* * * * *

Case 25-15: Whiz Calculator Company

In August, Bernard Riesman was elected president of the Whiz Clculator Company. Riesman had been with the company for five years, and for the preceding two years had been vice president of manufacturing. Shortly after

taking over his new position, Riesman held a series of conferences with the controller in which the subject of discussion was budgetary control. The new president thought that the existing method of planning and controlling selling costs was unsatisfactory, and he requested the controller to devise a system that would provide better control over these costs.

Whiz Calculator manufactured a complete line of electronic calculators, which it sold through branch offices to wholesalers and retailers, as well as directly to government and industrial users. Most of the products carried the Whiz brand name, which was nationally advertised. The company was one of the largest in the industry.

Under the procedure then being used, selling expenses were budgeted on a "fixed" or "appropriation" basis. Each October the accounting department sent to branch managers and to other managers in charge of selling departments a detailed record of the actual expenses of their departments for the preceding year and for the current year to date. Guided by this record, by estimates of the succeeding year's sales and by their own judgment, these department heads drew up and submitted estimates of the expenses of their departments for the succeeding year. The estimates made by the branch managers were then sent to the sales manager, who was in charge of all branch sales. He determined whether or not they were reasonable and cleared up any questionable items by correspondence. Upon approval by the sales manager, the estimates of branch expenses were submitted to the manager of marketing, Paul Melmed, who was in charge of all selling, promotional, and warehousing activities.

Melmed discussed these figures and the expense estimates furnished by the other department heads with the managers concerned, and after differences were reconciled, she combined the estimates of all the selling departments into a selling expense budget. This budget was submitted to the budget committee for final approval. For control purposes, the annual budget was divided into 12 equal amount, and actual expenses were compared each month with the budgeted figures. Exhibit 1 shows the form in which these monthly comparisons were made.

Riesman believed that there were two important weaknesses in this method of settng the selling expense budget. First, it was impossible for anyone to ascertain with any feeling of certainty the reasonableness of the estimates made by the various department heads. Clearly, the expenses of the preceding year did not constitute adequate standards against which these expense estimates could be judged, since selling

EXHIBIT 1

BUDGET REPORT CURRENTLY USED

Branch Sales and Expense Performance

Month: October   Branch A   Mgr: N. L. Darden

| | This Month | | | | |
	Budget(a)	Actual	Over*-Under	% of Sales	Over*-Under Year to Date
Net Sales	310,000	261,000	49,000		
Manager's Salary	2,500	2,500	--	0.96	--
Office Salaries	1,450	1,432	18	0.55	1,517
Sales Force Compensation	15,500	13,050	2,450	5.00	3,502*
Travel Expense	3,420	3,127	293	1.20	1,012*
Stationery, Office Supplies	1,042	890	152	0.34	360
Postage	230	262	32*	0.10	21
Light & Heat	134	87	47	0.03	128
Subscriptions and Dues	150	112	38	0.04	26
Donations	125	--	125	0.00	130
Advertising Expense (Local)	2,900	2,700	200	1.03	1,800*
Social Security Taxes	1,303	1,138	165	0.44	133*
Rental	975	975	--	0.37	--
Depreciation	762	762	--	0.29	--
Other Branch Expense	2,551	2,426	125	1.93	247*
Total	33,042	29,461	3,581	11.29	4,512*

(a) 1/12 of annual budget.

conditions were never the same in two different years. One obvious cause of variation in selling expenses was the variation in the "job to be done," as defined in the sales budget.

Second, selling conditions often changed substantially after the budget was adopted, but there was no provision for making the proper corresponding changes in the selling expense budget. Neither was there a logical basis for relating selling expenses to the actual sales volume obtined or to any other measure of sales effort. Riesman believed that it was reasonable to expect that sales expenses would increase, though not proportionately, if actual sales volume were greater than the forecasted volume; but that with the existing method of control it was impossible to determine how large the increase in expenses should be.

As a means of overcoming these weaknesses the president suggested the possibility of setting selling cost budget standards on a fixed and variable basis, a method similar to the techniques used in the control of manufacturing expenses. The controller agreed that this manner of approach seemed to offer the most feasible solution, and he therefore undertook a study of selling expenses to devise a method of setting reasonable standards. Over a period of several years, the accounting department had made many analyses of selling costs, the results of which had been used for allocating costs to products, customers, and territories, and in assisting in the solution of certain special problems, such as determining how large an individual order had to be in order to be profitable. Many of the data accumulated for these purposes were helpful in the controller's current study.

The controller was convinced that the fixed portion of selling expenses -- the portion independent of any fluctuation in sales volume -- could be established by determining the amount of expenses that had to be incurred at the minimum sales volume at which the company was likely to operate. He therefore asked Paula Melmed to suggest a minimum volume figure and the amount of expenses that would have to be incurred at this volume. A staff assistant studied the company's sales records over several business cycles, the long-term outlook for sales, and sales trends of other companies in the industry. From the report prepared by this assistant, Melmed concluded that sales volume would not drop below 65 percent of current factory capacity.

Melmed then attempted to determine the selling expenses that would be incurred at the minimum volume. With the help of her assistant, she worked out a hypothetical selling organization that in her opinion would be required to sell merchandise equivalent to 65 percent of factory capacity, complete as to the number of persons needed to staff each branch office and the other selling departments, including the advertising, merchandising, and sales administration departments. Using current salary and commission figures, the assistant calculated the amount required to pay salaries for such an organization. Melmed also estimated the other expenses, such as advertising, branch office upkeep, supplies, and travel, which would be incurred by each branch and staff department at the minimum sales volume.

The controller decided that the variable portion of the selling expense standard should be expressed as a certain amount per sales dollar. He realized that the use of the sales dollar as a measuring stick had certain disadvantages in that it would not reflect such important influences on costs as order size, selling difficulty of certain territories, changes in buyer psychology, and so on. The sales dollar, however, was the measuring stick most convenient to use, the only figure readily available from the records then being kept, and also a figure which everyone concerned thoroughly understood. The controller believed that a budget that varied with sales would certainly be better than a budget which did not vary at all. He planned to devise a more accurate measure of causes of variation in selling expenses after he had an opportunity to study the nature of these factors over a longer period of time.

As a basis for setting the variable expense standards, using linear regression the controller determined a series of equations that correlated actual annual expenditures for the principal groups of expense items for several preceding years with sales volume. Using these equations, which showed to what extent these items had fluctuated with sales volume in the past, and modifying them in accordance with his own judgment as to future conditions, the controller determined a rate of variation (i.e., slope) for the variable portion of each item of selling expense. The controller thought that after the new system had been tested in practice, it would be possible to refine these rates, perhaps by the use of a technique analogous to the time-study technique which was employed to determine certain expense standards in the factory.

At this point the controller had both a rate of variation and one point (i.e., at 65 percent capacity) on a selling expense graph for each expense item. He was therefore able to determine a final equation for each item. Graphically, this was equivalent to drawing a line through the known point with the slope represented by the rate of variation. The height of this line at zero volume represented the fixed portion of the selling expense formula. The diagram in Exhibit 2 illustrates the procedure, although the actual computations were mathematical rather than graphic.

The selling expense budget for the coming year was determined by adding the new standards for the various fixed components and the indicated flexible allowances for the year's estimated sales volume. This budget was submitted to the budget committee, which studied the fixed amounts and the variable rates underlying the final figures, making only minor changes before passing final approval.

The controller planned to issue reports each month showing actual expenses for each department compared with budgeted expenses. The variable portion of the budget allowances would be adjusted to correspond to the actual volume of sales obtained during the month. Exhibit 3 shows the budget report which he planned to send to branch managers.

One sales executive privately belittled the controller's proposal. "Anyone in the selling game knows that sometimes customers fall all over each other in their hurry to buy, and other times, no matter what we do, they won't even nibble. It's a waste of time to make fancy formulas for selling cost budgets under conditions like that."

Questions

1. From the information given in Exhibits 1 and 3, determine, insofar as you can, whether each item of expense is (a) nonvariable, (b) partly variable with sales volume, (c) variable with sales volume, or (d) variable with some other factors.

2. What bearing do your conclusions in Question 1 have on the type of budget that is most appropriate?

3. Should the proposed sales expense budget system be adopted?

4. If a variable budget is used, should dollar sales be used as the measure of volume?

5. (Optional -- requires calculator with linear regression routine.) Consider the following five-year time series of annual sales and some element of annual branch selling expense:

Year	Sales ($000)	Expense ($)
1	2,686	25,007
2	2,920	27,461
3	3,174	29,813
4	3,450	31,975
5	3,750	35,052

Find the least-squares linear regression equation that relates annual expense to annual sales. Describe how this equation can be used to determine a flexible budget for the expense on a monthly basis.

EXHIBIT 2
BUDGET FOR "OTHER BRANCH EXPENSE," BRANCH A

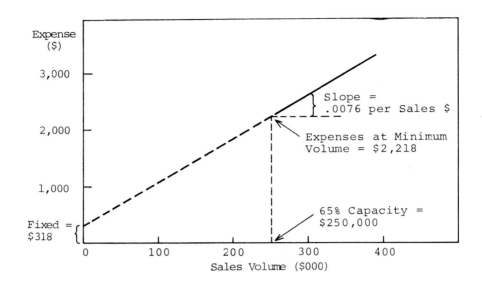

EXHIBIT 3
BUDGET REPORT PROPOSED BY CONTROLLER

Expense Budget Report				Branch: A Manager: N. L. Darden Month: October		
	Budget Factors		This Month			Year to Date
	Fixed	Variable	Flexible Budget	Actual	Over* Under	Over* Under
Net Sales			261,000	261,000		(a)
Manager's Salary	2,500	--	2,500	2,500	--	
Office Salaries	139	.0041	1,209	1,432	223*	
Sales Force Compensation	--	.0500	13,050	13,050	--	
Travel Expense	568	.0087	2,839	3,127	288*	
Stationery, Office Supplies	282	.0026	961	890	71	
Postage	47	.0006	204	262	58*	
Light and Heat	134	--	134	87	47	
Subscriptions and Dues	10	.0005	141	112	29	
Donations	20	.0003	98	--	98	
Advertising Expense (Local)	35	.0100	2,645	2,700	55*	
Social Security Taxes	177	.0036	1,117	1,138	21	
Rental	975	--	975	975	--	
Depreciation	762	--	762	762	--	
Other Branch Expense	318	.0076	2,302	2,426	124*	
Total	5,967	.0880	28,937	29,461	524*	

(a) The controller had not recalculated budgets for previous months, and figures
    were therefore not available for this column.

Chapter 26

Analyzing and Reporting Performance

Key Terms

Variance
Favorable and unfavorable variances
Gross margin variance
Unit margin variance
Sales volume variance

Mix variance
Industry volume variance
Market share variance
Control report
Exception principle

Discussion Questions

1. A person's performance can be measured only after he or she has performed; however, at that time there is nothing that management can do to change what was done. Of what value, then, are performance measurement techniques such as variance analysis?

2. Some responsibility centers, e.g., the legal department, do not have outputs that can be measured in monetary terms, because their function is to perform a service. How can performance be measured in such a responsibility center?

3. The text points out that management control systems inherently tend to focus on short-run performance. Can you think of an instance where too much emphasis on short-run results might hamper longer term performance?

4. Why is the total (or net) gross margin variance broken down into the unit margin, sales volume, and mix components? Why are labor and materials variances decomposed into usage and price components? Why is net overhead variance separated into a volume component and a spending portion?

5. For a variance number to be meaningful, the standard from which actual performance differed must be reasonable. Can one ever be certain a standard is reasonable?

6. There is no volume variance for direct labor or direct material, but there is a production volume variance for overhead. What accounts for this fact?

7. In a certain month, actual net income was $10,000 less than budgeted, and the entire $10,000 was accounted for by overhead spending variance. In what sense did the spending variance identify the <u>cause</u> of the $10,000 net income variance? In what sense did it <u>not</u> identify the cause?

8. Give examples of (a) "favorable" variances that may reflect situations that are not truly favorable; and (b) "unfavorable" variances that may not reflect a "bad" situation.

9. Distinguish between information reports and control reports.

10. What are the relative strengths and weaknesses of evaluating performance on the basis of (a) predetermined standards, (b) historical standards, and (c) external standards?

11. A thermostat and a control report are both feedback devices. What is the important difference between them?

12. What is the exception principle?

13. Of the departments listed in Prt B of Illustration 26-5, which one do you judge to have the best performance record from the information given? (Caution: You need to consider carefully which of several possible measures is best.)

14. Control reports often omit income tax expense. Why is this omission justified? Under what circumstances would it be desirable to include income tax expense in control reports?

Problems

26-1. The diagrams shown in Exhibit A can represent either gross margin, direct labor costs, or direct material costs. For each case, identify the letters.

EXHIBIT A

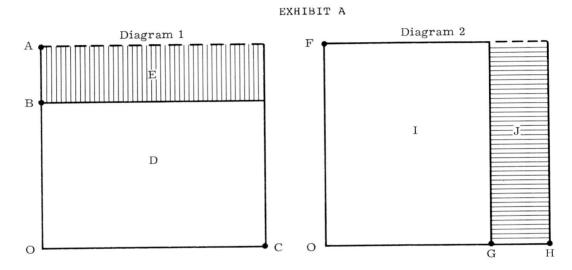

26-2. In its annual profit budget, Alpha Division of Gotham Industries, Inc., budgeted Product A's sales volume at 25,000 units. Product A's budgeted price was $30 per unit; its standard cost was $17 per unit. Actual sales of Product A turned out to be $724,500 for a volume of 23,000 units.

Required: Determine Alpha Division's gross margin variances.

26-3. Midwest Ice Cream's gross margin budget for the year was based on these assumptions: (1) average margin per gallon, $0.453; (2) total industry sales in Midwest's marketing territory, 11,440,000 gallons; and (3) Midwest's market share, 50 percent. Actual sales for the year turned out to be 12,180,000 gallons for the industry, of which Midwest sold 5,968,366 gallons.

Required: Calculate the gross margin sales volume variance and its two components.

26-4. Beta Division of Gotham Industries, Inc., makes three products. Last month's budgeted and actual sales and margins for these products were as follows:

	Budget		Actual	
	Unit Sales	Unit Margin	Unit Sales	Unit Margin
Product 1.........	3,200	$10.00	2,800	$10.40
Product 2.........	1,700	15.00	2,500	15.18
Product 3.........	5,100	8.00	4,200	7.60
	10,000	$9.83	9,500	$10.42

Required: Determine the gross margin mix, selling price, and sales volume variances. Calculate the net gross margin variance directly, then as a check see if it equals the sum of the three variance components you calculated individually.

26-5. Gamma Division of Gotham Industries, Inc., makes a product for which the standard raw materials cost per 100 pounds of finished product is as follows:

$$
\begin{array}{ll}
60 \text{ lbs. of material X @ \$.50/lb.} \ldots\ldots\ldots\ldots\ldots \$30.00 \\
\underline{40} \text{ lbs. of material Y @ } .75/\text{lb.} \ldots\ldots\ldots\ldots\ldots \underline{30.00} \\
\overline{100} \text{ lbs. of materials with total cost} \ldots\ldots\ldots \overline{\$60.00}
\end{array}
$$

Because materials were not supposed to be spoiled during production, these standards included no waste allowance.

During June, actual raw materials usage and costs were:

Material X: Used 5,500 lbs. @ $.50/lb. = $2,750
Material Y: Used 4,500 lbs. @ .80/lb. = 3,600
10,000 lbs. $6,350

Actual finished product: 9,800 lbs.

Required: Calculate the raw materials variances for June, referring back to Chapter 20 if necessary. Note: This problem contains a raw materials mix variance, analogous to the gross margin mix variance described in this chapter.

26-6. The Brandon Company has just completed its first year of operations. A condensed income statement follows, showing actual and standard amounts and the variances:

Income Statement
(000 omitted)

	Standard	Actual	Variance
Sales.................................	$2,660.0	$2,530.8	
Cost of goods sold @ standard........	1,710.0	1,520.0	
Manufacturing variances..............		(19.0)	
Gross margin.........................	950.0	991.8	$41.8
General and administrative expense...	66.5	57.0	9.5
Income...............................	$ 883.5	$ 934.8	$51.3

Other data pertinent to first-year operations:

Raw materials variances....$20,900F
Direct labor variances..... 3,800F
Both products have standard unit
  costs of $3.80

Overhead variances:
  Volume................$55,100U
  Spending.............. 11,400F

Marketing data:

	Standard Selling Price per Unit	Expected Sales in Units	Actual Units Sold
Product A..........	$6.08	250,000	270,000
Product B..........	5.70	200,000	180,000

Required: The president of Brandon Company has asked you as controller for the following data which you are to supply:

a. How much of the variance in income was due to the fact that we sold less than expected of Product B and more of Product A?
b. What would have happened to income if we had produced the number of units expected?
c. What would have happened to the total gross margin variance if we had sold the number of units of both A and B that we expected to sell, but

at the <u>actual</u> selling prices per unit?
d. What is the variance due to the fact that actual selling prices were less than expected? (Product A sold for $5.70 per unit.)

26-7. Delta Division of Gotham Industries, Inc., makes two products, A and B. Both products use the same raw material, and are produced in the same factory by the same work force. In preparing its annual statement of budgeted gross margin, delta's management used the following assumptions:

	Products	
	A	B
Sales (units)........................	2,000	3,000
Unit selling price....................$	100.00	$60,000
Standard unit costs:		
Raw materials (@ $.75/lb.)...........$	30.00	$22.50
Direct labor (@ $6.00/hr.)...........$	16.00	$ 9.00
Overhead (@ 150% of DL$).............$	24.00	$13.50
Other production standards:		
Production volume (units)...........	2,000	3,000
Overhead budget: $1.00 per DL$ plus $29,500 fixed		
Overhead absorption: based on <u>actual</u> DL$		

The year's actual results were as follows:

1. 1,800 units of A were sold for a total of $198,000.
2. 3,200 units of B were sold for a total of $192,000.
3. Production totaled 1,900 units of A and 3,400 units of B.
4. 191,200 lbs. of raw materials were purchased and used; their total cost was $149,136.
5. 10,666-2/3 hrs. of direct labor were worked at a total cost of $60,085.
6. Actual overhead costs were $90,000.

Required:

a. Do as detailed an analysis of variances as the data given permit.
b. Prepare a summary statement for presentation to Delta's top management showing the year's budgeted and actual gross margin and an explanation of the difference between them.

26-8. A condensed income statement for Weems Company is as follows for the month of October:

	Master Budget	Actual	Variance*
Units produced and sold..............	20,000	18,000	(2,000)
Sales revenue........................	$300,000	$288,000	$(12,000)
Costs:			
Direct materials..................	40,000	37,000	3,000
Direct labor......................	80,000	75,000	5,000
Manufacturing overhead............	95,000	89,000	6,000
Selling and administration........	65,000	62,000	3,000
Total Costs...................	280,000	263,000	17,000
Operating Income....................	$ 20,000	$ 25,000	$ 5,000

*( ) = unfavorable.

Further analysis revealed the following data on costs:

	Variable rate per unit	Fixed
Direct materials...................................	$ 2	
Direct labor.......................................	4	
Manufacturing overhead.............................	3	$35,000
Selling and administration........................	1	45,000
Totals...	$10	$80,000

Required:

    a. Prepare a report comparing the master budget with a flexible budget for October.

    b. Calculate the following variances:

        (1) Sales volume   (4) Direct labor (net)
        (2) Unit margin   (5) Manufacturing overhead (net)
        (3) Direct materials (net)   (6) Selling and administrative (net)

    c. Prepare a variance report that accounts for the difference between budgeted and actual operating income for Weems in October.

    d. Comment on the significance of the variances you calculated.

26-9. Brown Enterprises prepares monthly departmental reports in an effort to control its operating costs. Each department has a manager to whom the report is addressed and who is held responsible for the operating results in his or her department. The report made to Department C for September follows:

	Budgeted	Actual
Sales.................................	$39,000	$51,000
Cost of goods sold......................	23,400	31,800
Gross margin...........................	15,600	19,200
Direct operating expenses*..............	15,000	18,000
Contribution to indirect expenses........	$ 600	$ 1,200

    *Of which $7,200 are costs not varying directly with sales volume at the expected level of sales.

Required: Prepare a report that will be of more value in analyzing and appraising the performance of the manager of Department C for September. Comment on the operating results.

26-10. Hogate Company pays a bonus to any of its five division managers who increase their percentage of income to sales over that of the year before. The manager of Division A is displeased because of the results of operations of the line for the current year. The division showed a decrease in net income percentage, as can be determined from the following:

	Current Year		Last Year	
Net sales........................		$350,000		$300,000
Cost of goods sold:				
Division fixed costs.............	$ 40,000		$ 40,000	
Allocated costs.................	72,000		40,000	
Variable costs..................	100,000	212,000	100,000	180,000
Gross margin.....................		138,000		120,000
Selling and administrative expense:				
Division fixed expenses..........	35,000		30,000	
Allocated expenses..............	45,000		36,000	
Variable expenses...............	30,000	110,000	27,000	93,000
Income...........................		$ 28,000		$ 27,000

The items of allocated costs and expenses represent general costs and expenses of the company that were allocated to the divisions.

Required:

    a. Prepare a statement which shows more clearly the performance of Division A.

    b. Comment on the method used by the company to calculate bonuses.

26-11. The supervisor of the Machine Shop received the following monthly overhead cost report:

Item	Budget	Actual	Over (Under)
Materials handling.....................	$ 6,000	$ 6,150	$ 150
Supplies...............................	4,200	4,000	(200)
Depreciation--equipment...............	5,000	7,000	2,000
Training(a)...........................	3,500	4,300	800
Building and grounds(b)...............	2,700	2,700	0
General plant expense(a)..............	1,500	1,600	100
Maintenance(c)........................	4,000	3,800	(200)
Totals.............................	$26,900	$29,550	$2,650

Bases of allocation or assignment:
(a) Number of employees.
(b) Dollars of budgeted overhead cost.
(c) Number of hours of maintenance employees' time utilized times a standard rate.

Required:

a. Discuss the appropriateness of the individual items of the report.
b. Evaluate the performance of the machine shop supervisor.

26-12. Department A is one of 15 production departments in the Hopewell Company. On December 15, the following variable budget and planned production schedule for the coming year were approved:

Annual Variable Budget--Department A

Controllable Costs	Fixed Amount per Month	Variable Rate per Direct Machine-Hour
Salaries........................	$ 9,000	
Indirect labor.................	18,000	$0.07
Indirect materials.............		0.09
Other costs....................	6,000	0.03
	$33,000	$0.19

Production Plan

	Annual Total	Jan.	Feb.	Mar.	Balance
Planned output in direct machine-hours............	325,000	22,000	25,000	29,000	249,000

On March 1, the manager of Department A was informed that the department's planned output for March had been revised to 34,000 direct machine-hours. The manager expressed some doubts as to whether this volume could be attained.

At the end of March the accounting records provided the following actual data for the month for the department.

Actual output in direct machine-hours............	33,000

Actual controllable costs incurred:

Salaries..	$ 9,000
Indirect labor..................................	20,500
Indirect materials..............................	2,850
Other costs.....................................	7,510
	$40,160

Required:

a. Prepare a report on Department A's performance in March.   Suggest what items in this report are especially significant and what possible explanations for these items may be.

26-13. (C.M.A. adapted.) In late 1980, Win Sootsman, the official in charge of the State Department of Automobile Regulation, established a system of performance measurement for the department's branch offices. Sootsman was convinced that management by objectives could help the department reach its objective of better citizen service at a lower cost. The first step was to define the activities of the branch offices, to assign point values to the services performed, and to establish performance targets. Point values, rather than revenue targets, were employed because the department was not a revenue-producing agency. Further, the specific revenue for a service did not adequately reflect the differences in effort required. The analysis was compiled at the state office, and the results were distributed to the branch offices.

The system has been in operation since 1981. The performance targets for the branches have been revised each year by the state office. The revisions were designed to encourage better performance by increasing the target or reducing resources to achieve targets. The revisions incorporated noncontrollable events, such as population shifts, new branches, and changes in procedures.

The Barry Country branch is typical of many branch offices. A summary displaying the budgeted and actual performance for three years is presented in Exhibit 1 on the next page.

Sootsman has been disappointed in the performance of branch offices because they have not met performance targets or budgets. Sootsman is especially concerned because the points earned from citizens' comments are declining.

Required:

a. Does the method of performance measurement properly capture the objectives of this operation? Justify your answer.
b. The Barry County branch office came close to its target for 1983. Does this constitute improved performance compared to 1982? Justify your answer.

EXHIBIT 1

Barry County Branch Performance Report

	1981 Budget	1981 Actual	1982 Budget	1982 Actual	1983 Budget	1983 Actual
Population served	38,000		38,500		38,700	
Number of employees						
Administrative	1	1	1	1	1	1
Professional	1	1	1	1	1	1
Clerical	3	3	2	3	1.5	3
Budgeted Performance Points*						
1. Services	19,500		16,000		15,500	
2. Citizen comments	500		600		700	
	20,000		16,600		16,200	
Actual Performance Points*						
1. Services	14,500		14,600		15,600	
2. Citizen comments	200		900		200	
	14,700		15,500		15,800	
Detail of Actual Performance*						
1. New driver's licenses						
a. Examination & road tests (3 pts.)	3,000		3,150		3,030	
b. Road tests repeat-- failed prior test (2 pts.)	600		750		1,650	
2. Renew driver's licenses (1 pt.)	3,000		3,120		3,060	
3. Issue license plates (0.5 pt.)	4,200		4,150		4,100	
4. Issue titles						
a. Dealer transactions (0.5 pt.)	2,000		1,900		2,100	
b. Individual transactions (1 pt.)	1,700		1,530		1,660	
	14,500		14,600		15,600	
5. Citizen comments						
a. Favorable (+ 0.5 pt.)	300		1,100		800	
b. Unfavorable (- 0.5 pt.)	-100		-200		-600	
	200		900		200	

*The budget performance points for services are calculated using 3 points per available hour. The administrative employee devotes half time to administration and half time to regular services. The calculations for the services point budget are as follows:

    1981: 4.5 people x 8 hours x 240 days x 3 pts. x 75% productive time = 19,440 rounded to 19,500

    1982: 3.5 people x 8 hours x 240 days x 3 pts. x 80% productive time = 16,128 rounded to 16,000

    1983: 3 people x 8 hours x 240 days x 3 pts. x 90% productive time = 15,552 rounded to 15,500

The comments targets are based upon rough estimates by department officials.

The actual point totals for the branch are calculated by multiplying the weights shown in the report in parentheses by the number of such services performed or comments received.

CASES

Case 26-14: Woodside Products, Inc.

Phil Brooks, president of Woodside Products, Inc. called Marilyn Mynar into his office one morning in early July, 1983. Ms. Mynar was a business major in college, and was employed by Woodside during her college summer vacation.

"Marilyn," Brooks began, "I've just received the preliminary financial statements for our 1983 fiscal year, which ended June 30. Both our board of directors and our shareholders will want, and they deserve, an explanation of why our pretax income was virtually unchanged even though revenues were up by $175,000. The accountant is tied up working with our outside CPA on the annual audit, so I thought you could do the necessary analysis. What I'd like is as much of a detailed explanation of the $625 profit increase as you can glean from these data (Exhibit 1). I'd

also like you to draft a statement for the next board meeting that explains the same $625 profit increase, but in a fairly intuitive, summary way. Of course, that doesn't mean 'don't use any numbers'!"

Question

Prepare the detailed analysis of the $625 profit increase from fiscal 1982 to fiscal 1983, and draft an explanation for Woodside's board of directors, as requested by Phil Brooks. For the board's report, you may make any reasonable conjectures you wish as to what caused the variances you have calculated. For both years, assume that inventory was valued at $24 per unit. Assume also that none of the members of the board of directors has expertise in accounting calculations or terminology.

EXHIBIT 1

WOODSIDE PRODUCTS, INC.
Operating Results
For Years ended June 30

1982		1983
$3,613,125	Sales revenues	$3,788,100
2,115,000	Cost of goods sold	2,313,260
1,498,125	Gross margin	1,474,840
902,400	Selling and administrative	878,490
$ 595,725	Income before taxes	$ 596,350

Other 1982 Data

1. Sales = 88,125 units @ $41.
2. Cost of goods sold = 88,125 units @ $24.
3. Selling and administrative costs were $1.84 per unit variable selling cost plus $740,250 fixed S&A.
4. Production volume and sales volume were equal.
5. Production costs per unit were:
   Materials.....................$ 9.60
      (8 lbs. @ $1.20)
   Direct labor................ 4.80
      (.75 hrs. @ $6.40)
   Variable overhead.......... 1.60
      (per unit)
   Fixed overhead............. 8.00
      (based on long-term
      std. volume of
      88,125 units)
                   $24.00

Other 1983 Data

1. Sales = 82,350 units @ $46.
2. Cost of goods sold includes 1983 production cost variances.
3. Selling and administrative costs were $2.00 per unit variable selling cost plus $713,790 fixed S&A.
4. Production volume was 81,100 units; standard volume was 88,125 units.
5. 626,200 lbs. of material @ $1.40 were consumed by production.
6. 64,860 direct labor hours were worked @ $6.90.
7. Actual variable overhead costs were $152,000.

In ten years, Crompton, Ltd. had achieved noteworthy success in penetrating the highly competitive British abrasive products industry. Located in Sheffield, England, its factory employed more than 300 people, manufacturing grinding wheels for sale to steel converters and cutlery manufacturers in the Sheffield area.

From the time the company started in business, John Lucas, the factory manager, had controlled factory operations primarily by direct personal supervision. Because he had been so familiar with operations, he had known which departments were having difficulties and what they were doing to cope with them. He had worked very closely with the departmental supervisors and they, in turn, had never been afraid to call on him for help and advice.

With the growth of the company, this arrangement became more and more difficult. Lucas had to rely more and more on the individual supervisors to inform him of problems they were having, and he was quite sure that some of them, particularly the newer ones, were not as effective as they should have been. Unfortunately, he had no evidence on which to decide which departments needed attention. With this in mind, he asked Lou Field, a local accountant, to draw up a system of monthly reports that would supplement the knowledge that he would continue to gain by direct observation.

In the production of grinding wheels, abrasive grain was mixed with a bonding material according to the customer's requirements; molded in either a hot or a cold press, depending on the kind of bond; baked in a kiln; fitted with a bushing to take a motor spindle; "trued" to take off rough edges; shaped specially if needed; tested for balance and ability to withstand high speeds; and finally packed and shipped to the customer.

After several weeks of study and discussion with Crompton factory personnel, Field proposed that a report in the form illustrated in Exhibit 1 be prepared for each of the 18 production centers in the factory. One copy of the report would go to the supervisor in charge of that production center; a second copy would go to Lucas.

Field explained that the objective had been to produce a simple report, with as few figures as possible. Accordingly, the report had been limited to the following four items:

1. Gross production.
2. Rejection rate.
3. Net production per labor-hour.
4. Direct labor cost.

Gross production was measured by the total "list price" of the products passing through the department. Field considered using some other indicator of production volume, such as the total number of units or total weight of the output, but rejected all of these because the output varied so widely in size and complexity. The "list price" was a stabilized amount for each wheel, established several years earlier and

EXHIBIT 1
HOT PRESS DEPARTMENT OPERATION REPORT, NOVEMBER*

	Gross Production (£)**	Rejections (%)	Net Production per Labor-hour (£/hr.)	Direct Labor (£)
November (4 weeks)........	260,684	6.35	194.3	6,460
October (4 weeks).........	166,204	10.48	172.4	4,632
September (5 weeks).......	242,720	10.78	215.3	4,666
August (2 weeks)..........	62,567	9.10	140.6	1,758
July (4 weeks)............	158,915	13.41	168.7	4,477
January-June (26 weeks)...	1,112,202	8.90	155.8	32,183
Last fiscal year (52 weeks)...............	1,536,684	11.14	112.1	49,624

*Each "month" consists of either four or five full weeks, except August when the factory is closed for two weeks. A "year" consists of 52 weeks (50 working weeks plus two vacation weeks); approximately one year in every five, a calendar year includes 53 payroll dates, and that "year" consists of 53 weeks.
** £ = pounds, the British monetary unit.

unchanged since that time. Actual customer prices were set each year by multiplying the list price by a percentage (e.g., 145%) which management felt was "right" for the current market.

Rejections occurred in all production departments, although the majority were discovered in the testing department. At a weekly conference, the plant superintendent determined the source of the defect and allocated responsibility accordingly. Rejections were quoted as a percentage of gross production handled.

Net production per labor-hour was gross production, minus rejects, all measured at list prices, divided by the number of direct labor hours.

Direct labor costs were the actual direct labor hours for the month multiplied by the actual wage rates paid individual workers during the month, including any premium payments for overtime hours. Departmental supervisors were responsible for scheduling work in their departments and thus were expected to keep overtime premiums to the lowest level consistent with their delivery commitments.

Each report provided three sets of figures with which the most recent month's record could be compared: (1) the four immediately preceding months, separately for each month; (2) the six months prior to that, as semi-annual totals; and (3) the most recent complete fiscal year, as annual totals. Thus, the November figures could be compared with those for October, September, August and July; for January-June; and for the twelve months January-December of the preceding fiscal year.

Finally, Field suggested that the departments could be compared with each other to determine which were the most productive, which were showing the most improvement, and which seemed to need Lucas' attention the most.

Questions

1. In what ways does Exhibit 1 differ from the financial accounting reports you have studied?

2. What did Lucas mean by "control information? Why did he need it?

3. What suggestions would you make for improving Exhibit 1 so as to be more useful to Lucas?

* * * * *

Case 26-16: Glencoe County Hospital*

Glencoe County Hospital is located in the town of Springville, New Hampshire. The Springville area, besides being the location of several light manufacturing firms, is a popular recreational area. During the summer, Lake Springville attracts numerous tourists to local motels and lodges, as well as many families who spend the summer at cottages around the lake. In the snowy winter months, the Mount Springville ski area attracts many visitors.

Glencoe County Hospital enjoys the reputation of having a well-trained medical staff, who have been attracted to this relatively small hospital because of the pleasant surroundings and lack of big-city hospital pressures. However the hospital's trustees have been concerned about a series of annual deficits, and one year ago a nonphysician administrator was hired with instructions from the trustees to "improve the business management of the hospital."

Among the new ideas the new administrator, Lynn Richards, has introduced is responsibility accounting. This approach was announced to the hospital's various department heads in a memo, accompanied with a quarterly cost report for each department. Prior to Richards' arrival, department heads had been shown cost data for their departments infrequently. The memo said, in part:

"The hospital has adopted a 'responsibility accounting system.' Henceforth each of you department heads will receive quarterly reports comparing the costs of operating your department with budgeted costs. The reports will highlight the differences ('variances') so that you can focus on the departure from budgeted costs: this is called 'management by exception.'

"Responsibility accounting means that you are accountable for keeping the costs in your department within budget. The variances will help you identify which costs are out of line, and the size of the variances will indicate which ones are the most important. The first such report for your department is attached."

The first report for the laundry department is shown in Exhibit 1. To prepare the department reports, Richards had first constructed an annual budget for 1983. Quarterly budgets were one fourth of this annual budget. Richards had analyzed the previous three years' costs, an analysis that showed all cost items increasing each year, with the increases accelerating. Richards considered establishing the 1983 budgeted costs at the average of the previous three years' costs, hoping that the new control system would reduce costs to this level. However, in view of rapidly increasing prices for inputs, Richards decided to use 1982 costs less 4 percent for the 1983 budget.

Each report also showed at least one measure of activity level. The laundry department report used patient days and pounds of laundry as the activity measures. The 1983 annual budgeted activity levels for the department were the same as the 1982 actuals -- 38,000 patient days and 500,000 pounds of laundry. These activity levels had been essentially constant for each of the past three years.

Question:

Evaluate Lynn Richards' new budget system and the way in which it was implemented.

EXHIBIT 1

Performance Report
Laundry Department
July-September 1983

Activity Levels:	Budget	Actual	Variance	% Variance
Patient Days	9,500	11,900	(2,400)	(25)
Laundry Processed (lbs.)	125,000	156,000	(31,000)	(25)
Costs:				
Labor	$ 9,000	$12,500	$(3,500)	(39)
Supplies	1,100	1,875	(775)	(70)
Water, and Water Conditioning	1,700	2,500	(800)	(47)
Maintenance	1,400	2,200	(800)	(57)
Supervision	3,150	3,750	(600)	(19)
Allocated Administrative Costs	4,000	5,000	(1,000)	(25)
Laundry Equipment Depreciation	1,200	1,250	(50)	(4)
Total	$21,550	$29,075	$(7,525)	(35)

*Adapted from a C.M.A. examination.

Chapter 27

Management Accounting System Design

Key Terms

Cost Concepts (Review)

Full cost accounting
Differential accounting
Responsibility accounting
Expensed and capitalized costs
Product and period costs

Direct and indirect costs
Variable, semivariable, and fixed costs
Actual and standard costs
Controllable and noncontrollable costs
Engineered, discretionary and committed
   costs

Discussion Questions

1. Describe the basic differences between full cost accounting and responsibility accounting.

2. Why is differential accounting always future oriented?

3. What are some of the desirable characteristics of a good management accounting system?

4. Why is it difficult to determine the "right" level of detail in the account structure?

5. How does the goal congruence test aid in evaluating managemnt control system procedures?

CASE

Case 27-6: SIU Incorporated*

Divisional managers of SIU Incorporated have been expressing growing dissatisfaction with the current methods used to measure divisional performance. Divisional operations are evaluated every quarter by comparison with the static budget prepared during the prior year. Divisional managers claim that many factors are completely out of their control but are included in this comparison. This results in an unfair and misleading performance evaluation.

The managers have been particular-

ly critical of the process used to establish standards and budgets. The annual budget, stated by quarters, is prepared six months prior to the beginning of the operating year. Pressure by top management to reflect increased earnings has often caused divisional managers to overstate revenues and/or understate expenses. In addition, once the budget had been established, divisions were required to "live with the budget." Frequently, external factors such as the state of the economy, changes in consumer preferences, and actions of competitors have not been adequately recognized in the budget parameters that top management supplied

_____

*Adapted from a C.M.A. examination.

to the divisions. The credibility of the performance review is curtailed when the budget cannot be adjusted to incorporate these changes.

Top management, recognizing the current problems, has agreed to establish a committee to review the situation and to make recommendations for a new performance evaluation system. The committee consists of each division manager, the Corporate Controller, and the Executive Vice President who serves as the chairman. At the first meeting, one division manager outlined an Acheivement of Objectives System (AOS). In this performance evaluation system, divisional managers would be evaluated according to three criteria:

-Doing better than last year: Various measures would be compared to the same measures of the prior year.
-Planning realistically: Actual performance for the current year would be compared to realistic plans and/or goals.
-Managing current assets: Various measures would be used to evaluate the divisional management's achievements and reactions to changing business and economic conditions.

A division manager believed this system would overcome many of the inconsistencies of the current system be-

cause divisions could be evaluated from three different viewpoints. In addition, managers would have the opportunity to show how they would react and account for changes in uncontrollable external factors.

A second division manager was also in favor of the proposed AOS. However, he cautioned that the success of a new performance evaluation system would be limited unless it had the complete support of top management. Further, this support should be visible within all divisions. He believed that the committee should recommend some procedures which would enhance the motivational and competitive spirit of the divisions.

Questions

1. Explain whether or not the proposed AOS would be an improvement over the measure of divisional performance now used by SIU Incorporated.
2. Develop specific performance measures for each of the three criteria in the proposed AOS which could be used to evaluate divisional managers.
3. Discuss the motivational and behavioral aspects of the proposed performance system. Also recommend specific programs which could be instituted to promote morale and give incentives to divisional management.

Appendix Tables

Table A

PRESENT VALUE OF $1

Years Hence	1%	2%	4%	6%	8%	10%	12%	14%	15%	16%	18%	20%	22%	24%	25%	26%	28%	30%	35%	40%	45%	50%
1	0.990	0.980	0.962	0.943	0.926	0.909	0.893	0.877	0.870	0.862	0.847	0.833	0.820	0.806	0.800	0.794	0.781	0.769	0.741	0.714	0.690	0.667
2	0.980	0.961	0.925	0.890	0.857	0.826	0.797	0.769	0.756	0.743	0.718	0.694	0.672	0.650	0.640	0.630	0.610	0.592	0.549	0.510	0.476	0.444
3	0.971	0.942	0.889	0.840	0.794	0.751	0.712	0.675	0.658	0.641	0.609	0.579	0.551	0.524	0.512	0.500	0.477	0.455	0.406	0.364	0.328	0.296
4	0.961	0.924	0.855	0.792	0.735	0.683	0.636	0.592	0.572	0.552	0.516	0.482	0.451	0.423	0.410	0.397	0.373	0.350	0.301	0.260	0.226	0.198
5	0.951	0.906	0.822	0.747	0.681	0.621	0.567	0.519	0.497	0.476	0.437	0.402	0.370	0.341	0.328	0.315	0.291	0.269	0.223	0.186	0.156	0.132
6	0.942	0.888	0.790	0.705	0.630	0.564	0.507	0.456	0.432	0.410	0.370	0.335	0.303	0.275	0.262	0.250	0.227	0.207	0.165	0.133	0.108	0.088
7	0.933	0.871	0.760	0.665	0.583	0.513	0.452	0.400	0.376	0.354	0.314	0.279	0.249	0.222	0.210	0.198	0.178	0.159	0.122	0.095	0.074	0.059
8	0.923	0.853	0.731	0.627	0.540	0.467	0.404	0.351	0.327	0.305	0.266	0.233	0.204	0.179	0.168	0.157	0.139	0.123	0.091	0.068	0.051	0.039
9	0.914	0.837	0.703	0.592	0.500	0.424	0.361	0.308	0.284	0.263	0.225	0.194	0.167	0.144	0.134	0.125	0.108	0.094	0.067	0.048	0.035	0.026
10	0.905	0.820	0.676	0.558	0.463	0.386	0.322	0.270	0.247	0.227	0.191	0.162	0.137	0.116	0.107	0.099	0.085	0.073	0.050	0.035	0.024	0.017
11	0.896	0.804	0.650	0.527	0.429	0.350	0.287	0.237	0.215	0.195	0.162	0.135	0.112	0.094	0.086	0.079	0.066	0.056	0.037	0.025	0.017	0.012
12	0.887	0.788	0.625	0.497	0.397	0.319	0.257	0.208	0.187	0.168	0.137	0.112	0.092	0.076	0.069	0.062	0.052	0.043	0.027	0.018	0.012	0.008
13	0.879	0.773	0.601	0.469	0.368	0.290	0.229	0.182	0.163	0.145	0.116	0.093	0.075	0.061	0.055	0.050	0.040	0.033	0.020	0.013	0.008	0.005
14	0.870	0.758	0.577	0.442	0.340	0.263	0.205	0.160	0.141	0.125	0.099	0.078	0.062	0.049	0.044	0.039	0.032	0.025	0.015	0.009	0.006	0.003
15	0.861	0.743	0.555	0.417	0.315	0.239	0.183	0.140	0.123	0.108	0.084	0.065	0.051	0.040	0.035	0.031	0.025	0.020	0.011	0.006	0.004	0.002
16	0.853	0.728	0.534	0.394	0.292	0.218	0.163	0.123	0.107	0.093	0.071	0.054	0.042	0.032	0.028	0.025	0.019	0.015	0.008	0.005	0.003	0.002
17	0.844	0.714	0.513	0.371	0.270	0.198	0.146	0.108	0.093	0.080	0.060	0.045	0.034	0.026	0.023	0.020	0.015	0.012	0.006	0.003	0.002	0.001
18	0.836	0.700	0.494	0.350	0.250	0.180	0.130	0.095	0.081	0.069	0.051	0.038	0.028	0.021	0.018	0.016	0.012	0.009	0.005	0.002	0.001	0.001
19	0.828	0.686	0.475	0.331	0.232	0.164	0.116	0.083	0.070	0.060	0.043	0.031	0.023	0.017	0.014	0.012	0.009	0.007	0.003	0.002	0.001	
20	0.820	0.673	0.456	0.312	0.215	0.149	0.104	0.073	0.061	0.051	0.037	0.026	0.019	0.014	0.012	0.010	0.007	0.005	0.002	0.001	0.001	
21	0.811	0.660	0.439	0.294	0.199	0.135	0.093	0.064	0.053	0.044	0.031	0.022	0.015	0.011	0.009	0.008	0.006	0.004	0.002	0.001		
22	0.803	0.647	0.422	0.278	0.184	0.123	0.083	0.056	0.046	0.038	0.026	0.018	0.013	0.009	0.007	0.006	0.004	0.003	0.001	0.001		
23	0.795	0.634	0.406	0.262	0.170	0.112	0.074	0.049	0.040	0.033	0.022	0.015	0.010	0.007	0.006	0.005	0.003	0.002	0.001			
24	0.788	0.622	0.390	0.247	0.158	0.102	0.066	0.043	0.035	0.028	0.019	0.013	0.008	0.006	0.005	0.004	0.003	0.002	0.001			
25	0.780	0.610	0.375	0.233	0.146	0.092	0.059	0.038	0.030	0.024	0.016	0.010	0.007	0.005	0.004	0.003	0.002	0.001	0.001			
26	0.772	0.598	0.361	0.220	0.135	0.084	0.053	0.033	0.026	0.021	0.014	0.009	0.006	0.004	0.003	0.002	0.002	0.001				
27	0.764	0.586	0.347	0.207	0.125	0.076	0.047	0.029	0.023	0.018	0.011	0.007	0.005	0.003	0.002	0.002	0.001	0.001				
28	0.757	0.574	0.333	0.196	0.116	0.069	0.042	0.026	0.020	0.016	0.010	0.006	0.004	0.002	0.002	0.002	0.001	0.001				
29	0.749	0.563	0.321	0.185	0.107	0.063	0.037	0.022	0.017	0.014	0.008	0.005	0.003	0.002	0.002	0.001	0.001	0.001				
30	0.742	0.552	0.308	0.174	0.099	0.057	0.033	0.020	0.015	0.012	0.007	0.004	0.003	0.002	0.001	0.001	0.001					
40	0.672	0.453	0.208	0.097	0.046	0.022	0.011	0.005	0.004	0.003	0.001	0.001										
50	0.608	C.372	0.141	0.054	0.021	0.009	0.003	0.001	0.001	0.001												

Table B

PRESENT VALUE OF $1 RECEIVED ANNUALLY FOR N YEARS

Years (N)	1%	2%	4%	6%	8%	10%	12%	14%	15%	16%	18%	20%	22%	24%	25%	26%	28%	30%	35%	40%	45%	50%
1	0.990	0.980	0.962	0.943	0.926	0.909	0.893	0.877	0.870	0.862	0.847	0.833	0.820	0.806	0.800	0.794	0.781	0.769	0.741	0.714	0.690	0.667
2	1.970	1.942	1.886	1.833	1.783	1.736	1.690	1.647	1.626	1.605	1.566	1.528	1.492	1.457	1.440	1.424	1.392	1.361	1.289	1.224	1.165	1.111
3	2.941	2.884	2.775	2.673	2.577	2.487	2.402	2.322	2.283	2.246	2.174	2.106	2.042	1.981	1.952	1.923	1.868	1.816	1.696	1.589	1.493	1.407
4	3.902	3.808	3.630	3.465	3.312	3.170	3.037	2.914	2.855	2.798	2.690	2.589	2.494	2.404	2.362	2.320	2.241	2.166	1.997	1.849	1.720	1.605
5	4.853	4.713	4.452	4.212	3.993	3.791	3.605	3.433	3.352	3.274	3.127	2.991	2.864	2.745	2.689	2.635	2.532	2.436	2.220	2.035	1.876	1.737
6	5.795	5.601	5.242	4.917	4.623	4.355	4.111	3.889	3.784	3.685	3.498	3.326	3.167	3.020	2.951	2.885	2.759	2.643	2.385	2.168	1.983	1.824
7	6.728	6.472	6.002	5.582	5.206	4.868	4.564	4.288	4.160	4.039	3.812	3.605	3.416	3.242	3.161	3.083	2.937	2.802	2.508	2.263	2.057	1.883
8	7.652	7.325	6.733	6.210	5.747	5.335	4.968	4.639	4.487	4.344	4.078	3.837	3.619	3.421	3.329	3.241	3.076	2.925	2.598	2.331	2.108	1.922
9	8.566	8.162	7.435	6.802	6.247	5.759	5.328	4.946	4.772	4.607	4.303	4.031	3.786	3.566	3.463	3.366	3.184	3.019	2.665	2.379	2.144	1.948
10	9.471	8.983	8.111	7.360	6.710	6.145	5.650	5.216	5.019	4.833	4.494	4.192	3.923	3.682	3.571	3.465	3.269	3.092	2.715	2.414	2.168	1.965
11	10.368	9.787	8.760	7.887	7.139	6.495	5.937	5.453	5.234	5.029	4.656	4.327	4.035	3.776	3.656	3.544	3.335	3.147	2.752	2.438	2.185	1.977
12	11.255	10.575	9.385	8.384	7.536	6.814	6.194	5.660	5.421	5.197	4.793	4.439	4.127	3.851	3.725	3.606	3.387	3.190	2.779	2.456	2.196	1.985
13	12.134	11.343	9.986	8.853	7.904	7.103	6.424	5.842	5.583	5.342	4.910	4.533	4.203	3.912	3.780	3.656	3.427	3.223	2.799	2.468	2.204	1.990
14	13.004	12.106	10.563	9.295	8.244	7.367	6.628	6.002	5.724	5.468	5.008	4.611	4.265	3.962	3.824	3.695	3.459	3.249	2.814	2.477	2.210	1.993
15	13.865	12.849	11.118	9.712	8.559	7.606	6.811	6.142	5.847	5.575	5.092	4.675	4.315	4.001	3.859	3.726	3.483	3.268	2.825	2.484	2.214	1.995
16	14.718	13.578	11.652	10.106	8.851	7.824	6.974	6.265	5.954	5.669	5.162	4.730	4.357	4.033	3.887	3.751	3.503	3.283	2.834	2.489	2.216	1.997
17	15.562	14.292	12.166	10.477	9.122	8.022	7.120	6.373	6.047	5.749	5.222	4.775	4.391	4.059	3.910	3.771	3.518	3.295	2.840	2.492	2.218	1.998
18	16.398	14.992	12.659	10.828	9.372	8.201	7.250	6.467	6.128	5.818	5.273	4.812	4.419	4.080	3.928	3.786	3.529	3.304	2.844	2.494	2.219	1.999
19	17.226	15.678	13.134	11.158	9.604	8.365	7.366	6.550	6.198	5.877	5.316	4.844	4.442	4.097	3.942	3.799	3.539	3.311	2.848	2.496	2.220	1.999
20	18.046	16.351	13.590	11.470	9.818	8.514	7.469	6.623	6.259	5.929	5.353	4.870	4.460	4.110	3.954	3.808	3.546	3.316	2.850	2.497	2.221	1.999
21	18.857	17.011	14.029	11.764	10.017	8.649	7.562	6.687	6.312	5.973	5.384	4.891	4.476	4.121	3.963	3.816	3.551	3.320	2.852	2.498	2.221	2.000
22	19.660	17.658	14.451	12.042	10.201	8.772	7.645	6.743	6.359	6.011	5.410	4.909	4.488	4.130	3.970	3.822	3.556	3.323	2.853	2.498	2.222	2.000
23	20.456	18.292	14.857	12.303	10.371	8.883	7.718	6.792	6.399	6.044	5.432	4.925	4.499	4.137	3.976	3.827	3.559	3.325	2.854	2.499	2.222	2.000
24	21.243	18.914	15.247	12.550	10.529	8.985	7.784	6.835	6.434	6.073	5.451	4.937	4.507	4.143	3.981	3.831	3.562	3.327	2.855	2.499	2.222	2.000
25	22.023	19.523	15.622	12.783	10.675	9.077	7.843	6.873	6.464	6.097	5.467	4.948	4.514	4.147	3.985	3.834	3.564	3.329	2.856	2.499	2.222	2.000
26	22.795	20.121	15.983	13.003	10.810	9.161	7.896	6.906	6.491	6.118	5.480	4.956	4.520	4.151	3.988	3.837	3.566	3.330	2.856	2.500	2.222	2.000
27	23.560	20.707	16.330	13.211	10.935	9.237	7.943	6.935	6.514	6.136	5.492	4.964	4.524	4.154	3.990	3.839	3.567	3.331	2.856	2.500	2.222	2.000
28	24.316	21.281	16.663	13.406	11.051	9.307	7.984	6.961	6.534	6.152	5.502	4.970	4.528	4.157	3.992	3.840	3.568	3.331	2.857	2.500	2.222	2.000
29	25.066	21.844	16.984	13.591	11.158	9.370	8.022	6.983	6.551	6.166	5.510	4.975	4.531	4.159	3.994	3.841	3.569	3.332	2.857	2.500	2.222	2.000
30	25.808	22.396	17.292	13.765	11.258	9.427	8.055	7.003	6.566	6.177	5.517	4.979	4.534	4.160	3.995	3.842	3.569	3.332	2.857	2.500	2.222	2.000
40	32.835	27.355	19.793	15.046	11.925	9.779	8.244	7.105	6.642	6.234	5.548	4.997	4.544	4.166	3.999	3.846	3.571	3.333	2.857	2.500	2.222	2.000
50	39.196	31.424	21.482	15.762	12.234	9.915	8.304	7.133	6.661	6.246	5.554	4.999	4.545	4.167	4.000	3.846	3.571	3.333	2.857	2.500	2.222	2.000

Definitions of Key Terms

Chapter 1. THE NATURE AND PURPOSE OF ACCOUNTING

Operating information: data needed by an organization in order to conduct its day-to-day activities. This includes such information as payroll data, detailed records of stocks on hand, amounts owed by customers and the dates these amounts are due, records of orders that have been placed with suppliers but not yet received, and so forth.

Management accounting information: summaries of detailed operating information which are prepared for use by the organization's managers. These uses include controlling, coordinating, and planning the organization's activities.

Financial accounting information: information on a business's activities, prepared in monetary terms for use not only by management, but also by outside parties such as bankers, shareholders, and government agencies.

Control: the process by which managers try to ensure that organizational tasks are performed effectively (i.e., done properly) and efficiently.

Planning: the process of deciding what actions should be taken in the future. Planning takes place at all levels of an organization.

Budgeting: the process of planning the overall activity of the organization for a specified period of time, usually one year. Most budgetary information is expressed in monetary terms.

Generally accepted accounting principles: the foundation of principles underlying accounting in the United States. These principles, often referred to as "GAAP," are promulgated by the Financial Accounting Standards Board (FASB). As a practical matter, most corporations' financial statements are prepared in accordance with GAAP.

FASB: Financial Accounting Standards Board, created in 1973 and successor to the Accounting Principles Board (APB). Unlike the APB, the FASB has full-time members, and is financed, in part, by contributions from business firms.

Relevance: a criterion for acceptance of an accounting principle. Relevance relates to whether the principle results in meaningful and useful information to the readers of financial reports.

Objectivity: another accounting principle acceptance criterion, which relates to whether the principle results in information that is not influenced by the personal bias of those supplying the information.

Feasibility: the third criterion for acceptance of an accounting principle. A principle is feasible if it results in information that is obtainable without undue complexity, effort, or cost.

Status reports: those reports that reflect measures of stock at a given moment in time. The balance sheet is a status report.

Flow reports: those reports that reflect measures of movements of stocks during a specified period of time. The income statement is a flow report.

Chapter 2. BASIC ACCOUNTING CONCEPTS: THE BALANCE SHEET

Money measurement concept: accounting records only those facts that can be expressed in monetary terms.

Entity concept: accounts are kept for entities, as distinguished from the person(s) associated with those entities.

Going-concern concept: accounting assumes that an entity will continue to exist indefinitely, unless there is good evidence to the contrary.

Cost concept: accounting assumes that an entity will continue to exist indefinitely, unless there is good evidence to the contrary.

Dual-aspect concept: the total amount of assets equals the total amount of equities (liabilities plus owners' equity).

Balance sheet: a statement showing the financial position of an accounting entity as of a specified moment of time. Sometimes called a "statement of financial position," a balance sheet "balances" because of the dual-aspect concept.

Assets: economic resources controlled by an entity whose cost at the time of acquisition could be objectively measured. (A resource is "economic" if it provides future benefits to the entity.)

Current assets: cash and other assets that are reasonably expected to be realized in cash or sold or consumed during the normal operating cycle of the business or within one year, if that cycle is less than one year. These assets include cash, marketable securities, accounts receivable, inventories, and (usually) prepaid expenses.

Monetary assets: cash, or assets that can be converted into money at an amount that is ascertainable with reasonable certainty, including marketable securities and receivables.

Property, plant and equipment: tangible, relatively long-lived assets; also frequently called "fixed assets."

Equities: from a legalistic standpoint, claims against the assets. From a financial management viewpoint, equities are the sources of the funds invested in the entity's assets. A company's equities include its liabilities and its owners' equity.

Liabilities: the entity's obligations to pay money or to provide goods or services. (A few items, such as deferred taxes, do not fit this definition.)

Current liabilities: obligations that are expected to be satisfied either by use of assets classified as current in the same balance sheet, or by the creation of other current liabilities or obligations that are expected to be satisfied within a relatively short period of time, usually one year.

Owners' equity: the owners' claims against an entity's assets; i.e., the amount owners have invested in the entity. Owners' equity includes contributed capital and retained earnings. (Misleadingly called "net worth.")

Contributed capital: the amount that an entity's owners have invested directly in the business; also called "paid-in capital." Contributed capital includes the stated (or par) value of capital stock and other paid-in capital (or paid-in surplus) -- see Chapter 9.

Retained earnings: the cumulative difference between a company's earnings (net income) and the amount of dividends paid by the company.

Transaction: The technical name given to an event that affects an accounting number. Every accounting transaction can be recorded in terms of its effect on the balance sheet.

Chapter 3. BASIC ACCOUNTING CONCEPTS. THE INCOME STATEMENT

Income statement: a financial statement that summarizes the results of an entity's operations for a period of time. The income statement is a _flow_ statement that explains most, if not all, of the change in the retained earnings account between two balance sheet dates.

Revenues: the value of the goods and services sold by an organization. A revenue also can be defined as an increase in owners' equity resulting from the operation of the entity.

Expenses: the cost of the resources used in providing the goods and services which generate revenues. An expense can also be defined as a decrease in owners' equity resulting from the operation of the entity.

Net income: the excess of revenues over all expenses (including taxes) of a period. Revenue - Expenses = Net Income. If this difference is negative, it is termed a net loss.

Time period concept: accounting measures activities for a specified period of time, which is usually one year (called the "fiscal year"). Reports prepared for periods of less than one year are called interim reports.

Conservatism concept: revenues are recognized only when there is a reasonable certainty that the entity has earned income, whereas expenses are recognized as soon as they are reasonably possible.

Realization concept: revenues are generally recognized in the period in which they are realized, i.e., in the period in which goods are delivered to customers or in which services are rendered. The amount of revenue recognized is the amount that customers are reasonably certain to pay.

Matching concept: when a given event affects both revenues and expenses, the effect on each should be recognized in the same accounting period. Also, costs associated with the period's activities are expenses of that period, as are costs that cannot be associated with revenues of future periods.

Consistency concept: once an entity has decided on a certain method of accounting for a given class of events, it will use the same method for subsequent events of the same character unless it has a sound reason to do otherwise.

Materiality concept: insignificant events may be disregarded, but there must be full disclosure of all important information.

Expenditure: the transaction that occurs when an asset or service is acquired. Though many expenditures are made by cash and hence are disbursements, expenditures may also be made by exchanging another asset (other than cash) or by incurring a liability.

Gains and losses: increases (decreases) in owners' equity not associated with the production and sale of a company's goods and services, and therefore distinguished from revenues (expenses).

Cost of goods sold: an expense that is the cost of merchandise for which revenue has been recognized. In a service firm the analogous account is called "cost of sales."

Gross margin: the difference between revenues and cost of goods sold; also called "gross profit."

Cash-basis accounting: a concept of accounting in which "income" is regarded as the difference between receipts and disbursements, rather than between revenues and expenses. It is not a generally accepted accounting principle. (Note: What the IRS calls "cash basis" for a business is really a "modified cash basis"; this latter method does include inventories and plant and equipment as assets, but does not include receivables or payables on the balance sheet.)

Economic income: the difference between the value of a business at the end of an accounting period and its value at the beginning of the period. Interest on all equities is regarded as an element of cost.

Gross margin percentage: gross margin expressed as a percent of sales revenues.

Profit margin: net income expressed as a percent of sales revenues.

Chapter 4. ACCOUNTING RECORDS AND SYSTEMS

Account: an accounting device for accumulating increases and decreases relating to a single balance sheet or income statement item.

Debit and credit: as adjectives, these terms mean, respectively, "left-hand" and "right-hand," as the debit side of an account. As verbs, debit and credit respectively mean to make an entry in the left-hand or right-hand side of an account. The words, debit and credit, have no other meaning in accounting.

Ledger: a group of accounts. In manual systems, the ledger may consist of a set of pages in a binder, one page for each account.

Chart of accounts: a list of the names and numbers of an entity's accounts, organized in some systematic way.

Journal: a chronological record of accounting transactions that shows (a) the names of accounts to be debited or credited, (b) the amounts of the debits and credits, and (c) any other useful supplementary information about the transaction.

Posting: the process of recording transactions in the accounts in the ledger; these transactions are copied from the journal.

Trial balance: a list of accounts and their balances as of a given moment in time, with debit balances shown in one column and credit balances shown in another column. The equality of these two columns is a necessary, but not sufficient, condition for the preparation of arithmetically correct financial statements.

Adjusting entries: accounting entries made at the end of an accounting period which are not evidenced by "obvious" documents. Examples include interest accruals, depreciation, bad debt expense, and amortization of intangible assets.

Contra account: an account that is subtracted from some other account. Examples are Accumulated Depreciation and Allowance for Doubtful Accounts.

Temporary accounts: revenue and expense accounts; balance sheet accounts are called "permanent" or "real" accounts.

Closing entries: entries that transfer balances in temporary accounts to owners' equity (Retained Earnings). As an intermediate step, the revenue and expense accounts are first closed to "clearing" accounts (e.g., Cost of Goods Sold), which, in turn, are closed to an Income Summary account, which then is closed to Retained Earnings.

Chapter 5. REVENUE AND MONETARY ASSETS

Delivery method: revenue is recognized in the period in which goods are delivered or services are provided.

Percentage-of-completion method: the accounting method for long-term contracts in which a portion of the contract revenue is recognized in each accounting period of the contract. In many instances, the cumulative portion recognized is the ratio of cumulative costs to date over total estimated costs at completion.

Completed-contract method: the accounting method for long-term contracts in which no contract revenue is recognized until the period in which the contract work is completed.

Installment method: the accounting method which recognizes revenue on credit sales only when the cash installment payments are received.

Bad debt expense: the amount of accounts receivable that is believed to be uncollectible. The write-down of receivables to reflect anticipated bad debts is an adjusting entry.

Aging schedule: a table which shows the amounts of accounts receivable that have been outstanding for various lengths of time (see Illustration 5-4 in the text). Such a schedule is used, in part, to estimate bad debt losses.

Warranty costs: the costs of fulfilling an obligation (legal or voluntary) to repair or replace merchandise. These costs are future costs, whose amount is estimated and expensed in the period in which the merchandise is sold.

Unexpired cost: the amount at which a nonmonetary asset appears on the balance sheet. (Inventory is an exception.) For an item of plant or equipment, the unexpired cost is the original cost minus accumulated depreciation to date.

Realizable value: the amount at which a monetary asset appears on the balance sheet, reflecting the amount of money into which the asset can be converted with reasonable certainty.

Certificate of deposit: a document evidencing the fact that a company has loaned money to a commercial bank.

Marketable securities: monetary assets consisting of commercial paper, Treasury bills, bonds of other entities, and equity securities which are held for the sole purpose of earning dividends and/or capital gains. Marketable equity securities are divided into curent and noncurrent portfolios, with each portfolio reported at the lower of cost or market value on the balance sheet.

Investment: stocks in other companies held for the purpose of exercising some control over those companies; or untraded securities.

Current ratio: the ratio of current assets to current liabilities; a measure of liquidity.

Acid-test ratio: the ratio of monetary current assets to current liabilities; a shorter-term liquidity measurement than is the current ratio.

Days' cash: cash costs per day divided into the Cash balance. This ratio gives a rough approximation of how many days' operating expenses could be paid with the cash on hand.

Days' receivables: sales per day divided into the balance in Accounts Receivable; also called "collection period."

Chapter 6. COST OF SALES AND INVENTORIES

Gross margin: revenues less cost of goods sold (or cost of sales).

Periodic inventory method: the method of determining inventory by taking a physical count. Cost of goods sold is determined by subtracting ending inventory from goods available for sale (beginning inventory plus purchases).

Perpetual inventory method: the method of measuring inventory by maintaining a record of purchases and shipments. Cost of goods sold is the offsetting entry to shipments. A physical inventory is still taken at the end of the period, but for the purpose of verifying the perpetual inventory record and identifying the amount of shrinkage, rather than for the purpose of deducing cost of goods sold.

Retail method: the method by which retail stores find the approximate cost of goods sold for a period. The method involves multiplying the period's sales revenues by (100 percent - gross margin percentage), i.e., the complement of the gross margin percentage.

Inventory shrinkage: inventory losses due to pilferage or shoplifting, or "apparent" losses due to accounting mistakes. In the periodic method, shrinkage is "hidden" in the deduced cost of goods sold figure. In the perpetual method, shrinkage is the difference between the inventory balance indicated by the perpetual inventory records and the balance indicated by a physical count.

Cost accounting system: the perpetual inventory method in a manufacturing company. In a cost accounting system, the cost of each product is accumulated as it flows through the production process, and the amounts involved in the inventory journal entries are obtained directly from cost records rather than being deduced.

Product costs: the items of cost that are included in the cost of producing a product. Unless market value is lower, manufactured goods inventories are valued using these product costs.

Period costs: items of cost that are charged directly to the income statement as expenses, rather than "flowing through" inventory as product costs.

Production overhead: the costs of producing a product other than raw materials costs and direct labor costs. These are product costs, not period costs.

Full cost of a product: the sum of a product's materials, labor, and production overhead costs.

Specific identification: the inventory costing method in which a record is kept of the cost of each specific item in inventory. This method is commonly used by retailers of "big-ticket" items such as cars and expensive jewelry.

Average cost: the inventory costing method with which the average cost of physically identical goods in inventory is computed, and this average figure is used for determining ending inventory and cost of goods sold. If the perpetual inventory method is used, a new average cost is computed after each purchase.

First-in, first-out (FIFO): the inventory costing method in which it is assumed that the oldest goods in inventory are the first ones to leave inventory; hence the ending inventory is assumed to consist of the most recently acquired goods.

Last-in, first-out (LIFO): the inventory method in which it is assumed that the goods leaving inventory are the ones which most recently entered; hence ending inventory is costed at the cost of the oldest units available. (Note: Both LIFO and FIFO are accounting assumptions that may not coincide with the actual physical flow of goods through inventory.)

Net realizable value: the estimated selling price of an item in inventory less the costs that will be incurred in selling it.

Inventory turnover: the cost of goods sold for a period divided by the period's ending inventory (or, alternatively, the period's average inventory). This ratio indicates the velocity with which products move through a business.

Days' inventory: cost of goods sold per day divided into the balance in Inventory. This ratio shows roughly how many days' sales could be made from the inventory on hand.

Chapter 7. LONG-LIVED ASSETS AND THEIR AMORTIZATION

Long-lived tangible assets: an asset that has physical substance, and which is expected to provide service for more than one year. Also called "fixed asset" or an item of "property, plant and equipment."

Capitalized expenditure: an expenditure that is recorded as a long-lived asset, rather than as an expense.

Amortization: the general name given the process of matching the cost of a long-lived asset with the revenues that are generated as a result of the use of this asset. The term is also used specifically with respect to this process as applied to intangible long-lived assets, which are ordinarily amortized using the straight-line method.

Intangible asset: a long-lived asset without physical substance, such as goodwill, trademarks, and patents.

Depreciation: the specific term used to describe the amortization of plant and equipment assets. Depreciation is a process of cost allocation, and is not related to a diminution of market value (the nonaccounting meaning of the term).

Depletion: the specific term used to describe the amortization of natural resources or "wasting assets," such as coal, oil, other minerals, gas, and timber. The units-of-production method ordinarily is used.

Betterment: work performed on an item of plant or equipment that makes it better than when it was purchased or which extends its useful life (distinguished from maintenance).

Capital lease: a lease that gives the lessee essentially all of the rights of ownership of the leased asset; also called a "financial lease."

Service life: the number of accounting periods (usually years) over which a depreciable asset will be useful to the entity.

Residual value: the amount of a depreciable asset's cost that is expected to be recovered at the end of the asset's service life. This recovery may come through sale, trade-in, or salvage.

Straight-line method: the depreciation method that charges an equal amount of depreciation expense in each accounting period of an asset's useful life. If an asset has life of n accounting periods, then each period's depreciation expense is 1/n. This method is frequently found in financial accounting.

Declining-balance method: a depreciation method that applies a percentage of the straight-line rate to the beginning-of-the-year net book value of an asset to arrive at the year's depreciation expense. This is an "accelerated" method, and is the basis of ACRS allowances (see below).

Sum-of-years'-digits method: an accelerated depreciation method, with which each year's depreciation expense is arrived at by multiplying the asset's cost times a fraction whose denominator is the sum of the numbers 1, 2, 3, ..., n, where n is the estimated years of useful life. If this sum is called S, the first year's depreciation is n/S, the second year's is $(n-1)/S$, and so on. Note: The formula for finding S is $S = (1/2)(n)(n-1)$ for any integer n.

Units-of-production method: a depreciation method that charges as a period's depreciation expense u/U of the asset's cost, where U is the total number of "service units" the asset will provide during its service life, and u is the number of these units provided during the accounting period.

Net book value: an asset's original cost minus the sum of its depreciation charges to date. (This sum is called accumulated depreciation.)

ACRS: the accelerated cost recovery system, created under the 1981 Tax Act, places an asset into one of four recovery period classes for the purpose of determining the allowable cost recovery (depreciation) deduction for income tax calculations. Realistic services lives and residual values are ignored under ACRS rules.

Deferral and flow-through methods: the two methods used in financial accounting for the investment tax credit. The deferral method spreads the effect of the tax credit over the useful life of the asset giving rise to the credit. The flow-through method treats the credit as a reduction in income tax expense in the year in which the asset is purchased.

Chapter 8. LIABILITIES AND INTEREST EXPENSE

Contingency: an occurrence that might arise in the future, such as settlement of a pending lawsuit. Under some circumstances (described in the text), contingencies give rise to liabilities.

Term loan: a business loan with a maturity of more than one year, repayable according to a specified schedule, typically in periodic installments.

Bond: a certificate promising to pay its holder a specified sum (usually a multiple of $1,000), plus interest at a stated rate.

Mortgage bond: a bond that is secured by designated "pledged" assets of the issuing corporation, usually property, plant, and equipment assets.

Debenture: a bond that is not secured by specific assets of the issuing corporation.

Sinking fund bond: a bond for which a company regularly deposits money in a sinking fund. The fund is used to redeem the bonds, either gradually over their life or at maturity, depending on the conditions set forth in the bond.

Callable bond: a bond that the issuing corporation may, at its option, redeem before the maturity date.

Convertible bond: a bond that may be converted at the option of its holder into a specified number of shares of the issuer's common stock.

Bond par value: the sum that must be paid the bondholder when the bond is redeemed or "matures." Also called the principal or face value, it is usually a multiple of $1,000.

Coupon rate: the rate of interest on a bond's par value that a bondholder is periodically paid; also called the nominal rate or simply the bond's interest rate.

Bond discount and premium: the amount by which a bond's issuing price is less than (discount) or greater than (premium) the bond's par value. Bonds issued at a discount yield more than the coupon rate to an investor, whereas bonds issued at a premium yield less than the coupon rate.

Refund a bond issue: to call a bond issue (i.e., redeem it before maturity) and to float a new issue at a lower rate of interest to replace the funds used in the early redemption.

Debt/equity and debt/capitalization ratios: these ratios measure the degree of financial leverage in a company's capital structure. Debt/equity is calculated by dividing shareholders' equity into either total liabilities or just long-term liabilities. Debt/capitalization is a fraction whose numerator is long-term liabilities (plus perhaps the current portion of long-term debt), and whose denominator is the sum of the numerator plus shareholders' equity. (This sum of debt and equity is often called "invested capital.")

Times interest earned: the ratio of pretax income before interest expense to interest expense. This is a rough measure of "how many times over" a company can pay its interest obligations from cash generated by operations -- "rough" because pretax income is not equivalent to cash generated by operations.

Compound interest: interest is computed on the original principal plus all accumulated interest previously added to the principal. The future value equation is the formula for determining the total amount of compound interest plus principal at a future point in time.

Discounting: the process in which interest compounding is reversed to arrive at a present value given the future value.

Present value: the present value of an amount that is expected to be received at a specified time in the future is the amount which, if invested today at a designated rate of return, would cumulate to the specified amount.

Debt amortization: a process which correctly divides a level series of debt repayments into principal reduction and interest expense amounts. The compound interest method amounts are calculated such that interest expense is always a constant percentage of the principal outstanding for the given period.

Current yield: the annual interest payment on a bond divided by the bond's current price.

Yield to maturity: the discount rate which will make the present value of the series of future bond interest payments plus the present value of the bond's redemption proceeds equal the current market price of the bond. This rate is also known as the bond's effective rate of interest.

Chapter 9. OTHER EXPENSES, NET INCOME, AND OWNERS' EQUITY

Personnel costs: wages and slaries earned by employees and other costs related to the services furnished by employees -- social security taxes, employee insurance costs, and other "fringe benefits."

Normal cost: an entity's pension plan costs for the year. The amount involves complicated calculations; the idea is to contribute enough to the pension fund each year so as ultimately to be able to pay the future benefits that eligible employees have earned in that year.

Past service cost: pension plan costs associated with "sweetening" an existing pension plan's benefits, or with starting a new plan that in effect is made retroactive to prior years' service by eligible employees. Past service cost is not expensed or funded immediately, but is spread over 10-40 years.

Unfunded cost: the amount of past service cost that has not yet been contributed to the pension fund.

Permanent tax difference: a tax difference related to the difference between reported pretax income (a financial reporting item) and taxable income (on the tax return) that arises because tax regulations permit certain deductions (or omission of certain revenues) that will never be counted as expenses (or will be shown as revenues) for financial reporting purposes. Stated another way, permanent differences are those that will not (because they cannot) "reverse" in the future. Permanent differences are not reflected in the deferred taxes account.

Timing tax difference: a difference between reported tax expense and taxes paid that arises because revenues or expenses are reported in different periods for tax reporting than they are for financial reporting. Timing differences do "reverse" in later periods. (Note: A gradual increase in the Deferred Taxes balance does not mean differences are not reversing; rather it means the new deferrals exceed the reversals of earlier deferrals.)

Deferred income taxes: the amount of tax expense reported in financial accounting reports that has not yet been reported as income taxes in tax reports. This account appears as a liability, but is not an obligation in the same sense as are most other liabilities. It is to be distinguished from taxes payable, which definitely are a financial obligation to the government.

Extraordinary item: a transaction affecting revenues and/or expenses which is unusual (essentially unrelated to the ordinary activities of the business) and occurs infrequently (is not expected to recur in the foreseeable future). Extraordinary items are reported below the "income from continuing operations" line on the income statement.

Discontinued operations: operations of a company that have been abandoned or sold, or where such abandonment or sale is anticipated. Only identifiable segments of a company qualify for accounting treatment as discontinued operations (as distinguished from disposal of an individual asset or dropping one product in a product line).

Prior period adjustment: a transaction involving a direct adjustment to Retained Earnings and related to events that occurred in earlier years. Such adjustments are severely limited by the FASB.

Single proprietorship: an unincorporated business entity solely owned by an individual.

Partnership: an unincorporated business entity owned by two or mroe persons, called the partners.

Corporation: a legal entity that is chartered to operate by a state. Distinguished from a partnership or proprietorship primarily because of its essentially perpetual existence, its taxation as an entity, and its legal liability as an entity (as opposed to liability of its owners as individuals).

Stock certificate: a document evidencing ownership in a corporation. The number of shares of ownership is shown on the certificate.

Preferred stock: a stock that pays a stated dividend. This dividend has priority over the payment of common stock dividends; preferred stockholders also have priority over common shareholders in the event of the company's liquidation.

Book value of common stock: assets minus liabilities minus preferred stock, divided by the number of outstanding shares of common stock; equivalently, common stock (par plus paid-in capital) plus retained earnings, divided by the number of common shares outstanding.

Contributed capital: the amount of funds invested in a firm by its shareholders; equal to the sum of the par value of outstanding shares plus paid-in capital.

Paid-in capital: the excess of the issue price of stock over its par value; preferably called "capital contributed in excess of par value of shares."

Treasury stock: shares of stock of a corporation that have been issued and subsequently reacquired by the corporation by purchasing them.

Reserve: An appropriation (segregated portion) of Retained Earnings; hence an owners' equity account. Because such reserves reduce the amount of retained earnings, it is felt that they reduce shareholder pressure to pay larger dividends.

Stock options and warrants: rights to purchase shares of common stock at a stated price within a given time period. In general usage, warrants are negotiable (can be transferred to others) whereas options are not.

Earnings per share: a ratio computed by dividing net income minus preferred dividends (if any) by the number of outstanding common shares.

Chapter 10. FUNDS FLOW STATEMENTS

Statement of changes in financial position: the formal name for the financial statement that explains the flows that increase or decrease the various balance sheet accounts in a given period. Such a statement informally may be called "funds flow statement," "sources and applications of funds," or "cash flow statement." (Abbreviated below as "SCFP.")

Funds flow statement: strictly speaking, an informal synonym for any SCFP; but in practice, the name often given an SCFP that uses working capital as the definition of funds.

Sources of funds: the points of origin of funds. Cash and working capital can originate from operations, additional long-term debt, new equity issues, or the sale of fixed assets. Increases in current liabilities, such as accounts payable, are sources of cash, but not of working capital.

Uses of funds: the investments or financial payments made with funds. Primary uses are investments in fixed assets, repayment of long-term debt, and dividends. Payment of short-term debt is a use of cash, but is not a use of working capital.

Funds generated by operations: the net amount of funds inflow that has resulted from the company's production and sales of goods and services during the period.

Net current monetary assets: current monetary assets minus short-term monetary liabilities. The concept of funds is less liquid than the cash concept, and yet avoids treating inventory as a monetary asset.

Working capital: current assets minus current liabilities. Woking capital is used as a broader definition of funds than cash in preparing a statement of changes in financial position. Most corporations' SCFPs define funds as working capital.

Permanent capital: a term used to describe the sum of long-term liabilities and owners' equity; also called "invested capital."

Receipts and disbursements: respectively, inflows and outflows of cash.

Cash flow statement: an SCFP in which funds are defined to be cash. Unlike a statement of receipts and disbursements, a cash flow statement highlights the amount of cash generated by operations, and employs the all financial resources principle (see below).

Working capital flow statement: an SCFP in which funds are defined to be working capital. The working capital flow statement describes the flow of permanent capital, while disregarding the details of the continuous movement of resources between current liabilities and current assets that results from operations.

All financial resources principle: a concept used in preparation of a statement of changes in financial position to insure that all major financing and investing activities are shown in the SCFP, whether or not they impact directly on cash or working capital. Two examples are the acquisition of long-lived assets in exchange for long-term debt, and conversion of preferred stock to common stock.

Depreciation: the accounting process of allocating the cost of a fixed asset over its estimated useful life in order to match this cost with the periods of benefit. No cash actually flows at the time depreciation expense is recorded. Depreciation is neither a source nor a use of either cash or funds.

Cash flow earnings: the name given an estimate of the period's cash generated by operations that is calculated by adding the period's net income and depreciation expense.

Chapter 11. ACQUISITIONS AND CONSOLIDATED STATEMENTS

Cost method: the method of acounting for an investment in another company used when the investor holds less than 20 percent of the investee's outstanding stock, or does not have effective control of the investee. The investment is recorded at cost and dividends are treated as other revenue. Profits and losses of the investee are not reflected in the investor's books.

Equity method: the method of accounting for an investment in another company used when the investor holds more than 20 percent of the investee's outstanding stock. The investor's share of the investee's income (or losses) is added (or deducted) from the original cost of the investment as recorded on the investor's books. Dividends received from the investee are treated as reductions of the investment. The 20 percent rule was established by APB Opinion No. 18 (March 1971); 20 percent is the arbitrary point set at which the investor is presumed to have a controlling interest in the investee.

Parent and subsidiary: if Company A acquires Company B, Copmpany A becomes the parent of B, and Company B is the subsidiary of A. (The terms are used even if the parent does not wholly own the subsidiary, so long as the parent has a majority interest in the subsidiary.)

Horizontal combination: a business combination in which the combining firms are in the same line of business.

Vertical combination: a combination in which the combining firms are involved in different stages of the production and marketing of the same end-use product.

Conglomerate combination: a combination in which the combining firms are in unrelated lines of business.

Pooling of interests: the method of accounting for a business combination subject to various criteria set forth in APB Opinion No. 16. The pooling is treated as a "marriage" of the two entities, with all assets, liabilities, and owners' equities added together at book value (eliminating any intercompany transactions).

Purchase accounting: the method of accounting used for a business combination unless the criteria for "pooling of interests" are met. Tangible assets and liabilities of the acquired company are recorded by the parent at current values; "goodwill" may arise from the acquisition (see below).

Goodwill: the excess of the purchase price of an acquired company over the total market or appraised value of its tangible net assets. Goodwill is recorded as an asset, and arises only when accounting for an acquisition using the purchase accounting method. Goodwill must be amortized over a period not to exceed 40 years, using the straight-line method.

Consolidated financial statements: the combined financial statements of a family of corporations that are one economic entity, even though they are legally separate entities. Consolidated statements are prepared when they will be more useful to users than would be the individual statements of each separate corporation in the family.

Minority interest: when a parent owns less than 100 percent of a subsidiary, the ownership represented by the fraction of stock not held by the parent corporation is the minority interest; i.e., the equity of the subsidiary's other owners. On the consolidated balance sheet this minority interest appears as a separate equity item.

Chapter 12. ACCOUNTING AND CHANGING PRICES

Purchasing power: the value of a dollar at any given point in time. During a period of time, this value may increse or erode due to changing economic conditions (e.g., inflation).

Consumer Price Index: an index that tracks the price of typical consumer goods and services. The base year of the CPI is 1967.

GNP Deflator: an index which trades the price of all goods and services found in the U.S. economy, i.e., the Gross National Product. This index is the most general in nature because it is all-inclusive.

Specific prices: the price of only one narrowly defined good or service. Specific price indexes are less homogeneous than broad market-basket price indexes.

Constant dollar accounting: historical cost amounts reported in terms of units of general purchasing power. Conventional financial statements are restated from their units of money basis into "units of general purchasing power" using the CPI or GNP Deflator.

Holding gain or loss: the purchasing power gain that occurs when a company holds net monetary liabilities, or the purchasing power loss that occurs when a company holds net monetary assets, during a period of inflation. FASB-33 requires disclosure of this amount.

Current cost accounting: current cost data is used as the basis for the financial statements instead of historical costs. This method of accounting does not involve a restatement of the financial statements based upon general price indexes, but rather is based on specific prices.

Replacement cost: the cost of currently replacing an asset with one similar in kind or in its productive capacity.

Inflation-adjusted current cost: nominal current costs adjusted to units of purchasing power as of some point in time; also called a current cost/constant dollar amount.

Transaction gain or loss: exchange rate fluctuations between the date a transaction was entered into and the date cash is transmitted cause transaction gains or losses. The transaction gain or loss occurs because the transaction is denominated in a currency other than the dollar.

Translation gain or loss: a gain or loss that results from the translation of all the assets and liabilities of a foreign subsidiary at the balance sheet date's exchange rate. Such translation gains or losses do not flow through its income statement (per FASB-52).

Chapter 13. FINANCIAL STATEMENT ANALYSIS

Return on assets: return on investment (ROI) -- net income divided by investment -- with investment thought of as being total assets. This concept of ROI is usually the most meaningful one for an operating manager.

Return on owners' equity: ROI, with owners' equity used as the investment definition. This ROI concept is the most meaningful one for shareholders.

Return on invested capital: ROI, with the sum of long-term debt and owners' equity used as the concept of investment. This version of ROI is useful to a corporation's financial officers, and to division managers who control their division's assets and current liabilities.

Return on tangible investment: any of the three preceding ROI concepts, but with investment adjusted so as to eliminate intangible assets such as Goodwill.

Price/earnings ratio: price per share divided by earnings per share. This ratio is an indicator of investors' evaluations of a firm and its prospects.

Profit margin: net income as a percent of sales. This margin represents the average earnings per each dollar of sales. This ratio is also called "net income percentage" or "return on sales." It is a commonly used measure of overall profitability.

Investment turnover: sales divided by investment. (Investment can be defined any of the three ways noted above.) This ratio gives an indication of how effectively the investment is utilized in terms of sales volume. It is also a measure of how investment-intensive a company is; i.e., how many dollars of investment are required to "support" or "generate" a dollar of sales.

Capital intensity: sales revenues divided by property, plant, and equipment. This is really another investment turnover ratio, focusing only on the investment in fixed assets.

Working capital turnover: sales revenues divided by working capital. This ratio focuses on still another aspect of investment -- the amount of current assets not financed by current liabilities, and therefore financed by invested capital. The ratio is broader than inventory turnover, but narrower than investment turnover (as defined above).

Cash conversion cycle: the length of time for cash to complete the operating cycle; equal to days' receivables plus days' inventory minus days' payables.

Liquidity: a company's ability to meet its current obligations. This can be estimated by comparing current liabilities and current assets, the latter of which presumably will be converted into cash in order to pay the current liabilities.

Solvency: the ability of a company to meet the interest costs and repayment schedules associated with its long-term obligations.

Dividend yield: dividends per share for the year divided by market price per share. Strictly speaking, this is not a measure of financial condition, although it is used by many investors to appraise financial condition.

Dividend payout: dividends divided by net income. This ratio gives an indication of the extent to which a firm is reinvesting its earnings in new assets as opposed to distributing earnings to shareholders in the form of dividends.

Chapter 14. UNDERSTANDING FINANCIAL STATEMENTS

Auditors: independent, outside public accountants who examine financial statements and the records from which these statements were produced. An auditor is usually a certified public accountant (CPA) with a license to practice in a given state.

Scope paragraph: the first paragraph of the auditors' letter ("opinion") which describes the results of their examination of the company's financial statements. The auditors state in this paragraph that generally accepted auditing standards were used, and that such tests as the auditors considered necessary in their professional judgment were used.

Opinion paragraph: the second paragraph of the auditors' letter, in which the auditors state whether in their opinion the statements are (1) fairly presented; (2) in conformity with generally accepted accounting principles; and (3) that the GAAP are applied on a consistent basis.

"Clean" opinion: an auditors' opinion on a company's financial statements in which the auditors were not restricted in performing the tests they thought necessary and in which they found the financial statements to be fairly presented and in conformity with GAAP applied on a consistent basis.

Qualified opinion: an auditors' opinion on a company's financial statements in which the auditors state a consistency exception or a major contingency that precludes their giving a "clean" opinion.

Full disclosure: a fundamental accounting principle that requires that the financial statements and accompanying notes contain all material financial information about a company up to and beyond the balance sheet date. The general rule is that any financial information that would cause an informed investor to appraise the company differently than he or she would appraise it without that item of information should be disclosed.

Form 10-K: the annual report that companies under the jurisdiction of the Securities and Exchange Commission must file with the SEC. It contains more detailed data than the company's annual report does, and does not contain the "public relations" material that is in the shareholders' annual report (e.g., color photographs of the company's products and top officers).

Basic Concepts (Review): All eleven basic concepts are defined above under the headings for Chapters 2 and 3.

Chapter 15. BASIC MANAGEMENT ACCOUNTING CONCEPTS

Management accounting: the process within an organization that provides accounting information used by managers in planning, coordinating, and controlling the organization's activities. The information provided these managers is generally based on summaries of operating information (see below).

Information: a fact, datum, observation, perception, or any other thing that adds to knowledge.

Operating information: the stream of data from daily operations that serves as raw data for both financial and management accounting. The principal sources are production, purchasing, payroll, plant and equipment, sales and accounts receivable, and finance records.

Full cost accounting: the "full cost" of producing goods is the sum of the direct costs of these goods plus a fair share of the indirect costs that are incurred for the production of these and other goods. Full cost accounting measures these full costs, not only for goods, but also for services or other activities.

Differential accounting: this accounting construction estimates how costs, revenues, and/or assets would be different if one course of action were adopted as compared with an alternative course of action. Differential costs are always estimates of future costs.

Responsibility center: a specific unit (generically, "department") of an organization, headed by a manager who is responsible for the unit's activities.

Responsibility accounting: the tracing of costs, revenues, and/or assets to individual responsibility centers.

Chapter 16. THE BEHAVIOR OF COSTS

Variable costs: items of cost that vary directly and proportionately with volume.

Fixed (nonvariable) costs: costs that do not vary with volume. Fixed costs may change, of course, due to the passage of time, or as a result of management decisions to change them. The point is that they do not change "automatically" with volume changes, as do variable costs.

Semivariable costs: costs that vary in the same direction as, but less than proportionately with, changes in volume. A semivariable cost can be decomposed into its fixed and variable components.

Cost-volume diagram: a graph showing the relationship between costs (vertical axis) and volume (horizontal axis). The cost axis usually represents total costs, although it can represent costs per unit (as in Illustration 16-3).

Linear assumption: the assumption in a cost-volume diagram that variable, fixed, and semivariable costs bear a linear (i.e., straight-line) relationship to volume. This is a different assumption than one finds in economic texts; but it provides an adequate approximation of costs within the relevant range (see below).

Relevant range: the range of volume for which a straight-line segment gives a good approximation of the behavior of costs on a cost-volume diagram.

High-low method: the method of estimating a cost-volume relationship that involves estimating total costs at each of two volumes, and then drawing (or algebraically describing) the straight-line determined by these two points.

Linear regression: a mathematical procedure that finds the equation of the straight-line that gives the "best-fit" to a series of cost-volume data points; also called "the method of least squares."

Profitgraph: a diagram showing the expected relationship between total cost and revenue at various volumes; also called a "break-even chart." Illustrations 16-9 and 16-10 show two different formats for a profitgraph.

Break-even volume: the volume at which total revenues equal total costs, and thus profit equals zero.

Unit contribution margin: the difference between selling price and variable cost per unit. This amount is constant at all volumes within the relevant range.

Margin of safety: the amount or ratio by which the current volume exceeds the break-even volume.

Learning curve: a curve that reflects the decrease in unit cost of an item associated with productivity increases gained from cumulative experience in producing the item. Also called the "experience curve."

Chapter 17. FULL COSTS AND THEIR USES

Cost: generically, cost is a measurement, in monetary terms, of the amount of resources used for some purpose. The key points are: it is a measurement of re-sources used; it is expresed in the common denominator of monetary terms; and the cost measurement always relates to a stated purpose.

Cost objective: the technical name for the purpose for which costs are measured.

Direct costs: items of costs that are specifically traceable to, or are directly caused by, a cost objective. (Note that it is not meaningful to say a cost is "direct" without indicating with respect to what cost objective it is direct.)

Indirect costs: elements of costs that are associated with or caused by two or more cost objectives jointly, but that are not directly traceable to each of them individually.

Full cost: all the resources used for a cost objective. It is the sum of the cost objective's direct costs plus a fair share of its indirect costs.

CASB: the Cost Accounting Standards Board, created by the Congress in 1971 to set standards for measuring full costs on defense contracts. (These standards have also been adopted by many other government agencies.

Prime cost: the sum of a product's direct material cost and direct labor cost.

Overhead cost: the commonly used term for "indirect production cost," which ordi-narily includes all items of production cost other than prime cost.

Inventory cost: the sum of prime cost and overhead cost; also called "full produc-tion cost."

Selling cost: the cost of obtaining orders (marketing or order-getting costs) and of storing a product and transferring it to the customer (logistics or order-filling costs).

General and administrative cost: a "catch-all" category to cover costs other than prime, overhead, and distribution costs.

Normal pricing: setting selling prices at a level that is high enough: (1) to recover direct costs; (2) to recover a fair share of all applicable indirect costs; and (3) to yield a satisfactory profit.

Time and material pricing: setting prices using two rates. One pricing rate is established for direct labor and a separate rate for direct material. Each rate is constructed to include allowances for indirect costs and profit.

Billing rate: the name used in professional service firms for the time component in time and material pricing.

Contribution pricing: setting selling prices at a level below full costs.

Chapter 18. ADDITIONAL ASPECTS OF PRODUCT COSTING SYSTEMS

Job-order costing: collecting costs for each physically identifiable job or batch of work as it moves through the production process, regardless of the accounting period in which the work was done.

Process costing: collecting costs for all the products worked on during an accounting period, and determining unit costs by dividing the total costs by the total number of units worked on.

Equivalent production: the number of completed units to which the fully completed and partially completed units are equivalent. This common base is needed in calculating average unit costs in a process cost system.

Allocation: the process of assigning indirect costs to individual cost objectives.

Cost center: a cost objective for which costs of one or more related functions or activities are accumulated. In a cost accounting system, items of cost are first accumulated in cost centers, and then they are assigned to products; thus a cost center is often called an intermediate cost objective, and a product, a final cost objective.

Production cost center: a cost center that produces a product or a component of a product.

Service cost center: a cost center that provides services to production cost centers and to other service cost centers, or which performs work for the benefit of the organization as a whole.

Allocation basis: the basis on which indirect costs are allocated to cost objectives. Such bases may be payroll related, personnel related, material related, space related, or activity (volume) related.

Step-down order: the order in which service center costs are redistributed among other service centers. Generally, the least significant service centers are allocated first.

Overhead rate: the device used to allocate indirect costs to cost objectives. (To be consistent, this should be called indirect cost rate, but overhead rate is more often used for historical reasons. It is also sometimes called the burden rate.) The rate is determined for a production cost center by dividing the indirect costs assigned to the center by the center's level of activity (volume).

Flexible overhead budget: an overhead budget (actually, a series of budgets) that is prepared for a cost center based upon various volume levels. Total overhead costs will be different at each volume level because some cost elements are variable or semivariable.

Standard volume: the volume used as the denominator when calculating predetermined overhead rates. This standard or "normal" volume may be the volume expected during the period or the average volume expected over the next several years.

Underabsorbed or overabsorbed overhead: the difference between the actual amount of indirect costs incurred during the period and the amount of indirect costs allocated to products during the period. This difference arises when overhead rates are developed from estimates of costs and volume, rather than being developed after the fact from actual costs and volumes.

Chapter 19. STANDARD COSTS, JOINT COSTS, AND VARIABLE COSTING SYSTEMS

Standard cost system: a cost accounting system that is based on what amount of cost should have been incurred in the production of a product (as opposed to the cost that actually was incurred). Note: In practice, the term "standard cost" tends to be applied when referring to per-unit costs, and the term "budget" is used when talking about aggregate costs. Both "standard" and "budget" connote what costs should be, assuming a particular set of conditions.

Variance account: a repository for the differences, if any, between actual and standard costs.

Joint products: two or more dissimilar end products that are produced from a single batch of raw material or from a single production process.

By-products: a special type of joint product; one product is desired (the main product) but it is necessary to produce a certain amount of another product (the by-product) to obtain the main product.

Split-off point: the point after which separate end products are identifiable in a joint product production process.

Absorption costing: the use of a cost accounting system that assigns all production costs to the goods or services produced, regardless of whether these costs are fixed or variable with respect to production volume.

Variable costing: the use of a cost accounting system that charges only variable production costs to products, and which treats fixed production costs as expenses of the period in which they were incurred. Also commonly -- but conceptually incorrectly -- called "direct costing."

Chapter 20. PRODUCTION COST VARIANCES

Material usage variance: the difference between total standard quantity and total actual quantity of material, with each quantity priced at the standard price per unit of material. Both total quantities are based on the actual production volume.

Material price variance: the difference between the standard price per unit of material and the actual price per unit of material, multiplied by the actual quantity of material used.

Labor efficiency variance: completely analogous to material usage variance, above -- substitute "time" for "quantity," and "rate" for "price."

Labor rate variance: completely analogous to material price variance.

Joint variance: a variance that occurs when two variances (e.g., price and usage, or rate and efficiency) are both favorable or both unfavorable. Although the joint variance is in fact caused by both factors being off-standard, in practice the joint variance is arbitrarily assigned to one of the two components. For example, the rules in the text assign joint material variance as part of the price variance.

Budgeted overhead cost: the amount of overhead cost that was expected or planned to be incurred at a given volume. Budgeted overhead is a semivariable cost, except in rare instances.

Absorbed overhead cost: the amount of overhead cost assigned to (or "absorbed by") products. This amount is the overhead rate multiplied by the period's actual production volume.

Variable budget: an overhead budget showing the planned amounts of overhead at various possible production volumes -- often depicted in cost-volume diagram format. (Also called a flexible budget.)

Overhead production volume variance: the difference between absorbed overhead costs and budgeted overhead costs at the actual production volume. This variance occurs only when actual volume differs from the standard volume used in setting the overhead rate; only at the standard volume will fixed costs be properly "spread across" (actually, "absorbed by") the units produced. It is important to understand that if there were no fixed production costs to be allocated to products, there would be no volume variance.

Overhead spending variance: the difference between budgeted and actual overhead costs, measured at the actual volume. This variance is an indicator of cost control performance, after adjusting for the fact that the overhead cost budget changes if actual volume differs from planned volume.

Favorable variance: a variance that occurred because actual cost was lower than standard cost. This does not necessarily mean, however, that performance was "good."

Unfavorable variance: a variance that occurred because actual cost was greater than standard cost. It does not necessarily connote "poor" performance.

Chapter 21. DIFERENTIAL ACCOUNTING: SHORT-RUN DECISIONS

Differential costs: costs that are different under one set of conditions than they would be under another set of conditions. They always relate to a specific situation.

Differential revenues: revenues that are different under one set of conditions than they would be under another set.

Contribution margin: the name given the difference between total revenues and total variable costs for a company, product line, division, or any other cost objective. (As noted above, "unit contribution" is the term generally used when the cost objective is a unit of product.)

Alternative choice problem: a problem in which a manager chooses, from two or more alternative courses of action, the action that he or she believes to be best. "Best" refers to the alternative which is most likely to help accomplish the organization's objectives, including achieving a satisfactory ROI.

Base case: the alternative course of action which is to continue what is now being done (the "status quo"). It is the benchmark against which other alternatives are measured.

Opportunity cost: the value of the opportunity that is sacrificed when the choice of one course of action requires that an alternative course of action be given up. The student should recognize that the opportunity cost concept applies only if some resource is constrained (floor space, in the text's example.)

Sunk cost: a cost incurred because of past actions. If no decision made today can change the cost effect, it is not a differential cost.

Make-or-buy problem: an alternative choice problem in which the alternative is to pay an outside party to perform a function (e.g., making a certain component) presently performed by the organization's own employees.

Differential income: the difference between differential revenue and differential cost for an alternative course of action; also called "differential profit."

Contribution pricing: the practice of setting prices to recover more than differential costs, but less than full costs; distinguished from normal pricing (Chapter 17) where the price is set to recover full costs and a profit.

Economic order quantity: the number of a particular item to order (from the factory or from an outside supplier) at one time to ensure minimum total costs. This number reflects the offsetting influences of inventory carrying costs and ordering or setup costs.

Expected value: the sum of the products of the possible outcomes of an event times the probability of each outcome's occurring; i.e., value(1) x probability(1) + value(2) x probability(2) + ... This is the weighted average of the possible outcomes, with the outcomes' probabilities used as the weights.

Sensitivity analysis: techniques for identifying which factors have the greatest influence on the outcome of a calculation of differential costs or differential income.

Decision tree: a diagram that shows the several decisions or acts and the possible consequences of each act; these consequences are called events. Probabilities, revenues, and/or costs may be included in more elaborate versions of decision trees.

Linear programming: a method of determining the mix of activities which maximizes income or minimizes costs, while being limited by a set of resource constraints.

Chapter 22.   LONGER-RUN DECISIONS: CAPITAL BUDGETING

Capital investment problem: a problem in which it is proposed to commit funds (capital) today (at "time zero") in the expectation of earning a return on these funds over some future period. The assets purchased with these funds are called an investment.

Present value: the present value of an amount that is expected to be received at a specified time in the future is the amount which, if invested today at a designated rate of return, would cumulate to the specified amount.

Discounting: the process of converting a stream of future cash inflows to their present-value equivalents, in order to compare them with the amount of the investment (which is already stated at its present value or "time zero" amount).

Net present value: the difference between the present value of the future cash inflows and the amount of the initial investment.

Required rate of return: the rate at which the cash inflows are discounted in a net present value calculation; also called the "discount rate" or "hurdle rate."

Cost of capital: the cost to a company of the funds it acquires, both debt capital and equity capital. In theory, the cost of capital should be used as the required rate of return when discounting cash flows, but it often is not because of the difficulty in determining the cost of equity capital.

Economic life: the number of years over which cash inflows are expected to be received as a consequence of making an investment. The end of this time period is called the investment horizon for the investment.

Tax shield: a noncash expense which reduces taxable income, and hence reduces the cash outflow for income taxes. Such an expense -- most commonly depreciation -- is said to "shield" the pretax cash inflows from the full impact of income taxes.

Residual value: the amount of cash that will be freed up at the end of the economic life of an investment. Such residual value may arise from the salvage or resale of machinery or the liquidation of working capital.

Internal rate of return method: a capital investment analysis method in which is computed the rate of return which equates the present value of cash inflows with the amount of the investment; i.e., that rate which gives a zero net present value. Also called the "discounted cash flow (DCF) method," the "time-adjusted return method," or the "investor's method" (none of which is as descriptive as the term "internal rate of return method").

Payback method: a capital investment analysis method in which the ratio of investment to annual inflows is computed; this ratio is the number of years in which the (undiscounted) cash inflows will "pay back" the initial investment.

Discounted payback method: a conceptually superior version of the payback method, in which is determined the number of years in which the discounted cash inflows will equal the initial investment. (Mechanically, this is the NPV method with the NPV set at zero, and the time horizon used as the unknown variable.)

Unadjusted return on investment method: a capital investment analysis method in which the annual net income from a project is divided by the investment, or by one half of the investment; also called the "accounting rate of return method" or "average return method."

Screening problem: a capital investment problem in which the question is whether or not to accept the proposed investment.

Preference problem: a capital investment problem in which a number of proposals, each of which has an acceptable return, must be ranked in terms of preference.

Profitability index: the ratio of an investment proposal's present value (before subtracting the initial investment) to its initial investment. This index is used to rank projects in a preference problem.

Chapter 23. RESPONSIBILITY ACCOUNTING: THE MANAGEMENT CONTROL STRUCTURE

Management control: the process by which management assures that the organization carries out its strategies effectively and efficiently. Management control "links" strategic planning and operational control.

Strategic planning: the process of arriving at the organization's goals and broad strategies.

Task control: the process of assuring that specific tasks are carried out effectively and efficiently.

Responsibility center: an organization unit headed by a manager responsible for its activities. Responsibility centers are the focus of responsibility accounting.

Responsibility accounting: the type of management accounting that collects and reports both planned and actual accounting information in terms of responsibility centers.

Expense center: a responsibility center for which expenses are measured, but for which outputs are not measured in terms of revenues.

Revenue center: a responsibility center for which the outputs are measured in monetary terms (revenues), but which is not responsible for the cost of the products it sells. (It is responsible for its selling costs, however.)

Profit center: a responsibility center for which both revenues and expenses are measured. The revenues and expenses are those the company decides to recognize, and do not necessarily coincide with revenues and expenses shown on the company's income statement.

Transfer price a price used to measure the value of the goods or services furnished (i.e., "sold") by a profit center to other responsibility centers in the firm. Transfer prices may be market-based or cost-based.

Investment center: a profit center in which the manager is also held accountable for the use of the center's assets. ROI and residual income are alternative ways of relating the center's profit to the assets employed in the center.

Residual income: a measurement of an investment center's income defined as profit (before interest expense) minus a capital charge rate levied on the investment in the center's asets or net assets.

Chapter 24. RESPONSIBILITY ACCOUNTING: THE MANAGEMENT CONTROL PROCESS

Programming: the process of deciding on the programs that the organization will undertake and the approximate amount of resources that are to be allocated to each program. Programming is the first phase in the four-phase management control cycle.

Budgeting: the process of translating programs into quantitative (usually monetary) terms corresponding to responsibility centers and for a specified period of time (usually one year). Budgeting is the second phase of the management control cycle.

Controllable cost: a cost, the amount of which incurred in or assigned to a responsibility center is significantly influenced by the actions of the center's manager. Note that "control" here means to have substantial influence; it does not mean complete influence.

Engineered costs: items of cost for which the right or proper amount of costs that should be incurred can be estimated.

Discretionary costs: items of costs whose amount can be varied at the discretion of the manager of the responsibility center; also called programmed or managed costs. Unlike engineered costs, a "right" amount cannot be "scientifically" determined for discretionary costs.

Committed costs: costs that are inevitable consequences of commitments previously made. These costs are noncontrollable in the short run.

Extrinsic and intrinsic needs: extrinsic needs include "existence" needs, and needs for security, socializing, esteem, and self-control. Intrinsic needs include the needs for competence, achievement, and self-realization. Only extrinsic needs can be satisfied by outcomes external to the person; intrinsic needs are satisfied by outcomes persons "give" to themselves.

Expectancy theory: this theory states that the motivation to engage in a given behavior is determined by (1) a person's beliefs or "expectancies" about what outcomes are likely to result from that behavior, and (2) the attractiveness the person attaches to those outcomes as a result of the outcomes' ability to satisfy the person's needs.

Rewards and punishments: respectively, outcomes that result in increased or decreased need satisfaction; also called "positive incentives" and "negative incentives."

Goal congruence: the name given to the situation that exists when employees acting in their perceived self-interest are also acting in the best interests of the organization. Goal congruence is used as a primary criterion in evaluating any practice used in a management control system.

Chapter 25. PROGRAMMING AND BUDGETING

Zero-base review: an evaluation "from scratch" of the ongoing programs of a responsibility center; sometimes (erroneously) referred to as "zero-base budgeting." The review includes questioning the appropriateness of continuing existing programs, and evaluating their size, quality level, "methodology," and costs.

Benefit/cost analysis: an analytical technique in which the costs of a program are compared with a nonmonetary -- and often nonquantitative -- evaluation of the program's benefits.

Long-range plan: a plan that shows what programs an organization intends to carry out over the next few years.

Master budget: a budget "package" that includes an operating budget, cash budget, and capital expenditure budget. The operating budget consists of a program budget and a responsibility budget (see below).

Operating budget: a budget showing planned operations for the coming year (or other time period), including revenues, expenses, and changes in inventory.

Program budget: a budget consisting of the estimated revenues and costs of the major programs that the organization plans to undertake during the year. The programs include product lines, R & D programs, etc.

Responsibility budget: a budget that sets forth plans in terms of the responsibility center managers responsible for carrying out the plans. This budget serves as a benchmark in the management control process.

Project budget: a budget constructed for one particular project, as in the case of constructing major capital assets such as buildings, roads, bridges, and the like.

Variable budget: a budget that shows how the total costs in a responsibility center are expeted to vary with changes in volume; also called a flexible budget.

Management by Objectives: the term popularly applied to the process of planning and measuring performance related to nonfinancial objectives.

Rolling budget: a budget that includes amounts for each of the next four quarters. At the end of a quarter, the budget for that quarter is dropped, the budgets for the next three quarters are revised, and a budget for the fourth succeeding quarter is added.

Incremental budgeting: adjusting the current year's budget for expected differences in the coming year's activities, plus adjustments for inflation and salary increases.

Cash budget: the operating budget translated from terms of revenues and expenses to terms of cash inflows and outflows.

Capital expenditure budget: a list of what management believes to be worthwhile projects for the acquisition of new plant and equipment, together with the estimated cost and timing of expenditures for each project.

Chapter 26. ANALYZING AND REPORTING PERFORMANCE

Variance: the difference between the actual amount and the budgeted amount of gross margin, or of any revenue or cost item. (Note that this is a broader definition than the one originally given in Chapter 19.)

Favorable and unfavorable variances: respectively, variances that have the effect of making actual net income greater or less than budgeted net income. (This is also a broader definition than given in Chapter 20.)

Gross margin variance: the difference between the actual and budgeted gross margins. "Actual" gross margin is actual revenue minus the standard cost of the goods actually sold; "standard" gross margin is budgeted revenue minus the standard cost of the goods budgeted to be sold. (Note that this definition does not involve differences between actual and standard unit costs, which are production cost variances.) This variance can be decomposed into the three variances whose definitions follow.

Unit margin variance: the difference between actual and budgeted unit margin, multiplied by the actual number of units sold. This variance usually arises when the actual selling price per unit is different from the budgeted unit price, and it is therefore often called the selling price variance.

Sales volume variance: the difference between actual and budgeted sales volume (in units) priced at the budgeted unit margin. This variance arises when the number of units actually sold is different from the budgeted sales volume.

Mix variance: the variance in gross margin that arises when some products have higher unit margins than others and the actual proportions of products sold is different from the budgeted proportions. Although not described in detail in the text, mix variances can also be calculated for labor or material costs; in practice, calculating these cost mix variances is not so common as is calculating gross margin mix variances.

Industry volume variance: the difference between actual and forecast industry volume, multiplied first by the company's budgeted market share, and then by the budgeted unit margin. It is one component of the sales volume variance, and is often noncontrollable by the company.

<u>Market share variance</u>: the difference between actual and budgeted market share, multiplied first by the actual industry volume, and then by the budgeted unit margin. This second component of the sales volume variance is usually controllable by the company.

<u>Control report</u>: a management report whose purpose is to compare a responsibility center's actual performance with what performance should have been under the circumstances prevailing. (To be contrasted with information reports and economic performance reports.)

<u>Exception principle</u>: a control report should focus management's attention on those items for which actual performance is significantly different from standard. Following this principle is often referred to as "management by exception."

Chapter 27. MANAGEMENT ACCOUNTING SYSTEM DECISION

(All of the listed terms were defined previously; also, each can readily be found in Chapter 27 itself.)